COMPOSING APARTHEID

MUSIC FOR AND AGAINST APARTHEID

EDITED BY GRANT OLWAGE

WITS UNIVERSITY PRESS

Wits University Press
1 Jan Smuts Avenue
Johannesburg
South Africa
http://witspress.wits.ac.za

Introduction, selection and compilation: © Grant Olwage, 2008
Individual essays: © as per authors indicated, 2008
Artwork: © institutes and individuals indicated, 2008

First published 2008.

ISBN 978-1-86814-456-3

All rights reserved. No part of this publication may be reproduced, stored in a retrieval system, or transmitted in any form or by any means, electronic, mechanical, photocopying, recording or otherwise, without the express permission, in writing, of both the copyright holder and the publishers.

Cover, layout and design by Hybridesign
Printed and bound by Creda Communications

For Bronwyn

CONTENTS

Acknowledgements   vi

Introduction   1
Grant Olwage

Chapter 1   11
Back to the Future? Idioms of 'displaced time'
in South African composition
Christine Lucia

Chapter 2   35
Apartheid's Musical Signs: Reflections on black choralism,
modernity and race-ethnicity in the segregation era
Grant Olwage

Chapter 3   55
Discomposing Apartheid's Story: Who owns Handel?
Christopher Cockburn

Chapter 4   79
Kwela's White Audiences: The politics of pleasure
and identification in the early apartheid period
Lara Allen

Chapter 5   99
Popular Music and Negotiating Whiteness
in Apartheid South Africa
Gary Baines

Chapter 6   115
Packaging Desires: Album covers and
the presentation of apartheid
Michael Drewett

CHAPTER 7   137
Musical Echoes: Composing a past in/for South African jazz
Carol A. Muller

CHAPTER 8   155
Singing Against Apartheid: ANC cultural groups
and the international anti-apartheid struggle
Shirli Gilbert

CHAPTER 9   185
'Nkosi Sikelel' iAfrika': Stories of an African anthem
David Coplan and Bennetta Jules-Rosette

CHAPTER 10   209
Whose 'White Man Sleeps' Aesthetics?
and politics in the early work of Kevin Volans
Martin Scherzinger

CHAPTER 11   239
State of Contention: Recomposing apartheid at
Pretoria's State Theatre, 1990-1994. A personal recollection
Brett Pyper

CHAPTER 12   257
Decomposing Apartheid: Things come together
Ingrid Byerly

CHAPTER 13   283
Arnold van Wyk's Hands
Stephanus Muller

CONTRIBUTORS   301

INDEX   305

ACKNOWLEDGEMENTS

GRANT OLWAGE

This book, like many, began its life as a conference. That conference, unlike most, was a prelude to a music festival: the annual New Music Indaba of 2004, a contemporary music festival that then took place in Grahamstown, South Africa. Both the festival and conference were the brainchild of Michael Blake, a South African composer who more than anyone in the decades either side of the millennium has sought to assault and assuage the ears of the South African public with new art music. That Michael's vision has been able to extend to the academic project is to acknowledge him as one of the ideas-men of the South African music scene.

But how did a conference on the music of apartheid find a place on the programme of a new music festival? The year of the conference, 2004, was the first decade anniversary of South Africa's post-apartheid democracy. *Pace* the uncritical public festivities for which the arts are typically roped in to support, the New Music Indaba of that year sought also to explore the musics of the apartheid past. It was in that spirit that the parallel conference was conceived. My intentions for the conference were twofold. I wanted to gather together in person and then on paper as many as possible of the most interesting thinkers working on South African music and I wanted to focus their thoughts on the topic at hand: the musics of apartheid, on how apartheid was constituted through music. The themes of the topic I elaborate on in the Introduction and need not detain us here; save to say that a book-length exploration of this topic does not to date exist, a sure motivation for the enterprise.

Writing the Acknowledgements of course signals the end – finally! – of this four-year project. As such it is a pleasure to pen. It is also a pleasure to name those whose knowledge and skills have shaped the book. As a first-time editor I've had a pretty easy time of it I suspect. For this thanks both to my contributors and the Wits University Press team, the latter expertly managed by commissioning editor Estelle Jobson, who has guided the manuscript to publication and who has asked me to thank, specifically: Barbara Ludman as editor, David Lea for proofreading, Margie Ramsay for indexing, and Karen Lilje of Hybridesign for the book and cover design.

To conclude. In the spirit, if not quite in the form, of a *Festschrift* I want to dedicate *Composing Apartheid* to Christine Lucia: as personal thanks to her ongoing guidance of my thinking and career, as public acknowledgment of her influence on this book, and as celebration of her contribution to South African music scholarship at large. For many – and many of the contributors to this book – Christine has been chief interlocutor on many and diverse matters of South African music during the recent past. The conversations no doubt will continue.

The publishers and I wish to thank all those institutions from whom their publications and archives have been cited and those individuals who have been interviewed. Acknowledgement has been cited accordingly. Every effort has been made to trace copyright holders, but should any infringement have occurred, the publishers apologise and would welcome any information that would enable them to amend any errors in the event of a reprint.

INTRODUCTION

Grant Olwage

The dual terms of *Composing Apartheid* combine in a double act: primarily, the book explores facets of the musical make-up of apartheid, but simultaneously, and more broadly, it reveals how, through this cultural composition, apartheid itself was variously made.[1] But what is 'apartheid itself'? It was – is – a horror, notorious the world over; to the extent, as Jacques Derrida pointed out, that the word has never been translated, 'as if all the languages of the world were defending themselves, shutting their mouths against a sinister incorporation of the thing by means of the word' (1986a: 331). The word, importantly as Derrida emphasises, references a concept and reality (1986b: 362); or, in the case of apartheid: words, concepts and realities – plural. The relations among these are always complex, seldom stable. And so, while it would be irresponsible scholarship not to resolutely historicise apartheid – officially a period of South African history from 1948 to 1994 – we can only do so 'thickly' by looking beyond apartheid's geographic and temporal borders. Thus, as some of the concepts of apartheid preceded its naming, so some of its realities persist after its dethroning; and vice versa. *Composing Apartheid* endeavours to trace the relationships between some of the names, concepts and realities as they variously interacted, and continue to interact, on the musical landscape, and it does so as historically and socially responsible scholarship: genealogising our musical histories, as Michel Foucault would say, in the name of a critical 'history of the present'.

What a collection like this cannot do, and this Introduction does not attempt, is to map out the totality of that history. Rather, I want to explore just some of the topography of apartheid's musical landscape as revealed by the essays collected here. I do so by proceeding from the logic of apartheid, named in the word, which Derrida highlighted with typical deconstructionist flair:

> APARTHEID: by itself the word occupies the terrain like a concentration camp. System of partition, barbed wire, crowds of mapped out solitude ... the glaring harshness of abstract essence (*heid*) seems to speculate in another regime of abstraction, that of confined separation. The word concentrates separation, raises it to another power and sets separation itself *apart*: 'apartitionality', something like that (1986a: 331).

MUSICAL SEPARATIONS OF RACE AND ETHNICITY

In the popular imagination apartheid is synonymous with race and racism. For Derrida it was the apogee of racism and it is the racialisedness of apartheid on which he focuses. Unsurprisingly, then, several essays in this volume cast their analytical gaze on race. But if this volume looks back, it is also a body of thought situated in the present. For race of course is an inescapable part of dominant public discourses in post-apartheid South Africa: inquiries into racism, legislation on black economic empowerment, exposés on white poverty, the discourse of 'representivity' – our everyday existence is saturated with language on race. Our scholarly excursions too record this. These have been encouraged by the relatively recent appearance of postcolonial and race studies in music scholarship; it was not so long ago that Philip Bohlman and Ronald Radano spoke of the paucity of studies on music and race: 'the racial quietude of musical scholastics' (2000: xiii).

The effectiveness of apartheid's racisms was also to effect other separations from within race, to apportion other partitions. One of the most important of these separations was 'ethnicity', often conflated in the apartheid imagination with 'nation' (see Sharp, 1988).[2] It was particularly on the terrain of culture that ethnicity was separated from race and through which ethnicity itself was separated out into ethnicities (see Thornton, 1988: 26).

Martin Scherzinger's essay in this volume on Kevin Volans, one of the world's most successful art music composers of the late twentieth century, hinges on the duality of race-ethnicity. Much of Volans' early, internationally popular 'African' works of the early to mid-1980s are indebted to the musics of ethnicity, such as Shona *mbira*, *nyanga* panpipes, Basotho *lesiba*; Volans himself briefly ventured into the southern African field to record African music for German radio in the late 1970s. Scherzinger explores how Volans' composition provides a critique of certain racialising topoi commonly held about Africa. In so doing he suggests that Volans' music upsets commonplaces about race that were stereotypical of the apartheid imagination. As Volans composed *from* apartheid's ethnic musics, the white composer of the famous string quartet 'White Man Sleeps' dialectically composes out apartheid's racial logics. Scherzinger participates in a larger project, fronted by Kofi Agawu (2003: chap. 7), which aims to unseat colonialist – and apartheid – epistemologies still colonising our minds.

Scholarship on the musical constructedness of race, however, and unlike work on the musical performance of ethnicities, is in its infancy. Gary Baines' 'Popular Music and Narratives of Whiteness' is thus a timely intervention.[3] Following seminal American work on whiteness, he shows that whiteness in apartheid South Africa cannot simply be delineated by language – the white population divided into Afrikaans- and English-speaking whites – but that some popular musicians performed whitenesses that crossed these and other identifying boundaries, deconstructing a monolithic, state-sanctioned concept of whiteness. Johnny Clegg, for example, who was hugely popular in continental Europe during apartheid's terminal years, deployed a reimagined Zuluness that in the process also reconfigured whiteness. Akin to Volans' compositions, Clegg, the 'white Zulu', reperforms race by staging ethnicity.

In these cases race, even as it proceeds from ethnicity, is in the spotlight. In others, the apparent disappearance of race serves to highlight our racialisedness. Carol Muller's 'Musical Echoes' argues that the reception of jazz songster Sathima Bea Benjamin's music as neither sufficiently 'African' nor 'American' has had the consequence of excluding the singer from both the South African and American jazz canons, detaining her in historiographic exile long after her release from political exile. Muller's essay is thus a caution against homogenising nationalist histories (a hallmark of 'official' apartheid-era histories) that are under-written by race. And so Benjamin's music, migrated to the US because of apartheid's racial politics, now also offers us a lesson in exclusionary scholarship.

As does the essay 'Arnold van Wyk's Hands'. Stephanus Muller's work on Van Wyk, probably the most celebrated of apartheid-era art music composers within the country, follows a now well-established line of politically-engaged musical scholarship in South Africa. Initiated by John Blacking in the 1960s, such work at first aimed to give voice in the academy to black music, to proclaim its rights to full participation in South African music history. The concern of both Mullers, though differently, is that black music – 'black' music – does not now become South African music *tout court*, that a scholarship racialised *a priori* is also potentially exclusionary. Through an exploration of the musical Romanticism of Van Wyk, Stephanus Muller shows up another scholarly racism: the assumption that all white – especially Afrikaans – art music was in collusion with the apartheid state.

It is of course not simply the post-apartheid prevalence of the public and scholarly discourses on race that accounts for its centrality in this volume. Lest we forget, and to summon Derrida again, apartheid was 'the most racist of racisms' (1986a: 330), and music's place within the racial imagination made of it a double-agent: put to use sometimes for, sometimes against, apartheid's racisms. Thus Lara Allen's chapter on pennywhistle *kwela* reveals perhaps somewhat surprisingly that the black urban genre of *kwela* was popular with a range of white audiences, including conservative agents of the state – policemen – precisely during the time, the 1950s, of the first wave of apartheid's institutionalisation. The point is that music's potential to confuse and refuse racial categorisation at times problematised apartheid's wished-for separations. It is a point Ingrid Byerly's essay makes forcefully for the later apartheid and transitional years.

By contrast, Grant Olwage's essay, 'Apartheid's Musical Signs', intends to show how music could reinforce – and even bring into being – the ideologies of apartheid. Focussing on black choralism of the 1930s and its transactions with a complex of institutional players and their sometimes contradictory ideologies, 'Apartheid's Musical Signs' traces the lineage of apartheid's ethnicities to the musical practices of the segregationist era before apartheid. Olwage's essay reminds us of the usefulness of thinking about a 'long apartheid'. For many of the (ethnicised and racialised) ideological and institutional structures of apartheid were already in place by 1948, as novelist Bloke Modisane experienced first-hand in the 1930s and 40s: 'the doors into the art galleries, the theatres, the world of ballet, opera, classical music, were shut in my nose because I am black' (1963: 178-9).

INSTITUTIONAL SEPARATIONS OF MUSIC

To talk of music as being *pro* and *contra* – for example, for or against apartheid's racisms – positions music 'as position'. Once again music is separated: a part of one party or the other, and it is then institutionalised as such. We might thus write a history of apartheid music as institutional history. Certainly, music institutions of all kinds – radio stations, primary school music classes, choirs, universities – were by and large separated by race-ethnicity, and it was through these and non-music institutions – political parties, juridical apparatuses – that the musical separations of race and ethnicity discussed above were enacted.

Apartheid's institutional separations were often the formalisation through legislation of existing common practices. For example, in a report on the state of black music education in pre-apartheid South Africa, written just prior to the Reservation of Separate Amenities Act of 1953, music scholar and educationist Percival R Kirby found that the exclusion of 'non-Europeans' from white performances was 'usually by reason of custom, though at times because of local by-laws' (1949: 627). Commissioned by the South African Institute for Race Relations, Kirby's report tersely concluded that institutions of music education were governed by 'race relations'. They had long been so. Already in late nineteenth-century colonial South Africa, music education, in the many details of its practice, was structured by race. Black students, for example, received a largely vocal, specifically choral, training, their literacy for the most 'confined' to the tonic sol-fa system of notation (and many then and since have argued as to sol-fa's limitations), and their formal instruction rarely extending beyond school.[4] Such different, and unequal, schooling facilitated different, and separate, traditions of performance and composition.

It is the relationship between schooling and composition that is at the core of Christine Lucia's chapter on black choral composition, 'Back to the Future'. Focusing on the work of two choral composers, Joshua Mohapeloa and Michael Moerane, she argues that black choral composition is a unique tradition of twentieth-century composed, notated music precisely *because* of its separations: isolated from the aesthetics of Western modernism, it is in part the partial compositional education of the composers that accounts for their music. Lucia's essay also shows up the post-apartheid academy's continuing, implicit complicity with apartheid education: the teaching of composition and theory of music in South African universities, grounded in pedagogies borrowed from the Euro-American academy, and which bolstered white compositional practices during apartheid, has yet to take into account the discourse of black choral composition; yet to be accountable, if you will, to the majority of the country's composers. Lucia's critique goes further, revealing also the consequences of apartheid for musicology. Just as white art music composers, and the university training they received, attempted to keep abreast of the international new music scene, so the academy, beholden to the methods of Western ethnomusicology, has been cut off from black choral composition, has inhibited us from analysing – coming to understand the musical logics of – this music. Elsewhere, Lucia has written on apartheid South Africa's 'two separate communities of scholarship': musicology for 'conservatives' who engaged with the hegemonic discourse of Western classical music, and ethnomusicology for white liberals and black scholars interested mainly in African music and the discourse of resistance (2005: xxxv).

To account then for apartheid's music institutions we need, as Lucia's 'Back to the Future' reminds us, to heed the idea of a long apartheid, extending both prior to and post official apartheid. We also need to resist the conception of apartheid as monolith, to recognise it as an always unfinished project, and thus to chart its vicissitudes and contradictions; we need, to return to the opening thought in this Introduction, to pay attention to the different names, shifting concepts and changing realities that constitute(d) the apartheid story.

One institution that registered this was the State Theatre, bastion of white classical music and opera. Located in the heart of Pretoria, capital city of the apartheid state, the theatre was instituted to glorify state culture. Yet, as Brett Pyper argues in 'State of Contention', the theatre's operations problematise the assumed relationship between the apartheid state and 'its' culture, to the extent that we might question the facile copulation 'state culture'; Muller similarly shows this for the composer Van Wyk's relations with state institutions. Focusing on apartheid's twilight years during the 'transition to democracy', Pyper explores how the specific political landscape of the early 1990s (mis)aligned with the theatre's actual workings. What emerges is a picture of an 'official' culture less sure, certainly not wholly homogeneous. And also, that the state of contention in which the theatre became embroiled as regards its 'proper' function is in part attributable to the actions of theatre officials on the ground. This is an important point to bear in mind: institutions are constituted of individuals, who, for whatever reason, do not necessarily institute every letter of the grand plan. It is in this space, between the plan and its enactments (the concept and its realities), that individuals, from within or out, may undermine institutional cultures, and potentially, in the case of apartheid, their musical separations. Hence, in relation to essays already discussed, the individual protests of Volans and Clegg against the racially 'pure'.

There were, of course, also institutions of protest. And if it is difficult to pinpoint a unified state apartheid cultural policy it is no less so for anti-apartheid politics. Little critical work exists on the cultural policy and praxis of various players in the anti-apartheid movement.[5] Shirli Gilbert's work on the role of musical culture in promoting the struggle abroad in the 1970s and 80s, particularly by the African National Congress in exile, should thus be read in counterpoint to Pyper's essay. It should also be read as a follow-up to

Christopher Cockburn's reception history of Handel's *Messiah*. Attending to apartheid's first decades, the 1950s and 60s, Cockburn situates the oratorio's performance within the dominant mode of oppositional politics, both black and white, at the time: the 'liberal option'. Cockburn's and Gilbert's essays highlight that politics *within* institutions – here, political opponents of apartheid – changed during apartheid, and that at different stages during apartheid different politics were voiced through different music.

The politics of protest inaugurated perhaps one of apartheid's most dramatic separations: exile. Gilbert's 'Singing against Apartheid', Muller's 'Musical Echoes', and David Coplan's and Bennetta Jules-Rosette's 'Stories of an African Anthem' are, in different ways, case studies of South African musicians and musics in exile.[6] Almost always for political reasons, though sometimes self-imposed rather than forced, many South African performers and composers – Benjamin and Volans, for instance – lived in exile, separated from their country of birth because of apartheid. And as people migrate so their culture, and the concept of their culture, and its remembered realities, spread. The separations of exile indeed globalised South African music. Hence, for example, Coplan and Jules-Rosette explore how 'Nkosi Sikelel' iAfrika', in its incarnation as protest song, moved with exiled freedom fighters throughout Africa, and as it did so it was appropriated by various non-South African groups – churches, political parties, countries – for their own liberation and other politics. And as the hymn returned 'home' as the national anthem of post-apartheid South Africa it was appropriated again, de- or newly historicised by several popular music outfits. The story of 'Nkosi's' stories, then, is an old historiographical one: the meaning of music resides in its receptions, and often in its institutional receptions.

The life of exile was only the most visible of separations that impacted on the everyday lives of musicians. We should not forget that (often brutally) forced separations of the spaces of living and working – homelands, townships, facilities, and even marriage – materially affected South Africa's musicians – and music scholars too. And it was not only musicians who were variously banned but music; the state's institutions of separations also acted, often though parliamentary Acts, directly on the musical products themselves.

In all authoritarian states the institution of censorship is a well-oiled apparatus, and this was no less so for apartheid South Africa. Yet the history of apartheid's censorship of music is a murky area which, like the idea of 'state culture', circulates largely at the level of anecdote and assumption. Michael Drewett's 'Packaging Desires' begins to shed light on the practices of state censorship and consequently on the self-censorship of the popular music industry. He does so by scrutinising album covers, a neglected area of the study of the pop music package: censorship separated out – covered up – images deemed undesirable. The pop album cover, Drewett suggests, was thus a crucial site for *advertising* apartheid to the populace, for making apartheid desirable and therefore hegemonic.

INCONCLUSIVE CONCLUSIONS

To follow Derrida, as I have in this Introduction, and think of apartheid as a 'system of partition', is only one part of the story. As we read through *Composing Apartheid* it becomes clear that music, musicians and music scholars variously traversed apartheid's calculated separations. These negating activities, producing what Homi K Bhabha calls the 'unhomely' – moments of estrangement – are of course no less part of the apartheid story (1994: 8-10). Ingrid Byerly's 'Decomposing Apartheid' takes this evidence one step further: music, she argues, provided a space in late-apartheid South Africa for separated peoples and cultures to interact; as collaborative practice, performance and composition became arenas for potentially diffusing conflict, avenues for exploring conflict resolution. Thus Byerly presents music as a small, but crucial, 'catalyst on the road to democracy'. As *Composing Apartheid* shows how music was powerfully part of apartheid's logic of separations we should also allow music the space – and power – to have helped take apartheid apart.

The end of apartheid is of course not the end of the apartheid story, and I want to conclude with two thoughts about non-conclusions and continuations. The one I take from Byerly, who reminds us that in an exploration of the past, the realities of the present cannot, and should not, be ignored. Would 'a new *apart*-heid', she asks, 'replace the previous divide between black and white with one between rich and poor, healthy and dying, perpetrator and victim?'. And how, we might add, does music continue to be imbricated with not only an upbeat liberated post-apartheid South Africa, but also with the ongoing social fallout of apartheid? The other point I take from Stephanus Muller's essay: this book, *Composing Apartheid*, he reminds us, is itself implicated in the construction of 'apartheid'. The stories, including musical narratives, that circulate about apartheid now, and in the future, continue to constitute the apartheid story.

Hip-hop poet Tumi Molekane bespeaks these two thoughts in '76' (2003), an (anti)memorialising rap of the 1976 Soweto protest. Molekane's rapper-character takes part in, witnesses and survives the violent horrors of the protest, but now, in a post-apartheid world (he seems to be saying), we've 'got it worse'. This phrase, endlessly repeated, is passed on by Molekane as spoken word to RnB songster Pebbles as sung melody, who in spinning out the phrase in her soulful voice for the rest of the track silences Molekane's narration of the past. It's a bitter-sweet message, the beauty of Pebbles' singing voice and the distaste of the textual truth of the present – 'I've got it worse' – inseparable. I juxtapose '76' and *Composing Apartheid* to make the point that both are instances of the ongoing composing of apartheid through ambivalent narrations.

ENDNOTES

1. My thanks to Christine Lucia for her comments on this Introduction.
2. For an account of the state's shift from the rhetoric of race to that of the ethnic-nation, see McClintock and Nixon (1986: 341-4).
3. See also Christopher Ballantine's work on whiteness in post-apartheid popular music (2004).
4. White students in the pre-Union colonies were taught both to sing and play instruments, to read in tonic sol-fa (when it was in vogue) and staff notations; see Olwage (2003: chap. 3). Kirby thus found pianos in almost all 'European' classrooms, but very few in 'native' schools. Nor was this simply a matter of economics, some educators fearing that teaching blacks to play instruments would prove 'detrimental to the spontaneous expression of Africans through song' (1949: 621, 624-5).
5. Not much work has been done on the musical positions and practices of political organisations in South Africa, though see, for example, Ballantine (1993: chap. 3); and Bothma (1986).
6. Little work exists on the musics of exile, though see Lucia (2002); and Ansell (2004: chap. 7).

BIBLIOGRAPHY

Agawu, Kofi. 2003. *Representing African Music: Postcolonial Notes, Queries, Positions*. New York & London: Routledge.

Ansell, Gwen. 2004. *Soweto Blues: Jazz, Popular Music and Politics in South Africa*. New York & London: Continuum.

Ballantine, Christopher. 1993. *Marabi Nights: Early South African Jazz and Vaudeville*. Johannesburg: Ravan Press.

_. 2004. 'Re-thinking "Whiteness"? Identity, Change and "White" Popular Music in Post-apartheid South Africa'. *Popular Music*, 23(2), pp. 105-131.

Bhabha, Homi K. 1994. *The Location of Culture*. London & New York: Routledge.

Bothma, Erika. 1986. 'Die Bydrae van die Musiekkomitee van die FAK tot die Bevordering van Musiek in Suid-Afrika met Spesifieke Verwysing na die Volksmusiek van die Afrikaanssprekendes'. M.Mus. diss., University of the Orange Free State.

Derrida, Jacques. 1986a. 'Racism's Last Word'. In Henry Louis Gates, Jr. (ed.). *'Race', Writing, and Difference.* Chicago & London: University of Chicago Press, pp. 329-38.

_. 1986b. 'But Beyond... (Open Letter to Anne McClintock and Rob Nixon)'. In Henry Louis Gates, Jr. (ed.). *'Race', Writing, and Difference.* Chicago & London: University of Chicago Press, pp. 354-68.

Kirby, Percival R. 1949. 'African Music'. In Ellen Hellmann (ed.). *Handbook on Race Relations in South Africa.* Cape Town: Oxford University Press, pp. 616-27.

Lucia, Christine. 2002. 'Abdullah Ibrahim and the Uses of Memory'. *British Journal of Ethnomusicology,* 11(2), pp. 125-43.

_. 2005. 'Introduction: Reading South African Music'. In Christine Lucia (ed.). *The World of South African Music: A Reader.* Newcastle: Cambridge Scholars Press, pp. xxi-xlvi.

McClintock, Anne, & Rob Nixon. 1986. 'No Names Apart: The Separation of Word and History in Derrida's "Le Dernier Mot du Racisme"'. In Henry Louis Gates, Jr. (ed.). *'Race', Writing, and Difference.* Chicago & London: University of Chicago Press, pp. 339-53.

Modisane, Bloke. 1963. *Blame Me On History.* London: Thames & Hudson.

Olwage, Grant. 2003. 'Music and (Post)Colonialism: The Dialectics of Choral Culture on a South African Frontier'. Ph.D. diss., Rhodes University.

Radano, Ronald, & Philip V Bohlman. 2000. 'Preface'. In Ronald Radano & Philip V Bohlman (eds). *Music and the Racial Imagination.* Chicago: University of Chicago Press, pp. xii-xv.

Sharp, John. 1988. 'Ethnic Group and Nation: The Apartheid Vision in South Africa'. In Emile Boonzaier & John Sharp (eds). *South African Keywords: The Uses and Abuses of Political Concepts.* Cape Town & Johannesburg: David Philip, pp. 79-99.

Thornton, Robert. 1988. 'Culture: A Contemporary Definition'. In Emile Boonzaier & John Sharp (eds). *South African Keywords: The Uses and Abuses of Political Concepts.* Cape Town & Johannesburg: David Philip, pp. 17-28.

Tumi and the Volume. 2003. *Tumi and the Volume: Live at the Bassline.* Self-published.

1

BACK TO THE FUTURE?

IDIOMS OF 'DISPLACED TIME' IN SOUTH AFRICAN COMPOSITION

CHRISTINE LUCIA

INTRODUCTION

One evening in August 1997 I played a composition by a young black choral composer to one of my colleagues in the Fine Art Department at Rhodes University, Grahamstown, South Africa.[1] After listening to the strangely familiar yet unfamiliar language of the music, my colleague commented, 'it's postmodern'. It seemed to have arrived at a state of postmodernism without having been through European modernism, eschewing reference to art music of the early twentieth century (Schoenberg, Stravinsky, Bartók) and ignoring serial or post-serial techniques. What it lacked most conspicuously, however, made it what it was. It rearranged the codes and conventions from an earlier tonal era but projected them onto a flatter surface. Hence it sounded, to a colleague schooled in contemporary art but not music theory or composition, postmodern.

The codes this piece *did* employ belong to a substantial history and repertoire of written black South African choral music, but one transmitted half-orally because scores are scarce and choirs taught mainly by rote (see Lucia, 2005: xxvi). This is a tradition going back more than 125 years, with John Knox Bokwe (1855-1922) usually seen as colonial founding father (Olwage, 2006). The repertoire in this part of Africa has developed among hundreds of composers scattered throughout the region, adding idioms from various musical discourses encountered, including jazz, dance music, European classical, popular and folk music, African 'traditional' music, and church music of various kinds. Especially it feeds off its own histories; and along the way it has produced major composers and 'classics'. The annual national competitions in which it is mainly performed, a culmination of local and regional competitions held throughout the year, make it seem as if there is a unitary history of such music; but the surviving repertoire comes from several historical periods and many areas of a large country, and is far from homogeneous in style and especially language, since the texts of choral songs are composed in all eleven official languages. Text and musical language articulate the experiences of black South Africans from colonial times to the present, and thus these pieces are valuable social documents.

On the production side: where scores have been preserved (and many have not) they are invariably hand-me-down copies of copies of manuscripts or typescripts. Traditionally composers wrote in tonic sol-fa notation because this was prescribed in 'native' mission schools, and under apartheid's Bantu Education policy in the 1960s to 1980s choral singing and sol-fa continued to provide so-called 'music education' in approximately 67 percent of black schools.[2] On the reception side: choral music's history has been shaped by the church, school, and community choirs that have always sung it. The best composers have almost the same status as national poets or soccer heroes, but the music is seen as belonging to all, in much the same way as congregational music is. Hence composers have benefited little from royalties, and their music is illegally reproduced with abandon. The reception has taken a new turn since the 1980s, with the music's increased exposure to white South African adjudicators, composers, and audiences, and also to scholars. More pieces are appearing in print, often in dual (staff/sol-fa) notation, and with the publication of eight 'classics' in what amounts to the first 'critical edition' (the South African Music Rights Organisation (SAMRO) *South Africa Sings* Volume 1 (Khumalo, 1998)), the possibility arises for analytical scrutiny of such pieces in the academy. The need to investigate and critique reasons why such music has for so long been marginalised or misread as 'composition' also becomes more urgent.

For the choral repertoire has been dogged by mis-readings, mainly those of whites who see it as a poor imitation of Western music, a 'travesty' as someone remarked from the floor at a South African musicology conference in 1997.[3] As Veit Erlmann pointed out in 1991, in his study of the composer Reuben Caluza:

Percival Kirby and other South African musicologists [have claimed] that Bokwe's, Sontonga's, and Caluza's compositions were 'without a trace of the devices used by European composers to mitigate the 'squareness' of the design or to inject vitality into the melody or character into the harmony' (Kirby, 1979: 94 [93]). Such harsh criticism was of course motivated by racial prejudice and misinterpreted the composers' intentions (121).

The foundations for such misinterpretations were laid down long before the National Party's victory in 1948, continued through the 1950s when HF Verwoerd coined the term 'apartheid', throughout legislation that consolidated his philosophy, through to the official end of apartheid in 1994, and beyond it to the present day. This is largely because the misinterpretations are tied to notions of composition that stem from the academy, rather than from the music in question and its contexts. The move to classicise choral music in the post-apartheid era – calling it '[s]erious music in an African context' (Khumalo, 2003/4 and 2005/6: 13) – does historicise it in new ways, which is to be welcomed, but this also brings with it the dangers of a formalist analytical discourse being applied in order to prove this music's (new) status as art music. The danger is that it will be read using paradigms learned through an education system not in harmony with the music, that its musical syntax will be compared to the norms of Western music, to the detriment not only of the musical tradition itself but to all its acquired meanings, performative contexts, and other aspects of production and reception, not least of which are the texts it uses.

Words are integral to the meaning choral works hold for black communities. Composers usually write their own, adapted from liturgical or other ritual contexts or from folk music, often drawn from the Bible or other literature close at hand.[4] The words of songs are allegories of a personal or collective experience of history, notable examples from different periods being Caluza's 'iLand Act',[5] Tyamzashe's 'Zweliyabanzi',[6] Matyila's 'Bawo, Thixo Somandla',[7] or Madlopha's 'Kwenzenjani maAfrika'.[8] Given those experiences – hundreds of scattered authors voicing in many languages a century of political violence and social displacement, in which apartheid was one particularly brutal episode – the deconstruction of song texts alone would fill many pages.

It is not texts that I focus on here, but rather the music of three songs written at different moments in this indigenous composing tradition, moments framing the era of 'official' apartheid but underscoring the point that what choral music did under apartheid was set in motion long before, and continues now. I attempt through a brief reading of Joshua Pulumo Mohapeloa's 'U Ea Kae?' ('Where Are You Going?') (1935), Percival Kirby's 'A Sotho Lament' (1939), and Michael Mosoeu Moerane's 'Barali Ba Jerusalema' ('Daughters of Jerusalem') (1950s?[9]) to suggest how the musical idiom of such pieces reflects their experience of the 'contemporary' at different times, problematising the way such pieces are often seen as untrained attempts to compose in an old-fashioned idiom, and suggesting they might rather be seen as 'foreshadowing' (to use Jacques Attali's notion) a new compositional order, even a new socio-political one.[10] In short, I argue that in the way they displace notions of time-periods by not comfortably belonging in South African music history and sounding a-modern or postmodern, they can be said to 'look back to the future'.

'U EA KAE?'

Mohapeloa's 'U Ea Kae?' (Ex. 1) is based on a traditional Sotho threshing song,[11] although interestingly it is now known principally in Mohapeloa's version, which according to Mzilikazi Khumalo has been accepted as the 'clan-song of the Moletsanes' (1998: 28). The song has an 'A' section of 12 bars and repeated 'B' section of 11 bars: 44 bars in all. I suggest that because it has been carefully notated as a piece for four-part choir, is prescribed as an 'indigenous composition' in choral competitions rather than as a traditional piece and is therefore sung without traditional dance movements, and because it is one of the 'classics' included by Khumalo in *South Africa Sings*[12] – all of this points to reading it as composition rather than 'mere' arrangement.

There is no evidence that when Mohapeloa used traditional music he thought of it as only arranging. It seems as if some of his early uses of traditional material (in the 1930s) even met with disapproval because they did *not* represent traditional music in the way arrangements normally would. In an interview in 2004 Mohapeloa's brother Josias Makibinyane noted that when JP started writing songs based on folk music 'he did not know that they were going to be singeable [sic]' because of 'criticisms that arose saying that they did not quite depict proper Basotho music' (Mot'soane, 2004: 2). 'Singable' here implies acceptable as well as vocally manageable, the implication being that there were parts that singers might not manage (rarely true of traditional music), and that there were elders who disapproved of change. When he came to publish the small song collection *Khalima-Nosi tsa 'Mino oa Kajeno* in 1951, Mohapeloa stated his case very clearly.[13] The following is an extract from his 'Preface':

> Authorities on African music uphold the old type of folk song as the only sound basis for further development. While for purposes of research this

Back to the Future?

Ex. 1. 'U Ea Kae?' by J Mohapeloa © SAMRO. Bars 1-17.

Translation:
[Bars 1-12] Take your stick, and let us go to Taung, home of the Moletsanes; let us go and see how corn is threshed. The small boys have knobkerries [knobbed sticks] in their hands. They thresh hard with a flashy rhythmic stroke.
[Bars 13-23] Where are you going [x2], without even a knobkerrie? Here admission is with a knobkerrie; here [at Taung], home of the Moletsanes, we have brought ours. Fa-la-la-la [x2] (Khumalo, 1998: 10).

view holds good, it is however not always applicable to work intended principally for recreation. Here one has to bear in mind the fact that music is a thing of fashions and, as far as possible, incorporate[s] in the work the idiom of the time. This old type of African folk music has receded into the background in most parts, and the people who really appreciate it are quietly dropping out of the scene. In certain aspects African folk music has undergone many changes, and we cannot with any more justice stigmatize current practice as foreign for its taint of European influence than we could be justified in ostracising the modern African youth on the grounds of sartorial fashions (2002: [2]).

Mohapeloa kills several birds with one stone here: first, 'authorities' (in 1951 foremost among these would be ethnomusicologists Percival Kirby and Hugh Tracey) who condemn the development of the 'tainted' modern African composer with their preservationist attitude to African music; second, the old folks at home 'quietly dropping out of the scene'; third, the idea that folk music does not change. It is a complex and not fully worked out argument which continues, frustratingly, only for another two paragraphs, about the need for composition to reflect the new rather than the old. But many songs like 'U Ea Kae?' were just as concerned with 'the idiom of the time' as they were with the past, aimed at (in Mohapeloa's words) 'reflecting the feelings of the people who are actively alive today and not those of the dead and dying … [in order to] serve as a record of the popular trend in musical development *today*' (Ibid.; my emphasis).

What struck me on first hearing this song was the dramatic nature of the melodic line, from which the piece derives a major part of its expressive power, the fluid treatment of texture and rhythm, the use of new material every few bars, the way chords do not pile up into phrases with regular cadencing, and the unceremonious ending. Rhythm in the lower parts is sometimes almost *parlando* in style – as if echoing an operatic chorus (among the few treasures left in Mohapeloa's former home in Morija are vocal scores of *Lucrezia Borgia* and *Robert Il Diavolo*). Yet the SAMRO score has no tempo, dynamic, or expressive indications – prominent in choral pieces, and unusually absent here. The song repeats certain vertical configurations, but without using the dominant (V) chord they do not signify a harmonic progression that is teleological in the Western sense; they do not generate phrases, or cadences, and thus control overall structure. The predominant chords are A-C#-E alternating with D-F#-A in the first section, A-C#-E alternating with B-D-F# in the second, which begins on the upbeat to bar 13.

The fluid texture comes partly from avoidance of the dialectic uses of tonality: no V-I cadencing, no teleology of tonic key-quick modulation-return. No point here, I would argue, in doing an analysis that looks for deep structure. There is a point, though, in looking at how vertical constructions are driven: whether by the soprano, as I first heard it, or by the bass. Are the chords imagined theoretically from the bass line as if this 'carried' the harmony? There are two ways of looking at this: sonically and theoretically. The bass voice as sound was ingrained in Mohapeloa's early experience: he had six brothers and two sisters, and thus '[a]n intimate [vocal] chamber ensemble could be completed within the circumference of that thatch-roofed hut at the Mohapeloa homestead at Molumong', as Moroesi Sibandze (n.d.) puts it, although it would certainly be a male-dominated ensemble. He was familiar with the popular *mekorotlo* (folk) songs sung by BaSotho men, where, 'to the BaSotho ear, a rich deep bass [is] very beautiful and indispensable to a "good" song' (Huskisson, 1969: 163). Mohapeloa's first experiences as composer and conductor were works for male-voice choir (popular among many choral composers of the early twentieth century probably because of the migrant worker system in urban areas), and it was only when he left Lesotho and went to South Africa to study at Fort Hare (then called the South African Native College) that he evidently 'became more aware of the musical possibilities of the "mixed" choir' (Ibid.:161). 'U Ea Kae?' can be sung by either kind of choir: an SABC transcription recording of it by the Ionian Male Voice Choir conducted by Khabi Mngoma shows how effective it is for men's voices (SABC, n.d. [c1960]); and the traditional song on which it is based, to judge from the text, was clearly a men's song.

The second way in which the bass is important is related to its harmonic use. It is not a bass line that functions in terms of Western harmony, 'coming up' from the bass even if some chords are inverted. Mohapeloa probably only learnt about this later at the University of the Witwatersrand (Wits) – but even then he might not necessarily have composed thinking of the bass this way. More likely the bass line illustrates the way harmonies in traditional African instrumental music such as bow-songs – solo songs with one-string bow accompaniment – are formed from two or three fundamental notes and the overtones above them, which result in what are called 'parallel' harmonies (see Rycroft, 1977: 225-27; Dargie, 1988: 50-52; and Tracey, 1996 on this topic). The Xhosa bow songs of Nofinishi Dywili or the Zulu songs of Princess Constance Magogo are examples of the way 'bass notes' or fundamentals can dominate not only the sound but also the whole theoretical structure of the music. They also use quite short phrases often beginning on higher notes and moving swiftly down, circumscribing a pentatonic or hexatonic scale because of the way available notes from the overtone series of the two adjacent fundamentals suggest such a scale. The melody of 'U Ea Kae?', too, has this descending pentatonic quality.[14] So even while the G# rising to A in the bass suggests a leading note rising to tonic, the overriding shifts in harmonies in the song as a whole are not, I suggest, based entirely on a Western heptatonic scale, or on harmonies derived from it.

'U Ea Kae?' uses material in relation to the length of the composition in such a way that the piece feels open-ended, with gaps for performers or listeners to interpret; gaps that leave questions, too, about how it was made. Lying behind such notions of 'making compositions' in the academy are first, training in harmony, counterpoint, and form, and then, more advanced training in compositional techniques, usually beginning with serialism and quartal harmony. This immediately introduces composers to a particular notion of modernism in music – the sound-world of Schoenberg, Berg and Webern, and Stravinsky, Bartók, Hindemith. As I suggested at the beginning, it is the very avoidance of this world (not through choice one suspects) that makes Mohapeloa and his contemporaries – indeed the whole tradition of black choral music – interesting: the way it side-steps the world of European musical modernity and engages with modernities of its own. Some writers have shown how South African popular music does this (for example Erlmann, 1999), and others have explored African modernity in the spheres of literature and fine art (for example Couzens, 1985; Attwell, 2005; Nettleton, 2003). In terms of choral music, too, such modernity is unashamedly eclectic, drawing on everything available: in Mohapeloa's words, all 'the various music [the] African has tasted, chewed, swallowed, and assimilated till they formed part of his being' (2002: [2]).

Ex. 2. 'A Sotho Lament' by P Kirby © SAMRO. Bars 1-18.

Assimilation of such intensity rules out an interpretation using the idea of hybridity or syncretism between discrete African and Western elements, an interpretation often found in studies of black South African music (in relation to choral music see, for example, Mngoma, 1981; and Mthethwa, 1988). Drawing on Homi K Bhabha's notion of liminal cultural expression occurring in neither new nor old, nor even in hybrid spaces, but in a 'third space' (a notion he borrows from Frederic Jameson), where 'part of the "progressivist" division between past and present, or the archaic and the modern [does not] give rise to a "newness" that can be contained in the mimesis of "original" and "copy"' (1994: 227), I suggest that choral music, too, is deliberately concerned with 'staging of cultural difference' as Bhabha puts it (Ibid.). It has always operated in a kind of theoretical no-man's land, a cultural 'third space' undermining not only the views of preservationist scholars of the 1930s and 40s who, Mohapeloa recalls, made 'scathing remarks [such] as "mimicking European hymn tunes of the worst type"' (2002: [2]), but also surviving and indeed thriving throughout the apartheid era, because its very 'difference' was not a threat to the dominant culture. It refused to be exactly like any other musics, but took something from all of them.

'A Sotho Lament'

What, then, did Mohapeloa take from the academy? His study of history of music, harmony and counterpoint at Wits between 1938 and 43 enabled him to come 'face to face with Music Composition' as Huskisson puts it (1969: 162). Percival Kirby taught composition and WP Paff harmony and counterpoint (Khumalo, 1998: 28).[15] Mohapeloa's first song collection, *Melodi le Lethallere tsa Afrika*, had appeared three years earlier in 1935 (two other volumes followed in 1939 and 1947). Its title has been translated as *African Melodies in Decorative Counter-Display* (Huskisson, 1969: 161), or *Decorative Counterpoint* (Khumalo, 1998: 38). There is a tension, however, I suggest, between what Mohapeloa went on to learn from Kirby and what he felt able or inclined to apply.[16] Mohapeloa had written almost 100 songs before he was formally trained in music composition, and was therefore probably more experienced in a way than his teacher, even if only within the sphere of choral music. For this reason, 'U Ea Kae?' makes an interesting comparison with Kirby's arrangement in 1939 (the year after Mohapeloa began studying with him) of something Kirby called 'A Sotho Lament', No. 1 of his *Three African Idylls*, with (English) words also by Kirby (see Ex. 2).

There are many differences between this piece and Mohapeloa's. Kirby's belongs to a solo art-song or parlour-song genre familiar at the time to audiences of European music. The song is strophic, its three verses identical in melody although the accompaniment is elaborated with semiquavers in verses two and three. This kind of piano figuration, as well as the lyrics and Edwardian style of expression, make it composition, not arrangement. The tonality is clearly E major despite the modal inflections in the harmony, the extended phrasing in bars 19-24 is a technique learned in Grade 8 music theory, the piano embellishments in verses two and three are attempts to avoid the apparent boredom of repetition. What is interesting about it, though, is the way it shows how Kirby interpreted 'Sotho music' compositionally, how he saw its elements as exotic, in need of framing and embellishment, of the improving ways of Western harmony in order to bring them in line with standard rhythmic and pianistic practices. But it is dire as a composition, repetitive materially and structurally in comparison with Mohapeloa's piece; and – more to the point – it makes one curious as to what happened in those composition lessons.

Under the guidance of Kirby and Paff, we are told, Mohapeloa 'gained an inner confidence in his ability and the technical knowledge to facilitate it' (Huskisson, 1969: 162). In such a view, raw compositional talent is refined through the civilising ways of harmony and counterpoint, the language of African modernity bent to conform with Western expectations. How did this actually happen, though, in practice? I suggest it happened in much the same way as it does now in theory and composition lessons: through Mohapeloa having to take on board the self-contained theoretical system of 'scientifically' based rules of chord progression, voicing and voice-leading, largely abstracted from concrete compositional examples, and presented in a progression from simple diatonics to advanced chromatics.[17]

This way of learning to compose was not always so self-contained. It became so in the early nineteenth-century 'just as music attained [autonomous] status as high art', as Sanna Pedersen has pointed out (cited in Treitler, 1999: 374). Pedersen further argues that it had a social agenda: 'music instruction and music organisations were seized on to help consolidate a middle-class society by means of appreciating music for its own sake'. So the use of music 'for its own sake' still lay within an overriding ideology of cultural hegemony, as Leo Treitler points out (Ibid.).

The development in the academy of harmony and counterpoint studies as forerunner to composition was largely the work of Sir Frederick Gore Ouseley. As the new Professor of Music at Oxford in 1855, he instituted 'major reforms of curriculum over the next thirty-four years [until 1889], introducing exams in "Harmony and Counterpoint, Fugue, Canon, Formal Analysis, and Musical History", in addition to the submission of written composition of prescribed nature' (Rainbow, 1989: 239). Note the separation of theory and history. This 'set the pattern generally adopted' by other universities (Ibid.: 241). The academy – including the South African academy – was thus successfully able to separate historical and performing contexts of music from the rules around compositional abstraction. One of the universities that in the early years of apartheid still insisted on compositions being submitted as a requirement for obtaining a BMus degree was the distance education institution Unisa (University of South Africa), where Michael Moerane studied. This was perhaps the reason he wrote his orchestral tone-poem 'Fatše la Heso' (for more on this see http://chevalierdesaintgeorges.homestead.com/Moerane.html).

'BARALI BA JERUSALEMA'

Moerane's 'serious study of music' at Unisa (Khumalo, 1998: 14), was in the late 1930s, culminating in a BMus in 1941: he was 'the first black South African to achieve that distinction' (Ibid.). We do not know the date of his choral piece 'Barali Ba Jerusalema' ('Daughters of Jerusalem' from the *Song of Songs*) – it could have been written any time between the 1940s and 60s and was apparently not known until Khumalo discovered it in the SAMRO Music Library in the 1990s (Ibid.).[18] Once discovered, however, it was immediately put to use

Ex. 3. 'Barali Ba Jerusalema' by M Moerane for SATB © SAMRO. Bars 1-5 and 10-14.

Translation:

[Bars 1-16] O daughters of Jerusalem, I am black but beautiful as the tents of Kedar. Do not stare at me because I am black, because I am darkened, darkened by the sun. You, beloved of my soul, tell me, tell me, where you tend your flock.

in post-apartheid South Africa as a nation-building composition, and in two versions: one the original SATB version (see Ex. 3), the other a recomposition by Hans Rosenschoon as a solo song with accompaniment (see Ex. 4), which Rosenschoon also orchestrated.[19]

'Barali Ba Jerusalema' (see Ex. 3) strains against the conventions it proclaims at almost every turn. Dominated by a powerful melody, like the Mohapeloa, the four opening 4-bar phrases and certain parallelisms in the harmony recall Victorian hymns of Sankey and Moody. It is however more clearly in a key: C major. But there is a tension of part-writing below the surface that intensifies chromatically half-way through the first 16-bar section (with the words 'do not stare at me because I am black') and erupts towards bar 15 into a series of vertical textures inexplicable in terms of conventional harmonic voicing ('tell me, tell me'), whereupon this direction suddenly disappears in bar 16: submerged, as it were (in the phrase 'where you tend your flock') by a rapid unison descent to the 'tonic'. Rather than closure, however, this seems more like interruption, a displacement of the expectation set up by the previous bars. What starts out again in bar 17 as a contrasting middle section in the relative minor key, also deviates from its own path some bars later, with choral shouts, at a high register and more urgent tempo ('open for me, my love'), followed by a series of parallel clusters that descend into virtual stasis. Then the piece gradually picks up again and continues in a rich-textured vein much like the opening of the piece, but without any return of the opening melody, so this is not a 'reprise'.

The idiom is not placeable within contemporary Western European art music of the mid-twentieth century, and the form is not a conventional song form. The words are closely represented musically, and the resulting tensions in harmony and voice-leading can, I argue, be seen as political signifiers in the musical language. It is common in African choral songs to use biblical or liturgical metaphors as motifs of resistance: recall the song by Matyila mentioned at the beginning of this paper (see endnote 6). Recall, too, that in 1948 the National Party came to power in South Africa, that throughout the 1950s draconian apartheid legislation was implemented and the era of 'high apartheid' was the 1960s and 70s – the last twenty years of Moerane's life, which he spent mostly in Lesotho.

A glimpse into Moerane's life that offers a clue to his political sensibility is given in Kirby's correspondence with him. On 16 February 1966 Moerane writes in answer to Kirby's request to reproduce the score of 'Fatše La Heso' a warm letter of thanks, noting his 'complete failure' to get the work published himself, 'the publishers always regretting the smallness of the market for such things' (Letter from Moerane to Kirby 16 February 1966, Museums and Archives, University of Cape Town: Kirby Papers file BC 750, 'Correspondence'). In his reply Kirby asks for 'an account of your personal career, your family origins, your own education, and so on' (Letter from Kirby to Moerane 22 February 1966, Ibid.). This may have sounded too probing during a decade of escalating repression and censorship, for Moerane's reply is unexpectedly terse: 'I regret I cannot oblige with the particulars for which you have asked. I cannot even explain why. Please be satisfied with the bare statement that *the times do not permit*' (Letter from Moerane to Kirby 9 March 1966, Ibid.; my emphasis). It was the last time the two men corresponded for several years.

The times were difficult for all educated, high-profile black composer-teachers such as Moerane; schools were already sites of struggle. Even if he

Ex. 4. 'Barali Ba Jerusalema' by M Moerane, solo version by H Rosenschoon © SAMRO. Bars 1-9 and 14-17.

is not found to have been a political activist – more research would be needed to establish this – he may have been seen as a threat. Kirby's colleague and successor at Wits, Friedrich Hartmann, saw him so. He had given his opinion on Moerane in 1958, some years after Hartmann helped Moerane to complete 'Fatše La Heso': '[m]any years ago I have seen Moerane once more and also received a letter from him. He was then a very embittered man with clear communistic tendencies' (Letter from Hartmann to Kirby 11 March 1958, Museums and Archives, University of Cape Town: Kirby Papers file BC 750, 'Correspondence').[20]

Given the importance – musical or otherwise – of the seething texture in the lower parts of Moerane's original version, the obvious question to ask is how the piece translates into a solo song, in the modern era. Part of the rewrite by Rosenschoon is shown in Ex. 4.

In Rosenschoon's version the soprano is far more soloistic: note the dramatic octave transpositions in the 3rd and 4th bars of the melody (elsewhere in the song the soprano is forced up to high C – quite an odd touch in the context of an otherwise bland 'art-song' rewriting). But it is the piano accompaniment that most remakes the song, and it is the all-important lower voice parts that are made into this accompaniment. Semiquavers taken from the agitated chromatic bass line in bars 11 and 12 are brought into service in a totally different way, as rippling accompaniment wrapping the melody like a chocolate box. Black notes become white, perceived dissonances become (re)perceived consonances or disappear altogether. Rosenschoon's harmonic simplification signifies a reading of the song as 'simple', and he underscores this with a dynamic marking of *p* at the beginning (rather than Moerane's *f*) and with pretty jump-bass left-hand figuration, which replaces Moerane's tense counterpoint. The texture is stabilised, and harmonic convention reinstated. But the end result, to me, sounds like a serious misreading, a writing out of the script of anything that Moerane might have been trying to say. In terms of the politics of reconciliation of the immediate post-apartheid year, within which the piece was recomposed, the piece is indeed 'brought out of the closet', literally, but in the process the original composer's voice is dusted off and replaced with the idealised past of Romantic harmony: Schubert with a Sesotho text. The idiom forcing its way to the surface of Moerane's music, assertively expressing his immediate experience of what to him was 'contemporary', was clearly an idiom unrecognisable to a contemporary composer today.

Was it the absence of European modernism lying behind Moerane's idiom that caused such a reading? Or, turning the question around: what does the original piece foreshadow that was not visible in Moerane's time or later? How does the original look back, conceptually, to the future? And what (or whose) notion of 'history' does the rewriting belong to?

BACK TO THE FUTURE

Two concepts from the world of musicology are brought into service here, in order to interpret such music historically and analytically and perhaps point to a new kind of paradigm for reading other South African music of this kind. In 1999 Gary Tomlinson proposed a historiography of music in anthropological terms, as 'others', a view in which he challenges influential historiographer Carl Dahlhaus's notion that the role of historical hermeneutics is 'to make alien material comprehensible, i.e. material that is remote in time or in social or ethnic origin' (1983: 5). 'The prevailing winds have shifted,' says Tomlinson, 'far enough indeed that the historian's aim may at times seem fully the opposite of Dahlhaus's – an aim, precisely, of making comprehensible material alien (1999: 3).' Tomlinson calls this a 'defamiliarising impulse', and applies it to his own fascination with the irrational, the metaphysical, in seventeenth-century European opera.

Applying Tomlinson's view here, though, immediately begs the question: familiar to whom? What notion of historiography pertains in South Africa, where choral compositions have very different reception histories from other kinds of South African music, especially art music, making them familiar to some (the black community of choralism) and unfamiliar to others (white academics)? The answer lies, I suggest, largely in how such pieces are viewed by the academy as successful or not in terms of a Western theoretical tradition. All composers in South Africa to a greater or lesser extent are inducted into this tradition's closed scientific system of rules; a system in which music is disengaged from the complexity of its meanings in cultural or historical practice. This displacement allows the analyst to ignore the mystery, the otherness, the alienating effect, as Tomlinson would say, of such music's *unfamiliarity*. An analytical reading in which nothing familiar is assumed would not privilege a notion of how such music conforms or otherwise, to a discourse of only one familiarity.

Susan McClary puts the argument for rethinking history slightly differently. In *Conventional Wisdom* (2000) she proposes a 'de-centred' approach that asks not why composers deviate from the norm, but what the norm actually *was* and in what cultural circumstances it came to be that way. She shows how the tonal idioms of later eighteenth-century music solidified out of the more harmonically capricious modal-tonal music of the seventeenth and in what cultural circumstances the latter, too, came into being. In another context, her

'Afterword' to the 1985 translation of Attali's *Noise*, McClary explains how Attali views 'norms', pointing out that his radical notion of 'composition' – putting a piece together – is a de-mystifying and de-theorising process 'removed from the rigid institutions of specialised musical training in order to return it to all members of society' (1996: 156).

Returning composition to the two black composers examined here is not the point, though, for they already owned compositional process. But when they learnt the rules of harmony and counterpoint they were certainly expected to rethink and maybe abandon their own norms. For this reason, when I asked contemporary choral composer Phelelani Mnomiya in 2004 if harmony and counterpoint studies at university were useful to him he answered enthusiastically, 'oh yes'. When I pushed him a little on harmony, he said that what he had learnt from university was a 'harmonic vocabulary' (pers. comm., May 2004). What he meant, it seems, is having the conceptual knowledge to go with his aural knowledge. This conceptual knowledge – knowing which part has which note, what all the parts are doing, what everything is called – was not, I suggest, taken on board out of context in South Africa, and this further complicates the issue. Mohapeloa, Moerane, and other black choral composers were well versed in conventional harmonic wisdoms from a stock of church hymns, popular music, and Western part-songs and choruses, before they studied it at university. '[Y]ou see, we have been taught to sing European hymns and songs in four parts. So we are used to that,' as Ghanaian composer Ephraim Amu put it (Agawu, 1987: 57). Or as Bongani Mthethwa put it in an interview with me, also in 1987:

> in African schools you find these kids singing a Mozart mass in Zulu or Sotho or a Haydn piece translated into an African language … To [them] it's a piece by Haydn, who lived somewhere in Austria, but it's *their* music, they think of it as their music, even if they know that the composer did not come from Africa; because they sing it, they understand it, they enjoy it.

But in order to 'normalise' their music, a university training would have expected them to learn a new harmonic theory, new concepts of melody and texture. What composers learn in harmony and counterpoint is grounded (quite literally) in a distinction drawn in the early eighteenth century between the harmonic and fundamental bass, in the ordering principle of triads and their extension and inversion from a harmonic root. Yet in the choral examples I have explored, these principles and the long trajectories of tonal music they later supported are simply not there.

In the search for some kind of framework for reading them it is worthwhile remembering that both McClary and Tomlinson drew heavily on vocal composition of the seventeenth century to explore theories of historiography and analysis. Seventeenth-century Italian and French music, especially, articulated social and political fragmentation akin to that of twentieth-century South Africa, and the voice, in early seventeenth-century Italian opera and in twentieth-century South African black choral music, similarly 'embodies' new theories of composition. The seventeenth-century's uncomfortably modal-tonal language and unexpected use of dissonances, McClary says,

> seeks by definition to overflow its boundaries. If some of the formal conventions of the 1700s seem quite uncompromising, it is in part because they were designed to cope with the overwhelming momentum generated through [long] tonal trajectories. Yet regardless of how cleaned up tonality becomes, this unruly potential is always still sedimented in, always threatening to break out: seventeenth-century tonality is the skeleton in the closet, the capricious turtle beneath what we like to perceive as bedrock (2000: 19).

What both McClary and Tomlinson help us to see in black choral music is a language in which the capricious turtle is always forcing itself up, and a language that does not merely reflect what *were* contemporary social discontinuities and disunities, but one that prefigures the much more remote *future*, the now, of post-apartheid South Africa, in which our sense of music's past and present is displaced, our sense of what makes it 'contemporary' called into question. Moreover, 'theories of music that have shaped our perceptions and consumption of music', McClary says, 'have been instrumental in conditioning us not to recognize silencing – not to realize that something vital may be missing from our experience' (1996: 150).

Mohapeloa and Moerane had, or in Mnomiya's case have, to write music for the same performers and audiences before and after their formal training. Mnomiya told me that he could not really apply what he learnt about composition at university because his community would not understand it, and this speaks to a performative dimension to this music that affects the way it is written, that I have not been able to touch on here. Yet Mnomiya is well versed in harmony, counterpoint and orchestration. What I want to open up here is the possibility that we are missing something in these compositions, that something in our reading of them silences the 'noise' that they are making. Trying to read them as reflecting very different, modern African experiences of the 'contemporary' might, I suggest, then also allow us to see them as 'foreshadowing' both a new compositional (dis)order and a new socio-economic one – the political state of post-apartheid South Africa. For as Attali says, 'music runs parallel to human society, is structured like it, and changes when it does. It does not evolve in a linear fashion, but is caught up in the complexity and circularity of the movements of history' (1985: 10).

Endnotes

1 This material is based upon work supported by the National Research Foundation. Any opinions, findings and conclusions or recommendations expressed in this material are however those of the author, and therefore the NRF does not accept any liability in regard thereto.

2 In 1979 the Education and Training Act replaced the Bantu Education Act of 1953, providing (unequally funded) education along colour lines via fourteen departments of education. (The South African Institute of Race Relations published annual reports throughout the period, in which statistics about school enrolment and per capita expenditure paint a gloomy picture.) The largest was the Department of Education and Training which catered for black schools in 'white' urban areas of South Africa, and there were also education departments in the nine independent and non-independent black homelands. In black schools music education was in a situation that Khabi Mngoma described in 1985 – coining a phrase from Todd Matshikiza – as the 'back of the moon' (Christie, 1986: 115). '[C]urricula are rudimentary and the amenities poor' (116), but 'to the extent that the participants equate a sound to a symbol' (117), choral competitions using songs in sol-fa notation helped at the very least, Mngoma argues, 'to keep music literacy in [black] schools alive' (116).

3 The comment came at the end of a paper I delivered on '"Africanising Elements" in South African Composition' at the Twenty-Fourth Congress of the Musicological Society of Southern Africa, held at the University of Stellenbosch 4-5 September 1997 (see also Levy, 1998).

4 This is true of most parts of Africa where choral music occurs. In an interview with Ghanaian composer Ephraim Amu, Kofi Agawu shows how '[m]ost of Amu's oeuvre consist[s] of vocal anthems, the words of which are either written by him or arranged from traditional or Biblical sources' (1987: 63).

5 Composed to mark black opposition to the Native Lands Act legislation of 1913 (see Lucia, 2005: 172-75 and 336).

6 'The country is thundering', composed for the visit of the British royal family to South Africa in 1947.

7 'Lord God Omnipotent', written in protest against the Ciskei Government in the mid-1980s (Mavis Mpola, pers. comm. 1999), and quickly becoming a widely-sung protest song that was later assumed to be 'traditional' (Khumalo, 1998: 48).
8 Composed 1992. The inscription on the last page of the score reads, 'A lament on the ongoing black-on-black violence gripping our beloved country'.
9 The score, which was found by Mzilikazi Khumalo in the SAMRO library, Braamfontein, in 1998, is not dated.
10 Mohapeloa (1908-82) is a national figure in the history of Lesotho and his music is widely known in Sesotho-speaking areas of southern Africa. Moerane (1909-81) is the uncle of the current president of South Africa, Thabo Mbeki, and although less prolific than Mohapeloa still a figure of major importance in black choral culture. Hardly a year passes without works by one or both men being prescribed in national school and adult choir competitions that involve millions of South African choralists all over the country. No white South African composer can claim this degree of recognition, over so many decades.
11 It was described in 1969 by Yvonne Huskisson as a '[c]horal arrangement of a traditional threshing song' (1969: 164) and this view is supported by Khumalo (1998: 28).
12 In Lesotho the term 'Mmino Walinoto' was coined in the 1960s to describe modern choral music in classical style that incorporated traditional melodies.
13 The literal translation from Sesotho is 'He who shines alone of the music of today', i.e. 'The finest collection of today's music' (I am grateful to Paul Germond for this translation). The subtitle is in English: 'Harnessing salient features of modern African music'.
14 In the second of two unpublished interviews with David Coplan in 1978, Mohapeloa explains that the first phrase was his own invention but the 'main theme' ('U Ea Kae') was traditional (Coplan field notes 2 May 1978, card 3).
15 Percival Kirby was a major figure in African music scholarship and Professor of Music at the University of the Witwatersrand from 1921 to 52 where among other things he taught composition. See his autobiography *Wits End* (1967) for a detailed account of the way he established the music degree programme at the University.
16 In the first of two unpublished interviews with David Coplan in 1978, Mohapeloa referred to the aesthetic dilemma of making 'a harmonious agreement between the two systems' – African and Western (Coplan field notes, n.d. [early 1978], card 17).
17 Mohapeloa claims that he 'did very little of the studies' at Wits and his training in music theory brought him 'some confusion. Because thing[s] that I thought

personally were okay, I had to abandon or try to alter' (David Coplan field notes, n.d. [early 1978], cards 10 and 6.
18 Moerane's best-known competition songs, 'Sylvia' and 'Della', were written in 1968 and 69 respectively (Huskisson, 1969: 158).
19 Hans Rosenschoon is Professor of Composition at the University of Stellenbosch, South Africa.
20 Moerane 'could not manage [it]without guidance', was Hartmann's comment. 'Moerane [thus] came to Grahamstown where I gave him tuition for a full year, pro deo, of course. During this time he wrote also his symphonic poem "My Country", which is based on tunes of his people' (Letter from Hartmann to Kirby dated 11 March 1962, Ibid.).

Bibliography

Agawu, Kofi. 1987. 'Conversations with Ephaim Amu: The Making of a Composer'. *The Black Perspective in Music*, 15(1), pp. 51-63.

Attali, Jacques. 1985 [1977]. *Noise: The Political Economy of Music* (trans. Brian Massumi). Minneapolis & London: University of Minnesota Press.

Attwell, David. 2005. *Rewriting Modernity: Studies in Black South African Literary History*. Ohio: Ohio University Press.

Bhabha, Homi K. 1994. *The Location of Culture*. London & New York: Routledge.

Christie, Pam, Helene Perold & Dawn Butler (eds). 1986. *The Right to Learn: The Struggle for Education in South Africa*. Johannesburg: Ravan Press.

Couzens, Tim. 1985. *The New African: A Study of the Life and Works of H.I.E. Dhlomo*. Johannesburg: Ravan Press.

Dahlhaus, Carl. 1983. *Foundations of Music History* (trans. JB Robinson). Cambridge: Cambridge University Press.

Dargie, D. 1988. *Xhosa Music: Its Techniques and Instruments, with a Collection of Songs*. Cape Town: David Philip.

Erlmann, Veit. 1991. *African Stars: Studies in Black South African Performance*. Chicago & London: University of Chicago Press.

_. 1999. *Music, Modernity and the Global Imagination: South Africa and the West*. New York: Oxford University Press.

Huskisson, Yvonne. 1969. *The Bantu Composers of Southern Africa/Die Bantoe-Komponiste van Suider-Afrika*. Johannesburg: South African Broadcasting Corporation.

Khumalo, James S Mzilikazi (ed.). 1998. *South Africa Sings Volume 1: African Choral Repertoire in 'Dual Notation'*. Johannesburg: SAMRO.

_. 2003/4 and 2005/6. '"Serious" Music in an African Context'. *NewMusicSA: Bulletin of the International Society for Contemporary Music – South African Section*, Third and Fourth Issue, pp. 13-15.

Kirby, Percival. 1979. 'The Bantu Composers of South Africa'. In Jaques P Malan (ed.). *South African Music Encyclopedia Vol. 1*. Cape Town: Oxford University Press, pp. 85-94.

Levy, Michael. 1998. 'Burning Question: Report on the Twenty-Fourth Annual Musicological Congress'. *South African Journal of Musicology: SAMUS*, 18, pp. 100-103.

Lucia, Christine. 2005. 'Introduction'. In *The World of South African Music: A Reader*. Newcastle-upon-Tyne: Cambridge Scholars Press, pp. xxi-xlvi.

McClary, Susan. 1996 [1985]. 'Afterword'. In Jacques Attali. *Noise: The Political Economy of Music*. Minneapolis & London: University of Minnesota Press, pp. 149-58.

_. 2000. *Conventional Wisdom: The Content of Musical Form*. Berkeley & Los Angeles: University of California Press.

Mngoma, Khabi. 1981. 'The Correlation of Folk and Art Music Among African Composers'. In A Tracey (ed.). *Papers Presented at the Second Symposium on Ethnomusicology*. Grahamstown: International Library of African Music, Rhodes University, pp. 61-69.

_. 1986. 'Music in African Education'. In C Lucia (ed.). *Proceedings of the First National Music Educators' Conference*. Durban: University of Natal Press, pp. 115-21.

Mohapeloa, Joshua Pulumo. 1988a [1935]. *Meloli le Lithallere tsa Afrika, I*. Morija, Lesotho: Morija Sesotho Book Depot.

_. 1988b [1947]. *Meloli le Lithallere tsa Afrika, III: Buka ea Boraro*. Morija, Lesotho: Morija Sesotho Book Depot.

_. 1996 [1939]. *Meloli le Lithallere tsa Afrika, II*. Morija, Lesotho: Morija Sesotho Book Depot.

_. 2002 [1951]. 'Preface'. In *Khalimo-Nosi tsa 'Mino oa Kajeno: Harnessing Salient Features of Modern African Music*. Morija, Lesotho: Morija Sesotho Book Depot.

Mot'soane, PM. 2004. 'A Brief History and Background to JP Mohapeloa's Music Composition: An Interview with Prof JM Mohapeloa, a Brother of the above Music Composer'. Unpublished mimeograph.

Mthethwa, Bongani. 1987. Author's interview, April.

_. 1988. 'The Songs of Alfred A Kumalo: A Study in Nguni and Western Musical Syncretism'. In A Tracey (ed.). *Papers Presented at the Sixth Symposium on Ethnomusicology, 1987*. Grahamstown: International Library of African Music, Rhodes University, pp. 28-32.

Nettleton, Anitra, Julia Charlton & Fiona Rankin-Smith (eds). 2003. *Engaging Modernities: Transformations of the Commonplace*. Johannesburg: University of the Witwatersrand Art Galleries.

Olwage, Grant. 2006. 'John Knox Bokwe, Colonial Composer. Tales about Race and Music'. *Journal of the Royal Musical Association*, 131(1), pp. 1-37.

Rainbow, Bernarr. 1989. *Music in Educational Thought and Practice: A Survey from 800 BC*. Aberystwyth, Wales: Boethius Press.

Rycroft, David. 1977. 'Evidence of Stylisitic Continuity in Zulu "Town" Music'. In no ed. *Essays for a Humanist: An Offering to Klaus Wachsmann*. New York: The Town House Press, pp. 216-60.

South African Broadcasting Corporation. n.d. [c.1960]. 'The Music of South Africa: A Programme featuring a Choir of the Non-White African Population of South Africa'. LT 7445/L38, Side B (Prog. 10).

Sibandze, Moroesi. n.d. 'Mohapeloa: The Man and His Music'. www.africanchorus.org/Voam/Voam1014.htm, accessed 19 November 2005.

Tomlinson, Gary. 1999. *Metaphysical Song: An Essay on Opera*. Princeton, New Jersey: Princeton University Press.

Tracey, Andrew. 1996. 'Indigenous Instruments'. *The Talking Drum*, 19, pp. 8-11.

Treitler, Leo. 1999. 'The Historiography of Music: Issues of Past and Present'. In N Cook & M Everist (eds). *Rethinking Music*. Oxford & New York: Oxford University Press, pp. 356-77.

2

APARTHEID'S MUSICAL SIGNS

REFLECTIONS ON BLACK CHORALISM, MODERNITY AND RACE-ETHNICITY IN THE SEGREGATION ERA

GRANT OLWAGE

IMPERIAL RELATIONS

Like most South African genealogies, apartheid's origins are a mixed up, miscegenated affair. Apartheid's gestation, however, is typically said to have occurred during the segregationist era, the half-century or so immediately prior to apartheid's official birth in 1948.[1] Historians tell us that in the first decades of the early twentieth century, predominantly English-speaking 'liberals' sowed the seeds for a project of socio-political engineering they themselves named segregationism, 'a composite ideology and set of practices seeking to legitimise social difference and economic inequality in every aspect of life' (Beinart and Dubow, 1995: 4). Significantly, segregation was also in tune with imperial policy, both in the metropolis and in the colony for the representatives of Empire.[2] For, if the growth of segregationism in South Africa was in part British-led it was because it had British interests at heart. This has been well documented for the large-scale political economy.[3] But imperial relations were established also on the terrain of culture.

One area in which there's a clear (ongoing) relationship between imperialist capitalism and culture is, of course, the recording industry. The early history of the recording industry in South Africa is sketchy at best; the details we have pertain largely to the new media as it impacted on the black music market:

black listeners were buying gramophone records already in the first decade of the twentieth century, black consumption of recordings increased dramatically in the 1920s, and the first recordings of black South African musicians were made more often in Britain than in South Africa (see Coplan, 1979: 143).[4] Many of the first South African sonic products, then, were 'manufactured' elsewhere: materially produced in, and with, the Empire's capital, ideologically fashioning the Empire's subjects in order to make money. To put this bluntly: the segregated state of things in early twentieth-century South Africa, I argue, abetted imperial money-making in the music industry.

In the late nineteenth- and early twentieth-century form of British imperialism, Empire was imagined (even if it did not always act) as functioning like a sort of multinational corporation with its headquarters in London.[5] It follows that the idea, and ideologies, of Empire became important for consumerism in the Empire at large. In what Anne McClintock calls 'commodity racism', for example, race was imported into capitalism's marketing machinery (1995: chap. 5). Indeed, race became commodified to a remarkable degree in the 'race records' industry. This has typically referred to the US industry from circa 1920 on, when specific genres were pitched at different racial audiences – the blues for blacks, country for rural whites – but is also applicable to the early recording industry in South Africa: 'black' music was produced by black artists with black consumers in mind by white capital.[6] The race records model, however, accounts inadequately for the structure of the South African industry, which operated also, and from the outset, as an industry of ethnicity. Records thus turned on the dual subject of race-ethnicity, a duality borne of the fracturing of race into the plurality of ethnicities.

Exemplary of this is the career of Daniel Marivate, one of the black South African artists to record in Britain. A teacher and 'choralist' – choral composer, conductor and singer – from the then northern Transvaal, Marivate and others had accompanied the early vaudeville star Griffiths Motsieloa on a trip to London in 1931 to record for the Singer Gramophone Company; such were Singer's returns on Motsieloa that this was his second set of studio sessions in the metropolis in as many years (see *Bantu World* [hereafter *BW*], 9 April 1932: 9).[7] In South Africa, Marivate's recordings were sold not simply as black (or, at the time, African, Bantu, or native) music, but as ethnic, 'Shangaan' music.[8] Inscribed thus on the grooves of Columbia's discs, as illustrated in Figure 1, are 'Songs of the Africans', which are more specifically songs of the 'Machopi, Chikaranga, Shangaan', and so on.[9] Ethnic interpolations, even more than race, spoke of and for capitalist interests, for ethnicity was crucial to the migrant labour system that characterised early industrial South Africa. In

Figure 1. Advertisement by Columbia's local distributor Polliacks (*Bantu World*, 25 March 1933: 12).

short, Columbia's 'Bantu Records' were a catalogue of the music of ethnicity, lists of music arranged under the categories of Zulu, Xosa, Sesuto (see *BW*, 15 April 1933: 20).

As we will see, ethnic typographising was a sign of things to come. But how in the first place was ethnicity sonically mapped out? At its simplest, the ethnic subject presented its ethnicity: Xabanisa's Xosa Choir, which recorded for His Master's Voice (HMV), by 'royal appointment to their Majesties the King and Queen', in the early 1930s, sang only Xhosa music, or rather music in the language isiXhosa (*BW*, 22 July 1933: 20). As often, however, the performers' ethnicities did not match their performances. The Hope Fountain Native Girls' Choir from the eastern Cape recorded in isiNdebele and Setswana, not in the mother tongue, which is isiXhosa, of the choir's region (*BW*, 16 Sep. 1933: 16). For purposes of ethnic classification, then, a song's language was a more important element than its performers' identities. There were further, possibly musical, criteria. When HMV called on 'Zulus!' to 'hear [the] new records, specially made for you', the music they were being asked to buy into included Western-style hymn-tunes in isiZulu, but also music designated as 'folk' and 'traditional'. The broad, fluid concept-category of 'the traditional' was no more specific here than elsewhere, and included a Zulu 'folk song' with organ, a Zulu folksong in English, and a 'traditional' number with concertina (*BW*, 23 Sep. 1933: 16). Whatever the musical content of the traditional (about which I say more below), it was not, as we know, something precolonially aboriginal but thoroughly entangled in the processes and practices of modernity. Accordingly, several of Columbia's traditional Zulu records, sung by the African Zulu Male Voice Choir, were accompanied by the very contemporary Jazz Revellers Band (*BW*, 21 Oct. 1933: 16).

When exactly the traditional song entered the black choral repertory is unclear; it did not, for certain, exist as a genre in pre-Union (pre-1910) choral performance (see also Erlmann, 1991: 69-77; and Coplan, 1985: 70). Its emergence seems to trace the rise of segregationism, to leave sonic traces of, by singling out, the ethnic subject.

Hence whites, too, were ethnicised by the recording industry. In addition to black catalogues, the major labels also had Afrikaner lists, thereby capitalising on the newest of South Africa's ethnicities. They were able to do this because around the time that the traditional made an appearance on black choral programmes, traditional Afrikaans, or folk, music was being invented. Jan Bouws, the mid-century Dutch historian of, and propagandist for, Afrikaans folk music, identified 'the threatened turn-of-the-century years' (*'die bedreigde jare om die eeuwisseling'*) – the threat being Anglophone imperialism circa 1900 – as marking the beginning of the Afrikaans folk music project. Decades of collecting and editing ensued, a collective – folk – effort realised in the *Federasie van Afrikaanse Kultuurvereniginge*'s *Volksangbundel* of 1937 (Bouws, n.d. [c.1958]: 16; also Bouws, n.d. [c.1962/3]). The irony of British business profiting from Afrikaner folksong was something Bouws would not have commented on; after all, the imperialist's records probably spread the gospel of the folk far more effectively than the *Volksangbundel* ever did. However, when, by the mid-twentieth century, the authenticity of Afrikaans folk culture came to be questioned – that favorite 'Sarie Marais' was discovered to have Scottish origins! – Bouws had plenty to say: he argued for the recognition of a genre of sacred folksong (*'godsdienstige Afrikaanse volksliedere'*), which, as genuine folk music (*'egte volksmusiek'*), was 'own' music (*'eie musiek'*), and, through an appeal to especially German and Dutch folklore studies, he rescued 'Sarie' and similar 'immigrant' tunes: what was initially foreign becomes borrowed and then, through a process of adaptation, finally wins citizenship (*'Die lied het burgerreg verkry'*) (Bouws, n.d. [c.1958]: 21-2, 29-33). In the creation of a specifically Afrikaans musical culture – and its reproduction on disc – Afrikaner ethnicity was born.[10] The birth of such a cultural identity became in turn a necessary condition for the later development of theories of ethnicity that would underpin the thinking of apartheid ideologues and their politics. Culture, in its separations, at times not only augurs, but powerfully inaugurates, politics of segregations.

The division of the South African landscape by ethnicity, infamously from the 1960s, into 'self-governing' ethnic states, or 'homelands', was a cornerstone of apartheid.[11] As Bouws established the musical citizenship of Afrikaners, so the Afrikaner-led apartheid state would deny blacks full citizenship of South Africa because their ethnicities located them in the homeland states. Music, too, was unavoidably, if often ambiguously, enlisted in the service of 'separate development', its fullest elaboration to this end worked out by the state through the South African Broadcasting Corporation. In his seminal work on state radio, Charles Hamm (1991) details how radio broadcasting in pre-apartheid South Africa flirted at first only tentatively and then unwittingly with the music of ethnicity, but that by the mid-1950s it was producing it – aggressively dispatching recording teams to the native reserves – and by the late 50s, with the establishment of Radio Bantu, building ethnicity into its policy and developing separate ethnic radio stations to broadcast it. This fetishising of ethnicity, by the most exemplary of apartheid's music industries, pre-existed, we have seen, in the commodification thereof by the industry of an earlier era. In the relationship between these industries of Empire and apartheid, bound by a contract to produce ethnicity, I want to reflect briefly on two processes through which apartheid itself was produced.

The first is as much a matter of historiography as anything else. Histories of apartheid suggest that it 'evolved', specifically out of segregationism, through a process of rationalisation.[12] Radio Bantu could thus be said to have drawn on, while systematising, the structures and practices of the segregation-era recording industry. It even used the products of its precursor. The playlist for choral music, which featured prominently on Radio Bantu's programmes, was compiled from two sources: in large part from the SABC's own recording activities – in just 1963 alone its mobile recording units visited 435 black schools, adding 7 374 choral items to its collection – but also from the early commercial recordings of black choirs made from the 1930s on (Hamm, 1991: 162). Pre-apartheid sounds were played on apartheid radio because they played into Radio Bantu's *raison d'être*: to ethnicise the airwaves.

The rationalising imperative was effected by a second feature of apartheid: the magnitude of the state's interventions; government drew on previously extra-state ideologies and structures, drawing them into the state machinery. In the case of Radio Bantu, corporate practice was institutionalised as a matter of state. There is of course an important difference: recording ethnicity for the state was primarily for ideological reasons – to naturalise the idea of the tribe and ideal of the homeland – whereas recording companies, we assume, were motivated largely by profit. Even here, though, apartheid's use of music to explicitly produce ethnicity (as opposed to merely producing the music of ethnicity) was not new. British capital, again, provided a precedent. For if it is well known that the histories of the mining industry and ethnicity are closely related, it is also known that music was productive of that relationship: the mines fostered 'tribal' dancing and black miners were among the first to record the music of ethnicity (see *BW*, 9 April 1932: 9). It followed that miners' ethnicity would become the topic of choral songs; Marivate wrote a piece for choir about 'Shangaans going to the mines on a lorry'. The song was recorded – of course in Shangaan, by Shangaan singers, and, in Marivate's words, as it was 'sung by the uncivilised natives' (14 Nov. 1935).[13]

The producers of the music of ethnicity were, of course, not just the captains of industry or apartheid apparatchiks. Choralists themselves were actively, and willingly, involved in the production of such subjectivities. And for good reason: there were real benefits, sometimes powerful, often banal, to be had from performing ethnicity. For the banal: black choirs capitalised on the value of recording their ethnicity for several reasons. Recording presented rare opportunities for travel, as choirs from the Cape and Natal journeyed to Johannesburg's studios, and was good publicity, as gramophone records, often advertised nationally, built reputations, sometimes resulting in offers of performance far from a choir's home base. For the not so banal: Veit Erlmann, for example, has detailed the varied uses of choral music by various parties in the genesis of a Zulu consciousness for the time, especially during the 1910s to 1930s (1991: 69-79). But these boons were consequent on enabling conditions. If the printed word in its various manifestations has been an important source and resource for the imagining of community, recorded music, too, has powerfully produced and disseminated the idea of the ethnic-nation.

THE AMERICAN CONNECTION

Mise-en-scenes of South Africa's ethnicised aurality were commonplace: a picture of a 'group of Bantu men recording tribal songs' (*BW*, 4 June 1932: 9), or, as in Figure 2, the performers become listeners: five animal skin-clad and beaded auditors beside a mud and thatch hut huddle around a gramophone, enthralled, we are to believe, by sounds emanating from the magical music box. The scenario served both to advertise Columbia's black catalogue, and to promote 'the portable', the fairly new boxed and now easily transportable

Figure 2. Advertisement for Columbia (Programme, Second Transvaal African Eisteddfod, 12-17 Dec. 1932, South African Institute of Race Relations papers, AD843 B47.6).

gramophone player, the portability of which meant that the sound of records could be heard in rural villages throughout Africa. As writer Ezekiel Mphahlele recalled of his childhood in the early 1930s: 'Jeemee Roe-Jars (Jimmie Rodgers), then in fashion, yodeled plaintively from various parts of the village' (1971: 22).

But alongside – and against – this advertising of ethnicity occurred a counter discourse. Newspapers such as *The Bantu World* spoke of 'the Demon of tribalism', which it vowed to 'fight against and destroy' (3 Sep. 1932: 4). In part a hangover from missionary and colonial government proscriptions against 'the savage', and black, largely middle-class, aspirations in the name of a 'civilisation' that for the most part took Western bourgeois culture as its measure, this anti-ethnic discourse also had specific political resonances in the 1930s. Thus the *World*'s editorial of 27 April 1935, 'Detribalisation of Africans', was an exposé of the 'paradox of the policy of segregation': 'the Government's policy ... to encourage "the Natives to maintain their tribal organisations and cultures", or in other words to "develop along their own lines"' was 'none other than the traditional policy of White South Africa, namely that of "keeping the black man in his proper place"' (p. 8). The anti-ethnic discourse had several seemingly contradictory thrusts. One argued for racial unity. The *World* urged its readers to 'drop their tribal differences' for the sake of 'the oneness of the race', 'to foster racial pride' (28 Jan. 1933: 6).[14] How this black nationalist discourse manifested in black musical culture at the time has been attributed to two factors: black South Africans' engagement with black America and, somewhat contradicting the anti-ethnic discourse, a nascent interest in the local 'traditional'.[15]

It was partly in the wake of an *engagement*, a calculated political intervention, I want to argue, that an interest was strengthened: the pull towards the local traditional was galvanised by the magnetism of black America.

One strain of white liberal politics in the 1920s saw the solutions for South Africa's (racial) problems as having been worked out in the American South through the politics of 'race relations'.[16] Americans visited South Africa to campaign for this politics, while white South Africans undertook fact-finding missions to the US to see it in action. As a result, 'joint' institutions, often with American funding, sprang up throughout South Africa in an attempt to harmonise race relations; the Bantu Men's Social Centre in downtown Johannesburg was one, a 'centre for inter-racial goodwill and harmony' (*BW*, 4 Nov. 1933: 16). But if white liberals were sold on the idea of race relations, it was because it involved an ideal black man, a model that liberals and the black elite alike encountered in the New Negro of the Harlem Renaissance.[17]

A popular item in the Bantu Men's Social Centre library (funded by the Carnegie Corporation of America) was thus *The New Negro: An Interpretation* (1925), enthusiastically recommended by the white-authored *Literature for the South African Bantu* (1936) (Couzens, 1982: 324, 329-31). A crucial document of the Harlem Renaissance, *New Negro* defined the black American for 'the progressive Negro community'. *The New Negro* had a dual, partially contradictory, political purpose: to counter the 'fiction ... that the life of the races is separate', that is to encourage white and black contact, but also to 'build his Americanism on race values', to engender a 'racial awakening'; ideas that would persistently be restated in *The Bantu World*. The production of racial difference, as *The New Negro* admitted, had potentially segregationist implications, a difficulty that was finessed thus: by playing up difference, the New Negro would emphasise his Americanness, thereby downplaying his difference. And it was specifically in the field of culture, 'in terms of his artistic endowments and cultural contributions', that the black American was to be 'a conscious contributor and ... participant in American civilization' (Locke, 1925: x, 4, 11, 9, 12, xi, 15). Throughout the 1930s, lead stories in the *Bantu World* thus held up for its readers 'the theme of Negro advancement in the United States' (3 Sep. 1932: 1). In an article on 'Negro Progress in Art', black American musicians were heralded as having 'shared in the upliftment of their race' (16 April 1932: 9). Harlem had become a pregnant sign for black South Africans: of the birth of better times, of models to inspire and to which to aspire (see Ballantine, 1989). Thus the rhetoric of modernity, long racialised white in South Africa by the British civilising mission, now took on an alternative – black – provenance, located in what Guthrie Ramsey has called 'Afro-modernism' (2003: chap. 5).

Aesthetically, Afro-modernism shares similarities with classical or canonical modernism, such as the division of music into the categories of art and folk. At the same time black musical texts 'critiqued, teased, and taunted these boundaries', effecting what Ramsey calls a 'hybrid modernism' (p. 106-7). *New Negro* presents Afro-modernism in these terms. On the one hand, the editor of the volume, Alain Locke, has been charged with editorial 'smoothening' to fashion the artists and intellectuals represented in the anthology as modern New Negroes, to promote black artistic achievement on Eurocentric grounds, and to demote, through exclusion, black vernacular music, such as the blues (p. 114-15). On the other hand, in defining the New Negro Locke gave centrality to 'folk-expression'.

For Locke, the folk was above all expressed in the 'Negro spiritual', 'the most characteristic product of race genius as yet in America' (1925: xi, 199). His essay on the genre affirms both the spiritual's blackness – it is 'folk-expression', 'race music' – and its Americanness – it is 'nationally as well as racially characteristic'. Locke also highlights the genre's inherent modernity: the slave song 'transcends the level of its origin', having 'escaped the lapsing conditions and fragile vehicle of folk art, and come firmly into the context of formal music'. The spiritual's coming of age, coming into 'the formal', entailed a double process: recomposing it within the modern and performing it modernly. The former, for example, is most commonly identified with the 'arrangement', a mode of recomposing that deployed 'formal European idioms and mannerisms', and which was typically performed by classically trained solo singers or choirs on the concert stage (p. 199, 206-10). Locke thus concluded: 'We cannot accept the attitude that would merely preserve this music, but must cultivate that which would also develop it' (p. 210). It was all about keeping up with the times, and black South African choralism did similarly.

The spiritual had particular psycho-political resonances for black South Africans, especially during the 1920s and 1930s. As many have noted, the meta-theme of black oppression as an article of faith in an emancipated future spoke to the trials and aspirations of blacks in pre-war South Africa. As a black writer put it: in the spiritual 'there breathes hope and faith in the ultimate justice and brotherhood of man. The cadences of sorrow invariably turn to joy, and the message is ever manifest that ... every man will be free' (Ilanga Lase Natal (Natal Sun), 2 Nov. 1923, cited in Ballantine, 1989: 9). It was the arranged, modernised spiritual that black South Africans first heard on records, performed themselves, and even imitated in composition; Marivate wrote both words and music for a mock spiritual called 'No colour der' (see School Songs for Choir Competition).[18]

The year 1931 witnessed the founding of the Transvaal African Eisteddfod, an important institution for choral activity. One of its objects was the 'preservation (i.e. recording) of African traditional and "primitive" music'. But this, its manifesto stressed, was 'not enough': 'We should develop, reinterpret, and build on these tunes' (BW, 10 Dec. 1932: 1). Like the New Negro's relationship to the folk spiritual, black choral interest in the traditional was also in its modernising potential.[19] It was perhaps for this reason that, at this time, the traditional song arranged for choir was seldom allowed to speak for itself, typically being placed in a relational, teleological context.[20] Thus, with the appearance of the traditional song in the choral repertory, there emerged a new category in complementary opposition: the 'modern composition', penned by the 'modern Bantu composer' (BW, 10 Dec. 1932: 1; 20 May 1933: 3). The music designated by this category was not new, however; it had been composed since John Knox Bokwe's first composition of 1875 (see Olwage, 2006). What was novel was the modernist move of naming black choral composition 'modern'.

The traditional song arranged for choir was equally implicated in the modern. For the act of arranging the folk, we will see, was an act of modernising it. Of course, arranging the folk had become a global activity, one begun in early nineteenth-century Europe, gaining momentum throughout that century, and eventually capturing the imaginations of high modernists such as Bartók and Britten and New Negro musicians alike. What set the South African case apart from the black American example was that, while in America the category of the folk was productive of race, in South Africa it became productive also of ethnicity. And thus, while the engagement with Afro-modernism was intended to forestall the segregationist argument, did black choralism reproduce the ideas of segregation. The dialectic play of the complex of ideas on America and Africa played into, by sounding out, the ideology of segregationism.

A final irony is that this cultural production of difference was conceived, amongst other things, as a strategy to counter economic segregation. Like the African American example, black economic contribution was presented as also occurring within the field of culture: 'The most remarkable thing about the progress of Bantu music,' the *Bantu World* could claim of the Eisteddfod, was that it had 'brought European dealers in music into direct contact with Bantu singers and composers' (30 Dec. 1933: 1). To this end, the *World* could even concede that socially blacks and whites could be 'as separate as the fingers, and one as the hand in all things that are for mutual progress'; in other words, economic segregation was not on but culturally things were less clear-cut. For especially the revisionist school of South African history, the stories of capitalism and apartheid are inseparable. In a different sense, and as musical difference – race-ethnicity – became fetishised as a commodity, one might conclude that the logic of capitalism, which the black elite had largely internalised, fed into the logic of segregation, making of black choralism a potentially segregationist product.

Old relations continued

Black choralism's engagement with folk music in the 1930s was a commitment to the modern that exceeded the dictates of multinational capital, the internationalism of nationalist folkphilia, and Afro-modernism. For Marivate, as much as the discourse of Afro-modernism was inscribed in the spiritual he wrote, and the multinational industry produced the Shangaan music he recorded, his composing of ethnicity originated at 'home': in the mission school, the original context for the modernising of black South Africans and an enduring context for the practice of black choralism.[21]

Marivate was the principal of the mission school at Valdezia in the northern Transvaal, headed by the famous Swiss family of missionary-anthropologists, the Junods.[22] Their pioneering research on Tsonga culture complemented nascent ethnomusicological interest in the musics of southern Africa; 'European interest in Bantu folk songs is keen throughout the length and breadth of the sub-continent', reported the *Bantu World* (4 June 1932: 9; also 6 Jan. 1934: 4).[23] These efforts combined to put a more positive spin on aspects of black culture and music previously demonised by the mission.

Reasons for the mission's slowly shifting stance are complex, and here I want to point out only the following: the 'civilising mission' – the mission's own brand of modernity which aimed to assimilate its converts to Western ways of thinking and living – was in no way abandoned at this time, but rather came to be mediated by another feature of modernity: the folk-nation. The narrative of ethnicity, moreover, as the example of the Junods shows, was often written by missionaries themselves. It is thus that the mission, domesticator of the rest to the West, became also a home for the production of ethnicity, providing an unwitting context for the elaboration of segregationism, which the mission with righteous resolution typically gainsaid. The ambiguities of modernity, in short, put civilisation and segregation dialectically into play.

Curiously, it was literacy, long one of the mission's most cherished signs of modernity, through which the music of ethnicity was further publicised.[24] In 1934 Marivate published a collection of school songs for choir. The foreword, written by Henri Philippe Junod, eulogised the composer as 'a good student of European culture', but also as 'a true lover of his own'. To this end, Marivate had 'collected a great number of the folksongs of his tribe', some of which ended up in the collection (see *School Songs for Choir Competition*). Marivate himself wrote of his auto-ethnographic work:

> We are passing at an age when things purely African are being replaced by things European. We who are between ... have great responsibility for our race. We may either allow all native life, art, music, language to be crushed and wiped out or preserve all the present ideas, customs, life, music and art for those that will be born at the time when there will be not uncivilised Bantu ... My language is Shangaan and I am trying all I can to preserve some of Shangaan music and language (14 Nov. 1935).

For Marivate, the 'only way' of preserving music was 'by writing', and it was in the process of writing down traditional music that it was modernised (idem.). The song 'Ka Mpfumu' ('To the Authorities') – see Example 1 – shows this clearly. It was collected by Marivate in June 1933 on a trip to Rikatla, one of the Junods' mission stations, just north of present-day Maputo, Mozambique, and included in the school songbook. Unlike other songs in the book, some of

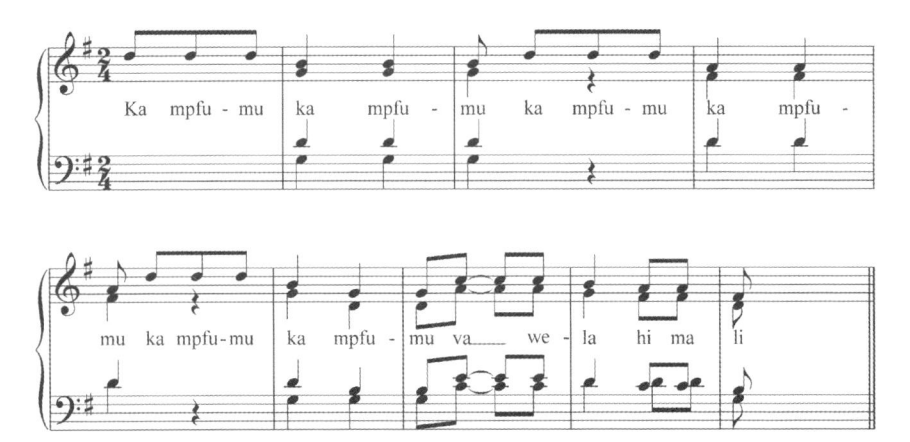

Ex. 1. Opening of 'Ka Mpfumu' by D Marivate.

which bear the signature 'composed by DC Marivate', 'Ka Mpfumu' is marked out as only being 'arranged by' the composer. Clearly, Marivate distinguishes between his newly authored – modern – compositions and music of folk origin, which he has not only notated but written down in the interventionist practice of arranging.

The interventions are easily identified. Whatever the unmediated, 'original' version of the song may have looked like, the song's introduction into the world of black choralism is its incorporation into the compositional world of four-part homophony, dominant-tonic progressions and phrasal cadencing (see also Coplan, 1985: 117). In fact, the content of the traditional is elusive, not especially evident, in the arranged song. And yet 'Ka Mpfumu' was named as traditional Shangaan music – by Marivate, Junod, and the recording company.

Some historians tell us that apartheid was not a preconceived 'grand plan' thought up by a group of Afrikaans-speaking intellectuals and implemented only by the state. Other actors – missionaries, capitalists and black South Africans – too were variously involved, sometimes willingly and actively, often unwittingly and accidentally, in the making of apartheid (see Posel, 1995: 207; Beinart and Dubow, 1995: 9-10). The multiple actors who operated on black choralism, and the contexts within which it operated, in the 1930s – the new mission, recording industry, Afro-modernism, amongst others – suggest that, from at least this time, black choralism did ethnic work, and that it did so in the hands of its black practitioners. This because of, we have seen, the ambiguities of modernity within which choralism developed. This despite the anti-ethnic discourse with which its members, the black elite and aspirant 'middling sort', spoke, and despite the 'civilised' status that choralism continued to hold. And so, while on the one hand the black elite almost uniformly argued against segregation, and presented choralism as one of a number of counter-arguments to it, on the other they prepared the ground, by grounding choralism in ethnicity, to be interpellated by what would become apartheid's signature cry: 'Develop along your own lines'. Choralism's protest at apartheid's making was also its, and its practitioners', participation in the genesis of apartheid.

The apartheid state would hence easily co-opt black choralism into its own story. When Yvonne Huskisson, who headed up the music section of Radio Bantu and whom Veit Erlmann called the 'Verwoerd of music' (1996: 253),[25] wrote her 'Story of Bantu Music' in 1968, she hardly mentioned indigenous black musics because choralism, which did feature prominently in the story, had long been ethnicised, had long inserted difference – and so, in the logic of segregation-apartheid: separateness – into the musical landscape.

ENDNOTES

1. This material is based upon work supported by the National Research Foundation. Any opinions, findings and conclusions or recommendations expressed in this material are however those of the author, and therefore the NRF does not accept any liability in regard thereto.
2. To take an early example: the Native Affairs Commission, whose report of 1905 was a key segregationist text, and which had been ordered during the tenure of the arch imperialist Lord Alfred Milner, Governor of the Cape and High Commissioner to South Africa, concluded that 'the rational policy ... is to facilitate the development of aboriginals on lines which do not merge too closely into European life' (cited in Legassick, 1995 [1972-3]: 47-9; also Davenport, 1991: 207-8).
3. A typical example is the mining industry's requirements of cheap, largely black, labour, readily supplied from the black 'reserves' that were a product of segregationist thought; see, for an early essay on the subject, Wolpe (1995 [1972]: 60-90).
4. The London-based Gramophone Company, owners of the HMV label, sent the first portable field-recording unit to South Africa in 1912. From the 1920s and into the early 1930s, however, it was common to ship South African musicians to the motherland (Rob Allingham in Meintjes, 2003: 275).
5. For an overview of the history and historiography of imperialism, see Young (2001: chap. 3).
6. There is no evidence for this period that the white producers of black records 'produced' recordings so as to further racialise the music. Lara Allen (2003: 241-2), pace David Coplan (1985: 136), argues that this was still the case at mid-century. As Louise Meintjes (2003) has so richly detailed, by the mid-1980s, however, national-racial-ethnic sounds were 'engineered' in South African studios under the impress of the expectations of musicians, producers, and audiences alike.
7. Singer was admittedly the label of entrepreneur Eric Gallo, who founded the local Brunswick Gramophone House in 1926, first as a retail business distributing overseas records. When he moved into the recording business he imitated metropolitan practices.
8. For a list of the music Marivate recorded under the label Shangaan, see the *Singer Bantu Records Complete Catalogue* (n.d. [c. early 1930s]).
9. By this time the Columbia label outside the US was owned by the British-registered company EMI, which also included HMV in its stable.
10. For an account of the role of language in this process, see Hofmeyr (1987).
11. Robert Ross (1999: 16) repeats the conventional wisdom that the apartheid government was as interested in ethnicity as race. Some argue that it was the

systematic development of 'ethnos' theory that in part distinguishes the apartheid and segregationist eras (see Bonner, Delius and Posel, 1995: 29-30).

12 For overviews of histories that draw on this metaphorics, see, for example, Beinart and Dubow (1995); and Bonner, Delius and Posel (1995).

13 The song 'A Yingelani Mova' (catalogue number GE 52) was recorded for Singer by Marivate and Company in the mid-1930s.

14 On the other hand, the *World* took 'the detribalisation of Africans' as a sign of 'an Africa that is fast becoming Europeanised', and consequently that blacks 'must evolve from the tribal state to that of a nation' (27 April 1935: 8). Here, 'nation' meant an inclusive, non-racialised South Africa: to 'think that there can be two or more nations and civilisations within one democratic state without conflict is to ignore political history' (18 Feb. 1933: 6). See also DDT Jabavu's *The Segregation Fallacy* (1928).

15 For an account of the uses of, and aims for the uses of, indigenous music in black South African vaudeville and early jazz from the late 1920s on, see Ballantine (1993: 23-5).

16 Tim Couzens discusses the South African reception of US race relations, tracing its impact especially on the cultural field (1982: 316-17).

17 If it is well known that from at least the 1920s the South African black elite began increasingly to take black America as its model, it is partly, we should acknowledge, because they were paternalistically encouraged to do so.

18 Reuben Caluza, whom the *World* described as 'the most famous Bantu composer today' (22 Dec. 1934: 9), became an advocate of the spiritual after a five-year sojourn in the US during the early to mid-1930s: 'I was very much interested in the study of Negro spirituals in America, and I hope to be able to spread the knowledge of them in South Africa – for they form a valuable link between the Negro race in the old and the new worlds' (*BW*, 21 March 1936: 20); cf. the early comparative musicologist Percival R Kirby's comparative work on spirituals and 'South African native music' (1930).

19 For related matters, see the black choral composer Joshua Mohapeloa's engagement with the traditional and contemporary in the 1930s in Lucia's essay in this volume.

20 When 'The People's Forum' debated the issue of folk culture in the *Bantu World*, one KE Mokgatle summed up the prevailing wisdom: 'Preservation of our traditions, customs and folklore stories should be the object of every educated Bantu writer or teacher who wishes to keep constantly the progress of his people from those "dark" days to these of light' (17 Dec. 1932: 6). Black elite discourse on the preservation of (select) traditions and customs was generally inscribed within the modernist discourse of 'progress'; see also

Bantu World (5 Jan. 1935: 8; 27 April 1935: 8). Of course, black interest in the traditional was also the re-evaluation of culture that had been demonised during colonisation, especially by the mission, and so part of the process of re-imagining black cultural identity in changing socio-political times.

21 Caluza's career summarised these strands too: he had 'made over 150 recordings of primitive and folk songs and also his own compositions' for HMV in London in 1930; was, as we saw, an enthusiast of both the spiritual and black South African traditional music; and, upon his return to South Africa in 1936, planned to teach 'the study of African music', including 'training in native folk song', at the 'Adams Mission' in then Natal ('Caluza Makes Musical History', 1936[?]: 272-4). This was part of a new curriculum devised by the institution's head, Edgar Brookes, a liberal segregationist whose *History of Native Policy* (1924) has been described as the first 'extensive analysis of segregation' (see Dubow, 1995: 152-5). For more on Caluza, see Erlmann (1991: chap. 5).

22 The Junods' researches were organised by, and so productive of, the idea of ethnicity. Henri-Alexandre Junod, for example, published numerous ethnographic works on the 'tribes' of northern South Africa and southern Mozambique.

23 Marivate knew of Kirby, who had done fieldwork in the area; see Marivate's letter to JD Rheinhallt Jones (14 Nov 1935).

24 For the mission's, specifically the Junods', involvement in matters of language and literacy and, amongst others, Tsonga ethnicity, see Harries (2001). The mission was also the primary pedagogue of black *music* literacy in South Africa; see Olwage (2003: chaps 1-3).

25 Hendrik Verwoerd, third prime minister of the apartheid state, is often referred to as the 'architect of apartheid'.

Bibliography

Allen, Lara. 2003. 'Commerce, Politics, and Musical Hybridity: Vocalizing Urban South African Identity during the 1950s'. *Ethnomusicology*, 47(2), pp. 228-49.

Ballantine, Christopher. 1989. '"Africans in America", "Harlem in Johannesburg": The Ideology of Afro-America in the Formation of Black Jazz and Vaudeville in South Africa Before the mid-1940s'. In Andrew Tracey (ed.). *Papers Presented at the Seventh Symposium on Ethnomusicology*. Grahamstown, South Africa: International Library of African Music, Rhodes University, pp. 5-10.

_. 1993. *Marabi Nights: Early South African Jazz and Vaudeville*. Johannesburg: Ravan Press.

Beinart, William, & Saul Dubow. 1995. 'Introduction: The Historiography of Segregation and Apartheid'. In William Beinart & Saul Dubow (eds). *Segregation and Apartheid in Twentieth-Century South Africa*. London & New York: Routledge, pp. 1-24.

Bonner, Philip, Peter Delius & Deborah Posel. 1995. 'The Shaping of Apartheid: Contradiction, Continuity and Popular Struggle'. In Philip Bonner, Peter Delius & Deborah Posel (eds). *Apartheid's Genesis, 1935-1962*. Johannesburg: Ravan Press & Witwatersrand University Press, pp. 1-41.

Bouws, Jan. n.d. [c.1958]. *Die Afrikaanse Volkslied*. Johannesburg: Federasie van Afrikaanse Kultuurvereniginge.

_. n.d. [c.1962/3). *Die Volkslied Weerklank van 'n Volk se Hartklop*. Cape Town: H.A.U.M.

'Caluza Makes Musical History in Africa'. 1936[?]. *Southern Workman*, pp. 272-74.

Coplan, David. 1979. 'The African Musician and the Development of the Johannesburg Entertainment Industry, 1900-1960'. *Journal of Southern African Studies*, 5(2), pp. 135-64.

_. 1985. *In Township Tonight! South Africa's Black City Music and Theatre*. Johannesburg: Ravan Press.

Couzens, Tim. 1982. '"Moralizing Leisure Time": The Transatlantic Connection and Black Johannesburg, 1918-1936'. In Shula Marks & Richard Rathbone (eds). *Industrialisation and Social Change in South Africa: African Class Formation, Culture and Consciousness, 1870-1930*. London & New York: Longman, pp. 314-37.

Davenport, TRH. 1991. *South Africa: A Modern History*, 4th ed. London: Macmillan.

Dubow, Saul. 1995. 'The Elaboration of Segregationist Ideology'. In William Beinart & Saul Dubow (eds). *Segregation and Apartheid in Twentieth-Century South Africa*. London & New York: Routledge, pp. 145-75.

Erlmann, Veit. 1991. *African Stars: Studies in Black South African Performance*. Chicago & London: University of Chicago Press.

_. 1996. *Nightsong: Performance, Power, and Practice in South Africa*. Chicago: University of Chicago Press.

Hamm, Charles. 1991. '"The Constant Companion of Man": Separate Development, Radio Bantu and Music'. *Popular Music*, 10(2), pp. 147-73.

Harries, Patrick. 2001 'Missionaries, Marxists and Magic: Power and the Politics of Literacy in South-East Africa'. *Journal of Southern African Studies*, 27(3), pp. 405-27.

Hofmeyr, Isobel. 1987. 'Building a Nation from Words: Afrikaans Language, Literature and Ethnic Identity, 1902-1924'. In Shula Marks & Stanley Trapido (eds). *The Politics of Race, Class and Nationalism in Twentieth-Century South Africa*. London & New York: Longman, pp. 95-123.

Huskisson, Yvonne. 1968. 'The Story of Bantu Music'. *Bantu*, 15(7), pp. 16-21.

Jabavu, DDT. 1928. *The Segregation Fallacy and Other Papers: A Native View of Some of South Africa's Inter-Racial Problems*. Lovedale: Lovedale Press.

Kirby, Percival R. 1930. 'A Study of Negro Harmony'. *The Musical Quarterly*, 16(3), pp. 404-14.

Legassick, Martin. 1995. 'British Hegemony and the Origins of Segregation in South Africa, 1901-14'. In William Beinart & Saul Dubow (eds). *Segregation and Apartheid in Twentieth-Century South Africa*. London & New York: Routledge, pp. 43-59.

Locke, Alain (ed.). 1925. *The New Negro: An Interpretation*. New York: Albert & Charles Boni.

Marivate, Daniel. Unpubl. note, 14 Nov. 1935, South African Institute of Race Relations papers, AD843 B47.2. Historical Papers, University of the Witwatersrand.

_. Unpubl. letter to JD Rheinhallt Jones, 14 Nov. 1935, South African Institute of Race Relations papers, AD843 B47.2. Historical Papers, University of the Witwatersrand.

_. *School Songs for Choir Competition*. Unpubl. Ms., South African Institute of Race Relations papers, AD843 B47.2. Historical Papers, University of the Witwatersrand.

McClintock, Anne. 1995. *Imperial Leather: Race, Gender and Sexuality in the Colonial Context*. London: Routledge.

Meintjes, Louise. 2003. *Sound of Africa! Making Music Zulu in a South African Studio*. Durham & London: Duke University Press.

Mphahlele, Ezekiel. 1971 [1959]. *Down Second Avenue*. London: Faber & Faber.

Olwage, Grant. 2003. 'Music and (Post) Colonialism: The Dialectics of Choral Culture on a Colonial Frontier'. Ph.D. diss., Rhodes University.

_. 2006. 'John Knox Bokwe, Colonial Composer. Tales About Race and Music'. *Journal of the Royal Musical Association*, 131(1), pp. 1-37.

Posel, Deborah. 1995. 'The Meaning of Apartheid Before 1948: Conflicting Interests and Forces Within the Afrikaner Nationalist Alliance'. In William Beinart & Saul Dubow (eds). *Segregation and Apartheid in Twentieth-Century South Africa*. London & New York: Routledge, pp. 206-30.

Ramsey, Jr., Guthrie P. 2003. *Race Music: Black Cultures from Bebop to Hip-Hop*. Berkeley: University of California Press.

Ross, Robert. 1999. *A Concise History of South Africa*. Cambridge: Cambridge University Press.

Singer Bantu Records Complete Catalogue. n.d. [c. early 1930s]. Johannesburg: Saxon Printing Co. South African Institute of Race Relations papers, AD843 B47.2. Historical Papers, University of the Witwatersrand.

Wolpe, Harold. 1995. 'Capitalism and Cheap Labour Power in South Africa: From Segregation to Apartheid'. In William Beinart & Saul Dubow (eds). *Segregation and Apartheid in Twentieth-Century South Africa*. London & New York: Routledge, pp. 60-90.

Young, Robert JC. 2001. *Postcolonialism: An Historical Introduction*. Oxford: Blackwell.

NEWSPAPERS

Bantu World. 1932. 'Bantu Records Create Interest'. 9 April.
Bantu World. 1932. 'Negro Progress in Art'. 16 April.
Bantu World. 1932. 'Bantu Artists Before a Microphone'. 4 June.
Bantu World. 1932. 'Negro Advancement'. 3 September.
Bantu World. 1932. 'Hands Off Our Languages!'. 3 September.
Bantu World. 1932. 'Transvaal African Eisteddfod'. 10 December.
Bantu World. 1932. 'The People's Forum'. 17 December.
Bantu World. 1933. 'Drop Your Differences and Unite'. 28 January.
Bantu World. 1933. 'The Policy of Segregation'. 18 February.
Bantu World. 1933. Advertisement for records. 15 April.
Bantu World. 1933. 'Well-Known Bantu Musician Conducts His Compositions'. 20 May.
Bantu World. 1933. Advertisement for records. 22 July.
Bantu World. 1933. Advertisement for records. 16 September.
Bantu World. 1933. Advertisement for records. 23 September.
Bantu World. 1933. Advertisement for records. 21 October.
Bantu World. 1933. 'Bantu Men's Social Centre'. 4 November.
Bantu World. 1933. 'Interesting Review of the Past Year'. 30 December.
Bantu World. 1934. 'Africans Recording Tribal Music'. 6 January.
Bantu World. 1934. 'Bantu National Eisteddfod'. 22 December.
Bantu World. 1935. 'Chaotic State of Native Education'. 5 January.
Bantu World. 1935. 'Detribalisation of Africans'. 27 April.
Bantu World. 1936. 'African Musician Coming Home'. 21 March.

3

DISCOMPOSING APARTHEID'S STORY

WHO OWNS HANDEL?

CHRISTOPHER COCKBURN

INTRODUCTION

In April 1959 several performances of Handel's *Messiah* took place in the City Hall in Johannesburg which attracted unusually widespread publicity and attention. An estimated 11 000 people attended (*Transvaler*, 1960) and according to one account, 'Johannesburg music lovers went mad with delight' (*Star*, 1963b). The performances were considered sufficiently significant to warrant newsreel coverage, and were so successful that they initiated a series of annual performances stretching over the following decade.

Since *Messiah* performances by a variety of choirs, most notably the Johannesburg Philharmonic Society, had been a regular feature of musical life in the city for many years, an obvious question arises: what was the reason for this sudden attention? The answer leads directly to the theme of this book: the relationship between musical activities and a society shaped (or deformed) by apartheid. At this time and in this place, the most surprising and therefore noteworthy feature of the performances was the identity of the singers: they were all black Africans. It was thus inevitable that the significance of these performances would be explicitly constructed in terms of race, apartheid's central category and concern.

Different socio-political positions, however, could inflect that construction in very different ways. The available positions were, at this moment, becoming more sharply defined than before, and facing people with choices that were made more difficult because they involved not only a programme of political action but also a struggle over identities imposed, chosen, or negotiated. This was a turning point in the history of twentieth-century South Africa. A space of three years (1959-1961) saw the formation of the Pan Africanist Congress (PAC) and the Progressive Party, British Prime Minister Harold Macmillan's 'winds of change' speech to Parliament in Cape Town, the shooting of demonstrators by police at Sharpeville, the introduction of a whole range of apartheid laws, South Africa becoming a republic outside the Commonwealth, and the start of the African National Congress's (ANC) armed struggle.

This historical context heightens the visibility of music's never-absent but often-hidden entanglement with politics. At this juncture, a black choir and soloists performing one of the greatest icons of Western classical music with a white orchestra and conductor, to (separate) black and white audiences in the heart of (white) Johannesburg, was entering exceptionally complex and fraught ideological territory. There can be no simple, singular, 'composed' assessment of the significance of these performances even after half a century, not only because of this complexity but also because many of the issues remain alive, albeit in changed ways, in what might seem the very different context of post-apartheid society. The performances initially discomposed the story which apartheid ideology wished to write, by their refusal to conform to its rigid categories. They also discompose those stories told about apartheid now in which there are simply two unified and opposed categories – stories told in black and white. Postcolonial theory might therefore find these performances at the 'uncanny crossroads' where metropolitan culture is simultaneously affirmed and subverted (Gikandi, 1996: 16), or entering debates about hybridity (see for example Loomba, 1998: 173ff.) or cultural imperialism (Tomlinson, 1991), although it is not possible within the scope of this chapter to explore these and other intersections more fully. While postcolonial theory and cultural studies have tended to focus on difference (a theme which can hardly be absent here), these performances also invite a consideration of affinities and the scope of universalist ideals (see the discussions of these issues in Nuttall and Michael, 2000: 9-10; and Thornton, 2000: 31).

I have based my account on the printed programmes, newspaper reports, and interviews with people who took part in or knew of the performances. The main outline is clear, though details differ – not only because of inevitable differences in perspective and the effects of time on memory, but also because this rapidly became the stuff of legend. Within four years, for example, estimates of the total attendance at the first performances rose from 11 000 to 15 000 (*Star*, 1964a).

Origins

In the latter part of 1958, a Johannesburg businessman, Leslie Dishy, invited members of a Soweto-based choir, the Jabavu Choristers, to provide entertainment at a party for his black staff. It seems that the singing drew an appreciative crowd in the street, as well as making a strong and favourable impression on Dishy himself. Among the pieces the choir performed was the 'Hallelujah' Chorus. According to one account 'Dishy said to them: "I will put you on the City Hall one day." They thought that was funny' (*Star*, 25 February 1963). Soon afterwards their conductor, Ben Xatasi, joined Dishy's staff, and this contact between the two men ensured that Dishy's idea for a City Hall performance by the choir was not forgotten.

The Jabavu Choristers was just one of many choirs in the townships around Johannesburg for which the 'Hallelujah' Chorus was standard fare – indeed, so well known that one of my informants described it as being for black choirs 'sort of a national anthem, a signature tune' (Masote, 2000). Other choruses from *Messiah* had also become familiar, especially since the advent in 1947 of the Johannesburg Bantu Music Festival and its choral competition, where *Messiah* excerpts were frequently prescribed. The Jabavu Choristers, under their previous conductor, Jabulani Mazibuko, had learnt enough of *Messiah* to present a whole programme of excerpts.

Dishy was a member of the Memorable Order of Tin Hats (MOTHS), an organisation which had taken on a significant role in raising money to support not only the ex-servicemen who were its members but also a variety of charities. The method favoured by Dishy's local branch, the 'Desert Lily' shellhole, was producing shows. He thus had access to an organisation likely to respond favourably to his proposal that the Jabavu Choristers should present a full performance of *Messiah* in the City Hall. The MOTHS decided to form a joint organising committee, chaired by Dishy, from two shellholes, 'Desert Lily' and 'Hole in the Wall'.

To conduct the performance, they invited Joseph Friedland, recently returned to Johannesburg after studies in Europe. The cover of the commercial recording of the 1960 performance states that he undertook it 'in the absence of an African conductor with sufficient experience in this type of work' (*Arias and Choruses*, 1960). At some point a decision was taken to form a much larger choir. Some accounts suggest that this was Dishy's original idea (for example, *Rand Daily Mail*, 1965c), but one specifically attributes it to Friedland, stating that in his view the 30 voices of the Jabavu Choristers would be too few (*World*, 1959b). The choirs of two churches were then invited to join the Jabavu Choristers: St Augustine's (Orlando West), conducted by Stanford

Gxashe, and Christ the King (which had been Trevor Huddleston's church in Sophiatown), conducted by Michael Rantho. Together with some additional individual singers, the choir numbered between 140 and 150. Assistance with the organisation and co-ordination of the singers, as well as copying of scores, was given by various people involved with choral activity in the townships. Programmes over the years paid tribute to the important role of these 'African choir organisers': JP Tutu, Osborne Ferdinand, and Itala Monkoe.

For the solo parts, it seems that the choirmasters proposed singers from within their choirs, or personally known to them, to be auditioned by Friedland. He chose two sopranos, Iris Letanka and Alice Mollson, the alto Mabel Modiga, and the bass Lucas Scott, while Ben Xatasi himself took the tenor solos. The well-known tenor, Webster Booth, assisted the soloists with private tuition for the first performance. The instrumentalists are described in the programme as 'The Handel Orchestra', a group consisting of musicians who also played in other Johannesburg orchestras, and who had accompanied many different choirs in performances of *Messiah* over the years. All the members of the orchestra were white, as was the organist.

The choirs worked independently under their own conductors and then came together for joint rehearsals with Friedland. These presented logistical difficulties. On the first occasion, about 100 singers were expected, but only about sixteen arrived. Transport turned out to be the major problem. In their efforts to make the venture work, the white organisers came face to face with the daily realities of life for their singers. Speaking to an interviewer a couple of years later, Les Dishy reminisced:

> Africans work miles from their townships and get home later than other people do. When they do get home, they're tired, but they have to face household chores and cooking. Those who have the flair for choral work live miles from any central place to which they can be gathered (*Star*, 1963b).

Once buses were organised, and food and refreshments provided at the practice venues, preparations for the performance could still not be insulated from other problems faced by the singers. Dishy continues:

> Just when we wanted a full tenor section for rehearsal, we'd find two of them beaten up by tsotsis, two others detained, perhaps for some pass offence, and others delayed in the long bus queues at city termini. Often, dozens of times, we felt like hurling the whole thing in.

But they, and their singers, persevered, and the performances duly took place between 8 and 13 April 1959.

Initial plans had been fairly modest, envisaging two performances. Racially mixed audiences were not permitted in the Johannesburg City Hall, so separate performances had to be organised for black and white audiences. However, as bookings were made and interest increased it was decided to add further performances. In the end such was the demand that a total of seven performances was given. *The World* reported that at the first performance for blacks there was a 'record crowd' of 1 600, while the gala performance for whites was fully booked (1959a). As a result of this success, plans were made to put the organisation on a more permanent footing.

The singers in the first performance had been identified simply as 'combined African choirs', with or without the three individual choirs being mentioned. The following year, enlarged by the Mofolo Choristers and the choir of Christ the King, Meadowlands, to a total of around 200, they were named the 'Johannesburg African Music Society' or JAMS. They were also frequently referred to, especially in the townships, as 'the Messiah Choir'. From 1961 the soprano Anne Feldman became involved, initially as singing coach for the soloists and later assisting with the training of the choir. The subsequent history of JAMS includes annual *Messiah* performances in Johannesburg, as well as in townships along the Reef, and tours to Pretoria, Kimberley, Durban, and Cape Town. In 1963 Joseph Friedland left for Israel and the conducting was taken over by Jeremy Schulman, who had recently retired as one of the conductors of the SABC Symphony Orchestra. From 1964 they began to present occasional performances of music other than *Messiah*, but it was Handel's oratorio that continued to be their mainstay.

Valuing: Audiences and performers

It is not often in South Africa that performances in the classical field have created the kind of stir which the first performances of *Messiah* by the combined choirs in 1959 produced. The 1961 programme recalls 'an unforgettable experience' and mentions 'wave after wave of applause'. A report in *The World* (1959a) describes the performances as a 'sensation', and notes that 'inquiries are pouring in from other Reef towns to find out if it is possible for the combined choir ... to go out and sing for them'. The following week the newspaper carried an editorial on the subject, headed: 'After Kong – The Choir' (*World*, 1959d). It draws a comparison between the *Messiah* performances and the recently staged musical play, *King Kong*:

Just as the 'King Kong' wonders were leaving Johannesburg for the Cape, a new wonder by African men and women was on again. This time it was not at the University Great Hall nor was it jazz-opera. It was a choir at the Johannesburg City Hall.

The element of novelty obviously played a role, but other values began to emerge more clearly as the performances continued in subsequent years.

For the choristers and audiences from the township, the scale of the performance was an important factor in its musical value, to which the large numbers of singers, presence of an orchestra, backing of a large organ, and size of the venue all contributed. Michael Masote (2000) recalls how at rehearsals Faye Smith had played on a portable harmonium, but then the time came for the dress rehearsal, with the orchestra and the City Hall organ: 'It was real exciting. I was still a student then, I was doing matric, and for some time I neglected my studies because of this excitement of sitting in the Messiah choir and with orchestra accompaniment.'

There was also a social value. The performances provided an opportunity for the singers to demonstrate their skills and establish their status in township society more generally. This was not only because of the support they received from their own communities, but also because they performed for white audiences. Their achievement was recognised by those whom racial ideology had defined as superior, those who had for so long been posited as the bearers of the civilisation to which black people had to aspire, and in relation to whose standards blacks would be seen as succeeding or failing. When I asked Sheila Masote (2000) how she felt about the question of segregated audiences, she mentioned the mixed emotions that this had evoked:

> It was an honour to play for whites. That's how reduced we were ... They never come to our concerts, now we have gone to them and showed them we can do it, and it was a success ... And also, wow, if you can sing for whites it means – and they applauded so much – it means we are up there, we are getting somewhere.

For most of those in the white audiences, it was their first exposure to a black choir of any kind, let alone one of this size, singing music of this kind, with this level of skill. Their reaction can be gauged from many of the reviews. The choir 'had a huge European audience stamping and clapping its enthusiasm at the end of the two-hour performance' (*Rand Daily Mail*, 1960). When the choir toured to Durban, the *Natal Mercury* (1963) commented:

Any production of *The Messiah* over Easter could expect an 'appreciative' audience. The three packed houses that heard the J.A.M.S. interpretation, however, were taken completely unawares. They found themselves applauding for as long as five minutes, floor thumping and shouting when their hands became too painful to clap.

Apart from reporting the audience response, the reviewers provide their own more detailed assessment. It seems that from the beginning Friedland was concerned not to give any opening to condescension. A reporter attending a rehearsal records him saying to the choir: 'It must be sung so well that there will be no apologies ... Nobody saying, "Sorry, we had difficulties"' (*Our Africa*, 1959). To a large extent he appears to have succeeded. The reviews in the newspapers aimed at a primarily white readership were overwhelmingly positive, and there seems to be general agreement that between 1959 and 1965 the standard of the choir steadily improved. All reviewers were nevertheless faced with the problem of how (or whether) to 'take account' of race in attempting to do justice to the particular qualities of this choir. Dora Sowden's review of the 1959 performance exemplifies the difficult balancing act involved:

> There may have been better performances of Handel's 'The Messiah' in the Johannesburg City Hall. There has not, within my memory, been one more inspiring ... What was thoroughly African was the freshness and impulse of the singing. What was lacking in art was more than compensated in unspoilt simplicity, easy-flowing part-singing and remarkable power to express sorrow and joy (*Rand Daily Mail*, 1959).

It was rare, however, for the issues to be faced with the openness displayed by the reviewer in *Die Burger*, who heard the choir on their Cape Town tour at the end of 1964. Having pointed out what was lacking in the performance (technical and musical deficiencies of the soloists, and choral balance are mentioned) the reviewer goes on to say:

> In spite of this the performance was one of the most enthralling and moving musical experiences that one could have. This writer and other audience members were literally brought to tears. It is naturally difficult to arrive at an objective, purely musical estimation of a Bantu undertaking such as this. The South African listener is all too aware of the cultural and organisational arrears that had to be made up. That this group could present a performance of notably high standard is in

itself already something that borders on a miracle. A comparison with a similar undertaking by whites would not reveal the full extent of this choir's true achievement. How does one measure them, then, in a work of European high culture, according to Western musical standards? (*Burger*, 1965; my translation).

Having placed a question mark over the intonation, the last section of the review identifies four qualities 'in which they would equal and even surpass many white choirs': rhythmic cohesion, dynamic control, clarity of diction, and deep familiarity with the work as a whole.

Review after review describes the performances with words such as 'moving' or 'inspiring'. As suggested above, the qualities of the performance itself were not the only reason for this. A contributing factor was the realisation of the odds which had to be faced; and if the assumption of a cultural backlog needing to be made up carries the danger of patronisation, failure to recognise the real difficulties that were overcome carries the danger of minimising the choir's achievement. But these reiterated words may be the surface markers of deeper reasons. For the black singers, this was a first experience, and the freshness of their encounter with *Messiah* may, paradoxically, have reinvigorated it for white listeners, providing them with a new and gratifying experience of the value of their own culture. It does seem likely that for some, a factor contributing to the 'moving' quality of the performance was a new-found awareness that 'they' (the members of the black choir) were not, after all, so different from 'us' (the members of the white audience, some of whom may also have been members of choirs that sang *Messiah*). That being so, what could justify 'their' continuing exclusion from a common cultural (or social, or political) life? To raise such a question is inevitably to confront the politics of the day, at the centre of which lay the Nationalist government's apartheid policy.

Positive assessment: The liberal position

In considering in more general terms the ways in which these performances and their significance were constructed in relation to the political field, it must be recognised that the written comments that have been preserved largely represent a position which can perhaps best be labelled as 'liberal' within the spectrum of political positions of the time. This label was attached to segments of both the black and white populations, recognising that, despite differences, there were significant points of ideological and social contact between them, the principal basis of which was their occupation of a similar (middle) class position within their respective racially-defined groups. On one level, the

JAMS performances can be seen as taking place in this contact zone, enacting shared interests and demonstrating the possibility of co-operative activity. This liberal discourse, however, does not speak only of itself: it was shaped by its awareness of the political discourse surrounding it, most notably that of the Nationalist government and that of the Africanists, against which the white and black liberal positions were most explicitly defined. Traces of this surrounding discourse can be clearly discerned in the way the various commentators use the JAMS performances as 'evidence' for the rightness of their positions. Two interrelated themes were particularly highlighted: the significance of JAMS as a revelation of the abilities of blacks, and as a manifestation of co-operation between blacks and whites.

In its treatment of the first theme, a passage from the previously quoted editorial in *The World* is especially illuminating:

What thrilled the listeners most was the fact that these Africans so entered the spirit of Handel in this oratorio as to bring the great choral work almost to life. This is a great achievement which shows that Africans can appreciate western culture and assimilate it without in any way lowering its standards or turning it into a hybrid. Rather, they enrich it and bring it to fuller life. There could be no better and more timely answer to some light-minded members of Parliament who think that all the African is capable of doing is to go back to the cave and jungle and to play at the game of throwing bones and witch-hunting (1959c).

What is crucial here is the ascription by the editors of two qualities to *Messiah*: greatness and Westernness. *Messiah* in fact becomes the vehicle for fusing the two concepts. For the editors of *The World* these performances of *Messiah* provided ammunition in the fight against the apartheid government's attempt to impose an unwelcome unitary identity on *all* black people. Government's version of Africanness constructed it in terms of a traditional tribal and rural identity that had to be preserved in all its purity (Ross, 1999: 116). This identity would both facilitate and justify the total separation (apartheid) that was the cornerstone of National Party policy. Against such ideas, the editors of *The World* sought to demonstrate, via their reading of these performances, the legitimacy of black aspirations to a different identity, from which Western elements were not excluded.

The greatness of *Messiah* had been constructed via a long process beginning in England in the eighteenth century. By the nineteenth-century, when it was introduced to both black and white choirs and audiences in South Africa, it had come to occupy a position of unique status and prestige within English musical culture. The programme notes for the 1959 performance thus reflect a long tradition of valuation of a Western masterwork, while at the same time contributing to its continuation: 'Generations throughout 200 years have lived and died in the firm faith that *Messiah* embraces all that is good and great in music'. This is the kind of hyperbole that caused *Messiah* to be viewed as the pinnacle of achievement for anyone involved with choirs, a focus of aspiration, cultural property of tremendous value. Now, at the very moment when blacks were at last within range of full possession of *Messiah* by giving a complete performance with an orchestra in the City Hall, was government policy going to attempt to deprive them of it? Who owns Handel? Who actually has the rights of ownership of *Messiah*? The programme provided an unequivocal answer: it is 'the common property of all mankind'. Underlying this statement is the assumption of a universal humanity characteristic of the liberal position. The government had a different view.

Contending: Nationalist government and white liberals

The first JAMS performances took place during the years that Deborah Posel identifies as marking a 'discrete second phase' of apartheid (1991: 227). It was characterised by a fundamental change in attitude towards blacks in white urban areas. The influx control policy of the 1950s had operated by making a clear differentiation between rural ('tribal') and urbanised ('detribalised') blacks, and sought to find some way of accommodating the latter within the 'white' urban areas:

> But by 1960 this 'practical' premise was overturned, inaugurating a new commitment to levelling the status of all Africans inside and outside the 'urbanised' group ... Indeed, the very notion of 'detribalisation' was scorned. Stressing the fundamental ethnic unity of Africans in the urban and rural areas, the BAD [Department of Bantu Administration and Development] expressly rejected the idea that there were 'two kinds of Africans', those who were urbanised and those who retained ties with the reserves (Posel, 1991: 232).

While there seems not to have been specific comment from the government on the performances, what it would have said is made sufficiently clear from the general position on such matters enunciated in Parliament during the same month as the first *Messiah* performances. Several opposition MPs had urged the government to give blacks, and particularly black choirs, a place in the proposed festival celebrating the fiftieth anniversary of Union. One stated: 'Their exceptional talent for singing should enjoy world recognition' (*World*, 1959c). Another maintained that this was an opportunity for South Africa 'to show that it could lead the continent of Africa by co-operating with the Non-European people in arranging the Festival'. Mr MC Botha was not to be persuaded by such arguments. Replying on behalf of the government, he insisted that 'the Bantu should be guided to celebrate in the reserves, in their own way ... They should be helped in their natural home to show what they had achieved within the framework of the Union, in farming, education, self-government and many other things that were typical of their own culture.' For those who were not on the reserves, the Minister of Finance, Dr Donges, provided the answer: 'There would be separate festivals for Indians, Coloureds and Africans.'

Who owns Handel? Not Africans, according to the government. They must be concerned with their own culture. For the architects of apartheid, events such as the *Messiah* performance were suspect in a number of ways. They could be seen as discomposing the story which apartheid wished to write, in two senses: they disturbed its composure, and they put together (composed) its components in illegitimate ways. Those involved were not following the script properly.

In the first place, the performances brought blacks physically into the centre of the city instead of locating their cultural aspirations in their own areas – if not the reserves at least the townships. Nor did the performances respect the supposedly 'natural' divisions – indeed, for Afrikaner Nationalists the 'God-given' divisions – between different ethnic groups, each connected to a different homeland: rather, the performers appeared as a homogeneous black group involved in a common cultural activity. The performances also presented them with an opportunity to pursue an activity which had clearly become important to them but which was not at all perceived to be part of their own traditional culture. They provided living proof of the refusal of at least some black people to be separated out into their own 'tribal' sphere. (Indeed, some black political activists viewed involvement with traditional African music as playing into the hands of the government: Khabi Mngoma mentioned to me that he had been criticised on exactly these grounds when he had performed African music (Mngoma, 1997).) *The World* (1960) presented the continuance of the performances after the first year precisely as a link to the wider world: 'The African choirs of Johannesburg have joined a great European cultural tradition by deciding to sing the 'Messiah' again this year. The tradition of singing the 'Messiah' every year is followed in a number of cities overseas.'

The performances showed not only that black people had a desire to participate in Western culture, but also, through the recognition of their success, that this desire was not unrealistic. This undercut the idea that blacks could not succeed in their attempts to become Westernised and were necessarily happier with their own traditional culture (an idea echoed, though for entirely different reasons, by some postcolonial theorists who insist that attempts by colonised peoples to 'mimic' the culture of the coloniser inevitably fail, and therefore reinscribe the oppressive relationship). By 1964, when the choir could no longer depend on novelty to make its impact, the reviewer in *The Star* wrote:

> We can remember the day, not long ago, when this choir first sang the Handel oratorio, and sang it like a group of enthusiastic township people who had been well drilled and had practised very hard. What last night's performance proved was that this is now a choir of the highest standards; so surely co-ordinated that it sings as one instrument, so deepened in musical understanding that it is sensitive to the subtlest nuance, and the smallest gesture of the conductor (1964b).

Nor was assessment of the choir as fully competent in this repertoire confined to the liberal English press. *Die Transvaler* (1964) carried the following: 'Last night this choir met the strictest requirements that can be set for a choir, namely the blending of the different voices. The JAMS Choir sings like one.' Commenting specifically on the 'Hallelujah' Chorus, the reviewer stated: 'It is a long time since I have heard this chorus with such conviction, feeling and discipline.'

For members of the white audience, therefore, or those who saw the newsreel in cinemas, or even simply read about the performances in the newspapers, there was the potential to unsettle the perceptions on which apartheid's story depended in order to be convincing. In many ways this was a performance in which looking was as important as hearing. As William Beinart says of the 1960s:

> Most whites were unable to see black South Africans during this critical period of the country's history. Homelands, passes, group areas, social amnesia, and powerful ideologies put them out of sight, literally and metaphorically ... Many of them came across Africans only as servants and workers (2001: 186).

Here was created the possibility that white people might 'see' black South Africans in a new way, as more like themselves, as able to excel in areas where it had been supposed this was not possible. Much more literally than in a show like *King Kong*, blacks were here occupying a space hitherto occupied by whites: not just the physical space of the City Hall stage but the symbolic space of Handel's *Messiah*, as an icon of the greatest Western music.

Perhaps most seriously from the government's point of view, these performances represented on many levels co-operation between black and white, which returns us to the second of the two themes mentioned earlier. There was co-operation between the white and black organisers, but they at least worked behind the scenes. Not so the black choir and white orchestra, black soloists and white conductor: they staged their collaborative effort in an extremely public way. All this tended to weaken the idea that apartheid was natural and desired by all. As Nigel Worden points out, the riots between Africans and Indians in Durban in 1949 had provided useful ammunition for the newly-elected National Party government in its claim 'that South Africans of different ethnicities could never co-exist peacefully' (1995: 105).

The performances of *Messiah*, in however small and limited a way, suggested a different possibility. A note in the 1964 programme, written from the point of view of the MOTHS, stated that: 'The mutual understanding and respect between the choir and organising committee is an object lesson in race relations of which the Desert Lily Shellhole is justly proud'. And a review in *The Star* began by suggesting that

> Dr Aggrey, the famous African educationalist, would have smiled benignly on last night's City Hall performance ... His favourite analogy was to compare society in Africa to a keyboard with black and white notes. You could get music from the notes separately, he used to say, but the best harmony of all came when they were played together. Here was living proof of black-white understanding at an exalted level (1959).

It was not only the white organisers and reviewers who noted this. Mr Joseph Zulu, one of the choristers, was reported as feeling that 'this kind of performance should be encouraged to continue because it improves relations between different racial groups' (*Our Africa*, 1960a). In the next issue of *Our Africa* (1960b), the caption below a photograph of the performance read: 'Probably nothing has done more to create good feeling between the races than the magnificent performance of 'The Messiah".' The accompanying article reports the comment of a black high school principal who brought 218 students from Pretoria to hear the performance: 'This helps our feelings toward each other in this country very much.'

Such sentiments were felt by many to be sorely needed, but also sorely tested when, barely a week after the 1960 performances, police opened fire on demonstrators at Sharpeville. It was an inauspicious time for people to attempt to bridge divisions, but the *Messiah* performances serve as a reminder that such initiatives continued to exist, keeping alive the hope for a nonracial democracy rather than one in which race would play a determining role, and preventing the composition (both then and now) of a black and white story in which two monolithic groups appear simply as enemies.

CONTENDING: AFRICANISTS AND BLACK LIBERALS

It was not only the Nationalist government that viewed co-operation with suspicion. When the editors of *The World* highlighted the significance of the performances – 'It is yet another proof of what can be done by co-operation' – it seems likely that they had in their sights not so much the National Party as African nationalism. At this time, the Africanist position was represented most strongly by the newly formed PAC, which held its first conference a matter of days before the 1959 performances. One of the crucial issues leading to the break with the Congress alliance was the question of co-operation with whites (as well as Indians): the Africanists were suspicious of the influence of whites in Congress and, growing impatient with the lack of political progress, decided that only blacks could liberate blacks. *The World* reported that 'Many would like to see an organisation which is purely African in thought, method and action' (4 April 1959).

Philip Frankel suggests that in contrast to the ANC, which had its

> ideological roots in European conceptions of multiracialism, the PAC drew inspiration from the intrinsically African struggle against imperialism and colonialism which, at this point [the late 1950s] was reaching its historic apogee on other parts of the continent, further to the North. This reinforced the notion of political action 'by Africans for Africans' as the means of building the collective racial identities necessary for resisting the white state (2001: 47).

Of course, a performance of *Messiah* was hardly political action in the relevant sense. As we have already seen, however, arguments forwarded in one area soon found application in others. No specific comment from the Africanists appears to have survived regarding the JAMS performances, but their perspective would likely have constructed black involvement in these performances as upholding rather than challenging the status quo. Khabi Mngoma told me of criticism leveled at his involvement with Western music because it was 'the colonialists' culture' (Mngoma, 1997). Such involvement suggests a 'collective racial identity' in which non-African culture plays a significant role. *Messiah* itself could be seen as a colonial imposition to be rejected, and similarly the aspiration to achieve in terms defined by the colonising West, the seeking of recognition and approval by whites, and the acceptance of a position of dependence on white organisers, instrumentalists, vocal trainer, and conductor. Who 'owns' Handel? Who can afford to acknowledge the *Messiah* as having value, as having something to say to black South Africans? Not Africans, the Africanist position would suggest. For them, the very prestige of Handel within Western culture contributes to the denigration of African culture by blacks themselves, who give consent to the idea that '*Messiah* embraces all that is good and great in music', thereby reinforcing white hegemony. As Robert Kavanagh points out, it was the more subtle forms of domination exercised by the liberal English-speaking group, especially in the area of culture and through their relationship with the black middle class, that became the primary target of the Black Consciousness Movement of the 1970s (1985: 19, 21).

The Africanist position was not, of course, monolithic. It included on the one hand Josias Madzunya, who called for 'God's Apartheid' (Africa for the Africans and Europe for the Europeans), and on the other Robert Sobukwe, who 'called upon sympathetic whites to adjust their outlook in such a fashion that the slogan 'Africa for the Africans ... could apply to them even though they are white"' (quoted in Lodge, 1983: 84). Nor did alignment with the Africanists necessarily entail a disowning of Handel, or even a refusal to participate in the JAMS performances. Amongst those who sang in the JAMS choir on various occasions were Urbaniah Mothopeng and Sheila Masote, the wife and daughter of Zeph Mothopeng, who had himself in previous years conducted choruses by Handel. Mothopeng was one of the leaders of the Africanist dissent that coalesced around a group of ANC Youth Leaguers in Orlando in the 1950s (Lodge, 1983: 80). He presided at the first PAC conference in 1959 and was elected to its executive. When I asked Sheila Masote whether *Messiah*, as an originally Western work, was not now something South Africa could better do without, she said emphatically, 'Don't make that mistake' (Masote, 2000), while Urbaniah Mothopeng confirmed that *Messiah* 'has helped us a lot' (Mothopeng, 2000). Sheila Masote also expressed appreciation for those whites who, during the dark days, 'would dare come this side' to provide training or instrumental accompaniment.

Nevertheless, in general terms the Africanists stood in opposition to the more inclusive Charterists of the ANC, the group sometimes described at this period as the 'liberals' within the black political spectrum. The latter followed the principles of the Freedom Charter adopted at the Congress of the People on 26 June 1955, which includes a statement implicitly supportive of black ownership of Handel: 'All the cultural treasure of mankind shall be open to all, by free exchange of books, ideas and contact with other lands' (quoted in Nolan, 1988: 223-4). The typically liberal universalism implied here echoes that already noted in the JAMS programme. The link between white and black liberals is confirmed by the comments of the ANC's Secretary-General, Duma Nokwe, made only a few days before the 1959 performances. Nokwe was explicitly defending, against attacks by the Africanists, the ANC's policy of co-operating with whites, and is reported as saying that the Liberal Party 'was now fully sympathetic with Congress policy'. Nokwe stated that the ANC 'had decided to co-operate with all races in the struggle for emancipation of the African oppressed' (*World*, 1959a).

This inclusiveness, which in different forms appears throughout the long history of the ANC, eventually became an important element in paving the way for the political settlement of the 1990s. From this point of view, the Westernness, even the Englishness, of *Messiah* did not require blacks to disown it. Handel could be owned by anyone. The meanings and values contained within *Messiah* could be put to use for purposes different from those of the Europeans who asserted exclusive rights to it. For blacks to reject it simply because it had European origins would be to impose on themselves the very impoverishment from which they sought liberation.

WHITE LIBERALISM AND ITS LIMITS

Harry Schwarz describes white liberalism in the South African context in a way which seems to fit the concerns of the organisers of these performances. He suggests that 'whatever this word may mean elsewhere in the world, in the Republic it means being against discrimination, supporting civil liberties and wanting to uplift under-privileged sections of the population' (1984: 142). This last statement applies not only to the cultural opportunities that Dishy had initially sought to open up for the choristers, but also to one of the principal charities to benefit from these performances, the African Children's Feeding Scheme.

Schwarz makes his comments in the context of outlining the political position of Jewish South Africans. The Jewish presence in the *Messiah* performances was notable, most visibly in the persons of Joseph Friedland and later Jeremy Schulman as conductors, but much more extensively in the list of MOTH committee members who promoted the event. Many South African Jews had fought against Hitler, which explains their presence in the MOTHS. Their experience of anti-Semitism inclined them to be opposed to various forms of discrimination and they became prominent in white liberal circles in South Africa. Stephen Cohen notes: 'When the Government embarked on its programme of apartheid ... Jewry was singled out for castigation and rebuke. This was mainly due to the high proportion of Jewish individuals among the Government's most vehement and articulate opponents' (1984: 11-12).

William Beinart (2001: 150) points out that there was significant opposition to the Nationalist government on the part of ex-servicemen generally. Their awareness that many National Party leaders had hoped for a German victory in the war predisposed them to see apartheid legislation as a threat to the values for which they had fought, and for which their comrades had died. All of this suggests that the organisers might have been well aware of the implicit opposition between the *Messiah* performances and apartheid policy.

The liberal position of course had its limitations. Traces of the paternalistic, if not patronising, attitudes of which white liberals are so often accused occasionally surface. One of the reviews of the first performance asked: 'And who, by the way, tipped off the non-White audience that it is the tradition to stand for the crowning 'Hallelujah' chorus?' (*Star*, 1959), as though this was not something they could already have known or established for themselves. Leslie Dishy is quoted as saying in an interview: 'The talent was there, for sure ... Guidance, tuition, organisation – well, these just did not exist. So we took them in hand' (*Star*, 1963b). The 1966 programme says approvingly that members of the choir 'have relied implicitly on the good judgement of the MOTH Committee to arrange performances and nation-wide tours as well as guide them generally'. It was not only the organisation that remained in white hands but also important aspects of the training, and the most visible aspect of control, the conducting. It could thus be argued that whites still 'owned' Handel in the most literal sense of having access to the resources required for mounting performances on this scale.

In some cases, self-interest simultaneously motivated liberal opposition to apartheid and ensured that it was kept within boundaries. Some English business interests opposed apartheid because labour unrest and resultant decline in foreign investment would affect profits. In 1960 a number of organisations representing commerce and industry (including even the Afrikaanse Handelsinstituut) published a joint memorandum urging the government to allow urbanised blacks greater freedom of movement and employment, and by removing the most obvious causes of grievance secure the support of what they called 'a loyal middle-class type Bantu' (quoted in Posel, 1991: 239). JAMS received considerable sponsorship from big business, particularly BP Southern Africa and the Anglo American Corporation. It could be argued that, while JAMS represented a challenge to the more obvious features of apartheid, it would not have received such corporate support without some complicity in more hidden forms of domination that co-opted the black elite in order to preserve racial-class privilege.

This may have been one of the reasons why political issues were not confronted explicitly in the discourse surrounding the JAMS activities. No criticism is voiced of the requirement to have segregated audiences, though the organisers may have regarded this as something that had to be accepted under the apartheid government and perhaps a small price to pay when set against the material and symbolic advantages of having the performances in the City Hall. The way the programme for the 1960 performance introduces the choir of Christ the King, Meadowlands, is perhaps symptomatic: 'Its members were originally with Christ the King, Sophiatown. This separate group was formed when a number of members moved to Meadowlands.' This politely effaces the responsibility of the agents of apartheid for one of the most notorious removals of the apartheid era.

CONFRONTATION

It was above all the failure of the liberals to prevent the advance of an increasingly determined and ruthless apartheid system into every corner of life that gave credibility to more radical positions. Sharpeville is often seen as the defining moment in this regard:

> Prior to 21 March 1960, the overwhelming majority of South Africans opposed to apartheid – indeed, most people of global repute – still believed that the country's deeply entrenched racial problems were tractable and could be resolved by the application of good civic sense lavished with a dose of mutual goodwill. Sharpeville rudely shattered this illusion (Frankel, 2001: 180).

The kind of initiative represented by the JAMS performances can therefore be seen as part of a political culture that was powerless to bring about fundamental change. Instead of helping to turn back apartheid, the JAMS performances eventually became its victims. In 1965, the performance of *Messiah* was forced to confront the system directly. Government Proclamation R26 of 1965 had the effect of tightening control in two areas which had long been of concern to apartheid legislators. Its provisions are summarised by Muriel Horrell:

Mixed audiences or mixed casts are prohibited at places of public entertainment except under the authority of a permit; and, unless a permit is obtained, a public hall in a group area proclaimed for members of one racial group cannot be hired by members of any other group (1967: 292).

On both counts, the *Messiah* performances turned out to be vulnerable.

The organising committee applied to present two performances on Ascension Day, a matinee for a black audience and an evening performance for a white audience. Permission was refused. The committee at first assumed that the problem was the black audience in a white group area, so they proposed that the matinee should instead be for whites. Inconsistently, a permit was then given for the matinee, but still not for the evening performance. It seemed that the real problem was the presence of two groups belonging to different races on the stage at the same time. As an urgent last-minute compromise, a proposal was put to the Minister of Community Development, Mr PW Botha, that the *Messiah* performance would take place with a black conductor and a lone white organist. With barely 24 hours to go, permission was given. The matinee was cancelled so that the conductor (Michael Rantho) and organist (Howard Bryant) could rehearse with the choir in the afternoon.

The government's action sparked almost as much outrage as the initial performances had sparked enthusiasm; but whereas the enthusiasm entailed at most an implicit criticism of aspects of apartheid policy, the outrage was explicit. *The Rand Daily Mail* was particularly outspoken. One issue carried a report on its front page that began: 'The latest victim of South Africa's no-mixing rule is the long-dead composer, Handel. His 'Messiah', due to be performed in Johannesburg on Thursday, has fallen foul of the Government' (1965a). The next day an editorial, headed 'What a Madhouse!', referred to the 'lunatic muddle' over the *Messiah* performance, and the 'fantastic regulations' according to which permits were given or refused (1965b). A week later, the paper carried a major article on JAMS by Dora Sowden, which began:

With one stroke of the pen, the South African Government struck a blow this week that crippled six years of painstaking build-up by the Johannesburg African Music Society. It struck a blow at musical achievement which is not likely to recover, and a blow at our human dignity that will leave it more tarnished even than it has lately been in the cultural field (1965c).

In these events there was not the violence and physical suffering which apartheid policy did not hesitate to inflict in other contexts, but its attempt to make every aspect of life conform to its singular story shows another kind of ruthlessness. Dora Sowden was at pains to emphasise that the reason for the combination of black choir with white orchestra, 'was not any aim to break the Colour Bar. It was pure necessity. There is no African orchestra available'. She lamented that JAMS, 'a purely music-loving, music-promoting body, has now become bewilderingly involved in politics' (*Rand Daily Mail*, 1965a). But whatever the intentions of its organisers, the JAMS performance of *Messiah* could no more escape from politics than any other aspect of life under apartheid. Perhaps, then, the clearest confirmation that these performances did after all constitute an implicit challenge to apartheid comes from the actions of the very people who might be expected to be most sensitive to such a challenge: those who administered the day-to-day workings of the system. Perhaps, too, by revealing the lengths to which they were willing to go, their treatment of the JAMS performance may have provoked or strengthened the resistance of at least some in the white community.

Concluding

That this may have been the case is suggested by the fact that the authorities did not entirely succeed in putting a stop to this venture in musical co-operation that crossed the racial divide they were so determined to entrench. JAMS was able to find a new home in St Mary's Anglican Cathedral and there continued to discompose apartheid's story. Leslie Stradling, Bishop of Johannesburg, replaced the Mayor as patron of the performances. His message printed in the 1966 programme expressed his feeling that 'the Cathedral will form an ideal setting for the performance. Not only is this basically a religious work, but in the house of God there are no arguments about who is welcome to sing or to listen to the singing.' The performances continued to take place at St Mary's until they ended in the early 1970s.

We look back on the performances of 'the Messiah Choir' from a South Africa which has passed its verdict decisively on apartheid, but in which some of the issues the performances raise remain, and (as new stories of racial purity and exclusivity are told) retain their urgency. What are the possibilities and limits of co-operation between different social groupings? Should identity (defined in terms of group membership) determine cultural affiliation – absolutely (because identity must be pure and unified), or not at all (because identity is socially constructed), or strategically (because while identity may have no 'real' existence, its social institution has real effects)? The JAMS performances continue to challenge the idea that the only legitimate owners of any given culture are the descendants of those with whom it originated. If the discourse of achievement that surrounded the JAMS *Messiah* performances too easily assumed the universality of Western cultural values (if not their superiority), insistence on universal access to the values of any culture remains an important principle. If the discourse of co-operation too easily overlooked existing inequalities, determination to find some common ground on which to transcend material and symbolic differences (that some would make absolute) remains a value without which conflict and oppression in ever-renewed forms seem inevitable.

Bibliography

'Arias and Choruses from The Messiah'. 1960. Notes to LP recording by the Johannesburg African Music Society, conducted by Joseph Friedland. Gallotone GALP 1097.

Beinart, William. 2001. *Twentieth-Century South Africa*, 2nd ed. Oxford: Oxford University Press.

Cohen, Stephen. 1984. 'Historical Background'. In Markus Arkin (ed.). *South African Jewry: A Contemporary Survey*. Cape Town: Oxford University Press, pp. 1-22.

Frankel, Philip. 2001. *An Ordinary Atrocity: Sharpeville and its Massacre*. Johannesburg: Witwatersrand University Press.

Gikandi, Simon. 1996. *Maps of Englishness: Writing Identity in the Culture of Colonialism*. New York: Columbia University Press.

Horrell, Muriel. 1967. *A Survey of Race Relations in South Africa: 1966*. Johannesburg: South African Institute of Race Relations.

Kavanagh, Robert Mshengu. 1985. *Theatre and Cultural Struggle in South Africa*. London: Zed Books.

Lodge, Tom. 1983. *Black Politics in South Africa Since 1945*. Johannesburg: Ravan Press.

Loomba, Ania. 1998. *Colonialism/Postcolonialism*. London: Routledge.

Masote, Michael. 2000. Author's interview, Soweto.

Masote, Sheila. 2000. Author's interview, Soweto.

Mngoma, Khabi. 1997. Author's interview, KwaDlangezwa.

Mothopeng, Urbaniah. 2000. Author's interview, Soweto.

Nolan, Albert. 1988. *God in South Africa: The Challenge of the Gospel*. Cape Town: David Philip.

Nuttall, Sarah, & Cheryl-Ann Michael. 2000. 'Introduction: Imagining the Present'. In Sarah Nuttall & Cheryl-Ann Michael (eds). *Senses of Culture: South African Culture Studies*. Oxford: Oxford University Press, pp. 1-23.

Posel, Deborah. 1991. *The Making of Apartheid, 1948-1961: Conflict and Compromise*. Oxford: Oxford University Press.

Programmes. 1959-1970. Performances of Handel's *Messiah* by the Johannesburg African Music Society. Box files, STC 783.3 MES, 1890-1969, 1970 –, Strange Africana Library, Johannesburg Public Library.

Ross, Robert. 1999. *A Concise History of South Africa*. Cambridge: Cambridge University Press.

Schwarz, Harry. 1984. 'Political Attitudes and Interaction'. In Markus Arkin (ed.). *South African Jewry: A Contemporary Survey*. Cape Town: Oxford University Press, pp. 131-145.

Thornton, Robert. 2000. 'Finding Culture'. In Sarah Nuttall & Cheryl-Ann Michael (eds). *Senses of Culture: South African Culture Studies*. Oxford: Oxford University Press, pp. 29-48.

Tomlinson, John. 1991. *Cultural Imperialism: A Critical Introduction*. Baltimore: Johns Hopkins University Press.

Worden, Nigel. 1995. *The Making of Modern South Africa: Conquest, Segregation and Apartheid*, 2nd ed. Oxford: Blackwell.

Newspapers

Burger. 1965. 'As Hierdie Koor So Volhou, Word Hy Nog Die Allerbeste Nie-Blanke Sanggroep in die Hele Afrika'. Review by E-Es, 1 January.

Natal Mercury. 1963. 'African "Messiah" Choir Enthrals'. Review by DM, 15 April.

Our Africa. 1959. 'Combined African Choirs Present – The Messiah'. April.

Our Africa. 1960a. 'The Year's Greatest Musical Event'. Sam Shabalala, March.

Our Africa. 1960b. 'African Singing of "The Messiah" Thrills Audiences'. April.

Rand Daily Mail. 1959. 'M.O.T.H.S. Make History With Oratorio'. Review by Dora Sowden, 10 April.

Rand Daily Mail. 1960. '200 Sing "Messiah"'. Review by Dora Sowden, 7 March.

Rand Daily Mail. 1965a. 'Handel is Latest SA Victim of Race Rule'. 25 May.

Rand Daily Mail. 1965b. 'What a Madhouse!' Editorial, 26 May.

Rand Daily Mail. 1965c. 'Government's Blow at Musical Achievement'. Dora Sowden, 29 May.

Star. 1959. 'Black Choir Gives Fervent Uplift to "The Messiah"'. Review by OW, 10 April.

Star. 1963a. '"Messiah" Choir Gets National Reputation'. 25 February.

Star. 1963b. '"The Messiah" Choir'. 2 May.

Star. 1964a. 'Drawn Together By Their Love of Singing'. 9 April.

Star. 1964b. 'African Choir Fervent in "The Messiah"'. Review by CJB, 13 April.

Transvaler. 1960. 'Bantoekoor Voer Weer, Messias' Van Händel Uit'. 18 February.

Transvaler. 1964. 'Messias Voortreflik Uitgevoer'. Review by PS, 13 April.
Vaderland. 1959. 'Bantoes Munt Uit in Puik, Messias". Review by MR, 13 April.
World. 1959a. 'Nokwe Attacks Africanists, Defends C.O.D., Liberals and Black Sash Movt'. 4 April.
World. 1959b. 'Glorious African Voices are a New Thrill'. 18 April.
World. 1959c. 'Give African Choirs a Place in the Union Festival – MP'. 18 April.
World. 1959d. 'After Kong – The Choir'. Editorial, 25 April.
World. 1960. '160 Voices for "Messiah" Rendering'. 13 February.

4

KWELA'S WHITE AUDIENCES

THE POLITICS OF PLEASURE AND IDENTIFICATION IN THE EARLY APARTHEID PERIOD

Lara Allen

In 1957 something curious and unprecedented happened. A South African recording company released a long playing record, *Something New from Africa* (Decca LK 4292), featuring visiting American clarinetist Tony Scott in collaboration with a local penny whistle band called the Solven Whistlers, led by Ben Nkosi.[1] What was unprecedented was the release of black South African music on LP, a format aimed exclusively at white audiences. What was curious was the new expectation that white South Africans would buy music by black musicians just at the very moment that the separation of different racial groups was beginning to be effectively enforced under various apartheid laws. The record company had not made a miscalculation: within a year other penny whistle LPs were being released in South Africa, and one track almost managed to top the British Hit Parade.[2]

This penny whistle style, the first within the *marabi*-tradition of urban, hybrid, black South African popular music to effectively cross over into the white market, became known as *kwela*.[3] A fusion of American big band swing with local compositional elements, *kwela* evolved on township streets, in shebeens and at stokvels.[4] Initially it was played on penny whistles and guitars by boys, adolescents and young adults; later a string bass and drum-set were added. By the late 1950s the penny whistles were replaced by saxophones, the acoustic guitars and bass by electrified instruments, and *kwela* evolved into sax jive.

White South Africans had been introduced to music and dance variety shows performed by black artists during the Second World War when Ike Brooks organised the *Zonk* show to entertain troops. This variety show tradition was continued by Alf Herbert's *African Jazz and Variety*, and various productions organised by the Union of Southern African Artists that played to white audiences throughout the 1950s. It was, however, *kwela* musicians who consistently brought township music into white areas by busking in city streets and playing in public parks. By the mid-1950s the myriad of small groups of penny whistling buskers had made *kwela* a familiar part of white Johannesburg's soundscape, and penny whistle *kwela* came to be identified by white South Africans as a manifestation of their own cultural identity.

In this chapter I am not concerned with the production of *kwela*, nor with the meanings it held for its musicians; rather, I am interested in the multivalent reception of *kwela* during the 1950s, and what this reveals about the complexities of apartheid at its genesis. Specifically, I investigate the popularity of *kwela* among white audiences because this was so directly antithetical to the social engineering project that apartheid constituted. The fact that *kwela* was appreciated as meaningful by a number of different identity groups that crossed the racial categories on which apartheid was premised suggests that the reality of South African cultural production and consumption was far more complex than the social engineers acknowledged. It is not surprising that this occurred precisely at the moment that apartheid was being entrenched legally and politically: the 1950s constituted a brief phase during which it was apparent that identities could be chosen, before separate, exclusive racial categorisation became hegemonic.

The conflicts and contradictions raised by the reception of *kwela* amongst different white audiences not only reveal the generally unacknowledged complexities of cultural politics in the early apartheid era; they also expose the gaps and slippages that arise within individual processes of identification. Most importantly these contradictions uncover the politics of pleasure, the politics of identity, and the politics of the relationships between the two. *Kwela*'s white audience may be roughly divided into two types: those who consciously patronised the genre as a statement about their identity, and those who appreciated *kwela* for its ability to give them pleasure, usually as dance music. Roughly these types correlate with two types of resistance politics: against exclusionary racial categorisation and separation, and against the moral and behavioral strictures imposed by older generations. Amongst white *kwela* fans, however, these modes of resistance and reasons for patronage were constantly fused and confused: the politics of patronage became complex when, for instance, the process of identification, particularly recognition of self, was pleasurable; when the self was recognised in the music of the other; when the pursuit of pleasure was punished as if it were the pursuit of illegal identification.

The politics of identification

In many ways the patronage of *kwela* as an overt statement of identification is relatively straightforward. Both conservatives and liberals found ways of using *kwela* to buttress their respective political ideologies. Each group used *kwela* to articulate their concerns, finding the genre meaningful in different ways.

In 1953 the multiracial Liberal Party was formed by a group whose political ideals could not be accommodated by the official opposition, the United Party. According to Tom Lodge:

> [T]he Liberal Party's chief importance was in helping to shape African political perceptions, firstly as a result of the friendships which existed between some of its principals and Congress politicians, and secondly as a source of hope and inspiration for the conciliatory brand of nationalism characteristic of the Luthuli [then president of the ANC] era (1983: 87).

Patronage of black culture was a distinct political statement for white liberals and radicals, because any multiracial activity 'was in itself an act of defiance in a society where inter-racial contact invoked official disapproval' (Lodge, 1983: 73). Music was frequently utilised to facilitate such inter-racial contact. For instance, a 1958 newspaper carried a picture of a white woman dancing, the caption for which read: 'Mrs. Sonia Bunting "does the Kwela" at party at home of Adv. J. Slovo to celebrate the withdrawal of the indictment against the ninety-one treason trialists during the week'. As black people were present, the party was raided by police on the pretext that liquor was being consumed illegally (*Golden City Post*, 19 October 1958). Pat Williams (co-author of the script for the musical *King Kong*) explains the euphoria and excitement for white liberals who socialised across the race barrier:

> Everyone was terribly hopeful. I think why was because this interface between black and white had just started. We were mixing socially, which had happened very little in the previous generation, except

amongst very serious political people. Suddenly it was happening socially, and *King Kong* actually accelerated that in the sense that, for the first time ever I can remember, there were black celebrities and white 'whoopies'. You know – that had never happened before. But when we went off to parties there was this marvellous feeling of – God we're doing it! You know? It's happening, and it's going to happen more and more (Williams, 1990).

The liberal agenda in the patronage of shows like *King Kong* was clearly recognised by conservatives. A concerned citizen writing as an 'Afrikaans theatre goer', for instance, noted in a letter to the press: 'Surely, the success of these South African plays can be attributed, in large measure, to the fact that they are in tune with the political feelings of the English speaking section, the protesting opposition' (*Rand Daily Mail*, 1 April 1959).

The co-option of *kwela* and other contemporary black music genres to serve conservative political ends did, however, also occur. The South African Information Service, for example, produced a film about forced removals, *The Condemned are Happy*, in which *kwela* was used as the background music for almost every township scene.[5] Furthermore, in 1959 Miss J Coertze, head of the Cultural Section of the Information Service, announced that 'copies of the LP record of the all-Native musical *King Kong* have been bought by the South African Information Service for sixteen of the Union's Embassies and Legations'. *King Kong* was to join Lionel Bowman, Mimi Coertze, Moira Lister, Cato Brink, and *boeremusiek* in the government's representation of South African culture (*The Star*, 11 March 1959).

Kwela's major tonality and fast swing beat made the genre irrepressibly upbeat. It was therefore easily utilised in support of the 'happy Africa' myth adhered to by white liberals and conservatives for different reasons. Liberals wished to convince the rest of white South Africa that black people were creative, cheerful, and unthreatening. For instance, Anthony Sampson (centrally involved in the evolution of *Drum*) claimed: 'Bitter though some moments are, Africans have not yet turned to hating: they have a resilience, a gaiety and humour and vitality, and a capacity for suffering and patience that will not easily turn to despair' (1956: 256). The conservative agenda in the cultivation of the 'happy Africa' image reasoned that singing and dancing black people were clearly content, and there was therefore no reason to alter the status quo.

The politics of pleasure

The politics of pleasure becomes interestingly embroiled in the politics of identification when people enjoy the music of a group to which they do not belong, and with whom they are not supposed to have anything in common. Such strictures make certain kinds of pleasure political.

On occasion the fact that some white people liked *kwela* was used to suggest – in the spirit of the Defiance Campaign – that the idea of apartheid was not only unjust, but also unrealistic, given some people's desire to cross racial boundaries. The desire of white people to play *kwela* was sometimes interpreted as such in the black press. For instance, a black journalist reported seeing a white youth playing the penny whistle in the Johannesburg suburb of Malvern East in the following way:

> I stopped and listened. The chappie was playing Spokes Mashiyane's 'Kwela Claude'. Not only that, but he held the instrument just like they do it in the townships ... I must hand it to this Kwela craze. It's breaking all those silly barriers some people waste a lifetime dreaming up (*World*, 11 October 1958).

In similar terms *Drum* reported that Spokes Mashiyane was frequently asked to give penny whistle lessons to white children (December 1958).

Kwela, rock 'n' roll and blue jeans

For the most part, however, white *kwela* enthusiasts did not perform the music themselves. Rather, they appreciated it as dance music. For these fans, *kwela* functioned as localised rock 'n' roll because the two genres are musically similar enough to accommodate the same dance steps. In terms of fulfilling the function of dance music, the most important common element is the fast shuffle rhythm. Differences, such as the instrumentation and harmonic progressions, would not have interfered with the dancers' movements. *Kwela* musicians even recorded rock 'n' roll-type compositions. The first penny whistle recordings to gain fame – Willard Cele's 'Penny Whistle Blues' and 'Penny Whistle Boogie' (Gallo New Sound GB 1123) – were, in fact, fast numbers in the 12-bar blues form with a shuffle beat. In 1951, when these were recorded, Cele's American model would have been rhythm and blues, one of the genres from which rock 'n' roll directly descended. A good example of a later rock 'n' roll-based penny whistle number is Spokes Mashiyane's recording 'Phenduka Twist' (Gallo New Sound GB 3402): a 12-bar blues that includes a guitar solo stylistically influenced by country-and-western music. (It is possible that this number is a cover version of a rock 'n' roll song, since the composer's credits on the record label are indicated as 'arr. Mashiyane".) Other examples are: Ben Nkosi's 'Ben's Hawk' (HMV JP 622), a fast double-penny whistle blues number with a prominent walking base, and 'Time Square' (Envee NV 3069) by Peter Makana.

Expressing the common South African desire for international recognition (see Allen, 2005), black journalists read the interchangeability of *kwela* and rock 'n' roll as significant. Noting the international prestige of rock 'n' roll, they intimated that *kwela* might reach, and even overtake, the American genre in terms of global recognition: 'South Africa's penny whistle kwela music, invented by Africans, may eventually replace rock 'n' roll. It is fast growing international fame," claimed *Ilanga* (26 April 1958); while the *Golden City Post* declared: '"Tom Hark" is the hottest thing in England. It is shattering all box-office records, shouldering aside "rock 'n' roll" (Hurray!) and the skiffle' (13 July 1958).

Memories of young white rock 'n' rollers who danced to *kwela* suggest, however, that they were neither particularly interested in *kwela's* international prestige, nor in overtly defying apartheid race laws. Rather, they were expressing a generational rebellion against the moral strictures of the establishment: white adolescents who wore jeans and danced rock 'n' roll both to *kwela* and American rock 'n' roll recordings were associating themselves with an international youth movement that desired greater sexual and personal freedom. Albert Ralulimi asserts, for instance, that by 1957 the King Kwela Trio had a 'very large white following ... We had conquered the whole of Johannesburg: north, south and eastern suburbs. We had followers who could fill up the Johannesburg City Hall ... Most of our followers were students and the young working-class' (Ralulimi, 1990b). Irene Menell, one of the organisers of the musical *King Kong*, broadly corroborates Ralulimi's categorisation of *kwela's* young white audience, describing them as 'the swingers – the young Hillbrow people who went to clubs' (Menell, 1990). One of those swingers, Elsa Nell, secretary of the Official Elvis Presley Fan Club of South Africa in the early 1990s, remembers: 'We all used to go to the Zoo Lake in our stove-pipes, and we would get up on tea boxes and play penny whistles with the black guys there' (*Weekly Mail*, 24-26 August 1990).

Stove-pipe jeans were one of the primary distinguishing factors that marked rock 'n' roll and *kwela* fans from other sectors of the white youth. Albert Ralulimi recounts some of the tensions between these different white interest groups in the following account of the first live performance of *kwela* in the east rand town of Brakpan, an event he refers to as 'the Brakpan Fiasco":

Guys who came from places like Nigel, Brakpan – they used to be called the bell-bottoms. The people who jived to our *kwela* type of music used to wear the stove-pipe type of pants ... So our friends here in Johannesburg had accompanied us to attend the show at Brakpan. So the stove-pipes and the bell-bottoms – they did not really share one time of peace. So else our guys here could dance to the *kwela* music and those fellows there were really behind with the adoption of the times. They became jealous and a fight broke out. Everything just went haywire, whereby we were even attacked by those guys. We came back to Johannesburg here bruised after we were assaulted by those farmers that end, because surely they didn't like the Johannesburg guys grabbing their girls. Girls always went for those who could dance this *kwela* music to be shown the proper positions – so that's when the fight started (Ralulimi, 1990b).

Jeans, rock 'n' roll and *kwela* became syntactically associated in the South African public imagination. Indeed, both jeans and the relatively blatant sexuality of rock 'n' roll dance elicited the same polemical, horrified response from conservative spokespeople on both sides of the Atlantic. Charles Hamm reports an article in the Johannesburg newspaper *The Star* that claimed that 'rock 'n' roll sounded like nothing more than "beating on a bucket lid"' and identified its audience as those 'hordes of sloppy, aggressive, be-jeaned louts and their girl friends who cause so much trouble in South Africa' (Hamm, 1985: 159). The connection between rock 'n' roll and black music and dance culture that underwrote much of the prejudice against the genre in the United States generated similar responses in South Africa. In 1958, for instance, *The Star* published a letter from twenty citizens who objected to rock 'n' roll on the grounds of its supposed connection with 'primitive' music. The letter claimed: 'The exact same ritual and war dances may be seen at less cost, and in greater safety, at our own mine compounds' (Hamm, 1985: 160). Hamm also reports that one Reverend DFB de Beer of the Transvaal Secretary for Morals issued a statement on behalf of the *Nederduits Gereformeerde Kerk* (Dutch Reformed Church) in which he took 'strong exception to rock 'n' roll, dancing and music exhibition, [which exert a] demoralising influence on youth and aggravate the youth problem. We are now sowing the wind and will reap the whirlwind' (1985: 159-63).

While on the surface the moral depravity that the Reverend wished to police was similar to that decried elsewhere in the world with reference to rock 'n' roll, the whirlwind to which he referred is likely to have been raised by the spectre of 'immorality' in its peculiarly South African form. The Immorality Amendment Act of 1950, one of the legal cornerstones of apartheid, outlawed sexual relations between people of different race groups. I suggest that it was fear of miscegenation that fuelled the most virulent public outcry against white youngsters enjoying *kwela* music. *Drum* journalist Basil 'Doc' Bikitsha described the furor for the benefit of his township readers:

> [T]hese whites did not hesitate to rock 'n roll and to jive 'n gyrate in the fiercest modern tradition. Someone wrote an indignant letter to a Johannesburg newspaper about the 'goings on' at the Zoo Lake, where white boys and girls were 'jiving disgustingly' to the music of a black flute-player. The newspaper subsequently published a picture of such dancing. Then the fat was in the fire. Outbreaks of holy horror were expressed by various people in the press, so the authorities had to move. Penny whistle music was banned – and so was dancing (*Drum*, October 1958).

The authorities filled the customary dance floor – the children's paddling pool – with water, and the penny whistle band was moved to another section of the park. The white *kwela* fans searched the area until they found the music and started to dance again. However, *World* reports that, 'after the Africans had pleaded with them not to come dancing in the African section of the grounds, as this would cause trouble with the authorities', the white teenagers left voluntarily (30 August 1958).

This series of incidents at Zoo Lake reveals a complex merger of the politics of pleasure and issues of generational control with the politics of racial identification. On the surface, what seems to have concerned the upstanding citizens who wrote to the press was the sexual impropriety of the dancers. The reaction of the authorities, however, suggests that the underlying fear was the emergence of a situation that could ultimately result in breaches of the Immorality Act, specifically the perils of inter-racial dancing. While no such dancing was reported – the press is clear that white youngsters were partnering each other – the excitation of white bodies by black musicians seems to have been threat enough. The authorities did not stop the offensive public display: white youngsters continued to dance to rock 'n' roll records; they simply separated the white youth from black music.[6] However the ban on *kwela* music at Zoo Lake did not last long and the following scene was described as the status quo in 1963:

> A little distance from the gambling, cooking and praying set is reserved a patch of ground for Spokes Mashiyane and his band ... He draws a regular crowd of Africans and Whites. There is jiving, twisting and all the latest dances from the townships. Police cars zoom past unconcerned. The revellers – and they are there too – don't even bother about police on this day. Everyone forgives and forgets on a Sunday at Zoo Lake (*World*, 1 July 1963).

Although *World* suggests that the Zoo Lake series of incidents was over, it might be argued that the authorities had made a tactical error, the results of which would only manifest two decades later: by reacting to youth rebellion as if it were defiance of apartheid, the authorities made the two types of resistance synonymous.

The enjoyment of *kwela* by some white youths was matched by an equivalent move amongst black youngsters. While *kwela* was widely appreciated by township dwellers across generations, there existed an active group among black adolescents who demonstrated their identification with American youth culture through wearing jeans and dancing to rock 'n' roll. It is in relation to these youngsters that I wish to revisit aspects of Charles Hamm's reading of the reception of rock 'n' roll in South Africa. Hamm asserts that rock 'n' roll was not popular amongst the black population; although he somewhat undermines this claim by prefacing it with an analysis of opinions expressed in the black press, citing seven positive and one negative response to rock 'n' roll in the years 1956 and 1957, and noting that from the end of 1956, 'many new releases by local performers were identified, in advertisements or reviews, as being examples of indigenous rock 'n' roll', and that throughout 1957 '*Zonk*, *Drum*, and *Hi-Note!* continued to carry reviews of newly-released discs advertised as rock 'n' roll music' (1985: 166-68). The arguments that Hamm presents to support his claim are somewhat problematic (169-72).

First, Hamm maintains that all early rock 'n' roll discs available in the country were by white artists, and because of this, and because visiting rock 'n' roll artists were white, black South Africans 'apparently took this music to be an exclusively white product', and were therefore uninterested. However, statements made in interviews and in the press at the time suggest that at least some black South Africans were aware of African American rock 'n' roll artists, and enjoyed the music of both black and white artists. One *Drum* journalist reports:

> I go to the back of the house, where there's a tent pitched for 'rockagers' who now and again want to shake a leg ... A busty young girl in jeans slides a disc on the battered gramophone, and some rockagers begin to

dance while the Elvis of Presley accuses each and everyone of being 'Nothing but a Hound Dog' (May 1958).

When asked if he ever played rock 'n' roll, penny whistler Jake Lerole replied, 'Ja, I did play rock 'n' roll as well. I did like rock 'n' roll. Like with that guy Holly something, Elvis Presley, Little Richard ... Yes, we used to enjoy the music: we loved it! That's when the jeans, you know these denims, came in fashion' (Lerole, 1990). Similarly, Barney Rachabane suggests that Presley was particularly inspirational in his early aspiration towards a performance career:

> One day we went to the bio and Elvis Presley was on the screen in some flick called 'Loving You'. I watched the guy swinging and swaying and lording it over just like he was the greatest thing in the world. I burned to do the same (*Golden City Post*, 4 January 1959).

The second claim Hamm makes is that rock 'n' roll could not compete with the enthusiasm for jazz that he suggests peaked in the 1950s and early 1960s, partially because jazz was ideologically more in accord with the rise of black nationalism. I would argue, however, that any rising popularity of jazz is unlikely to have severely affected the appreciation of rock 'n' roll because the two genres attracted different audiences. Contemporary press reports and comments made by interviewees suggest that black rock 'n' rollers were primarily interested in pleasure rather than politics.

Third, Hamm suggests that rock 'n' roll was rejected because 'black musicians in southern Africa were forging an indigenous urban popular style which drew important elements from their own traditional music' (1985: 172). Describing this genre as 'jive', he collapses together a number of genres within the *marabi*-tradition (specifically African jazz, *kwela*, saxophone jive, and *mbaqanga*), all of which were constituted through the merger of indigenous musical elements with elements from the genres that were concurrently popular in America. Thus *kwela* drew strongly from rock 'n' roll, making it possible for fans to dance to *kwela* and rock 'n' roll interchangeably. All this suggests that, in fact, the wearing of jeans and the adoration of American rock 'n' roll stars (black and white) was common amongst South African adolescents across the race barrier. It is possible that Hamm's overriding interest in a racialised politics of identification (a common enough concern of left academics in the mid-1980s) made it difficult for him to be alive to the possibility of an overriding cross-racial politics of pleasure.

KWELA AND BOEREMUSIEK

Musically, and to some extent socially, the relationships between *kwela* and both white and 'coloured' Afrikaans musical culture was closer than apartheid ideologues would have wished. It is important to clarify the confusion that exists between *kwela* and a particular form of *boeremusiek*, a type of Afrikaans folk music. The misunderstanding results primarily from the concurrent development of the *quela* dance amongst the Cape coloured population and the rise in popularity of Reef-based penny whistle *kwela* in the mid-1950s. In 1956, Todd Matshikiza explained the new genre:

> [S]omething different happened among the Coloured bands. They've stopped playing 'Squares a specialty.' A new style, the Quela (pronounced kwela), has evolved. Quela is the brainchild of the squares and the modern samba, so that you get a vastrap which is both South African and yet continental. You can dance the squares to quela and you can also samba to it. Example, 'Shuel se Kwela' on Phillips SC 14 by Mike Adams's Dance Band (*Drum*, April 1956).

Confusion between *kwela* and *quela* was exacerbated when *boeremusiek* recordings were issued with *kwela* in their titles: for example, 'Carnival Kwela, 'Jamboree Kwela', and 'Kalahari Kwela', by Nico Carstens and the Penny Serenaders (Columbia (Carnival Series) TSA3 side B, TSA7 sides A and B respectively). These recordings, however, do not include penny whistle. In a discussion about his brand of *quela* music, Nico Carstens, a well known white *boeremusiek* musician, was clear about the genre his band played: 'They had a rhythm which we called *quela* in the Cape, but it was more like a *klopse* ... I quite honestly can't tell you where is the dividing line between a *vastrap* and a *quela*' (Carstens, 1990). A contemporary press review of 'Laura Kwela' and 'Handy's Samba' by Bobbie's Ballroom Orchestra was similarly explicit about these recordings' style and function: 'This is a typical "Capie" or "Kapenaar" recording with the usual line-up of lead alto-sax, accordion, banjo and piano. Both sides offer very little musically but the rhythm appeals to dancing' (*Bantu World*, 16 November 1955).

While the Cape *quela* and penny whistle *kwela* were separate genres, played by different musicians for different audiences, there was a subtle but significant musical dialogue between *kwela* and *boeremusiek*. Apart from the occasional use of the term *kwela* by *boeremusiek* musicians, there were a few popular recordings made by white penny whistlers within the *boeremusiek* idiom. 'Die Wapad' and 'Haak Vrystaat' (Protea P.A. 205) by Chris Smit en Sy

Pennie Fluitjie, for example, might be thought of as a type of penny whistle-*vastrap*: the instrumental line-up features a penny whistle in addition to the typical *boeremusiek* instrumentation of accordion, guitar, string bass, and drum-set.

That the musical influence of *boeremusiek* on *kwela* is quite significant is not unprecedented. The aesthetic debt to Afrikaans folk music of other early genres in the *marabi*-tradition of black, urban, hybrid music is well acknowledged (see Coplan, 1985: 13-14). Christopher Ballantine states that 'types of "coloured"-Afrikaans and white-Afrikaans dance music known as *tikkie-draai* and *vastrap*, as well as the *ghommaliedjies* of the Cape Malays', influenced 'the melodic and rhythmic structures of *marabi*' (1993: 27). Similarly, David Rycroft claims that 'African dance-hall music in the smaller South African towns, and even such town dances as the *Tsaba-tsaba* of the Rhodesias, owe much to the *Vastrap*' (1958: 55).

The most important influence of *boeremusiek* on *kwela* was the addition of the banjo to the backing section. The musician who introduced the banjo was Saul Malahela from White River in the then eastern Transvaal (now Mpumalanga). According to Albert Ralulimi, one of Malahela's studio colleagues, Malahela grew up in the eastern Transvaal and originally played guitar in a Nelspruit band. His employer, a farmer in the White River area and a keen *boereorkes* musician, gave Malahela a banjo, which he soon adopted as his primary instrument. In Nelspruit Malahela met Billy Zambi, a saxophonist from Rhodesia (now Zimbabwe), and in 1957 they traveled together to Johannesburg to join Gallo, a leading recording company. At Gallo, Billy Zambi, Saul Malahela, Allen Kwela, and Spokes Mashiyane formed a 'brotherhood', making numerous recordings together. Banjo quickly became integrated into the *kwela* sound and Malahela was frequently 'borrowed' by other studios. Other banjo players who also recorded *kwela* were Marks Mankwane (later to become the lead guitarist of the Makhona Tsohle Band), and Saul Nkosi (Ralulimi, 1990b).

Ralulimi suggests that the appeal of the banjo lay in the customary technique of continuous strumming that increased the volume of the backing section and filled in the gaps: 'Let's say the guy [the rhythm guitarist] is playing 4/4 type of strumming – it leaves open gaps, but now the banjo fills in' (Ralulimi, 1990b). In 'Deep Heat', by Lemmy Special and the Alexandra Bright Boys (Gallo New Sound GB 3479), the banjo plays triplet quavers continuously from the second motif to the end, providing continuous sound and the zest Ralulimi describes. The influence of the Afrikaans *boereorkes* is evident in the banjo style of several *kwela* recordings. Example 1 illustrates the banjo rhythms of three such releases by Spokes Mashiyane. All three recordings are extremely

a) 'Caledon River' by Spokes Mashiyane and his Big Five.

b) 'Lona Na Lona' by Spokes Mashiyane and his Big Five.

c) 'Phesheya' by Spokes Mashiyane and his All Star Flutes.

Ex. 1. Banjo rhythms that indicate the influence of Afrikaans *boereorkes* music.

fast: In 'Caledon River' (Gallo New Sound GB 3149) and 'Lona Na Lona' (Gallo New Sound GB 3189) the bass moves on the minim; and the crotchet beat of 'Phesheya' (Gallo New Sound GB 3001) is metronome marking 224. The banjo is the only instrument that takes a solo in 'Caledon River'.

'Phesheya' is one of the best examples of what might be called *vastrap-kwela*. Apart from the characteristic *boeremusiek* rhythm illustrated above, the melodic structure is that of a verse of a folk song (see Example 2), and not constituted of the short repeated and varied motifs typical of *kwela* melodies (see Allen, 1999).

Ralulimi's account of the incorporation of the banjo into the typical *kwela* instrumental line-up is entirely aesthetic; there is nothing in his explanation to suggest that there was any conscious politics of identification at work on the part of the musicians who chose to use either the banjo or characteristic elements of *boeremusiek* in their recordings. In terms of reception, however, the presence of such elements is likely to have increased the appeal of *kwela* for *boeremusiek* followers who would, as a result, have been able to recognise something of themselves in the music. Indeed, tales abound of an appreciation of sorts demonstrated by a sector of the population iconic of conservative Afrikaans values: white policemen. Duze Magwaza, for instance, recalls: 'The SAP [South African Police] used to come and grab us, take us to the police station. Let us play "Skokiaan" for three, four hours for nothing' (Magwaza, 1990). Ralulimi similarly notes the importance of keeping popular Afrikaans songs in one's repertoire, for they were frequently demanded by police under such circumstances. However, some white policemen developed a particular

Ex. 2. The melody of 'Phesheya' by Spokes Mashiyane and his All Star Flutes.

taste for *kwela* music, as an arrangement between Ralulimi's penny whistle group and officers at the Yeoville police station attests. Ralulimi and his fellow musicians were arrested on a suspected pass offence and, after entertaining at the police station until four in the morning, were taken home to the township Alexandra in a police van, making their addresses known to the police. As a result, Ralulimi reports, they 'became victims of their weekend activities. Whenever one sees that his girlfriend is putting up a party, they used to come and grab me and Jerry to go and play just for their entertainment.' Although members of Ralulimi's group were never paid for their services, it was arranged that they could busk freely within the jurisdiction of the Yeoville police station without fear of arrest (Ralulimi, 1990a).

While exploitation and bullying were clearly fundamental to such incidents, something else was, arguably, also happening. Forcing penny whistlers to play popular Afrikaans songs to demonstrate knowledge of their oppressor's culture is a display of power. But we must assume that the policemen and their friends who regularly chose to dance to *kwela* at their private parties also derived pleasure from the music. Was this a case of pleasure overriding identification, or was there something more complex going on? It is possible that part of the policemen's and their friends' enjoyment may have been achieved through identification: they may have heard traces of their core culture through the *boeremusiek* elements within *kwela*; they may, however, also have appreciated being able to dance to local music for, compared to non-Afrikaner white South Africans, Afrikaners often demonstrate greater aesthetic alignment with local cultural forms as opposed to international trends. It is also possible that the threat raised by the acknowledgement of a common humanity through deriving pleasure from the same music was diluted, the forbidden recognition of self in black culture excused, because the pleasure was exhorted through force: apartheid's racial power hierarchies remained in place.

Whatever the reasons for Afrikaner appreciation of *kwela*, it is this kind of history, alongside the genre's internal musical characteristics that were akin to those of *boeremusiek*, that explains the phenomenon that so surprised John Leyden 30 years later. Leyden, a member of the pop group Mango Groove, a 1980s band that derived its musical idiom strongly from *kwela*, was astounded that elderly Afrikaans people formed the largest sector of the band's market: 'We have sold to people who normally buy Bles Bridges. It's unbelievable – we have sold to the mainstream Afrikaner!' (Leyden, 1990).

Exposure, syncreticism and the multivalent appreciation of *kwela*

So why did record companies release *kwela* on LPs before any other black South African music? How did it happen that the genre attracted white audiences and, at its height, a following amongst Indian youth (*World*, 3 December 1958; *Drum*, January 1962)? The primary reason for *kwela*'s success in crossing racial barriers was probably exposure. The young buskers who hawked their music in the city centres and white residential areas repeatedly exposed large numbers of white people to township music for the first time. It is widely believed in the music industry that familiarity generates appreciation; this is why recording companies go to such great lengths to ensure that their products receive as much radio airplay as possible. Perhaps *kwela* buskers achieved such high rates of 'airplay' that non-black South Africans started to identify with the sound of the penny whistle. *Kwela* became part of the general soundscape of 1950s Johannesburg.

For those attempting to entrench apartheid consciousness, such shared identification and common aesthetic appreciation was problematic: it proved the theory that achieving separation between race groups was fundamental to the success of the apartheid project. Whether the authorities understood this clearly at the time, or whether it formed a minor part of a general crack down, from 1958 the police started seriously to harass penny whistle buskers. Eventually the streets became unviable as a venue for *kwela* musicians, and the cross-racially shared soundscape that created the patterns of identification and pleasure that so undermined the apartheid project was silenced.

It is frequently bemoaned that researchers assert a strong relationship between music and identity but fail to explain exactly how a certain genre expresses the identity aspired to, or espoused by, a particular interest group (Street, 1985: 18; Hamm, 1987: 354). I have shown here that during the period of its popularity *kwela* music boasted a large and heterogeneous following: different, occasionally opposing, interest groups were able to associate the genre with their experience and find it meaningful. I suggest that this was possible because the syncretic nature of *kwela*'s musical structure allowed individuals to select certain musical elements that had particular meaning for them, and to articulate these elements with their lived identities. Syncreticism, as initially defined by Melville Herskovits, is 'the tendency to identify those elements in [a] new culture with similar elements in the old one, enabling the persons experiencing the contact to move from one to the other and back again, with psychological ease' (1945: 57-58). This requires 'reinterpretation', which Herskovits describes as the process 'by which old meanings are ascribed to new elements or by which new values change the cultural significance of old forms' (1948: 119).

Both rock 'n' rollers and *boeremusiek* fans were able to identify elements in *kwela* with their own music to dance their own dances to the new genre: they reinterpreted *kwela* and gave it old meanings that made them comfortable and gave them pleasure. These dancers were enjoying the pleasure of identification: the (mis)recognition of the self in the music of the legislated other that syncretic reinterpretation allows. Conversely, the journalists who interpreted the significance of white youngsters playing the penny whistle, and Mrs. Sonia Bunting doing the *kwela* at the treason trialists' party, as well as the concerned citizens who complained about 'the goings on at Zoo Lake', were ascribing new meanings to an established form. These commentators believed that new patrons and new contexts changed the significance of an old form. Instead of being recognised as a vehicle to facilitate the pleasure of dancing as it was in the townships, *kwela*'s cultural and political significance was interpreted as an expression of resistance against racial segregation. In fact, as the evidence above suggests, this was probably not generally the case: for the most part the politics of pleasure overrode the politics of identification, at least for *kwela* audiences if not for their observers.

This multivalent reception of *kwela* by its different white audiences reveals the complexity of cultural consumption in South Africa during the 1950s. The conflicts and contradictions raised by musical appreciation across the race barrier, the confusion of resistance against racial segregation with youth rebellion, and the fusion of pleasure and identification, all suggest that some music was capable of decomposing apartheid even at its genesis.

ENDNOTES

1. This material is based upon work supported by the National Research Foundation. Any opinions, findings and conclusions or recommendations expressed in this material are however those of the author, and therefore the NRF does not accept any liability in regard thereto.
2. The number that became popular in the United Kingdom was 'Tom Hark' by Elias and his Zig-Zag Jive Flutes (Columbia YE 164). Other *kwela* LP releases include: *Tony Scott in South Africa: Tony Scott with the Tony Scott African Quartet and the Alexandra Dead End Kids* (RCA Popular Record 31 104); *King Kwela* (Rave RMG 1107); *Kwela with Lemmy and other Penny Whistlers* (Gallotone GALP 1246).
3. Styles within this tradition that emerged prior to *kwela* are *marabi*, *tsaba-tsaba*, African jazz and vocal jive; see Coplan (1985); Ballantine (1993); and Allen (2003).
4. For a discussion of the musical structure of *kwela*, see Allen (1999); for an overview of the style's evolution see Allen (2005).
5. *The Condemned are Happy*, presented by the South African Information Service, was produced and directed by Jamie Uys Film Productions, Johannesburg.
6. A lobby within the city council tried to use the incident to further the apartheid project and create a separate park for blacks near Alexandra, but this failed (*World*, 13 August 1958).

BIBLIOGRAPHY

Allen, Lara. 1999. 'Kwela: the Structure and Sound of South African Pennywhistle Music'. In Malcolm Floyd (ed.). *Composing the Music of Africa*. Aldershot: Scholar, pp. 225-262.

_. 2003. 'Commerce, Politics, and Musical Hybridity: Vocalising Urban Black South African Identity during the 1950s'. *Ethnomusicology*, 47(2), pp. 228-249.

_. 2005. 'Circuits of Recognition and Desire in the Evolution of Black South African Popular Music: The Career of the Penny Whistle'. *South African Journal of Musicology*, 25, pp. 31-51.

Ballantine, Christopher. 1993. *Marabi Nights: Early South African Jazz and Vaudeville*. Johannesburg: Ravan Press.

Coplan, David. 1985. *In Township Tonight! South Africa's Black City Music and Theatre*. Johannesburg: Ravan Press.

Hamm, Charles. 1985. 'Rock 'n' Roll in a Very Strange Society'. In Richard Middleton & David Horn (eds). *Popular Music 5: Continuity and Change*. Cambridge: Cambridge University Press, pp. 159-174.

_. 1987. 'Review of *In Township Tonight! South Africa's Black City Music and Theatre* by David Coplan'. *Popular Music*, 6(3), pp. 352-354.

Herskovits, Melville J. 1946. 'Problem, Method and Theory in Afro American Studies'. *Phylon, 7(4)*, pp. 337-354.

_. 1948. *Man and his Works: The Science of Cultural Anthropology*. New York: Knopf.

Lodge, Tom. 1983. *Black Politics in South Africa since 1945*. Johannesburg: Ravan Press.

Rycroft, David. 1958. 'The New Town Music of South Africa'. *Recorded Folk Music*, 1, pp. 54-57.

Sampson, Anthony. 1956. *Drum: A Venture into the New Africa*. London: Collins.

Street, John. 1985. '"No Satisfaction": Politics and Popular Music'. *International Association for the Study of Popular Music: Working Paper 5*. East Anglia: University of East Anglia.

Interviews

Carstens, Nico. 1990. Author's interview. Johannesburg, 12 July.

Lerole, Jake. 1990. Author's interview. Johannesburg, 13 July.

Leyden, John. 1990. Author's interview. Durban, 11 March.

Magwaza, Duze. 1990. Author's interview. Durban, 11 March.

Menell, Irene. 1990. Author's interview. Johannesburg, 3 September.

Ralulimi, Albert. 1990a. Author's interview, Johannesburg, 12 February.

Ralulimi, Albert. 1990b. Author's interview, Johannesburg, 15 July.

Williams, Patricia. 1990. Author's interview. Durban, 17 January.

Discography

Carstens, Nico and the Penny Serenaders. 'Carnival Kwela'. Columbia, Carnival TSA3.

Carstens, Nico and the Penny Serenaders. 'Jamboree Kwela'. Columbia, Carnival TSA7.

Carstens, Nico and the Penny Serenaders. 'Kalahari Kwela'. Columbia, Carnival TSA7.

Cele, Willard. 'Penny Whistle Blues'. Gallo, New Sound GB 1123.
Cele, Willard. 'Penny Whistle Boogie'. Gallo, New Sound GB 1123.
Mabaso, Lemmy 'Special' and the Alexandra Bright Boys. 'Deep Heat'. Gallo, New Sound GB 3479.
Makana, Peter. 'Time Square'. Envee, NV 3069.
Mashiyane, Spokes. 'Caledon River'. Gallo, New Sound GB 3149.
Mashiyane, Spokes. 'Lona Na Lona'. Gallo, New Sound GB 3189.
Mashiyane, Spokes. 'Phenduka Twist'. Gallo, New Sound GB 3402.
Mashiyane, Spokes. 'Phesheya'. Gallo, New Sound GB 3001.
Nkosi, Ben. 'Ben's Hawk'. His Masters Voice, JP 622.
Scott, Tony with Ben Nkosi and the Solven Whistlers. *Something New from Africa*. Decca, LK 4292.
Smit, Chris. 'Die Wapad'. Protea, PA 205.
Smit, Chris. 'Haak Vrystaat'. Protea, PA 205.

Newspapers

Bantu World. 1955. 'Disc Delight'. Review by Elbee. 16 November.
Drum. 1956. 'Gramo-go-round.' Review by Todd Matshikiza, alias 'Hot Toddy'. April.
Drum. 1958. 'On the Beat'. Casey Motsisi, alias Kid Hangover. May.
Drum. 1958. '"The Magic Piper" Masterpiece in Bronze'. Nathaniel Nakasa. December.
Drum. 1958. 'We Look Into All This Trouble at Zoo Lake'. Feature by Basil Bikitsha. April.
Drum. 1962. Letter. J. Jugmohun. January.
Golden City Post. 1958. 'Elias Gets 'Em Raving in London'. Bloke Modisane. 13 July.
Golden City Post. 1958. 'What a Party'. 19 October.
Golden City Post. 1959. Interview with Barney Rachabane. 4 January.
Ilanga. 1958. '"Kwela Music" Popular'. 26 April.
Rand Daily Mail. 1959. Letter. 'Afrikaans Theater Goer'. 1 April.
Star. 1959. Article. 11 March.
Weekly Mail. 1990. 'He Hasn't Got the Pelvis. But Elvis Lives ... in Turffontein'. Charlotte Bauer and John Perlman. 24-26 August.
World. 1958. 'Africans Banned from City Hall: Apartheid "Blitz" Begins'. 13 August.
World. 1958. 'Europeans Stay Away from Zoo Lake Jive sessions'. 30 August.
World. 1958. 'King Kwela - Spokes Mashiyane and his accompanist, Jerry Mhlanga dole out torrid notes to the delight of their fans'. Picture caption. 3 December.
World. 1958. 'White Youths Play Kwela'. Usiyazi. 11 November.
World. 1963. Article. 1 July.

5

POPULAR MUSIC AND NEGOTIATING WHITENESS IN APARTHEID SOUTH AFRICA

Gary Baines

Whiteness studies is a relatively new humanities subfield (regarded by some of its critics as race studies in a new guise) which emerged in America. Employing a social constructionist approach to identity formation, whiteness studies attempts to trace the economic and political history behind the invention of 'whiteness', examining how whiteness functions in social practices and analysing the cultural practices that create and perpetuate whiteness. If, so the argument goes, whiteness is not an immutable essence but is historically produced, and if its production requires something more than the physical characteristic of skin colour, then whiteness as a form of political identification, if not racial identity, can be abolished (Wiegman, 1999: 136). Thus whiteness studies is not merely of academic interest (in both meanings of the phrase), but also a political project to dismantle the structures of power and privilege accorded whites (Jay, n.d.).

If whiteness studies is in its infancy in America, in South Africa it has barely seen the light of day. One of the few studies of South African society that explicitly employs a paradigm that holds that whiteness is a master signifier of a race system that is an entirely linguistic, cultural construct is Melissa Steyn's *Whiteness just isn't what it used to be* (2001). Her focus is on how whites have reinvented their identities during the period of transition in which they effectively lost control of the state. Whereas in America there have been inquiries as to the meaning of whiteness in literature and culture (see, for example, Babb, 1998), there has been little work of a similar nature in South Africa. Indeed, attempts to investigate the cultural imagination of whiteness represented in South African art, music, literature, and popular media is largely uncharted terrain. Ballantine (2004) has offered some insights into how musicians have negotiated white identity and positioned themselves in relation to the re-racialisation of political discourse in post-apartheid South Africa. But there has been no attempt to date to explore the construction of whiteness prior to 1994.

IDENTITIES AND WHITENESS

Historically, white people are an invented 'race', constituted of various ethnic groups perceived to have a common ancestry in parts of Europe. 'White' was invented as a category when previous notions of national groups (Dutch, French, German, English, etc) were lumped together to create a single powerful coalition. In part, 'whiteness' is thus an ideological fiction used by one social group to dominate others. The history of the invention of whiteness may strengthen arguments against the very notion of 'race' itself, since this history reveals that there is no such thing as a 'pure' race, and that all human population groups are historical mixtures of different ethnicities. Like other racial categories, then, whiteness is more than a classification of physical appearance; it is largely an invented construct intertwining history, ideology and cultural practice (Babb, 1998: 10).

Part of the difficulty characterising whiteness lies with it having no content other than a culturally manufactured one, developed unevenly over a period of time, influenced by and responding to a variety of historical events and social conditions: among them, the need to create a historical past, the need to create national identity, and the need to minimise class warfare. As whiteness evolved in response to these demands, it did so in no linear or orderly fashion, had no single abiding vision that created it, had no single source from which it sprang. In different periods, a variety of symbols, laws, and institutions have been mobilised to sustain the concept of whiteness, and over time repeated representations have reified its identity (Babb, 1998: 16).

Whiteness, then, should be understood as a positionality of power and privilege, and not some fixed, immutable essence. In varying instances specific whitenesses are constructed through concrete social relations and within concrete historical socio-economic situations, while they may have an overall coherence through exercising domination (Steyn, 2001: xxxi). Whiteness is sustained through hegemony, a complex network of political, economic, and cultural institutions. These institutions give coherence to the conception of what it means to be white, without specifically naming it (Babb, 1998: 5). In other words, whiteness is a cultural construct even though it functions as a naturalised social category in commonsense thought and the discourse of ordinary people.

Employing a Lacanian analysis, Seshadri-Crooks (2000) confronts the most intractable aspect of race thinking, namely the (apparently obvious) visibility of racially marked bodies. She addresses people's immediate, commonsense certainty that seeing is believing; that the visibility of defining characteristics such as skin colour, hair texture, and facial features is irrefutable evidence of the other's race. Seshadri-Crooks argues that, on the contrary, believing precedes seeing; that the cultural order determines what we see. And she claims that it is the anxiety that springs from a sudden encounter with the historicity of race, with evidence of its purely cultural, symbolic origins that engenders the perception of racial features in the other. Race, then, is ultimately a matter of the subject's projection of his or her own need for race fantasy onto the visualised body of the other. Seshadri-Crooks thus aims at a fundamental transformation in the way we see, in the regime of looking that founds race (Wyatt, 2004: 1142-4). Her intervention in the debate, however, is not likely to have much impact on prevailing realist/positivist perceptions in society at large, nor is it likely to have any impact on existing relations of power.

The devices employed in creating and sustaining white hegemony are for the most part devices of exclusion. They articulate not necessarily who or what is white but rather who or what is not white. As such, they reveal the fundamental paradox of whiteness: the persistent need of 'non-whiteness' to give it form and expression. The very existence of whiteness embodies an odd duality of distinguishing itself from non-white while appropriating the non-white to justify its being (Babb, 1998: 43). The unequal nature of the bipolar relationship allowed whites to fix meanings of the self and the other.

Constructing South African whiteness

The development of whiteness in South Africa has many resonances with other settler societies such as Australia and the United States. South African settlers of European descent defined themselves primarily in contradistinction to the 'other'. This included employing binaries such as Christian/heathen, civilised/savage, European/non-European, and white/non-white in which the other was always defined negatively. This provided a rationale for excluding non-whites from full participation in the nation-state. Restrictions on movement, rights to sell labour, rights to vote and own property ensured the exclusion of non-whites from political and economic power. By establishing itself as a naturally superior racial identity, whiteness legitimated the political and legal structures that denied non-whites the rights of citizenship and condoned discrimination against them. Simultaneously, whiteness became a marker of political power. It was able to function as a unifying device, continually co-opting the white working class and so-called 'poor whites', as well as integrating new European immigrants into the fabric of white South Africa.

According to Steyn (2001: 25-26), two major factors have distinguished South African whiteness from the global master narrative of whiteness. First, whites were vastly outnumbered by the indigenous populations which they subjugated but never decimated. Despite their domination, white South Africans always harboured a fear of being overwhelmed demographically and culturally. Whiteness in South Africa has always, at least in part, been constructed around discourses of resistance against a constant perceived threat posed by blacks. Second, the two major groups of European stock (English and Afrikaners) were not drawn into a common identity as early, nor as seamlessly, as white ethnic groups in, for example, the USA. They distinguished themselves from each other through adopting a different standpoint to blacks, their political and racial ideologies and their construction of 'home' being fundamentally different. On the one hand, English-speaking white South Africans adopted an identity by which they regarded themselves as part of an imagined global community with ties to Anglophone culture. This is readily apparent from the popular music they consumed (see Muller, 1997). White Afrikaans speakers, on the other hand, emphasised their identification with the African continent – but with the land and soil rather than with the people. In spite of their commonality of identity whites were obviously not a monolithic group. But while these differences manifested themselves in party politics, white supremacy, for most, was not negotiable.

Initially appealing to a narrow white Afrikaner ethnic constituency, the National Party deemed it imperative to promote the cause of a broader white South African nationalism after the party assumed power of the South African state in 1948. Essential in the making of such an exclusive white national identity was the construction of an imagined common past. Leslie Witz has shown that the 1952 Van Riebeeck festival, celebrating the tercentenary of the Dutch settlers' arrival in the Cape, was a symbolic event in the promotion of a broader exclusive racial past. It was about reconstituting the white nation of English and Afrikaans speakers. This white nation-building project became a crucial component of Nationalist political strategy, playing a major role in constructing a history and identity for whites as whites that reinforced and legitimated their notion of supremacy (2003: 96-7).

Active in furthering this project was the national broadcaster, the South African Broadcast Corporation (SABC), whose charter was developed in accordance with the policies of the Nationalist government. The SABC used its monopoly of the airwaves to establish a radio station for blacks known as Radio Bantu, as well as a string of regionally-based stations which broadcast in the black vernacular languages (see Hamm, 1991). While these stations promoted (neo-)traditional musical styles, white South Africans were served a fare of Anglo-American popular music on the separate Afrikaans- and English-language stations and on the bilingual Springbok Radio. State agents obviously believed that control of radio programming was essential, for, as we will see, even the content of popular songs could undermine its ideology. Censorship was thus used to silence the voices of both local and foreign artists that criticised the regime.[1]

Steyn holds that apartheid was an attempt to institutionalise the master narrative of whiteness through state mechanisms and controls (1997: 11), with the SABC an example of this. The emphasis was always on group identity and the cultural and ethnic complexity of the South African situation: the white group in contradistinction to the many African 'tribes'; the unchanging tribal nature of the black African one of apartheid's many ideological constructs. This reification of whiteness over other cultural markers had the effect of promoting an exclusive form of nationalism. Thus an apartheid version of the master narrative of whiteness underwrote white power, privilege, and wealth. It was a master narrative that provided the dominant frame for making sense of and legitimating the socio-political status quo. For narrative is not specifically a literary form but an epistemological category. Narratives are historical social constructions that provide a frame of interpretation through which we make sense of the world and our place in it, and thus constitute our sense of identity (Steyn, 2001: xxxviii).

Narrating whiteness in South African popular music

Artists, like other individuals in society, have multiple identities as they have to negotiate the intersection of different worlds. Class, ethnic, gender and racial identities are not fixed and so artists are invariably cultural straddlers: white and English, white and Afrikaans, and even white and black. The musicians that I discuss here all represented some aspect(s) of their experience of being white in South Africa: in their music by virtue of their language and accents, lyrical content, the spatial location of their stories (usually in the white suburbs), and the nature of the performance. Moreover, most of the artists discussed below have adopted personae for purposes of performance but have found that these assumed identities became part of their public image. These personae did not necessarily mask their identities. Rather, they afforded them the space to consciously construct identities that were thought to have some resonance with local audiences.

Jeremy Taylor made his home in South Africa in the late 1950s and was employed to teach English to the boys of St Martin's School in Rosettenville. He made his name as a performer on the show *Wait a Minim!* (1961) with a repertoire which included 'The Ballad of the Southern Suburbs' (aka 'Ag Pleez Deddy!'). As a single, it proved hugely popular despite being banned by the SABC for 'incorporating slang and mixing the [Afrikaans and English] languages' (Taylor, 1992: 30). The song with its good-humoured satire of Johannesburg's white working-class culture captured the idiomatic language of teenagers or 'woozers' who spoke Sow Theffricun Innglissh (STI) as Robin Malan was to dub it (Malong [sic], 1986: 5). Ironically, it took the gumption of an English-born *uitlander* (foreigner) to become the first artist to take off a South African English accent in a local recording. Yet, when Taylor attempted to satirise the social practices of what he termed the 'English-speaking G and T brigade' (1992: 30), his song 'Northern Side of Town' (1962) was banned because the SABC regarded it as 'insulting to the Afrikaner'. The offending verses were presumably the third and sixth:

We're from the northern side of town
To belong to the club we make our application
We're from the northern side of town
It protects us from all outside infiltration
One day a chap called Labushane tried to join our company
We really couldn't admit him when we discovered after tea
That his real name to his frightful shame was actually *Labuschagggne*
He was not from the northern side of town.

We're from the northern side of town
The language parallel's below our breeding
We're from the northern side of town
We couldn't give a rap which lingo's leading
Cousin Ethel fresh from England, to the best of her belief
Tried to greet us all in Afrikaans when arriving on the Reef
For she shouted from the comet '*Moenie spoeg nie, asseblief!*' ['Please don't spit']
Yes, we're from the northern side of town.

The fact that Taylor had pilloried the social snobbery of the mink and manure set with their condescending attitude towards Afrikaners was clearly lost on the SABC censors. But the official language policy which regarded Afrikaans as an expression of a discrete white culture was sacrosanct. And the language issue was particularly sensitive so soon after South African whites had voted to leave the Commonwealth. It was easy to dismiss Taylor as an 'outsider' but he exposed the fault lines of white South African society.

The Afrikaans musician David Kramer, by contrast, invented a stage and public persona which provided him with a voice to satirise whites from within the laager. Following his return to Worcester in the Cape from study in England, he started playing the Cape folk club circuit in the guise of a Boland *joller*. Kramer constructed a character from old family photographs consisting of a style of dress which included a white shirt with rolled-up sleeves, a waistcoat, baggy trousers and red shoes. He reckons that his 'whole sense of self was caught up in that character' (Kramer, 1998). This image was projected in his repertoire of songs, public performances and reinforced in the visual images of the cover of his 1980 *Bakgat!* album and the publication *David Kramer: Short back and sides* (1982). The role-playing included an accent or vocal costume (Frith, 1996: 198) with guttural diction, a bilingual vocabulary and a 'raw' musical style. Drewett (2002) suggests that Kramer's image as '*almal se pêl*' (everybody's friend) – transformed into the happy-go-lucky little guy of the Volkswagen commercials – appealed primarily to a white conservative Afrikaner community. Certainly his most popular songs, such as 'Hak Hom Blokkies' and 'Die Royal Hotel', which are set to *sakkie sakkie* (a type of Afrikaans folk dance) sounds and trade on the reminiscences of a former Springbok rugby player or on the nostalgia of a forgotten community, broadened his appeal. But Kramer also had a harder, satirical edge. For instance, he satirised the small town mentality of the white working class in sketches such as 'Hekke van Paradise' ('Gates of Paradise') and 'Suburban Dream'. But he did not (in his words) only 'take the piss out of the Afrikaner' (Kramer, 1998). In 'Tjoepstil' he parodied the perceived hypocrisy of white English-speakers who call their Afrikaner counterparts derogatory names such as 'rock spider' and 'crunchie', live off the fat of the land, but flee overseas 'when the shit starts to fly'.

Kramer not only commented on Afrikaans- and English-speaking identities, but on whiteness in general. Perhaps the most poignant satire in this respect is evident in the following lines from the song 'I Had a Dream':

But *Here* (Lord) did I have a dream
One of those dreams

That give you a helluva fright man
Because I dreamt I had been reclassified
Non-white
And when I told my wife she started crying
I said 'Don't worry, Skattie
I'm sure it'll come right'
But then the dog came in
And started to growl
Like he wanted to bite
And there's this ou looking through the window
With a bright torchlight

The biting pathos which had earlier elicited ripples of laughter from the (presumably white) audience on the live recording on the *Bakgat!* album is replaced by silence, then the laughter is tinged with unease. The bizarre and contradictory stories of race classification were – and still are – legendary, providing suitable material for comedians and newspaper cartoons. For many people this scenario was not beyond the bounds of possibility. The application of the Population Registration Act could actually destroy lives, and the apartheid regime employed the Act to uphold its definition of whiteness with no thought to the hurt and trauma imposed on its victims. Kramer's (tongue-in-cheek) dream of married bliss in white suburbia is turned into a nightmare by the arbitrariness of racial classification. Kramer is an example of an artist who questioned the value systems that made whiteness more than a label of racial classification and allowed it to become an ideology.

Johnny Clegg is widely known as the 'White Zulu' or, in France, where he is popular, Le Zulu Blanc. He earned this appellation as a result of his embrace of Zulu culture. As a teenager, Clegg immersed himself in the Zulu migrant culture of the mining compounds and inner city of Johannesburg. Under the tutelage of street musicians, he learned Zulu guitar styles, *indlamu* (traditional Zulu) dance steps, and stick fighting. He admits, in retrospect, that as a young person there was 'a great attraction in exploring the other'. He conceptualises his experience as 'a personal journey to try and discover my place as a white African', 'to explore what it is for me as a white person to be an African'. Clegg's identification with Zulu culture was more than skin deep and his academic training as an anthropologist caused him to reject an essentialist notion of ethnic identity. Indeed, he acknowledges celebrating the life force behind activities such as Zulu dancing precisely 'because the social construction of Zulu masculinity was a key aspect of his entry into Zulu culture' (Clegg, 1998).

Clegg argued that his constructed identity as the 'white Zulu' was a complete contradiction of apartheid ideology and discourse (Taylor, 1997:178).

In the 1970s Clegg formed a musical partnership with Sipho Mchunu. This led, in turn, to his fronting the multiracial group Juluka which played a hybrid of Zulu *maskandi* (traditional styles played on Western instruments) with rock arrangements and both English and Zulu lyrics. Their first release was titled 'Woza Friday' but was rejected by SABC's Zulu radio station because the use of English with the vernacular was regarded as an 'insult to the Zulu people'; a form of cultural censorship by language purists. Being banned from the airwaves meant that Juluka had to find other spaces in which to reach out to audiences, and they played in church halls and township venues in order to minimise harassment by the apartheid government. However, this alienated Clegg from part of his white audience. With Juluka, Clegg did not engage in a blatant confrontation with the state on political and cultural issues. Rather, the band's resistance to the regime was coded: in the way band members dressed, moved, and the lyrics that they sang (Clegg, 1998). The adoption of traditional Zulu attire in combination with Western dress, and the appropriation of Zulu dance routines amounted to a politicised cross-cultural collaboration. In the song 'Heart of the Dancer' on the album *African Litany* (1982), Clegg sings:

> I went to look into the heart of the dancer
> His movements have a magic mystery
> They must have a message and meaning
> 'Cause he's doing something to me
> Please don't let the drum stop beating
> I have to understand
> How he dances our future and our destiny
> And how we became part of this land

This is about as autobiographical as Clegg allows himself to become in his lyrics. His embrace of Zulu (male) culture leads him to express a wish to identify with the land and its indigenous peoples; to become a white African.

Juluka's performances challenged an apartheid taboo which regarded whiteness as an inviolable concept. As Coplan (2005: 3) puts it: 'Juluka's very existence was perceived as a threat by the apartheid regime with its notions of the absolute separation of strictly bounded cultures'. Clegg's actions actually amounted to an audacious political statement for he rejected the narrow ethnic chauvinism (i.e. tribalism) of the apartheid ideologues. And, musically, he crossed cultural boundaries by exploring his own, and a more general white, fascination with Zuluness. Clegg's performances suggest that whiteness (and also Zuluness) is a matter less of race than of style, and that style is itself a cross-cultural phenomenon, working against the grain of racial essentialism.

The final artist I briefly discuss is the Afrikaans writer and poet Andre du Toit (aka Andre le Toit), who reinvented himself as Koos Kombuis in the 1980s when he turned to music in order to appeal to younger members of his audience (Hopkins, 2006). Consequently, this 30-something self-proclaimed *boomelaar* (bum) found himself performing for an audience that was receptive to questioning hegemonic apartheid discourse. In the late 1980s he became part of the *Vöelvry* (literally, free as a bird) movement which opened up a cultural space for young Afrikaners to renegotiate their identities and narratives of self in a society undergoing transformation (see Grundlingh, 2004). But it was his iconoclasm and irreverence rather than his politics that rocked the Afrikaner establishment. In his autobiography, Kombuis (2000) refers to himself, with his usual touch of irony, as a *volksverraier* (traitor of his people). He interrogates the existence of a monolithic group of Afrikaners who constitute 'the *volk*' and the right of the establishment to speak on his behalf. Such concerns are also reflected in his musical repertoire. For instance, his album *Niemandsland and Beyond* (1990) included the track 'Paranoia in Parow-Noord':

> Ek weet ek is verslaaf aan drank
> Ek is oortrokke by die bank
> My dogter is 'n 'Boerepunk'
> Maar dank God ek's ten minste blank!

[I know I'm a slave to drink / I'm overdrawn at the bank / My daughter is a 'Boerepunk' / But thank God I'm white at least!]

There might well be a confessional element in (the first of) these lines. But in cataloguing the symptoms of paranoia amongst the outwardly respectable citizens of white suburbia, Kombuis also brings to bear a bitter irony and sarcasm. Despite his many failings, Kombuis' character sees his saving grace as his whiteness. He resorts to the fiction perpetrated by apartheid that there existed a superior race which deserved special privileges and protection of their way of life simply because they were white. Kombuis was more attuned and sensitive to human rights discourses than the ideology of apartheid with its privileging of whiteness. Indeed, Kombuis and other artists contested the meaning of whiteness at a time when South Africa's apartheid policies made her a pariah state.

The discussion, so far, has been confined to the construction and subversion of whiteness in the work of select white South African popular music artists. Obviously, whiteness is not a singular phenomenon but a social construct that can be articulated, as well as challenged, in musical lyrics and performance. Equally obviously, class position also affects an understanding of one's whiteness. Thus white middle-class artists are likely to conceive of their whiteness in rather less binary terms than their working-class counterparts. Similarly, South African audiences during the apartheid era were also segmented along racial and class lines. The relative success of the abovementioned artists in terms of record and concert sales suggests that they struck a chord with the experiences of (primarily but not only) white listeners. In apartheid South Africa this meant that audiences negotiated different expressions of whiteness with musicians.

Negotiating whiteness in South African popular music

It is a truism that individuals establish self-awareness in relation to their social worlds. This process involves the formation by the individual of an image of the 'generalised other': the assumed attitudes and values of those with whom one interacts socially. The individual may construct an image of self by refracting it from others with whom one has an affinity so that a self-image mirrors others in society. The individual's sense of self is thus mediated between its awareness of its own differences from, and its commonalities with, others in society. Identity is affirmed both with and against others. However, under conditions of (post)modernity, forming an image of the 'generalised other' in relation to which one may negotiate one's sense of self has become increasingly difficult. In a globalising world, the attitudes and values of those with whom one interacts become more and more diverse. Owing to the loosening of social controls such as religious institutions and family, and because of increased communication with those geographically distant from oneself, a sense of identify is not necessarily bounded by space nor by one's association with a local community. Indeed, identity formation has become increasingly a matter of personal choice (Jansen in Kivikuru, 2001: 59ff.).

The groups to which individuals see themselves belonging constitute 'imagined communities'. Benedict Anderson famously argued that imagined communities were constructed in the minds of the members of nation-states, and that especially two literary forms – newspapers and novels – were crucial in enabling individuals to imagine the community of the nation by reinforcing an awareness of certain standardised experiences of the citizens and residents within national boundaries (1983: 30). Whilst this might have been true of the late nineteenth and early twentieth centuries with which Anderson is concerned, the imagined communities of our contemporary global society, where the consumption of cultural forms often transcends national boundaries, are likely to assume different configurations. In the case of popular music, audience preferences are as likely to be for a particular transnational style or genre as they are for the music from a specific region or country.

Music, then, is capable of creating and reinforcing an awareness of shared experience among individuals irrespective of their geographical location. Thus English-speaking listeners living in apartheid South Africa were able to affirm an identity which was not 'first and foremost South African' (Muller, 1997: 8). They were able to imagine themselves as part of a world-wide Anglophone community, differentiated from white English-speakers elsewhere only by virtue of the fact that they happened to be resident in South Africa. Many white Afrikaans-speakers, especially amongst the youth, also listened to Anglo-American popular music. But not all whites identified with Europe or regarded themselves as being rooted in that continent. Their heritage tied them to Africa and this did not prompt a sense of cultural inferiority. In fact, some whites took pride in music performed and produced by South African artists and identified with their music. The appeal of the music of bilingual artists like David Kramer and Koos Kombuis transcended language barriers. This suggests that English- and Afrikaans-speaking whites might have imagined themselves as part of the same community on certain occasions, even when, on other occasions, they cultivated discrete identities. As Simon Frith (1996: 121) has put it: the experience of music is both personal and cultural, for the listener absorbs the music and the meaning into her/his life and becomes part of a broader collective which has experienced music in the same way.

Mary Robertson (2003) has conducted a case study amongst a small sample of white South African university students in order to determine what their listening habits reveal about the process of identity formation. From her analysis of one such (male) student who consumes locally-produced rock/ crossover music as a way of affirming a South African identity, Robertson asserts that her subject is able to 'imagine a community... united by the shared experience of growing up in South Africa' (2004: 133). The informant also listens to the music in order to define himself as someone who 'consciously tries to relate to those different from himself in the country' (134). As an English-speaker, he purposefully chooses to listen to artists such as Koos Kombuis and Johannes Kerkorrel whose songs have mainly Afrikaans lyrics. He also listens to artists such as Johnny Clegg and Bright Blue whose songs draw on the artists' experiences of living in South Africa and have an (ill-defined) South

African sound. As such, listening to South African music allows the subject to imagine himself in relation to other South Africans – both individuals and groups – and allows him to affirm or renegotiate his own self-perception (136-7). While Robertson's case studies were conducted amongst students who probably have little recollection of life under the apartheid regime and white South African identity is, to an extent, in the process of being renegotiated in post-apartheid South Africa, the same music is able to speak to experiences on both sides of this divide.

This seems to bear out the view of Louise Meintjes that the 'potency of music lies in the way and the extent to which the listener can feel meaningful connections to other experiences' (1990: 53). There is good reason to believe that music's power to create resonances between individual and collective identity narratives stems from both the lyrics and the sound. Born and Hesmondhalgh (2000: 32) insist that music, unlike the visual and literary arts, has particular powers of connotation and therefore a capacity to evoke a wide range of meanings. Whilst this understates the connotative power of non-musical cultural forms, there can be little doubt that music's lack of denotative meaning makes for a particularly flexible text that allows for an open-ended reading. This is true of both the music and the lyrics, which are equally open to interpretation.

By exploring select articulations of whiteness in popular South African music of the period circa 1960 to 1990, I have suggested exactly how explorative, shifting and malleable white identities during the apartheid era were at times. Although the regime invested much in racialised identities, being (classified) white did not necessarily mean that individual identities were closed to negotiation and self-reinvention. Given the constructed and subjective nature of identity formation, South African whiteness was not unchanging. In fact, neither articulating nor appropriating an identity through the medium of music is simple and straightforward. This is partly because artists have no monopoly on the shaping of personal and/or collective identities, and partly because audiences do not 'passively consume a product: they actively absorb it and rework it to construct their own meaning of self, of social identity and group cohesion' (Teer-Tomaselli, 1997: vi). Negotiating whiteness through music in apartheid South Africa was often a contested process.

Endnotes

1   For more on the censorship of music in apartheid South Africa, see Drewett's essay in this volume.

Bibliography

Anderson, Benedict. 1983. *Imagined Communities: Reflections on the Origin and Spread of Nationalism*. London: Verso.

Babb, Valerie. 1998. *Whiteness Visible: The Meaning of Whiteness in American Literature and Culture*. New York: New York University Press.

Ballantine, Christopher. 2004. 'Re-thinking "Whiteness"? Identity, Change and "White" Popular Music in Post-apartheid South Africa'. *Popular Music*, 23(2), pp. 105-131.

Born, Georgina & David Hesmondhalgh (eds). 2000. *Western Music and Its Others: Difference, Representation, and Appropriation in Music*. Berkeley: University of California Press.

Clegg, Johnny. 1998. Interview with Michael Drewett, Johannesburg, 20 April.

Coplan, David. 2005. 'God Rock Africa: Thoughts on Politics in Popular Black Performance in South Africa'. *African Studies*, 64(1), pp. 9-27.

Drewett, Michael. 2002. 'The Use of Satire in Popular Music in Apartheid and Post-apartheid South Africa'. In Kimi Kärki, Rebecca Leydon, Henri Terho (eds). *Proceedings of the 11th Conference of the International Association for the Study of Popular Music, Turku, Finland, 6-10 July 2001*. Saarijärvi, Finland: IASPM-Norden, pp. 583-97.

Dyer, Richard. 1993. 'White'. In *The Matter of Images: Essays on Representation*. London: Routledge, pp. 126-148.

Frith, Simon. 1996. 'Music and Identity'. In S Hall & P du Gay (eds). *Questions of Cultural Identity*. London: Sage, pp. 108-127.

Grundlingh, Albert. 2004. 'Rocking the Boat in South Africa? Vöelvry Music and Afrikaans Anti-apartheid Social Protests in the 1980s'. *International Journal of African Historical Studies*, 37(3), pp. 483-514.

Hopkins, Pat. 2006. *Vöelvry: The Movement that Rocked South Africa*. Cape Town: Zebra Press.

Hamm, Charles. 1991. '"The Constant Companion of Man": Separate Development, Radio Bantu and Music'. *Popular Music*, 10(2), pp. 147-173.

Hyslop, Jonathan. 2000. 'Why Did Apartheid's Supporters Capitulate? "Whiteness", Class and Consumption in Urban South Africa, 1985-1995'. *Society in Transition*, 31(1), pp. 36-45.

Jansen, A. 2001. 'Contested Meanings: Audience Studies and the Concept of Cultural Identity'. In Ullamaija Kivikuru (ed.). *Contesting the Frontiers: Media and Dimensions of Identity*. Goteborg: Nordicom, pp. 57-78.

Jay, Gregory. n.d. 'Whiteness Studies: Deconstructing (the) Race'. http://www.uwm.edu/%7Egjay/Whiteness/index.html.

Kombuis, Koos. 2000. *Seks & Drugs & Boeremusiek: Die Memoires van 'n Volksverraaier*. Cape Town: Human & Rousseau.

_. 2001. *Koos se Songs: 'n Versameling Lirieke en Kitaarakkoorde*. Cape Town: Human & Rousseau.

Kramer, David. 1982. *Short Back and Sides*. Cape Town: Maskew Miller.

_. 1998. Interview by Michael Drewett, Cape Town, July.

Malong, Rawbone [pseud. for Malan, Robin]. 1973. *Ah big yaws: A guard to Sow Theffricun Innglissh*. Cape Town: David Philip.

Meintjes, Louise. 1990. 'Paul Simon's *Graceland*, South Africa, and the Mediation of Musical Meaning'. *Ethnomusicology*, 34(1), pp. 37-73.

Muller, Carol. 1997. 'White Pop and an Imagined English-speaking Community in South Africa 1950-90'. In A Tracey (ed.). *Proceedings of the 13th and 14th Symposia on Ethnomusicology*. Grahamstown: International Library of African Music, Rhodes University, pp. 8-12.

Robertson, Mary. 2003. 'Imagining Ourselves: Music as a Vehicle of Identity Among Young White South Africans'. BA Honours thesis, Rhodes University.

_. 2004. '"Imagining Ourselves": South African Music as a Vehicle for Negotiating White South African Identity'. *Journal of the Musical Arts in Africa*, 1(1), pp. 129-137.

Seshadri-Crooks, Kalpana. 2000. *Desiring Whiteness: A Lacanian Analysis of Race*. London: Routledge.

Steyn, Melissa. 1997. 'New Shades of "Whiteness": White Identity in the New South Africa'. Paper presented at an IDASA conference on 'Multicultural Citizenship in the "New" South Africa'. Cape Town, December.

_. 2001. *Whiteness Just Isn't What It Used To Be: White Identity in a Changing South Africa*. Albany: State University of New York Press.

Taylor, Jeremy. 1992. *Ag Pleez Deddy! Songs and Reflections*. Pretoria: Jeremy Taylor Publishing.

Taylor, Timothy D. 1997. *Global Pop: World Music, World Markets*. New York: Routledge.

Teer-Tomaselli, Ruth. 1997. 'Shifting Spaces: Popular Culture and National Identity'. *Critical Arts*, 11(1-2), pp. i-xv.

Wiegman, Robyn. 1999. 'Whiteness Studies and the Paradox of Particularity'. *Boundary 2*, 26(3), pp. 115-150.

Witz, Leslie. 2003. *Apartheid's Festival: Contending South Africa's National Pasts*. Bloomington: Indiana University Press.

Wyatt, Jean. 2004. 'Review of *Desiring Whiteness: A Lacanian Analysis of Race* by Kalpana Seshadri-Crooks'. *Signs 29 (4)*, pp. 1141-1144.

6

PACKAGING DESIRES

ALBUM COVERS AND THE PRESENTATION OF APARTHEID

Michael Drewett

When deciding whether or not to ban a publication the official apartheid-era state censor, the Directorate of Publications, would consider whether or not it was 'undesirable'. Over the decades the Directorate declared thousands of publications undesirable. These included approximately 100 music albums, some of which were found to be undesirable wholly or partly because of their record covers. Although these decisions about album covers are in themselves interesting, my focus is not exclusively on government censorship decisions. For it was not only government censors who had an interest in the desirable: when deciding how to present their music to potential consumers, musicians and/or their record companies chose covers with which they wanted to associate themselves and their music. In this sense they too had an interest in the desirable, specifically in desirable marketing images.

Using the idea of 'packaging desires', I explore a variety of record cover images used by musicians and record companies during the apartheid era. I consider the ways in which race, ethnicity, sex, and gender were often integrally presented on album covers in a manner which reinforced a racist, ethnocentric, sexist, and heterosexist view of South African society. It is argued that record covers promoted apartheid hegemony in two ways: first, through the promotion of dominant ideas and second, through the omission of dissenting ideas, as a result of censors who, and threat of censorial action which, policed the boundaries of the dominant discourse, ensuring that the undesirable remained unseen. The prevalence of album cover images which either actively promoted or simply did not challenge the dominant apartheid discourse contributed towards a context in which South Africans were not encouraged to question the dominant order and were less likely to encounter alternatives.[1]

PACKAGING MUSIC: THE ART OF THE ALBUM COVER

Much sociological and musicological discussion of popular music focuses on the lyrics or music itself. Far less attention is paid to the album covers within which the music is packaged as part of a marketing strategy. Yet Brian Griffin, one of Britain's most prolific rock photographers of the 1980s, emphasises the importance of album covers as a medium. His comments are particularly apt for the 1960s to 1980s pre-compact disc context, when long playing records were the most popular format for recordings (and the period under discussion here). Griffin argues that the album cover:

> is *the* vehicle (for artistic expression), because it gets into the living room, as opposed to some art sanctum. It's on the streets, it's in the shops, it's in the home, and it stays around for a very long time. The most important aspect of it is the psychological one. The twelve-inch square is just right when you hold it at arms' length; it's an absolutely perfect viewing space, in feel, space and size (in Dean et al., 1984: 10).

The immediacy of the album cover makes it an ideal conduit for musicians and/or record companies to portray images with which they want audiences to associate their music. Indeed Kasper de Graaf states that record covers are a means by which musicians are able 'to express themselves in a medium which is not their medium', an extension of 'the ways they can express themselves' (in Dean et al., 1984: 9). This expression on album covers is made possible by what Barthes calls various 'signifying units' (1977: 23), enabling people and objects in the cover art to connote particular meanings. On occasion the meaning is an extension of the music's meanings, while at other times it provides additional meaning which is not, and perhaps cannot be, captured in the music. For example, in the apartheid era when there was severe lyrical censorship on state radio, images of defiance on album cover images could connote meanings not possible to present in the lyrics.

However, as much as album covers might work as an art form they are typically a marketing convention for packaging and selling music. Griffin notes that: 'We can chat about art ... but it's a packaging design really. You're selling cornflakes, you're selling the Bunnymen, you're selling Depeche Mode, you're selling detergent. It's exactly the same' (in Dean et al., 1984: 11). In an extremely competitive market the commercial value of album cover design is high. Colman Andrews argues that it therefore 'makes good commercial sense for each album to look different, to look appealing to its segment of the market, and to convey some philosophical or emotional sense of the kind of music it masks' (1974: 118). Andrews indicates the importance not only of packaging the music in a way which accentuates its difference in a competitive market, but which also emphasises its sameness by placing it within market niches. As I show in this chapter, many records were aimed at particular segments of the South African population, using signifying units clearly designed for specific audiences. Very often the way in which albums were designed to appeal to a particular sector of the population included a sense of the musicians' or marketers' philosophical and political underpinnings.

Marking the boundaries of apartheid desirability

It is useful to begin an exploration of apartheid desirability with a cursory inspection of Section 47(2) of the Publications Act of 1974. This section of the Act, in a sense, marked the boundaries of acceptable discourse, endorsing some ideas while excluding others. According to the Act, materials were undesirable if they were indecent, obscene, offensive, damaging to public morals, blasphemous, brought any section of the inhabitants of the Republic into ridicule or contempt, caused conflict between South Africans, or posed a threat to the security of the state. Political, religious, sexual, and moral interests were drawn together in an interrelated way in the form of a dominant discourse upheld by the state. These were the limits of desirability. Failure to conform placed individuals on the outside, to be brought in line by coercive state power.

Those granted the power to censor used the censorship processes to draw the boundaries of acceptable discourse within their field of jurisdiction. To begin with, state censors launched attacks on controversial material from a self-created and imagined centre, acting as 'arbiter between contending social forces' (Coetzee, 1996: 186), and policing the boundaries of the dominant discourse. Director of the apartheid government's Publications Appeal Board, Jacobus van Rooyen, admitted this much when he suggested that the role of the state censor was to provide 'for a framework within which the arts may be performed'. This constituted the state's duty to maintain 'order in society' (1987: 3). Van Rooyen literally envisaged the state censor ensuring this order by patrolling the country's geographic borders: 'the aim of legislation is to keep pornography and blasphemy out of the country' (p. 20); as though pornography and blasphemy only came from the extreme margins, off the country's map. Van Rooyen also imagined a space in which the state censor's duty was to 'strike a balance between opposing interests' in an attempt to serve the supposed 'general interests' of the public (1987: 106, 3). Operating from a position of centralised political power, the state censor hoped to foster conditions favourable to the dominant discourse by upholding apartheid desires.

Judith Butler argues that censorship preserves such desires not only through external exertion of control or the deprivation of liberties, but is also formative of subjects and the legitimate boundaries of speech (1997: 132). Thus censorship is a form of moral instruction bestowed upon citizens by the state but also operates on a more fundamental level, labelling certain citizens and objects as desirable and others as undesirable. Censorship is therefore not primarily about speech, but is exercised in the interests of deeper social and state goals. Its productive capacity is in developing certain types of subjects rather than others or in achieving consensus. Thus Catharine Lumby suggests that 'censorship is not a weapon (to oppress natural desires and sexualities) or a necessary evil (to protect the virtuous from the wanton) but a tool, whose shape and purpose changes according to who's wielding it. Nor is censorship simply a set of laws, regulations and procedures used to police images and information – it affects the meaning we give those images and information' (1997: xxi). In passing certain narrow forms of judgement, the apartheid censors were therefore producing, reinforcing and maintaining the principles that guided their decisions.

According to John Street, censors' decision-making needs to be regarded as part of the politics of judgment. Influenced by Pierre Bourdieu's (1984) writing on the sociology of judgment and taste, Street argues that censorship should be understood as political judgment, a product of political ideology, interests and institutions (1997: 181). Accordingly, censorship forms part of a process of shaping or reshaping the political landscape, supporting certain interests while marginalising others (p. 179-80). For example, Christopher Merrett argues that censorship was integrally connected to the apartheid state's desire

> to keep to a minimum the contact between the different racial groups into which the country's population was divided, so as to perpetuate the myth that the differences between people are greater than their common humanity ... Censorship was a device used to maintain the illusion that the fine-sounding ideas of apartheid were not only desirable and moral, but realisable. It was the fiction that counted, not the reality (1994: 3).

The South African state certainly implemented the censorship of publications as an intended limitation of discourse, part of a system of classification, order and distribution designed to prevent the emergence of ideas that subverted apartheid's fictions. These publication 'fields' were governed by the dominant political discourse according to the government's moral-political framework.

For Street, instances of music censorship are an inevitable consequence of music's political character (2001: 243-255). He argues that it is the ability of music to shape society that leads to its censorship, as a reaction linked to the preservation of particular interests (1997: 181; 2001: 246). In this sense, struggles over censorship can be conceived in terms of tensions over moral-political considerations between production and reproduction. The habitus of musicians prevented 'total contingency' as musicians negotiated the 'constant tension between the urge to create and the urge to conserve' (Bourdieu, 2000: 40), where 'creation' is incorporated to refer to uttering and publishing ideas which subverted the dominant discourse. To be sure, the dominant discourse is not fixed, it is negotiated and renegotiated; or, as Bourdieu puts it, is 'constantly broken and restored', perpetuated, or subverted (1990: 141). This hegemony is most susceptible to contest when there is a 'mismatch between the expectations of habitus and the opportunities offered by the fields' (Swartz, 1997: 290). Even in contexts like apartheid South Africa where a 'malevolent state' attempts to control music through a heavy reliance on force and surveillance, Keith Negus cautions that attempts to erect cultural boundaries by making 'people play and listen to particular types of music have always led to resistance and opposition' (1996: 201). Importantly, Negus locates the censorship of music within the context of a hegemonic struggle whereby hegemony's vulnerability to contestation makes allowances for counter-hegemonic processes, and this is clearly attested in the ensuing discussion.

Packaging apartheid desires

The moral-political framework outlined in the Publications Act integrally connected moral, religious, and political criteria so that opposition to the state's stance on any one of these areas implied an attack on the entire hegemonic project. The fight against the undesirability of certain sexual and religious images, for example, could be integrally linked to the politics of apartheid. Nevertheless, as race and ethnicity obviously formed a core component of apartheid thinking, they unquestionably informed notions of desirability as reflected on album covers aimed at South African markets.

Patriotic images during the 1970s in particular portrayed nationalism as an

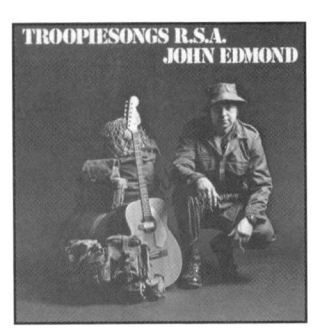

Images 1a-e. Record covers promoting patriotic militarised masculinity.

exclusive domain of white South Africans. Nowhere is this clearer than in the image of the military man, fighting to protect white South Africa. The covers for seven-inch singles by Esmé Solms (Image 1a) and Dennis East (Image 1b) in support of defence force recruits reveal white males as defenders of their country. Solms' 'Soldier, Son' is a particularly poignant image: a white male soldier reading a letter against the backdrop of the (apartheid) South African flag. Thus the separation of the 'front' (at which the white soldier is protecting his country) from the home (a letter of support) is supported by the patriotic image of the flag. East's 'Love manoeuvres' (1985), a comic song from the soundtrack to the film *Boetie op Manoeuvres*, portrays a white male being pursued by a white female, the soldier straddling the tank in a sexually suggestive manner. The defence of white (and heterosexist) hegemony is an implied ideal of apartheid militarisation in these examples. Album covers that reflected support for those in the army also tended to portray white militarised masculinity. John Edmond (Image 1c, *Troopiesongs R.S.A.* 1977) and Ge Korsten (Image 1d, *Huistoe* 1979) emphasised the significance of the body as a text when they donned military uniforms and rifles to signify empathetic support for military recruits. While the image of disciplined white masculine bodies on the 1982 Infantry School's

Exerce Perfectioni (Image 1e) emphasises the importance of the military as a means of attaining manhood for young white males.[2]

By contrast, any suggestion that the struggle in which army recruits were involved was illegitimate or any attempt to undermine the South African Defence Force (SADF) or support the liberation struggle was, for government censors, distinctly undesirable. The covers to the Special AKA's 'Free Nelson Mandela' (1984) and Eddy Grant's anti-apartheid 'Give me hope Jo'anna' (1988) were declared undesirable by the Directorate, to be banished from the public eye. 'Free Nelson Mandela' featured a photograph of Mandela's face. According to the Internal Security Act, photographs of Mandela's face were not to be published in South Africa because Mandela was a banned person. The picture cover to Grant's seven-inch single was politically confrontational, including the slogan 'Soweto lives, aparthate kills'. It brazenly defied the legitimacy of apartheid and was thus declared undesirable.

Meanwhile, support from those South Africans protected at home by the SADF was also imagined in racial (and sexist and heterosexist) terms. The cover of a compilation album, simply titled *Hit Power 1* (Image 2a, 1973), depicts a white woman wearing a military-style camouflage shirt and leaning on a rifle. A similar idea informs the cover of a later compilation album, *Forces Favourites* (Image 2b, 1979), in support of the 'Forces Favourites' propaganda radio request programme: a white woman wearing a bikini and army headgear holds a rifle. These images both sexed-up the military and implicitly suggested the support of white women for white males in the army, literally decorating themselves in military garb as a symbolic reflection of their support for absent men fighting to protect them. There were thus multiple points of desirability: for white military men to view white women as desirable, for white women to

Images 2a-b. White women's patriotic support for the military.

support men in the military and the military itself, and ultimately, for men to serve South Africa by fighting in the military.

It was not only the military that was sexed-up in this way: many record companies marketed compilation albums by combining patriotism with sexuality in a process of sexing-up nationalism. The most obvious example was the *Springbok Hit Parade* and *Springbok Hits of the Week* series (see Images 3a and b) which displayed semi-naked white women in suggestive poses. If the naming of the compilations showed that the songs were popular (Springbok Radio was a national symbol and thus connoted national popularity, at least amongst whites), the marketing of the albums revealed more than a desirable selection of songs. For the sexing of album covers followed distinctly racial and ethnic lines: white, never black, women accompanied reference to national symbols such as the 'springbok' in the belief that these symbols represented white aspirations.

The appearance of white women on these album covers symbolically demarcated South African patriotism as a white terrain. Interestingly, the depiction of these women became a site of contest over the constitution of white female desirability. There was an ongoing contest between the sexist white male quest for showing as much of white women's bodies as possible and the Directorate's attempt to show as little as possible, through the application of what Van Rooyen referred to as the 'lust criterion' (1987: 61). While Van Rooyen admitted that the lust criterion was difficult to apply and to a large extent depended on the eye of the beholder, state censors took into account such factors as 'the proximity of the camera to the breast or pubic area or the lewdness of the model's pose'. Given that in most instances censors were male, this contest amounted to a power struggle between different male gazes in which women's freedom to represent themselves was extremely limited. The 1960s *Dan Hill Sounds Electronic* series especially demonstrates this struggle (see Images 4a-b). The series marketed instrumental covers of contemporary pop music by way of depicting near naked white women posing for the camera. On several occasions censors believed that the record company had pushed the boundaries of desirability too far, and banned the album on the basis of the record cover. On each occasion the record was withdrawn from the market place and reissued with the same image, but with additional clothing sketched onto the offending image. Thus did the censors win the battle against the record company, bringing it into line with the state's ideas of desirability.

In the 1970s and 1980s many albums were similarly banned for revealing too much of people's bodies on their covers. For example, the *Forbidden Fruit* (1978) album by South African studio disco group Hot RS included a

Images 3a-b. Reflections of white patriarchal patriotism.

Images 4a-b. Contest over the desirability of Dan Hill's depictions of white South African women in the 1960s.

Images 5a-b. Depictions of racial and ethnic desirablity.

photograph of a naked (but strategically covered) couple on the cover sitting within an apple, which features again on the back sleeve this time with a bite taken out of it, thus providing the viewer with a religious context within which to interpret the images. The Directorate banned the cover because 'The naked figures on the cover are shameless and displayed in a manner which is provocative and which panders to the prurient minded. Considering the people who are likely to buy the record it is definitely harmful to public morals' (Directorate of Publications P78/12/82). The record company RPM appealed the decision, arguing that the cover was 'subdued and tasteful'. The ban, however, was upheld. In justifying the decision, the Director of the Publications Appeal Board, JN Snyman, maladroitly explained that although 'the genitalia are not shown and the breasts of the woman and her buttocks are not nude or substantially nude, a large past of the feminine breast is, however, nude – the outer part of the nipple being visible'. For Snyman, the significance of the cover art was that the 'two persons are nude in embarrassing circumstances ... The intimate foreplay or contemplation of the sexual act is deprived of all privacy in this photo ... Furthermore, it is the view of the Appeal Board that the photo is calculated to excite lustful thoughts' (Publications Appeal Board 8/79).

Guided by this prudish approach to depictions of the human body the Directorate also banned more revealing depictions of white topless women, such as Bachelet's *Emmanuelle* (1978), the soundtrack to a soft porn film already banned in South Africa, and the German compilation album *Sexy: Lässt die Puppen Tanzen*. The censors believed it was undesirable for the general populace to see too much of white women's breasts and what Van Rooyen referred to as 'pubic and genital nudity' (1987: 60). Examples of banned record covers which fitted the latter category included John Lennon and Yoko Ono's *Two virgins* (1968) album, on which the couple pose fully naked, and Man's self-titled album (1971), which included drawings on the front and back covers depicting full frontal images of a white man and a white woman respectively. In a clear indication that revealing images of men could also be regarded as undesirable, the Directorate banned Prince's *Dirty Mind* (1980) cover, on which Prince poses in a slightly revealing pair of scants. The Directorate believed that Prince's pose encouraged homosexuality, arguing that 'the cover is definitely designed to stimulate erotically in a "gay" context' (Directorate of Publications P81/1/177).

The official reason for banning images involving nudity or partial nudity was 'respect for the privacy of the sexual act, for the privacy of the nude human body ... (and to prevent the) dishonour of the female body '(Van Rooyen, 1987: 3, 59). Clearly, as JM Coetzee (1996: 191) points out, this right to privacy was a metaphorical right, given that the censors were not acting to protect a physical space in which one could be secluded, undisturbed and unobserved. The right to privacy evoked by the censors, therefore, had to do with the invasion of a conceptual space, of one's respect for other people's privacy. Accordingly, male censors viewed images on behalf of 'average' (white) South Africans in order to protect their respect for yet others' privacy and honour. Through this process of multiple displacement, censorship committees comprising or dominated by male censors routinely acted on behalf of women (and sometimes men), imposing a dominant Calvinist framework upon their representation.

As can be seen in Dan Hill's *Music to Watch Girls By* (Image 4a and b above) and the centrespread of Sam Sklair's *Dance Date '68* cover (a white woman submissively displayed before the camera wearing a bikini, with the caption 'yummy, yummy, yummy'), neither of which were banned, it was not sexism nor the degradation of women that perturbed the censors, but the extent to which parts of their bodies were revealed. White women were to appear with their breasts obscured by objects, clothing or at the very least printed stars. In order to meet the specificities of the censors' prudish yet patriarchal framework of desirability, these cover-ups had to be absolute to satisfy. But while such criteria applied to white women and (as will be shown) Western black women, they did not apply to black South African women; when the latter appeared topless on album covers they were never officially declared undesirable. Hence no South African album cover depicting topless black women was ever banned for this reason, despite the intermittent appearance of such covers on the shelves of record stores aimed primarily at the black market.

Examples of such covers include a compilation album titled *Soweto Hits* (year unknown), which shows a naked black woman adorned in (possibly African) necklaces, while Lakhiza Ndawonde appears topless but otherwise adorned with African beads on the front of *Wenzani Umakoti?* (Image 5a, 1983). In explaining the Directorate's approach to censorship in such cases, apartheid censor Van Rooyen explained that 'various sections of the black community do not regard the display of nude breasts of young black women in tribal dress as indecent and whites respect this view' (1987:60-1). As was typical of apartheid discourse, Van Rooyen's statement was obfuscatory. He neglected, for example, to explain that racist white ideologues respected this view because it conformed to the apartheid notion of separate (and inferior) black ethnicities. And of course, while censors opted to respect the black community's beliefs about depictions of black topless women, they disregarded black political aspirations. In addition, through acknowledging the permissibility of such images, the censors also unwittingly legitimised a racial and imperialist form of male scopophilia, subjecting African women to what Laura Mulvey (1995: 324) refers to as the 'controlling and curious gaze' of, in this case, white South African males.

It is important to emphasise that the application of measures of desirability was not applied simply along ethnic lines: race was integrally connected to ethnicity, as is intimated by the way Van Rooyen combines 'black' with 'tribal'

Images 6a-b. Juluka album covers promoting racial integration.

Images 7a-b. Contesting images of South African nationalism.

Images 8a-c. The quest for alternative images of the desirable.

in his account of the Directorate's rationale for not banning such images. This is best illustrated through reference to the cover of Sam Sklair's album of African tunes entitled *Pop Goes the Gumboot* (Image 5b, 1969) aimed at a white market. On the front and back covers a semi-naked white woman appears in neo-traditional African attire, but the strategic positioning of an arm, gumboot and necklaces prevent the need for censorial intervention. A white woman could pose in neo-traditional African attire, but was not allowed to pose topless. However, although the album cover stops short of depicting a topless white woman, it does allow for a degree of flirtation with the idea of crossing over to the 'ethnic other'. Conservative white males were permitted the opportunity to gaze upon a white women substituting for a black woman, without actually crossing the forbidden line of inter-racial sexual fantasy. And therein lies an important aspect of apartheid desires. These images were regarded as 'not undesirable' precisely because, in the eyes of white censors, they were not desirable and therefore not potentially harmful. As Rita Barnard (2000: 352) has argued, such images only become problematic to the white racist if they serve as ideals of attractiveness to a heterogeneous audience. By denying that such images might be sensuous, the censors relegated the black female body to a position of inferiority. It is therefore significant that images that were not banned were never declared 'desirable' but rather 'not undesirable'.

By contrast, the Directorate did declare images of topless Western black women undesirable. The most notorious instance involved the cover of Jimi Hendrix's *Electric Ladyland* (1969), on which naked black and white women posed topless alongside each other. Quite clearly for the Directorate the mixing of races in this way was undesirable, as was the appearance of a number of naked white breasts. The album cover in question was banned without any reasons given, so the censors' views of the topless black women can only be surmised. However, an insight into the Directorate's stance can be gained through a consideration of the front cover of the British *Dance Paarrrty* (1977) compilation album, declared 'undesirable' in 1984 because it featured a topless black woman. The Directorate decided that this image was undesirable because in its view the woman was Western, and therefore not representative of any African cultural group. It would therefore have been ludicrous for the censors to have defended her right to 'tribal tradition'. This point was accentuated by the fact that the censors regarded her as 'coloured' and not a black South African, as defined by the apartheid state. According to the Directorate, 'the photograph of the coloured girl on the cover, bare breasted, wearing only hat, cuffs and tie amount [sic] to a blatantly shameless intrusion upon the privacy of the female body and thus offensive [sic] under the meaning of the act' (P84/9/37). This clearly reveals that Western women of colour were granted a different, more 'civilised', status to that of South African black women, contained as they were by the apartheid ideologue's conceptions of the black African body. Censorial decisions about the undesirability and non-undesirability of bodies were therefore far more indicative of the apartheid state's need to undermine black South Africans than a concern for South African citizens' moral welfare.

The preoccupation with the privacy and honour of the white South African female body was not the only area in which race and ethnicity combined to affect the appearance of record covers and thereby preserve apartheid desires. The apartheid government's strategy of separating ethnic groups impacted heavily on the way record companies recorded and marketed musicians. The South African Broadcasting Corporation's (SABC's) Radio Bantu service provided separate radio stations for different ethnic groups, and maintained a system of apartheid of the airwaves by, amongst other things, forbidding the mixing of languages on these stations. This meant that record companies could only be assured of radio play if they recorded and marketed musicians on ethnic lines, particularly ensuring that musicians recorded albums in a single language. Not only were black musicians encouraged to restrict their lyrics to a particular language, but albums marketed ethnicity. Thus it was common for album covers to include a statement about the ethnicity of the group, in addition to the particular music genre. Covers advertised 'Zulu traditional', 'Sotho vocal', 'Zulu disco', and so on. Although white musicians were similarly affected by the state broadcaster's language policy, record companies did not label their albums in a similar way. Perhaps this was because the English and Afrikaans-language titles were sufficient for white SABC employees to realise the intended market. Songs by musicians such as Juluka, Sankomota and David Kramer, in which languages were mixed (and which thus confused the policy of separate development), were barred from airplay. It was commercially necessary for record companies to conform to a level of apartheid packaging in order to promote the possibility of airplay. For consumers browsing records in the stacks, the ethnic demarcations of music further perpetuated the ethnic divisions of apartheid policy more generally.

A final area in which record covers promoted apartheid discourse was religion. Given the integral part which religion (particularly a specific brand of nationalist Christianity) played in the defence of apartheid, it is to be expected that record covers also reflected the Christian values of the censors and the dominant discourse they represented. When Chris de Burgh's song 'Spanish Train' (1976) was banned because it was regarded as blasphemous, the record company opted to drop the offensive song from the top selling album in order to keep the record on retailers' shelves. However, it was not a matter of simply dropping the song from the album (as had happened with Peter Sarstedt's 'Take off your clothes' on Sarstedt's *The Best of Peter Sarstedt* (1975) album and Peter Tosh's 'Apartheid' on Tosh's *Equal Rights* (1977) album) because the album itself was called *Spanish Train and Other Stories*. The album cover was therefore redesigned and released as *Lonely Sky and Other Stories*. The re-released album cover therefore hid the 'undesirable' – the blasphemy – from the public eye, and Calvinist apartheid values were consequently upheld. A similar case occurred with South African group the Kalahari Surfers' *Bigger than Jesus* (1989). The album cover was banned because the censors thought it undesirable for such a boldly 'blasphemous' title to be openly displayed on the shelves of retail outlets. The Surfers changed the title to *Beachbomb*, and re-released the album. In these instances the censors' actions once again led to the 'undesirable' being obscured, in an attempt to protect South Africans from confronting ideas which may have challenged those of apartheid.

Repackaging images of South African life

The actions of the censors, and the concomitant pressure on South African musicians and record companies not to release inappropriate record covers had the effect of supporting the apartheid state's hegemony. However, this does not mean that the state's interests were not challenged. Indeed, some musicians used visual imagery on their album covers to subvert and resist apartheid desires. Whether text, image or combination thereof, this provided a framework within which to listen to the album, almost a guide on how to read the music. For instance, independent and progressive record label, Shifty Records, produced subversive anti-censorship logos by manipulating the 'His Master's Voice' logo to 'His Muzzled Voice' and by replacing the 'Home taping is killing music and its [sic] illegal' warning to 'Censorship is killing music and its [sic] legal'. In this way Shifty was able to expose, challenge and undermine the state censors' actions and decisions. The central moral space, which the censor claimed to occupy, became an openly political space. This was repeatedly borne out in resistant album covers, a few of which I explore now.

In contrast to the record covers designed for Radio Bantu's separate development programme, Juluka album covers typically included photographs of white and black musicians, Johnny Clegg and Sipho Mchunu, *together* wearing traditional Zulu dress. The images were always of equality and strength. For example, the cover of *Universal Men* (Image 6a, 1979) is a photograph of Clegg and Mchunu posing together defiantly on a mine dump. A cryptic message lay in the representation of the group's name, positioned in the sky. Richard Pithouse elaborated:

> The name of the band appeared as an engraving on a gold bar. Its shimmering glitz clashed, pointedly, with the more organic colours of the sky, the rocks, the men and their clothes. Juluka means sweat in Zulu and the message couldn't have been clearer: Johannesburg's wealth and glamour is built not just on gold but also on the sweat of the men, the migrant labourers, who mined that gold (2000:40).

On Juluka's follow-up album, *African Litany* (Image 6b, 1981), Clegg and Mchunu are shown in a smiling, friendly co-operative pose, Mchunu helping to put a bangle on Clegg's arm. These images strongly dismissed the apartheid policy of racial separation and mistrust and accordingly disrupted the apartheid fiction to which Merrett earlier referred.

Whereas patriotic apartheid albums such as the *SA Weermagkerkkoor en Konsertgroep's* (South African Army Church Choir and Concert Group's) *Langs ver Paaie* (Image 7a, 1978) series typically juxtaposed images of patriotic South African soldiers against a backdrop of the Voortrekker Monument, the Kalahari Surfers chose to subvert the meaning of the Monument. The booklet that accompanies their *Living in the Heart of the Beast* (Image 7b, 1985) combines two photographs: in the foreground is a whites-only beach scene, and in the background the overbearing Voortrekker Monument. The Monument acts as a symbolic reminder of the pact made by the Voortrekkers with God whereby God gave his approval to the slaughter of Zulus at the battle of Blood River in 1838. The Surfers' image suggests that white privilege existed because of the repression that made it possible.

In response to the government propaganda request programme 'Forces Favourites' and pro-South Africa Defence Force compilation album of the same name discussed earlier, Shifty also released a *Forces Favourites* anti-militarisation compilation album (Image 8a, 1985). On the cover a portable radio (labelled 'ECC Autodance'[3]) separates two images: on the top a line of soldiers stand at attention, capturing the essence of military conformism (and, in a sense, the conformism of the sexist and apartheid nationalist expectations underlying the original bikini-clad *Forces Favourites* (1978) model). In contrast, the lower image shows a diverse group of people dressed in colourful clothes dancing to resistant music. Shifty Record's *Voëlvry* (Free as a Bird) compilation album cover (Image 8b, 1988) also makes good use of symbolism. The cover illustration is of a young Afrikaans woman dressed in traditional Voortrekker dress and bonnet ecstatically flying as 'free as a bird' over the Johannesburg cityscape. She has clearly been freed of traditional expectations, of the rural conservatism that often acts as a backdrop for the dour women usually depicted in Voortrekker garb. The reverse side of the album cover is subtitled *Afrikaanse Musiek Vir Vandag* (Afrikaans Music for Today). The suggestion is that the music acts as a soundtrack for the liberated Afrikaner, freed of the conservatism of tradition. And she is indeed an independent woman, freed from the patriotic male gaze, typified in the *Springbok Hits* covers, which seeks to trap her in chauvinist expectations. Through the *Voëlvry* image Shifty perhaps unwittingly stumbled upon a space in which women are freed not only from the male gaze directed at the likes of the woman on the cover of *Sakkie Sakkie met Oom Sakkie* (Image 8c, 1978), but also from the gaze of the censors, who, by means of their 'lust criterion' force the *Sakkie Sakkie* model to falter in restrained uncertainty, not sure whether to cover up or not, caught between two gazes, neither of which, it seems, is her own. Certainly, these oppositional record covers reflected (some) South African musicians' attempts to resist the stifling gaze of the state's censors, thereby challenging dominant apartheid discourse. In so doing they suggested a more alluring way forward, which, perhaps, contributed towards the composition of a different tune.

Endnotes

1 My intention in exploring apartheid state censorship decisions in this essay is part of an attempt to interrogate apartheid desires. It is not possible here to provide an in-depth summary of the general literature on censorship, both in South Africa and further afield. Examples of work which cover various aspects of censorship as dealt with this in this chapter include: Nadine Gordimer (1988, 1990), Jack Cope (1982), Miriam Tlali (1984), André P Brink (1985), and JM Coetzee (1996), who have provided extensive discussion of censorship in relation to literature in apartheid South Africa. Muff Andersson (1981), David Coplan (1985, 2000), Jeremy Marre and Hannah Charlton (1985), Jacobus van Rooyen (1987: 114), John Street (1986: 19-23), Robin Denselow (1989: 186-202), and Ingrid Byerly (1996) are among those who have briefly alluded to popular music censorship in apartheid South Africa; while Barry Gilder (1983), Phillip Page (1986), Ian Kerkhof (1986, 1989), Ole Reitov (1998a, 1998b), Michael Drewett (2003, 2005), and Jonathan Clegg and Drewett (2006) have written more detailed pieces on the topic.

2   For more detailed discussion of popular culture imagery and South African militarisation see Drewett (forthcoming, expected November 2007).
3   The End Conscription Campaign (ECC) was an anti-apartheid organisation opposed to the conscription of white males into the state military, the SADF.

Bibliography

Andrews, C. 1974. 'Pop Rock Beat'. In W Herdeg (ed.). *Graphis Record Covers*. Zürich: Graphis Press.

Andersson, M. 1981. *Music in the Mix: The Story of South African Popular Music*. Johannesburg: Ravan Press.

Barthes, R. 1977. *Image. Music. Text*. New York: Hill & Wang.

Barnard, R. 2000. 'Contesting Beauty'. In S Nuttall & C Michael (eds). *Senses of Culture*. Cape Town: Oxford University Press, pp. 344-362.

Bourdieu, P. 1984. *Distinction*. Cambridge: Harvard University Press.

_. 1990. *The Logic of Practice*. Cambridge: Polity Press.

_. 2000. 'Social Space and Symbolic Space'. In D Robbins (ed.). *Pierre Bourdieu*, vol 4. London: Sage, pp. 3-16.

Brink, A. 1985. *Literatuur in die Strydperk*. Cape Town: Human & Rousseau.

Butler, J. 1997. *Excitable Speech: A Politics of the Performative*. New York: Routledge.

Byerly, I. 1996. *The Music Indaba: Music as Mirror, Mediator and Prophet in the South African Transition from Apartheid to Democracy*. Ph.D. diss., Duke University.

Clegg, J, & M Drewett. 2006. 'Why Don't You Sing About the Leaves and the Dreams? Reflecting on Popular Music Censorship in Apartheid South Africa'. In M Drewett & M Cloonan (eds). *Popular Music Censorship in Africa*. Aldershot: Ashgate, pp. 127-136.

Coetzee, JM. 1996. *Giving Offense: Essays on Censorship*. Chicago: University of Chicago Press.

Cope, Jack. 1982. *The Adversary Within: Dissident Writers in Afrikaans*. Cape Town: David Philip.

Coplan, D. 1985. *In Township Tonight: South Africa's Black City Music and Theatre*. Johannesburg: Ravan Press.

_. 2000. 'Popular Music in South Africa'. In R. Stone (ed.). *The Garland Handbook of African Music*. New York: Garland, pp. 333-354.

Dean, R, et al. (eds). 1984. *Album Cover Album 3*. Limpsfield: Dragon's World.

Denselow, R. 1989. *When the Music's Over: The Story of Political Pop*. London: Faber & Faber.

Directorate of Publications. 1978. File on Hot RS's *Forbidden Fruit* album. P78/12/82.

_. 1981. File on Prince's *Dirty Mind* album. P81/1/177.

_. 1984. File on the compilation *Dance Paarrrty* album. P84/9/37.

Drewett, M. 2003. 'Music in the Struggle to End Apartheid South Africa'. In M Cloonan & R Garofalo (eds). *Policing Popular Music*. Philadelphia: Temple University Press, pp. 153-165.

_. 2005. '"Stop this Filth": The Censorship of Roger Lucey's Music in Apartheid South Africa'. *Journal of South African Musicology*, 25, pp. 53-70.

_. forthcoming. 'The Construction and Subversion of Gender Stereotypes in Popular Cultural Representations of the Border War'. In G Baines & P Vale (eds). *Bounded States and Bordered Wars: South Africa and the Cold War*. Pretoria: UNISA Press.

Gilder, B. 1983. 'Finding New Ways to Bypass Censorship'. *Index on Censorship*, 12(1), pp. 18-22.

Gordimer, N. 1988. 'Censorship and the Artist'. *Staffrider*, 7(2), pp. 10-16.

_. 1990. 'Censorship and its Aftermath'. *Index on Censorship*, 19(7), pp. 14-16.

Kerkhof, I. 1986. 'Music and Censorship in South Africa'. *Rixaka: Cultural Journal of the African National Congress*, 2, pp. 27-31.

_. 1989. 'Music in the Revolution'. *Keskidee: A Journal of Black Musical Traditions*, 2, pp. 10-21.

Lumby, C. 1997. *Bad Girls: The Media, Sex and Feminism in the 90s*. St. Leonards: Allen & Unwin.

Marre, J, & H Charlton. 1985. *Beats of the Heart: Popular Music of the World*. London: Pluto Press.

Merrett, C. 1994. *A Culture of Censorship: Secrecy and Intellectual Repression in South Africa*. Cape Town: David Philip.

Mulvey, L. 1995. 'Visual Pleasure and Narrative Cinema'. In J Munns & G Rajan (eds). *A Cultural Studies Reader: History, Theory, Practice*. London: Longman, pp. 323-332.

Negus, K. 1996. *Popular Music in Theory*. Cambridge: Polity Press.

Page, P. 1986. 'Forbidden Music: Songs Against Apartheid'. *Ear Magazine of New Music*, 10(4), pp. 4, 5, 27.

Pithouse, R. 2000. 'A National Treasure Turns 21'. *Mail and Guardian*, 20-26 October, pp. 40-41.

Publications Act (Number 42) of 1974.

Publications Appeal Board. Decision on Hot RS's *Forbidden Fruit*. 8/79.

Reitov, O. 1998a. 'White Zulu'. *Index on Censorship*, 27(6), pp. 82-3.

_. 1998b. 'Only Doing My Duty: Interview with Cecile Pracher'. *Index on Censorship*, 27(6), pp. 83-5.

Street, J. 1986. *Rebel Rock: The Politics of Popular Music*. Oxford: Basil Blackwell.

_. 1997. *Politics and Popular Culture*. Cambridge: Polity Press.
_. 2001. 'Rock, Pop and Politics'. In S Frith, W Straw, & J Street (eds). *The Cambridge Companion to Pop and Rock*. Cambridge: Cambridge University Press, pp. 243-255.
Swartz, D. 1997. *Culture and Power: The Sociology of Pierre Bourdieu*. Chicago: University of Chicago Press.
Tlali, M. 1984. 'Remove the Chains'. *Index on Censorship* 13(6), pp. 22-26.
Van Rooyen, J. 1987. *Censorship in South Africa*. Cape Town: Juta.

Discography

Bachelet, Pierre. 1978. *Emmanuelle*. Bide Musique.
De Burgh, Chris. 1976. *Spanish Train and Other Stories*. A&M.
De Burgh, Chris. 1976. *Lonely Sky and Other Stories*. A&M.
East, Dennis. 1985. 'Love Manoeuvres'. David Gresham Record Co.
Edmond, John. 1977. *Troopiesongs R.S.A.* Jo'burg Records.
Grant, Eddie. 1988. 'Gimme Hope Jo'anna'. EMI.
Hendrix, Jimi. 1968. *Electric Ladyland*. Reprise Records.
Hill, Dan Sounds Electric. 1967. *Music to Watch Girls By*. CBS. ASF 1188.
Hill, Dan Sounds Electric. 1967. *Music to Watch Girls By*. CBS. ALD 8033.
Hot RS. 1978. *Forbidden Fruit*. RPM.
Infantry School. 1982. *Exerce Perfectioni*. Universal Recordings.
Juluka. 1979. *Universal Men*. CBS.
Juluka. 1981. *African Litany*. CBS.
Kalahari Surfers. 1985. *Living in the Heart of the Beast*. Recommended Records.
Kalahari Surfers. 1989. *Bigger than Jesus*. Shifty Records.
Kalahari Surfers. 1989. *Beachbomb*. Shifty Records.
Korsten, Gé.1979. *Huistoe*. EMI.
Lennon, John and Yoko Ono. 1968. *Two Virgins*. Apple.
Man. 1971. *Man*. United Artists.
Ndawonde, Lakhiza. 1983. *Wenzani Umakoti?* Teal Records.
Prince. 1980. *Dirty Mind*. Warner Brothers.
Sarstedt, Peter. 1975. *The Best of Peter Sarstedt*. United Artists.
Sklair, Sam. 1968. *Dance Date '68*. RCA Victor.
Sklair, Sam. 1969. *Pop Goes the Gumboot*. RCA Victor.
Solms, Esmé. n.d. 'Soldaat-Seun'. Brigadiers.
SA Weermagkerkkoor en Konsertgroep. 1978. *Langs Ver Paaie* 8. Brigadiers.
Special AKA. 1984. 'Free Nelson Mandela'. 2 Tone Records.
Tosh, Peter. 1977. *Equal Rights*. CBS.
Various. 1973. *Hit Power 1*. EMI.

Various. 1976. *Springbok Hit Parade*, Volume 28. EMI.
Various. 1977. *Dance Paarrrty*. Atlantic/Contempo Records.
Various. 1978. *Springbok Hits of the Week*, Volume 39. MVN.
Various. 1978. *Sakkie Sakkie met Oom Sakkie*. Disc Jockey Music Co.
Various. 1979. *Forces Favourites*. Dynamite.
Various. 1985. *Forces Favourites*. Shifty Records.
Various. 1988. *Voëlvry*. Shifty Records.
Various. n.d. *Sexy: Lässt die Puppen Tanzen*. Miller International.
Various. n.d. *Soweto Hits*. Creative Sounds Record Co.

7

MUSICAL ECHOES

COMPOSING A PAST IN/FOR SOUTH AFRICAN JAZZ

Carol A. Muller

> And I'm glad to say that I'm home
> I'm home to stay.
> Africa, Africa.
> I've come home; I've come home.
> To feel my people's warmth,
> To shelter 'neath your trees,
> To catch the summer breeze;
> Africa, Africa.
> I've come home, I've come home.
> I'm home to smell your earth,
> To laugh with your children,
> To feel your sun shining down on me;
> Africa, Africa.
> I've come home, I've come home.
> ('Africa' by Sathima Bea Benjamin)

I have extraordinarily vivid memories of hearing South African musicians Sathima Bea Benjamin and Abdullah Ibrahim in two specific live performances in the United States.[1] The first occasion was the JVC Jazz Festival in New

York City in c. 1990. Abdullah performed a solo piano concert in the Weill Recital Room at Carnegie Hall. The second was a performance by Sathima at the Kennedy Center's *Women in Jazz* series held in Washington DC more than a decade later. Neither occasion was the first or only time I heard the couple perform. Nevertheless, these two events stand out in my memory for the profound way in which the sounds emanating from the grand piano, and those carried by the human voice, evoked a full-bodied, multi-sensory response in me. In the first moment, it seemed as if I could see, smell, feel, and hear the Bo-Kaap district of central Cape Town. The second moment elicited a deep sense of longing, an aching in my body for the space called 'Africa' that Sathima sang about. These utterances were musical echoes in diaspora, and probably I had been away from South Africa far too long.

Though I was born in Cape Town, and spent my childhood in South Africa, what I heard in those moments were not the actual memories of sounds and places I had experienced earlier in my life. Rather, these were poetic invocations expressed out of a longing to return home that I felt in the music of the two South Africans. In each performance the voice and instrumental sounds made contact with me as an audience member, acoustically generating images of faraway places for a fellow South African in America. Of course, Abdullah Ibrahim is not actually from the Bo-Kaap – but this was the place of my imagining, the place I had visited a few years earlier in search of understanding Cape Muslim history;[2] and certainly the words of Sathima's 'Africa' suggest 'a space of longing. It evokes images of home, warmth, earthy smells, the innocent laughter of children, and [the sounds] of trees and summer breezes' (Muller, 2001: 147). A song recorded in the 1970s, after more than a decade of movement outside of South Africa, 'Africa' is an early articulation of a new, diasporic desire for Africa as a place of beauty, innocence and certain kinds of freedom.

Five decades ago, in January 1959 in Cape Town, Sathima performed at a fundraising event, *Just Jazz Meets the Ballet*, where she met Abdullah and discovered they were both working on the same piece: 'I Got It Bad and That Ain't Good'.[3] The Cape Town performance was reviewed in the *Golden City Post*:

> There is no doubt [about] it, Beatrice Benjamin is the mostest, the greatest and the most appealing girl singer in the Cape, whispers Howard Lawrence.[4] What she did to the audience at Post's show, 'Just Jazz Meets the Ballet' was wow. I got it bad when she sang 'I Got It Bad.' Everybody else got it bad too and they kept shouting for more of that FEELING. Most promising singer for 1959. Agreed (25 January 1959).

A much younger woman in this performance, Benjamin's voice made contact with Cape Town audiences through the emotional echoes resounding in the clearly articulated words and melodies of a foreign musical form. 'I Got It Bad' is one of American jazz composer Duke Ellington's most cherished songs.[5] While the words of the song resonated universally, it was the sound of her voice and the bodily presence, both vessels of feeling and human connection conveyed live by a local singer, which particularised Ellington's composition for South African audiences. In this period of South African entertainment history, being local often meant becoming the first live rendition of an imported product for South African audiences in a process I have called 'musical surrogacy' (see Muller, 2006b).

Born before apartheid was officially named and legislated, Sathima Bea Benjamin lived through its harshest years, went into cultural and ultimately political exile, and has lived to see its legal demise. After honing her vocal skills on white English and American girl singers of the 1940s, in the late 1950s Sathima 'borrowed' American-made jazz as her musical home because it provided a space for the individual voice in a collective fabric, for expressive freedom, and her growing political consciousness of the plight of people of colour in South Africa and the world at large. I use 'borrowed' because for Sathima and the Cape Town community she inhabited in the 1940s and 1950s, jazz was the musical discourse completely naturalised through radio, film, sound recordings, and live renditions of the American derived repertory in postwar South Africa. These English and American voices inhabited her home in mediated form or in live family renditions, operating as voices of distant kin, shaping everyday life for Sathima and her extended family and friends. From the early 1960s, Benjamin has applied the principles of jazz performance to a peculiarly South African songbook, songs that intermingled in her home and community in the 1930s-1960s, drawn from local renditions of British music hall, American Tin Pan Alley, and increasingly, her own compositions. Nevertheless, the tension between views of jazz and its ancestral repertories in South Africa and by South Africans as belonging versus being borrowed has plagued the composition, performance, and reception of Sathima's music, regardless of historical or physical location. In reality, much of her energy in exile in the United States from the mid-1970s has been spent trying to help the larger jazz world see the connections between the pasts in jazz from a US perspective and those from its distant musical kin in the southernmost part of Africa.

The complicated identity of much music making in twentieth-century South African popular music and jazz performance is poignantly articulated in Benjamin's 1983 LP *Memories and Dreams*, her third recording on her own

Ekapa Label. Side A contains three original compositions in her *Liberation Suite: Nations In Me*: 'New Nation A' Coming', 'Children of Soweto', and 'Africa'. Side B has four songs drawn from 1940s Hollywood musicals and jazz standards popular in her youth in Cape Town. It is hard not to see her 'memories' as American and the 'dreams' as her originals, projecting forward to a new South African nation and society. So the question that needs addressing is how American music, in its popular, film, or jazz forms, came to be so deeply embedded in South African experience in the mid-twentieth century, because one cannot listen intelligently to Sathima's singing without some knowledge of this period of South African music history in the Cape. It is precisely this confluence of styles, places, and possibilities, which constitutes the store of musical, family, and community memories Benjamin and other South African musicians drew on in their years of cultural and political exile in Europe and the United States.[6]

My primary concern then is to move beyond the individual experience and first, to rise to the challenge of defining a usable and inclusive past for South African jazz; and second, to speak to the persistent struggle to locate that past in close proximity to *the* standard history of jazz produced in America and about American jazz musicians, a history that only reluctantly includes narratives from elsewhere in the world as legitimate subjects of its scholarly output. I have divided what follows into three parts. In the first, I reflect on the acoustical image of the 'musical echo', as a poetic, but useful metaphor for widening the lens/microphone into new ways of seeing/hearing, or at least imagining a more inclusive narrative of South Africa's past through jazz performance than we have managed thus far. In the second, I draw on my discussion of the musical echo to suggest a new set of possibilities for thinking about the past in South African jazz by positing a series of keywords that may enable South Africans to create a chronicle, or a usable past, that is not overshadowed by the present shape of jazz historiography generated in and about the United States. Rather, I use the image of the echo to suggest new ways of thinking about the past that reflect the realities of music worlds constituted by mass-mediation. Finally, I extend these ideas to address the question of how South African jazz history, itself exiled from the conventional narratives of the official US-centred history of jazz, might be inserted into a global, quintessentially comparative, perhaps even dialogical narrative of, and about, the past in jazz not only in South Africa but elsewhere in the world as well.[7]

WHAT EXACTLY IS A MUSICAL ECHO?

As a common noun, the echo is often portrayed simply: as mere repetition or imitation of a sound emanating from a source. Visually we represent the echo as a movement of concentric circles of resonating sound. If we scrutinise the visual image it becomes clear that at the core of the definition of the echo is a notion of displacement, the displacement of sound from its point of origin. In other words, the echo is a spatial metaphor: it maps out distance generated by a central node. The echo also has a temporal dimension to it. In one definition the echo is the 'persistence of a sound after its source has stopped', introducing the idea of time lag, of temporal displacement, but also perhaps of fashion and its consequences, or indeed, of the capitalist notion of uneven development in the so-called Third World.[8] If we think of the cultural consequences of the echo, we realise that each repetition of the initial sound makes contact with an ever-widening circle of possibility. One source defines the echo as a 'reply that repeats what has just been said', pointing to its responsorial and interactive uses. Echolocation is one further use of the echo and it is crucial to this project. It is defined as 'a sensory system in certain animals, such as bats and dolphins, in which usually high-pitched sounds are emitted and their echoes interpreted to determine the direction and distance of objects'. In other words, the reverberation of the acoustical echo is used to measure distance by sending out a sonic signal. With its return comes the capacity to measure proximity. In this sense, echolocation signals the pressure to constantly evaluate the relationship between parts in space and time.

Rendering the echo poetically I suggest that there is more to the gesture than mere repetition. By creating an exact likeness, the echo pays homage to the acoustical source and generates sympathetic responses. In this frame the echo may exhibit a human and relational dimension as the sound emanating from its point of origin fosters moments of contact and engagement. Ethically, the echo signals the possibility of repercussion and consequence, at times even suggesting a political character in its waves. Articulating an emotive and humane quality one might, for example, hear in the echo resonances of similar social or political experiences elsewhere in the world. In this instance, the acoustical echo transcends the local, the regional, even the national: invoking transnational configurations of parallel processes in a global frame.

As a proper noun, 'Echo' surfaces in Greek mythology: 'Echo is the name of a nymph whose unrequited love for Narcissus caused her to pine away until nothing but her voice remained.'[9] A second definition provides more detail and greater violence. Echo: 'a nymph deprived of speech by Hera in order to stop her chatter, and left able only to repeat what others had said. On being repulsed by Narcissus she wasted away with grief until there was nothing left of her but her voice.' And in a third account she was vainly loved by the god Pan, who finally caused some shepherds to go mad and tear her to pieces; Earth hid the fragments, which could, nevertheless, still imitate other sounds. There are several versions of this myth, but these three excerpts convey the core idea that I will work with here. In this frame, musical echoes are the aural vestiges of the human, and more specifically in this instance, the female/feminised voice. Here, when the body is dismembered and suffering inflicted, the voice, quite remarkably, retains its presence and its capacity to bear witness to cruel treatment and bodily disintegration.

In one reading, the myth foreshadows sound recording technology in the contemporary world, where the body is absent as the whole person is compressed and conveyed alone in the sound of the voice or its supplement, the musical instrument. The voice or its supplement, and not the living human being, transmits remnants of distant places, experiences, and sounds to far-flung people. It is the objectified voice or its supplement that makes contact.[10]

In a more dramatic, and some might argue realist, reading of jazz under apartheid, the story of Echo foretells the acts of violence inflicted by the state on many South Africans: silenced voices, dismembered bodies, grieving women – tearing, shredding, narcissism, driven to madness; the ancient myth resonates trans-historically with the experiences of many South Africans, and, more specifically, with dozens of musicians, jazz and otherwise, in the era of grand apartheid: the state and its keepers (as Narcissus/Pan) against the people (as the feminised character, Echo).[11]

In sum, there are three distinct modes of operation for the musical echo. First, as pure imitation or repetition, the echo is conventionally reduced to something hollow or fading, a mere copy, which abides by a currency of diminishing returns (see Epstein, 2004). The copy has no intrinsic value in the marketplace or even in scholarship, which tends to value innovation and originality, but for those hearing it far from its sites of original production and translating it locally through exact repetition, entire communities absorbed, re-enacted, and mastered foreign repertory and style. Second, by means of echolocation, the echo demonstrates the capacity for measurement between points inside a circumscribed territory, invoking the possibilities of an inherently comparative position, and increasing its value to both constituencies. A striking characteristic of South African oral history is its persistent reference to the American model: there is less of a sense of a self-contained, nationally bounded participation in the making of local renditions that in contrast characterises much writing about (American) jazz. Third, the schematic representation of the echo in acoustics portrays the waves of sound as always moving outwards, further and further away from the centre, suggesting the capacity to quite literally cover the globe. The problem is that each subsequent copy of the primary sound becomes less and less audible to its site of original transmission – here I am reminded of Salman Rushdie's comment (cited by James Clifford) that the problem with the English is that their history happened overseas, so they don't know what it means. For those who are overseas, however, the echo is known to generate points of contact and realise new relationships at other places on the acoustical landscape, which while it resonates with, or bears a resemblance to, the original, only reverses its path in rare instances. In other words, the point of origin (the United States) has remained largely untouched by, or at least largely oblivious to, the increasingly wider but less audible resonances of music made in America and sold to the world at large. In this context, the echo transforms into a mere vestige of the source, increasingly nomadic, rationally distributed or more randomly dispersed, and becomes an acoustical parallel to physical displacement or diaspora.[12]

Composing a past

The question we surely need to pose at this point is whether a past can actually be composed for communities of jazz performance constituted out of the resonating echoes of music originating elsewhere in the world. If one simply considers the first definition of the echo, as mere repetition, or perfect facsimile, it is clear there is nothing to say, there is no past to be measured by innovation and stylistic rupture. And to some extent, we might see this as the first consequence of mass-mediated musical transmission. People learn by exact repetition. If, however, we begin to think about the past in jazz along the lines of the two additional functions of the echo, a far richer picture of a past in jazz is realisable.

And it is my contention that the musical echo does indeed provide a rich and useful nexus of ideas for composing such a past in/for South African jazz in the twenty-first century. To move you into this shifting intellectual space, take a moment to imagine what a visual representation of the musical echo might look like. Close your eyes, and insert into the mind's eye a large dot on a page representing the source of the sound. As the sound is heard it sends out sound waves. Each wave repeats what has just been heard in an ever-widening pattern of concentric circles. In this acoustical image of the echo, we conventionally presume the space into which the waves are set in motion to be the air around us. It is not a place-specific model.

In contrast to this, would you now transfer the acoustical image of the single dot and its resonances onto a place-specific surface, like a world map. Insert the dot representing the sound in a recording studio in New York City, for example. Let it sound once, and then allow the waves to ripple outwards, making sure that at least portions of the concentric circles of sound reach out to the southernmost tip of Africa. Begin to name the regions, cities, or towns on other continents situated on the rim of the waves. Put a date on that image; then repeat the process with a new date, perhaps a few days later with either the same musicians or another constellation of stars in your studio in New York City, Chicago, Philadelphia, or Los Angeles. Finally, imagine that you began your acoustical imaging on sheets of transparent or at least opaque paper. Now place one sheet on top of another in order to capture a glimpse of the new paradigm for thinking about jazz in a global perspective through the trope of the musical echo. What does this layering of time, place, and acoustical event tell us about the potential for jazz history to become a multi-sited, even global musical phenomenon? At the very least, it is no longer a single narrative that moves from one place on the American map to another, following a linear chronology of significant musical events, personalities and the emergence of new styles every decade or so – the structure of conventional jazz historiography. While it is clear that particular performances and recordings heard and re-enacted have set the sound of jazz in motion, both inside and well beyond the geopolitical borders of the United States, this newer picture of the past in jazz is dense, multilayered, and three-dimensional. It works more as a palimpsest than the evolutionary chronicle of musical progress characteristic of much writing about jazz history. And it certainly presents a wider palette of musical possibilities for incorporation into its archive.

At this point, we might usefully invoke Dipesh Chakrabarty's notion of the two histories of capital, transmuted here into two (or many more) histories of twentieth-century jazz. Chakrabarty's 'History One' is the universal narrative of *the* history of capital. It originates in Europe and catches up elsewhere in the world through a discourse of 'uneven development'. In my work, History One is the universalising narrative of the production, circulation, and distribution of musical commodities that begin, for this paper, in the United States and subsequently spread elsewhere. This narrative is conventionally categorised as the history of jazz and/or popular music. There are several versions of the jazz/popular music narrative that are continually updated with the emergence of new technologies, modes of distribution and consumption, and the merging and acquisition of transnational entertainment corporations. It is a history that is both celebratory in its demonstration of the powers of the free market economy to spread to the smallest corners of the earth, and characterised by anxiety as the global entertainment industry is read as a key mechanism of twentieth-century cultural imperialism and homogenisation (Feld, 2000).

While History Two is indelibly tied to History One, it is not merely the dialectical other (Chakrabarty, 2000: 66). History Two is a category 'charged with the function of constantly interrupting the totalising thrusts of History One' (66-69). Significantly in dealing with music, History Two is the affective history that allows for narratives of human belonging and diversity, which the totalising narrative of History One sublates. In my version of History Two the consumption of American jazz (and popular music) in commodity form works in several ways depending on the consumer constituency. It is first a model of 'American'-styled modernity and cosmopolitanism; second, it provides a narrative of modernity tied to the Harlem Renaissance, the civil rights and other radical social movements striving for racial equality and full citizenship for Africans in America in the postwar era;[13] and third, it speaks of the power of musical sound to work as a centripetal force in shaping real and virtual communities in one's neighbourhood, across the nation, and around the world.[14]

I have found Chakrabarty's notion of Two Histories a particularly useful one as I have struggled over the years to constitute what feminist philosopher Lorraine Code (1995) calls a 'rhetorical space' for writing about South African jazz so that it strikes up a conversation with the American canon, rather than existing in a 'regional studies' cocoon, as if there was no point of contact between the two places and their musical pasts. Chakrabarty's richly textured suggestions certainly provided the initial bridge. My concern, however, is with the inherent feminisation in Chakrabarty's characterisation of History Two, that is, as disruptive and affective relative to the rational, established Master Narrative presumed by History One. In response, I have developed a small ensemble of keywords that seem appropriate to the different kind of historicism required in writing a history of jazz that was derivative of, but also quickly departed from, the models and stylistic categories generated in the United States by American musicians in the twentieth century, and sent out, largely (though not exclusively) by the entertainment industry in the form of mass-mediated products and broadcast programming. And it is to these keywords I turn.

KEYWORDS[15]

To transmute the image of the musical echo into a usable and broadly representative narrative about the past in South African jazz presents enormous challenges to the music historian for a host of reasons that simply don't apply in the United States – though they may in places that have endured repressive regimes. First, in thinking about South Africa's past, in jazz and popular music – themselves terms borrowed from the metropolitan centres of the global entertainment industry – it is useful to invoke Veit Erlmann's notion of the **global imagination**, a kind of individual and collective subject formation that emerges in nineteenth-century South Africa primarily amongst black South Africans (1999). Such an expanded sense of being-in-the-world is stimulated by a host of forces: Erlmann names the invention of the diorama, the experience of traveling musicians – such as the Christy Minstrels (1870s), and African American Orpheus McAdoo (1890s) to South Africa, its towns and countryside – as well as South African travel abroad – the South African Native Choir is a most compelling example. I extend this idea of imaginative travel (largely with Europe and the United States in mind), to the idea of musical surrogacy – fantasies of movement that emerge with the arrival of recordings, radio broadcast, and popular films from a range of places in the northern hemisphere to all parts of South Africa.

Second, we are confronted with the problem of **the archive**. The apartheid era drove its music and musicians away from home, underground, apart from fellow musicians, or into the banalities of commercial music-making. There was no parallel kind of music industry that could or would have created the recordings to support a coherent history of jazz. Under apartheid, those like Sathima Bea Benjamin who sang in the English language and used foreign forms were rarely recorded locally, either by the dominant commercial outfit Gallo Records or by the state-controlled South African Broadcasting Corporation. For several decades the apartheid state prohibited the broadcast of music of those who went into exile and declared their opposition to the government. What was recorded locally was hard to distribute without access to mass-mediation or because it was often banned or heavily censored by the state as soon as it was released. When these exiled musicians did record their music overseas, the changing rate of exchange of the South African Rand to the US Dollar, for example, made their imported recordings prohibitively expensive for many South African consumers. And, the attitude of some South Africans who remained behind and endured the apartheid regime has sometimes been less than welcoming to those who have returned. Adding insult to injury, when some South Africans began to think about writing South Africa's jazz history, they found that the state had destroyed the archives – not deeming African jazz, for example, worthy of a remembered past. These issues exacerbate the recuperation of a nationally unified cultural memory or even consensus of what should constitute a past in South African jazz.

In other words, the process before us as writers of the past in music is to recuperate a narrative of South African jazz as one searches through a topography composed primarily of fragments; the ruins of a past ravaged by time, but more so, a past constituted of a meta-narrative of profound loss, absence, destruction, and frequently, resounding silence. It is a past that will not come predominantly from a single source – scores or sound recordings or the stories attached to the objects. Without the material object, which has traditionally constituted a past in music, we are required to think afresh about both method and representation if we are to constitute a past in/for South African jazz.[16]

As much as some might wish to move on from the politics and ideologies of **racial difference**, and the imposition of racial categories on South Africans under apartheid specifically, it is imperative that we continue to reflect on the implications of race in constituting a past for South African jazz. This is important internally – because jazz has both a racially divided past and one that strove for a non-racial musical community – and externally, because while many South Africans looked beyond the nation to find models of identity and forms of belonging in racial terms, some prefer to recall jazz as a musical discourse that transcended racial divides. Furthermore, the ways in which race plays itself out in the world varies according to where one is located. The word 'coloured', for example, continued to be used in South Africa as an official category of the state well beyond its use in the United States. And to be part of a powerful white minority in South Africa meant something quite different from being white and part of a numerical and cultural majority in the United States in the same period.

I reflect on the parameters of a concept of **living history** in detail elsewhere (Muller, 2006a). Suffice to say, this is a notion of the past that is more open-ended than the conventional chronology allows. It is a past shaped more in the manner in which jazz musicians quote and recycle materials from prior performances. It calls for a process that connects to the past by 'animating memories of earlier times in the present', by viewing the past not as 'shut off from the present in closed containers of historical periods that are over and done with' (such as the use of scores/recordings enables), but continually weaves personal pasts into a larger historical narrative. As living history, historiography and jazz performance shift from being narratives of innovation and rupture to ones where there is a far stronger connection between living people and their pasts. Similarly it is shaped out of a past newly imagined and recreated in live performance, and comprises open-ended, revisable texts. It gives greater agency to the living, and a new lease of life to those already dead.

This notion of living history also requires us to think about the past not as linear chronology, moving from one moment in time to the next and never returning to any of those pristine but forever finished moments. Rather we imagine its capacity for representation as palimpsest, a worldwide web or even just a web-link with its layers of prior performances embedded in the text. Each musical moment bears the traces of other performances, elsewhere and in another time. In the metaphor of the echo, each acoustical event has the capacity to generate new waves: to locate that event in relationship to a host of resonances heard from other places.

A living history has at its core then the **human voice**, as a particular kind of utterance: as an acoustical signature, in its capacity to bear witness, and in the particular way in which it combines words and music as a vehicle of deeply felt emotion. The focus on the voice places the human body and the heart back into narrations of the past. So if we think about the South African reception of jazz, we have to re-evaluate the workings of musical transmission and media. And we do so through the process of **musical surrogacy** – where the media of musical transmission are constituted as vessels of a disembodied person-to-person musical transmission between far-flung communities of music-makers. Appointed as a 'replacement for oneself', the musical commodity/surrogate becomes the appointed carrier of musical sound replacing the musician. Here the recording or radio broadcast brings new forms to other communities in the absence of the original musicians themselves. The recording stands in for the musician: it intervenes in local transmission of traditions, and fosters the idea of new musically conceived families and kin groups. Such imaginative links are often created out of the sound of the music itself – its warmth, romantic sentiment, but also its capacity to fuel political consciousness through its stress upon freedom, improvisation, self-expression, and insistence on the right of an individual to articulate a voice in the collective fabric of the music, and society itself.

This living history requires a revision of prior ideas of the Old and New **African diasporas**. The Old African diaspora is the one we are more familiar with – it is the diaspora generated by slavery. The New African diaspora is quite simply a way of being in the world that inhabits two places simultaneously – the physical environment you currently live in on one hand, and the vivid memories of places you have been to previously, or imagine yourself traveling to in the future, all creatively invoked through musical iteration live or in mediated form. Furthermore, there can be no doubt that defining a past for South African jazz has to be both about what had been made locally, in terms of vernacular languages (and there are 11 official languages in South Africa) and culture; and what was brought in from outside. It is a problem of simultaneously inhabiting the here and the elsewhere, of living **inter-culturally** or 'between two or more regimes of knowledge, or living as a minority in the still majority, white, Euro-American' world (Marks, 2000: 1). The question has to be how we deal with the essentially hybrid, creolised, mixed, and certainly de-centred character of these kinds of cultural formations and musical practices.

Finally, we must be concerned with **restoration**, a process of folding into a single space in the present what was impossible to achieve in its time of lived experience: the coeval performances of jazz in the range of racially distinct residential areas that the Group Areas Act enforced on South Africans in the apartheid era. In that era, Indians played jazz for the Indian community; in the same decade 'coloured' dance bands performed weekly for their constituencies; while white jazz musicians were moving between Durban, Johannesburg, Margate, and Cape Town; black South African swing bands played in the townships of Johannesburg; and the inter-racial groups of Chris McGregor (Blue Notes) and Abdullah Ibrahim (Jazz Epistles) insisted on progressive and experimental jazz as non-racial 'free spaces'.

Conclusion

In this paper I have invoked the possibilities embedded in the trope of the musical echo – an acoustical versus literary image – and suggested its usefulness in reconfiguring a past in South African jazz, a past shaped by the worldwide distribution of recordings and musicians who traveled – shaping a 'global imagination' amongst South Africans. In striving to find ways out of the singularity of a US-centred jazz canon and historiography, I have suggested that we cannot simply keep writing a linearly conceived narrative of regional or even comparative and global pasts in jazz: one that starts in one place and that travels in a 'progressively' circumscribed area. I have suggested that for South Africans, invoking the musical echo in narrating a past in jazz requires a consideration of a range of acoustical memories pertaining to the apartheid years: mass-mediated from local and foreign sources; live and communal in familiar places; representing 'tradition' and resisting its confinement; while allowing a breadth of political position and forms of representation. It urges a reassessment of the sources, or vestiges of past musical performances, that might be included in shaping a peculiarly South African history.

The question we now must ask is whether the image of the echo enables a productive mechanism for thinking about jazz history more generally in the twentieth century: where the technologies of innovation send out waves to multiple sites simultaneously, frequently generating a range of responses, real and imagined, which incorporate themselves into the archive of US- and European-generated musical performances and force the archives to expand their criteria for inclusion and extraction. For those producing canonical histories of jazz in the United States, the echo requires a similar capacity to open ears and minds far beyond the geopolitical borders of the US and elsewhere. Indeed, it is critical that the musical echoes resounding between the United States and its twentieth-century markets for jazz performance be heard: these include factoring in the consequences of travel, human and mediated, through US State Department tours; the journeys of individual musicians; and the less obvious but in some places far more influential journeys of jazz recordings to various parts of the world from the earliest days of the music industry. I wonder, for example, how we might reconfigure the contribution of Ellington or Holiday when we think of them as not just American but as two musicians with a very specific impact in many sites around the world: both in the places to which they personally travelled and in those sites where their recordings traveled without them.

Clearly, it is time for those of us concerned about jazz as a world of music to work critically inside of dominant narratives, while simultaneously creating new, emergent flights/lines of inquiry. We need to build a language that allows for the kinds of musical experiences, values, histories, and performances created by those who strive to live concurrently inside of, and self-consciously beyond, places, histories, and communities, who embody the state of in-between-ness that jazz composition, and living in diaspora/exile, simultaneously invokes and resolves. Such language emerges with a movement away from the profound colonisation of consciousness that apartheid forced upon its people, and the narrow vision of America that living in such a large and powerful nation as the United States supports. We need to move beyond these ways of thinking into a more intercultural space of musical, intellectual, and globally distributed thinking, a mode of being that many musicians have long engaged with, but seldom had the rhetorical spaces to name as such. Having posed the possibilities for new ways of thinking about a collective South African past, I urge us to similarly reflect on the place of South African jazz history in conversation with *the* narrative of jazz history disseminated from and about the United States and to reflect on the stories about jazz as a truly global phenomenon in the twentieth and twenty-first centuries.

ENDNOTES

1   'Musical Echoes' is an idea/title I have borrowed from Sathima Bea Benjamin's most recent recording made in Cape Town in 2002 with American jazz pianist Steven Scott, and South Africans Basil Moses on bass and the late Lulu Gontsana on drums. It is also the name of the book that Sathima and I have written together

(Muller with Benjamin, forthcoming). The idea of the echo encompasses and reevaluates my recent work on Sathima, and contemplates the travel of American music to South Africa as a kind of musical diaspora on one hand, and the common practices of copying, covering, and translating American music in postwar Cape Town on the other.

2   Ibrahim grew up in the Kensington area of Cape Town, a place I don't recall ever having visited as a child growing up with the Group Areas Act, which required South Africans to live in different residential areas according to racial classification.

3   A slightly later version of Benjamin's rendition of 'I Got It Bad' is available on *A Morning in Paris* (recorded with Ellington and Strayhorn in 1963, and issued in 1997).

4   Sathima was born Beatrice Benjamin, named after her father's sister, remembered as Auntie Beatty.

5   Duke Ellington played a key role in South African jazz history, particularly of the late 1950s and early 1960s. Even though he never actually travelled in person, his music and even personal presence certainly did (see McGregor, 1996).

6   See Lucia (2002) for parallel discussion of the effect of memory on Abdullah Ibrahim's compositional output.

7   Key to such a project must surely be to consider how South Africa's past in jazz might diverge, for example, from European pasts in jazz: where the one place finds resemblances between music making of Africans in America, who experienced and challenged racism, and articulated new places for themselves through jazz; and the other place that had no parallel set of struggles.

8   See Chakrabarty (2000) for comment on the problem of the Third World in relationship to a European centre.

9   These definitions of the echo are from the *American Heritage Dictionary*, http://dictionary.reference.com/browse/echo, accessed 22 June 2004.

10 Elsewhere I expand on the central place of radio broadcast, film, and sound recordings in Benjamin's childhood and early adult life in South Africa (Muller, 2006b). See also Allen (2004), Ballantine (1993), Coplan (1985), and Hamm (1995) for discussion of the importance of audio-visual technologies in shaping local popular music and jazz sensibilities in twentieth-century South Africa.

11 The Emmy award-winning documentary, *Amandla! Revolution in Four-Part Harmony* (2002), directed by Lee Hirsch, constitutes a contemporary take on the Greek myth of the Echo.

12 Sathima has suggested to me the mythical narrative of the echo is indeed the key metaphor in her own story. There are many places to read pieces of this story: Muller and Benjamin (forthcoming); Muller (2004: chap. 3); Molefe and Mzileni (1997); and Rasmussen (2000).

13 Robin Kelly's *Freedom Dreams: The Black Radical Imagination* (2002) provides a rich set of narratives about this process from the African American civil rights struggle as a struggle of international proportion in the mid-twentieth century.
14 Recently, there has been a surge in publication of what are commonly termed acoustical cultures, or histories of sound. See, for example, Erlmann (2004); and Bull and Back (2003).
15 The keywords are in bold typeface.
16 Despite the challenges endemic to recuperating a recorded history of South Africa's past in jazz performance, there has been remarkable production of oral history/photographic evidence collected and published recently by, among others, Allen (2005; 2003); Rasmussen (see the list of references); and Ansell (2004).

Bibliography

Allen, Lara. 2005. 'Circuits of Recognition and Desire in the Evolution of Black South African Popular Music: The Career of the Penny Whistle'. *South African Journal of Musicology*, 25, pp. 31-51.

_. 2004. 'Music, Film and Gangsters in the Sophiatown Imaginary: Featuring Dolly Rathebe'. *Scrutiny 2*, 9(1), pp. 19-38.

_. 2003. 'Commerce, Politics, and Musical Hybridity: Vocalising Urban Black South African Identity during the 1950s'. *Ethnomusicology*, 47(2), pp. 228-249.

Ansell, Gwen. 2004. *Soweto Blues: Jazz, Popular Music and Politics in South Africa*. New York: Continuum.

Ballantine, Christopher. 1993. *Marabi Nights: Early South African Jazz and Vaudeville*. Johannesburg: Ravan Press.

Bull, Michael, & Les Back (eds). 2003. *The Auditory Culture Reader*. New York: Berg.

Chakrabarty, Dipesh. 2000. *Provincializing Europe: Postcolonial Thought and Historical Difference*. Princeton: Princeton University Press.

Code, Lorraine. 1995. *Rhetorical Spaces: Essays on Gendered Locations*. New York: Routledge.

Coplan, David. 1985. *In Township Tonight! Black South African Music and Theater*. New York: Longmans.

Epstein, Jules. 2004. Notes to *Cape Town Love*. Cape Town: Ekapa Records.

Erlmann, Veit. 2004. *Hearing Cultures: Essays on Sound, Listening and Modernity*. New York: Berg.

_. 1999. *Music, Modernity and the Global Imagination*. New York: Oxford.

Feld, Steven. 2000. 'Lullaby for World Music'. *Public Culture*, 12(1), pp. 145-171.

Hamm, Charles. 1995. *Putting Popular Music In Its Place*. Cambridge: Cambridge University Press.

Hirsch, Lee (dir.). 2003. *Amandla! A Revolution in Four-Part Harmony*. DVD. Santa Monica, CA: Artisan Home Entertainment.

Kelly, Robin. 2002. *Freedom Dreams: The Black Radical Imagination*. Boston: Beacon Press.

Lucia, Christine. 2002. 'Abdullah Ibrahim and the Uses of Memory'. *British Journal of Ethnomusicology*, 11(2), pp. 125-43.

Marks, Laura. 2000. *The Skin of the Film: Intercultural Cinema, Embodiment and the Senses*. Durham: Duke University Press.

McGregor, Maxine. 1996. *Chris McGregor and the Brotherhood of Breath*. Flint, MI: Bamberger Books.

Molefe, ZB, & Mike Mzileni. 1997. *A Common Hunger to Sing: A Tribute to South Africa's Black Women in Song (1950-1990)*. Johannesburg: Kwela Books.

Muller, Carol, with Sathima Bea Benjamin. forthcoming. *Musical Echoes*. Durham: Duke University Press.

Muller, Carol. 2006a. 'The New African Diaspora, the Built Environment, and the Past in Jazz'. *Ethnomusicology Forum*, 15(1), pp. 61-84.

_. 2006b. 'American Musical Surrogacy: A View from Postwar South Africa'. *Safundi: A Journal of South African and American Studies*, 23. http://www.safundi.com/issues/23/default.asp, accessed 15 April 2007.

_. 2004. *South African Music: A Century of Traditions in Transformation*. Santa Barbara: ABC-CLIO.

_. 2001. 'The "Spirit of Africa" in the Jazz Singing of South African Sathima Bea Benjamin'. *Research in African Literatures*, 32(2), pp. 133-152.

Rasmussen, Lars (ed.). 2003a. *Jazz People of Cape Town*. Copenhagen: The Booktrader.

_. (ed.). 2003b. *Mbizo: A Book About Johnny Dyani*. Copenhagen: The Booktrader.

_. (ed.). 2001. *Cape Town Jazz, 1959-1963: The Photographs of Hardy Stockman*. Copenhagen: The Booktrader.

_. (compiler). 2000. *Abdullah Ibrahim: A Discography*, 2nd ed. Copenhagen: The Booktrader.

_. (ed.). 2000. *Embracing Jazz: Sathima Bea Benjamin*. Copenhagen: The Booktrader.

Discography

Benjamin, Sathima Bea. 2002. *Musical Echoes*. Cape Town: Ekapa Records.

_. 1999. *Cape Town Love*. Cape Town: Ekapa Records. SA 001.

_. 1997. *A Morning in Paris*. Germany: Enja Records. ENJ-93092.

_. 1983. *Memories and Dreams*. New York: Ekapa.

8

SINGING AGAINST APARTHEID

ANC CULTURAL GROUPS AND THE INTERNATIONAL ANTI-APARTHEID STRUGGLE

Shirli Gilbert

Introduction[1]

In 1989, an in-house African National Congress (ANC) seminar in Lusaka heard Albie Sachs's thoughts on 'Preparing Ourselves for Freedom', beginning with his famously controversial proposition that the phrase 'culture is a weapon of struggle' be banned.[2] The phrase was 'not only banal and devoid of real content', Sachs claimed, 'but actually wrong and potentially harmful'. In explanation, he gave his impressions of the current state of ANC art: it confined itself to a narrow range of politically acceptable themes ('fists and spears and guns'), portrayed the anti-apartheid struggle in simplistic terms of good and evil, and shunned nuance and ambiguity for 'solemn formulas of commitment'. He insisted, however, that the very power of art lay in its capacity to expose complexity and contradiction; furthermore, the ideal art 'is that which bypasses, overwhelms, ignores apartheid, establishes its own space'. As the promise of national liberation neared in the late 1980s, Sachs argued that art needed to be able to express not only the formulae of struggle, but also the richness and diversity of the newly emergent South African nation (1998).

Sachs – a highly respected lawyer and ANC activist whose pronouncements at this time carried particular weight, given his survival of an assassination attempt in 1988 – openly acknowledged that he had himself long endorsed the very conception of art as a 'weapon of struggle' that he now repudiated. A decade earlier, it had been legitimate and necessary to mobilise artists in service of the struggle, and this conception of culture had constituted an important focus for ANC thinking on the subject (Langa, 1990: 30). But the 1980s had seen the rise of an increasingly sophisticated discourse within the movement about the ways in which culture might contribute to the process of national liberation, as well as a steady increase in the number of publications, events, and institutions devoted to the issue. By the time Sachs delivered his call, culture occupied a firm place on the ANC's agenda. What he was emphasising was that the changing context of the struggle required a corresponding shift in how cultural activity was conceived and implemented.

This article takes its starting point approximately fifteen years earlier than Sachs's proclamation, when cultural life was still largely regarded within the ANC as peripheral to organised political activity. Through the lens of two of the ANC's most significant projects in exile, it explores the ways in which culture was actively recruited to promote the anti-apartheid struggle internationally. First, it chronicles the work of the Mayibuye Cultural Ensemble, a London-based ANC grouping that achieved considerable success in Europe with its agitprop performances incorporating narrative, poetry and song. Mayibuye was established in early 1975, and despite its rapidly shifting and amateur membership, functioned successfully for approximately five years, raising international awareness about the anti-apartheid cause, and simultaneously raising consciousness within the movement about the practical ways in which cultural activity could further the project of national liberation. The article then considers the work of the Amandla Cultural Ensemble, which originated in the late 1970s amongst ANC exiles based largely in *Umkhonto we Sizwe* (MK) training camps in southern Africa, principally Angola.[3] Led for much of its existence by trombonist Jonas Gwangwa, Amandla became, during the decade that followed, a popular ambassador for the ANC throughout Africa and further afield in Europe, South America, the Soviet Union and elsewhere. Unlike Mayibuye, it offered large-scale, increasingly professionalised performances incorporating choral singing, jazz, theatre, and dance. Its performances were intended not only to raise international awareness about apartheid, but also to present an alternative vision of a more dynamic, inclusive South African culture.

An initial motivation for this article was documenting the work of these two ensembles, both of which made significant contributions to the development of cultural activity and yet remain virtually undocumented in the history of the movement and the struggle.[4] The article's primary analytical focus is on how culture came to play a role in the movement's work in exile, the ways in which representations of 'fists and spears and guns' were used to appeal to the international community, and the relationship between this and cultural activity that was more internally focused. While a significant body of scholarship exists on the broader subject of black South African music, there has as yet been little investigation of how music was used by political movements during the struggle, either within the country or in exile. In addition, little detailed research has been conducted on freedom songs, the ubiquitous but largely informal and un-professionalised genre that was probably the dominant musical medium of popular political expression.[5] Given the presence of freedom songs at mass gatherings, celebrations, funerals, protests, and myriad public events in South Africa, this is a significant gap. This examination of the ANC's two professional ensembles thus represents an initial contribution towards understanding a significant dimension of South African cultural and political life, namely the deliberate and focused role that music was mobilised to play in the struggle. The development and activities of these two groups also shed some light on the ANC itself, its changing attitudes towards culture, and its broader diplomatic strategies in exile.

Two qualifications should be stated at the outset. First, Sachs's comments mark the end-point of this discussion, rather than its focus: the article does not engage with the larger debate that erupted from his paper.[6] While his observations affirmed the increasingly valuable role that cultural activity had played until that time, he was primarily concerned with the ways in which art could address itself to the demands of a new era in the process of national liberation. Second, beyond the Sachs debate the role of culture in the struggle was always a contested one: perspectives and priorities within the movement varied, and the complicated, shifting dynamics that characterised the broader discussion on this issue are a topic for another time.

Sachs's generalised comments, as well as the debate that they sparked, nonetheless help to illuminate some of the larger dynamics shaping ANC cultural endeavours during the 1980s, and thus constitute a useful frame for this discussion. In particular, they suggest that the movement had indistinct and sometimes conflicting conceptions of what culture's role should be in external propaganda work as opposed to the internally-focused work of nation-building. ANC discourse on the subject often did not distinguish clearly between these roles. Initially, this was probably in part because the crucial task was moving culture into the mainstream of the movement's work, an initiative in which both Mayibuye and Amandla played a significant part. As debate and activity on the cultural front intensified and deepened during the 1980s, however, and increasingly as transition neared, culture's manifold potential roles began to be examined more carefully, as exemplified in the Sachs debate. The distinction between internal and external roles, although seldom consciously made by the movement, helps to situate the particular contributions of these two groups in the larger context of culture and the struggle. Further, it helps to explain the difficulties faced by those trying to revive Amandla in post-apartheid South Africa, an initiative that has yet to come to fruition. In exploring how culture was mobilised by the ANC in the international arena, this article seeks to understand the importance and distinctive value of propaganda-focused cultural activity to the movement, as well as its necessary and inevitable limitations.

THE MAYIBUYE CULTURAL ENSEMBLE, 1975-1980

On Sunday, 10 November 1974, the Mermaid Theatre in London staged *Poets to the People*, billed as 'a dramatic presentation of South African freedom poems'.[7] The event was a book launch for a poetry anthology of the same title, edited by ANC activist Barry Feinberg and published earlier that year. The performance consisted of dramatic readings of 31 poems, including works by Mongane Wally Serote, Dennis Brutus, Cosmo Pieterse, Oswald Mtshali, Mazisi Kunene, Arthur Nortje and Feinberg himself. Interspersed with these poems were a variety of political and traditional songs, as well as rhetorical segments where British actors explained various aspects of the apartheid state – separate amenities, racial classification, Bantu education, and so on – in a dramatised conversational style. These dramatic sections were arranged thematically so as to illuminate the meaning of the poems and any allusions that might have been unclear to a British audience.[8]

Poets to the People was to become one of the central impetuses for the gradual integration of culture into the organised activities of the ANC in exile. The potential role of culture in the struggle had been a topic of discussion within the movement long before the 1974 event, and had informed the work of individual artists, writers and musicians who devoted their work to the anti-apartheid cause. In addition, cultural activities, particularly spontaneous group singing, had always played an integral role at celebrations, funerals and most other mass gatherings. According to Feinberg, however, despite their tangible significance in these contexts, there had been little attempt to incorporate them more systematically into the movement's mainstream political work as a medium for raising consciousness and achieving change. As the concept of Mayibuye was beginning to take root in England, a growing number of activists across the diaspora of exile were similarly arguing that culture should play a more active and important role, though perspectives varied widely as to how this might be practically achieved. Living in exile in London, Feinberg and his friend, Ronnie Kasrils, had come into contact with other liberation movements that were making use of culture to promote their cause. Increasingly feeling the need for action, they began to make contact with other like-minded ANC activists (Feinberg, 2004).[9]

Feinberg's book, promoting itself as the first of its kind to make a direct link between poetry and revolution in South Africa, was faulted by some for its propagandistic nature.[10] Nonetheless, the collection was on the whole enthusiastically received, and the launch-performance of *Poets to the People* was an enormous success. This was partly due to the high-profile nature of the production, which included well-known British theatre personalities such as director Peter Coe and actors Dame Peggy Ashcroft, Janet Suzman, Joss Ackland, and Edward Bond. The production also included an eight-member 'freedom choir', a makeshift group of South African singers who, though not particularly politicised, were willing to lend their voices to the production.

Based on the success of this performance, Feinberg and Kasrils decided to establish a more permanent ensemble. They named the group Mayibuye, echoing the familiar liberation slogan '*Mayibuye iAfrika*' (let Africa return). According to an internal report, the initial motivation for the group was to integrate artists into the struggle, particularly in the realm of international solidarity; in addition, it was seen as an opportunity for engaging younger South Africans who might otherwise have remained uninvolved in ANC activities. In January 1975, Feinberg and Kasrils recruited two members with whom to launch the initiative: John Matshikiza, a young South African studying drama in London, and Billy Nannan, a former leading member of the South African Indian Congress. The four engaged in vigorous debate about the envisaged nature of the group: some endorsed a more inclusive approach to membership, while others argued that only a professional approach would achieve the desired political results.[11]

The group's beginnings were modest. Although passionate and enthusiastic, the four performers were inexperienced, and their early performances were – by their own account – amateurish and unsophisticated (Feinberg, 1977: 41). In addition, lacking confidence in their singing ability, they initially relied on gramophone recordings of freedom songs, which suffered from repeated technical hitches. Nonetheless, they enjoyed encouraging responses from British audiences, and through a combination of training in basic performance skills and continued discussion, gradually refined their presentation. They also soon began to recruit new members.[12]

Mayibuye's presentation was based on the structure of the original *Poets to the People* performance, incorporating poetry, narrative and freedom songs. In place of British actors, it comprised a cast of between six and eight South African performers telling a moving story of life under apartheid and the struggle for liberation under the banner of the ANC.[13] The agitprop-style narrative marked a noticeable shift in kind from the 1974 production, where poems and songs had been interspersed with lengthy, rather dry narrative interludes detailing specific aspects of the apartheid state. The Mayibuye version was fast-paced and emotive, clearly intended to inspire sympathy and support for apartheid's victims. The poetic content of the performance remained largely the same, drawn from the *Poets to the People* anthology. ANC Kumalo's 'Red our colour', for example, was frequently used as an opening:

Let's have poems
blood-red in colour
ringing like damn bells.

Poems
that tear at the oppressor's face
and smash his grip.

Poems that awaken man:

Life not death
Hope not despair
Dawn not dusk
New not old
Struggle not submission
(Kumalo, 1974: 58).

Many of the poems used were similarly combative and rebellious in tone, and made explicit references to life under apartheid and the potential power of poetry in the struggle.

For its musical repertoire, Mayibuye drew largely on freedom songs. While the term 'freedom songs' has a long history, particularly in the United States – where it has been used to refer to protest songs from the abolitionist, civil rights, and labour movements – its usage in the South African context refers to a distinct local repertoire associated with the struggle for racial equality in the twentieth century, preceding as well as during apartheid.[14] Freedom songs have their stylistic origins in *makwaya* (choir), a syncretic and widely popular genre that combined southern African singing traditions with Christian hymnody (James, 2000: 155). They are perhaps more accurately described as short slogans – in indigenous languages (primarily Zulu and Xhosa) and/or English – set to simple melodic phrases, sung *a cappella*, and repeated over and over in a call-and-response style. They are created and sung collectively, are frequently modified as politics, attitudes and circumstances change, and are almost exclusively non-commercial.

From the enormous repertoire of freedom songs in circulation both at home and in exile, Mayibuye drew particularly on those that were popular in South Africa at the time – in contrast, as we shall see, with what Amandla was later to do. Some of the favourites among these were 'Naants'indod'emnyama Vorster' ('Here is the black man, Vorster'), 'Thina sizwe' ('We African people') and 'Dubula ngembayimbayi' ('We will shoot them with cannons'):[15]

> Thina sizwe esimnyama sikalela izwe lethu
> Elathathwa ngaba mhlophe
> Sithi mabayeke umhlaba wethu

[We African people are crying for our land / Which was taken by white people / We say they must leave our land]

> Bazobaleka soba dubula we mama
> Sizoba dubula ngembayimbayi

[They will run away, we will shoot them / We will shoot them with cannons]

According to Feinberg, after 1976 the group also incorporated many additional songs that had grown out of the Soweto uprising (pers. comm., 4 July 2005).

The freedom songs were performed in three- or four-part harmony by the small group of performers, an approximation (albeit unlikely) of how they would be sung by large crowds at mass gatherings inside South Africa. The stage set-up for these performances was basic. The performers would stand in formation on the platform, generally clustered in groups of two or three behind microphone stands; there was no theatrical element to the performance, although a minor dance component was introduced in the latter years of the group's existence, and apart from simple banners or posters, there were no stage sets.[16]

Mayibuye's narrative was regularly adapted to incorporate recent news and events, and was tightly interwoven with poems and freedom songs, arranged thematically so as to produce a coherent 'plot'. In the following example, the spoken introduction exposes the brutality of the apartheid state and the resistance actions of MK, while the song *'Abantu Bakithi'* ('Our people') asserts confidence in the revolutionary movement's ultimate success and urges further action:[17]

Speaker 1: In the wake of the Soweto uprising, an ANC leaflet was distributed by leaflet bombs in the major city centres of South Africa. The leaflet included the following declaration:

'We shall harass the enemy, his police, soldiers, officials and spies wherever we can. Above all we shall arm ourselves with modern weapons and hit back through our organised fighting force, *Umkhonto we Sizwe.*'

These racist murderers, who slaughter unarmed children and women, fled in panic when they came face to face with the armed freedom fighters of *Umkhonto* in Zimbabwe in 1967 and 1968. Their racist arrogance shrank when our MPLA comrades thrashed them in Angola, and now the time is coming when *Umkhonto* will punish the racists on our own soil. The mass struggle of our people helps to bring that day nearer.

Speaker 2: These are not empty phrases. Since the leaflet, a number of sabotage and guerrilla actions have indeed taken place within South Africa. Our song calls on our people to rise up and fight for our country. We will destroy Smith and Vorster with grenades and bazookas.

Abantu bakithi bahluphekile
Vukani madoda silwelwe ilizwe lethu elathathwa

Siqale ngoSmith, sigcine ngoVorster, baphele bonke
Vukani madoda silwelwe ilizwe lethu elathathwa

Siphons' igraned', sishaya ibhazuk',
bulala amabhunu baphele bonke
Vukani madoda silwelwe ilizwe lethu elathathwa

[Our people are suffering / Wake up men and fight for our land that was taken from us ... We will begin with Smith, and end with Vorster / Wake up men and fight for our land that was taken from us ... / We will throw in a grenade, we will hit with a bazooka, / kill all the Boers until they are finished / Wake up men and fight for our land that was taken from us]

Although Mayibuye's more mature performances progressed away from the wordiness of this early excerpt, the quote nonetheless illustrates the group's characteristic style in two primary regards: the agitprop tone of the narrative, which condemns the actions of the 'racist murderers' and confidently asserts the growing successes of the struggle; and the use of song to mark the narrative's emotional climax and rouse support for the revolutionary cause.

Mayibuye initially performed primarily in England, and soon elicited interest from anti-apartheid groups throughout Britain and more widely in Europe. Its practice from the outset was to make adjustments (often substantial) to its performance in order to optimise its relevance for different audiences. For its first Amsterdam performances in March 1975, for example, it included special sections on Afrikaans poets like Breyten Breytenbach who had opposed apartheid, and made specific references to Dutch trade figures, and to Dutch businessmen or politicians who had tried to justify their involvement with apartheid South Africa. In addition, a renowned Dutch writer, Jan Wolkers, was recruited both to translate the script, and to read the translation alongside Mayibuye's performance.[18] The use of popular local personalities as translators and co-performers became a standard technique in the group's performances. Where translators could not be found, simultaneous translations would be projected on a screen, or provided in booklets.

Mayibuye was first and foremost an agitprop group, intended to raise awareness about apartheid, strengthen international solidarity, and obtain financial support for the ANC. Organisations that hosted the group were required to cover transport, accommodation and maintenance costs, and all additional money raised went to the ANC. Through its travels, the group was able to consolidate existing relationships with Anti-Apartheid Movement (AAM) representatives across Europe, and to build new political friendships. An important objective was also to make contact with exiled South Africans dispersed in Europe, and to reinvigorate their connection with the liberation movement. Mayibuye's work was generally conducted in association with political organisations, anti-apartheid and anti-racist groups, trade unions and minority groups, and it was frequently invited to perform on university campuses. On occasion it performed in conjunction with similar groups from other countries, and participated in solidarity events with southern African liberation movements like the Zimbabwe African People's Union (ZAPU), the

Popular Movement for the Liberation of Angola (MPLA) and the Liberation Front of Mozambique (FRELIMO), all movements with which the ANC had ongoing diplomatic friendships. Its work was not limited to its performances: members consistently engaged audiences and organisers in political dialogue and gave interviews to the press. They also travelled with a photography exhibition exposing some of the injustices of apartheid.

The Mayibuye Cultural Ensemble gave almost 200 performances throughout Europe during its approximate five years of activity. Through its numerous live, television and radio performances, as well as a record released in the Netherlands in 1978, the group secured a reputation as the cultural voice of the ANC.[19] Within the first few years of its existence, however, Mayibuye began to strain under mounting personal and organisational pressures. Membership posed practical difficulties from the outset, as most people had full-time jobs elsewhere and performed on a voluntary and unpaid basis. As a result, membership was constantly shifting: people came and went as political, personal and career circumstances dictated, and stand-in performers frequently needed to be called in on short notice. As the group's work became increasingly demanding, fewer and fewer individuals were left to shoulder the bulk of the responsibilities. This reached critical point when a substantial number of experienced performers left the group in order to focus on their careers or engage more directly in political work. Although they were gradually replaced, few new members were able to acquire the skills and commitment necessary to cope with increasing demand.

By 1978, requests for performances were pouring in, but organisational problems were intensifying. Feinberg, who in addition to his work at the International Defence and Aid Fund acted as the group's formal leader, made repeated appeals to the ANC leadership in London that 'younger people from down South' – a reference primarily to the MK camps – be sent in order to assist in Mayibuye's administrative and performing work. In several reports and letters drafted in 1978-9, he indicated that the current part-time arrangement could no longer work. He advised that the optimal response would be to set up a professional group, preferably made up of young comrades from southern Africa, who would take over on a full-time basis the 'tried and tested vehicle' that they had built in London.[20]

The Amandla Cultural Ensemble, c.1978-1990

As previously suggested, when Mayibuye began its work in the mid-1970s culture was not yet on the ANC's mainstream agenda. As the decade progressed, however, culture gained increasing presence in the movement's formal discourse, and the 1980s saw a dramatic upsurge in the amount of airtime and energy devoted to the issue. Mayibuye was an important contributing factor to these developments, together with the cumulative efforts of groups and individuals elsewhere, particularly inside South Africa. Indeed, one of the key objectives that emerged at this time was the need to start organising these dispersed forces, and to encourage them to direct their activities in a more unified manner in service of the struggle (Feinberg, 2004; Moema, 1980: 1-3; Feinberg, 1977: 41-5).

As these diverse efforts built up momentum, the issue of culture began to rise steadily in prominence within the movement. In July 1982, the watershed Culture and Resistance conference was held in Gaborone, Botswana under the auspices of the Medu Art Ensemble, an organisation formally unaffiliated but whose members were, at least by the early 1980s, largely ANC (Seidman, 2004). Later the same year, the Department of Arts and Culture was established (Masekela, 1993), and in 1985, following a National Executive Committee (NEC) address in which ANC President Oliver Tambo made prominent reference to the role of 'cultural workers', the movement launched its own in-house cultural journal, named *Rixaka* (see 'Render South Africa Ungovernable!', 1985). This intensifying interest in culture saw rising numbers of workshops, festivals and seminars devoted to the issue, interviews and public pronouncements by leading ANC figures, and the high-profile Culture in Another South Africa (CASA) conference held in Amsterdam in December 1987. The Amandla Cultural Ensemble undoubtedly grew out of, and participated in, this burgeoning interest in culture, and it came to be considered within the ANC as one of its greatest achievements in this realm.

As Mayibuye struggled to cope with rising pressure in the late 1970s, the conception of Amandla was slowly beginning to take root 'down South'. Although Feinberg's 1978–9 reports explicitly suggested an ensemble in the Amandla mould, there was no direct connection between the two groups: more precisely, there were no formal meetings between Mayibuye and prospective members of a new group, and members of Amandla rarely mentioned Mayibuye when describing the origins of their group. At the same time, a large consignment of Mayibuye's records was sent to ANC headquarters in Lusaka, which increased awareness of the group's work. In addition, one of Mayibuye's leading members, Ronnie Kasrils, had been relocated from London to Angola to play a commanding role in MK in 1977 (Gastrow, 1995: 109). Although Kasrils' attention was focused on other matters, his experiences of cultural activity probably filtered through to those around him, even if only through occasional conversations.

Mayibuye was also an important conceptual precedent. It had established itself as an active representative of the ANC abroad, and was successfully winning support and funds. The movement, in turn, acknowledged the value and importance of the initiative, and encouraged its continued existence. Initially, however, there was little support for the idea of a more permanent, professional touring ensemble made up of younger activists. Ironically, one of the reasons for this early reluctance to support professional cultural activity was precisely the ubiquitousness of culture (particularly freedom songs) at mass gatherings and political events – also a key factor underlying Mayibuye's difficulties in sustaining commitment from its members. As Feinberg observed, 'it was difficult to elevate [this commonplace political culture] into Art, with all the organisation and discipline that implies, in the consciousness of people' (pers. comm., 4 July 2005). In addition, in the late 1970s there were more pressing priorities: in the MK camps in particular, daily life was focused primarily on military training and organisation. Though the camps were home to an active and abundant cultural life, many saw this merely as recreational activity that took second place to the more important task of getting back into South Africa (Simons cited in Ansell, 2004: 247). When Amandla finally took root, it did so independently, without any direct relation to Mayibuye (Feinberg, 2004).

Amandla's conceptual origins date back to the World Black Festival of Arts and Culture (FESTAC), held in Lagos, Nigeria in 1977. Participating in the festival were artists, poets and musicians from all over Africa, Europe, and the United States, many appearing under the banner of the ANC. Inspired by the diversity of talent represented at the festival, exiled musician Jonas Gwangwa was motivated to put together a temporary ensemble that he called Amandla (meaning 'power', and drawing on another popular liberation slogan), which included musicians like Dudu Pukwana and Julian Bahula (see Ansell, 2004). A popular musician who rocketed to success as a young trombonist in 1950s Sophiatown, Gwangwa had left South Africa in 1961 with the touring *King Kong* ensemble, and by the time of FESTAC had established a successful career in the United States alongside South African contemporaries Hugh Masekela, Miriam Makeba, and Caiphus Semenya (Szymczak, 2003). His impromptu ensemble's concerts were successful, and after the festival it accepted invitations to tour Tanzania and Zambia. According to Gwangwa, this was where the idea of Amandla was born; it should be stressed, however, that most of those who performed in the temporary FESTAC ensemble did not participate in the later establishment of Amandla itself. Key figures in the ANC – among them Thabo Mbeki, who was then Head of Information and Publicity – supported the idea of a permanent cultural group, and Gwangwa was called on to draft a memorandum for the formation of a cultural department (Gwangwa, 1985; Gwangwa, 1989-91).

It took some time before either of these initiatives materialised. The core of what was later to become the Amandla Cultural Ensemble itself was established at the 11th World Festival of Youth and Students, a meeting of the World Federation of Democratic Youth held in Havana, Cuba in 1978 ('World Federation of Democratic Youth'). During the festival, a small group of ANC representatives put together a performance, which turned out to be an enormous hit with the young international audience. On the basis of this success, a decision was taken to establish the group more formally and maintain its activities. In the months that followed, formal cultural activities under the banner of Amandla were enthusiastically developed in MK training camps in Angola. Much work was required to get the group on its feet: it was initially inexperienced and disorganised, and although there were many talented musicians, dancers and actors among the soldiers (both male and female), most were not professional performers, and needed to be trained. Many of the prospective recruits had never even seen a professional stage show, let alone performed in one (Khuze, 1985).

Added to this was the pressure of the surrounding context: these performers were for the most part young soldiers in training camps, political activists for whom engaging in military activity took priority. Some, like Man (Santana) Ntombela – one of Amandla's principal members in both performance and organisation – made forthright requests, with the support of MK commanders, to leave the group in order to go to the frontline. Ntombela was emphatically turned down by the ANC leadership, who he explains emphasised Amandla's importance in mobilising the international community (Ntombela, 1993). At the outset, young women and men like Ntombela struggled to balance their activities as 'cultural workers' and soldiers. Their primary duties were in Amandla, but when problems arose they would be called on to assist in military activities. Some performers, including Nomkhosi Mini (daughter of activist and composer Vuyisile Mini), were killed in the course of these activities ('Obituary'; Ntombela, 1993).

Certain locations, generally large halls, were designated as both residential and rehearsal spaces, where the group could practise and perform for regional audiences. In the first few years of Amandla's existence, performances were limited to the local scene around Luanda and in the camps. Its first international exposure came in 1980, when a 32-member group embarked on a tour of the Scandinavian countries, after three months' intensive preparation (Ntombela, 1993).[21] It was at this point that Gwangwa – who had not been present at the 1978 Youth and Students' festival in Cuba, and had until now not been formally involved with the group – was called to Luanda to assist with the instrumental component of the performance (Gwangwa, 2004; Gwangwa, 1985). Excited by the range of undeveloped talent he found, he set to work with the performers, planning choreographic routines, shaping a plot line, developing the show's instrumental and vocal components, and introducing traditional dances. With his arrival, the show that was to earn the group an international reputation began to be developed in earnest. Gwangwa became the group's artistic director, and Ndonda Khuze its 'political commissar' (Ntombela, 1993).

Mayibuye's performances, as mentioned earlier, were often substantially modified: choices of poems and songs varied widely, narrative was changed dramatically depending on where the group was performing, and performance length could range from twenty minutes to two hours. Amandla's presentation, by contrast, was a theatrical production of around three hours' length, carefully crafted and staged, with a segment towards the end devoted to a regularly updated discussion of current events in South Africa. It also involved a much larger cast of around 35 members, who trained on a full-time basis and became increasingly professionalised. It incorporated dramatic segments, a variety of vocal pieces, a medley of traditional dances with elaborate costumes, and an instrumental jazz band that eventually grew to fourteen members. It also boasted its own Amandla stage backdrop created by the well-known activist and graphic artist Thami Mnyele, displaying the words 'Amandla: Cultural Ensemble of the African National Congress' alongside an image of a raised fist clenching a spear.[22]

Amandla's musical repertoire also differed substantially from that of its precursor. While Mayibuye drew primarily on freedom songs and produced no original musical material,[23] much of Amandla's music was newly composed or arranged by Gwangwa and other ensemble members. The group's repertoire drew additionally on the culture of exile and the MK camps, including freedom songs like 'Umkhonto' and 'Sobashiy'abazali' ('We will leave our parents'), one of the most popular songs in the camps at the time:[24]

Sobashiy'abazal'ekhaya
Saphuma sangena kwamany'amazwe
Lapho kungazi khon'ubaba no mama
silandel'inkululeko

Sithi salan, salan, salan'ekhaya
Sesingena kwamany'amazwe
Lapho kungazi khon'ubaba no mama
silandel'inkululeko

Sobashiy'abafowethu
Saphuma sangena kwamany'amazwe
Lapho kungazi khon'ubaba no mama
silandel'inkululeko

[We will leave our parents at home / We go in and out of foreign countries / To places our fathers and mothers don't know / Following freedom
We say goodbye, goodbye, goodbye home / We are going in to foreign countries / To places our fathers and mothers don't know / Following freedom
We will leave our siblings / We go in and out of foreign countries / To places our fathers and mothers don't know / Following freedom]

'Sobashiy'abazali', like many of the songs popular in the camps, projected a markedly different character to those that were popular inside South Africa. Particularly in its Amandla incarnation, the music itself was faster, more upbeat and energetic, and its militaristic rhythm – with accompanying marching actions – was a gesture towards the marching step of the soldiers. The lyrics, too, avoided the more powerless and despairing sense of songs like 'Senzenina' ('What have we done') and 'Thina sizwe' ('We African people') – two of the most popular songs in South Africa at the time – preferring a more positive, encouraging and affirmative outlook: the idea of 'following freedom' despite the difficulty of leaving home. Amandla also sang favourites like 'Sikhokhele Tambo' ('Lead us, Tambo') and 'Rolihlahla Mandela' – songs that were also included in Mayibuye's performances, but sung by Amandla at a faster tempo, with a distinctively more militaristic and optimistic flavour.[25] The difference in character between the two ensembles was also partly the result of Mayibuye being a small amateur group, as opposed to the increasingly polished, professional production that was Amandla.

The dramatic segments of Amandla's performance offered a potted history of racial oppression in South Africa. The show opened with the idyllic depiction of life in a peaceful precolonial village, followed by the arrival of the white colonists, the formation of the ANC, the advent of industrialisation and the destructive effects of forced migration to the cities. The dramatic action was accompanied by a live onstage band, and interspersed with songs like 'Ekhaya lam' ('My home') and 'Before they came', lamenting the effects of colonialism on South Africa's indigenous peoples. These songs were not the unaccompanied call-and-response style freedom songs, but Gwangwa's frequently sentimental offerings sung by swaying vocalists behind microphones with backing singers, dressed in attractively co-ordinated outfits. The show continued with more historical vignettes of South Africa under apartheid, interspersed with scenes about women, the Freedom Charter, some dramatised conversations with current political content (about the ANC, the United Democratic Front, and particularly MK), and a portrayal of the 1976 Soweto uprising.[26] One of the most prominent scenes was a dance medley incorporating Zulu, Venda, Xhosa, Shangaan, Sotho and other traditional dances; former members emphasised that these dances were deliberately intended to assert the value of indigenous South African cultures as part of a larger, shared conception of national identity, and to refuse apartheid's distorted notions of ethnic particularity and separate development (Gwangwa, 2004; Khuze, 1985).[27]

On one level Amandla was, as Gwangwa put it, a 'highly political show' (2004). It contained some echoes of Mayibuye's agitprop style, including rousing declamations against apartheid and the use of popular political slogans, such as 'an injury to one is an injury to all', and sections of the Freedom Charter; it also included several freedom songs and a *toyi-toyi*.[28] The primary elements and aims of the liberation struggle were plainly portrayed, as were the conditions of life under apartheid. The overriding spirit, however, was affirmative rather than angry, forward-looking rather than vengeful. With Amandla, the open antagonism and sarcasm that characterised Mayibuye were toned down, and channelled into a more positive, dynamic representation of black South African culture.

In addition to freedom songs and new compositions, for example, the group's musical repertoire featured popular township music, including instrumental penny whistle *kwela* and *mbaqanga*, at the time also referred to as African jazz.[29] This fitted with the goal of exposing 'indigenous South African culture', or at least the kind of music that was popular amongst ordinary black South Africans (Gwangwa, 2004). The show also echoed some of the theatrical ideas that had gained prominence at home. The 1970s had witnessed a flourishing of theatrical initiatives amongst urban black populations within South Africa, including the development of radical Black Consciousness theatre (which became influential particularly amongst the youth) and popular township musicals by Gibson Kente and others. Gwen Ansell has written that Amandla had clandestine contact with this 'flowering new theatre scene' (2004: 247); even if direct interaction was not extensive, the large influx of youths into the MK camps after the 1976 uprising, many of whom themselves joined Amandla, undoubtedly meant that the group was in touch with current cultural trends in South Africa.[30]

Amandla was well regarded within the ANC, and its work was considered a valuable contribution to the project of national liberation. This contribution was seen to consist of two key elements: first, increasing international awareness about apartheid and raising funds; and second, presenting an alternative vision of culture in a future democratic South Africa. Raising international awareness was of course a crucial part of the ANC's wider mission, and a cultural ensemble was – as the experience of Mayibuye had shown – an effective medium for rousing emotions and mobilising support. Amandla became a successful ambassador for the ANC, travelling throughout Africa and as far afield as South America, Canada, Europe, Southeast Asia, Australia and the Soviet Union. The group also produced two records during its Soviet trips in 1982 and 1987.[31] NEC member Ruth Mompati claimed that Amandla educated international audiences more successfully than many conferences and seminars were able to do (1986: 19). The group also distributed informational literature at its shows and directed interested persons to the local ANC offices, where representatives could provide further information and organise volunteer work. Where they had occasion to address their audiences after performances, Amandla members were vocal in calling on individuals and governments to boycott South Africa and cut all ties with the apartheid regime.

It is worth noting that although Mayibuye and Amandla were official representatives of the ANC, there was little formal intervention from the movement regarding the kind of material they could present. However, both were closely engaged with broader trends that defined cultural activity within the movement, and stood at the helm of efforts to establish culture's role in the larger process of national liberation. A considerable number of their songs made reference to ANC leaders like Luthuli, Tambo, Sisulu, and especially Mandela, honouring their leadership and calling for political guidance. They also regularly updated their performances in response to shifting political circumstances, and Mayibuye in particular took pains to align its efforts 'in accordance with the political needs of solidarity work' (Feinberg, 1977: 43). In turn, they were enthusiastically supported by the ANC leadership. ANC President Tambo himself, in addition to assisting Amandla with the acquisition of costumes and instruments, wrote the lyrics to some of the choral items in the show (Gwangwa, 2004; Mbeki, 1985).

A second, equally important part of Amandla's objective was projecting an affirmative image of culture in the envisaged united, democratic South Africa. Official ANC discourse regarding the group emphasised that the imposed culture of the coloniser, and the concomitant devaluation and neglect of 'inferior' indigenous culture, needed to be actively resisted. Speaking on the British documentary *Song of the Spear*, Thabo Mbeki, as Head of Information and Publicity, stressed that affirming black South African culture was integral to the process of liberation, since what was necessary was not only eliminating the outward manifestations of oppression, but also its attendant individual and collective psychological effects. Asserting culture was a rebellious act of asserting national identity and refusing colonised status. A democratic and expressive 'people's culture', in other words, was not something that would come after liberation, but was an essential psychological requirement for *achieving* liberation (Mbeki, 1985).[32] Barbara Masekela, who served as Head of the Department of Arts and Culture from shortly after its establishment in 1982, similarly stressed that in addition to international mobilisation, the conscious intention behind Amandla was to counteract perceptions of black South Africans as mere victims of apartheid. Through Amandla's performances, she argued, the humanity of black South Africa in all its richness and diversity became more palpable, and audiences were presented with an affirmative, dynamic vision of an alternative South African culture (Masekela, 1985).

A Vision for Whom?

During the time that Amandla was functioning, an increasingly coherent conception of culture and its role in the struggle was emerging across a wide range of forums within the ANC, including conferences, journal articles, speeches and interviews with both artists and leadership. It was widely agreed that the ideal art was not elitist or exclusive, but was intimately connected with 'the people'. Its purpose was not only to portray their plight – according to artist Thami Mnyele, this in isolation was the theme of 'defeatist' township art – but to articulate their 'hopes and aspirations', to encourage commitment to the struggle, and to promote the affirmative values of a democratic South Africa. The kind of art that provided mere entertainment for the masses was also considered unacceptable: truly revolutionary art served to educate, awaken political consciousness and galvanise people to action. Finally, art was a vehicle for condemning the regime and informing the world about apartheid.[33] In short, culture was emphatically promoted as 'a weapon in the struggle for national liberation and democracy in our country' (Langa, 1988: 26-7).

Amandla's performance echoed these conceptions to a certain extent, and the official discourse around it promoted it as the epitome of 'the emerging culture of liberation'.[34] At the same time, however, this discourse existed in tension with a simultaneous emphasis on producing a show that would first and foremost appeal to international audiences. As suggested at the outset, the tension relates primarily to a lack of conscious distinction in the movement's conception between culture's roles in the internal nation-building process and international solidarity work – in short, between its internal and external roles. Amandla's declared intention was to promote an affirmative vision of an alternative South African culture: but a vision for whom?

In order to untangle this issue it is worth considering briefly how these questions about culture relate to the ANC's broader political strategy in exile. Underlying the movement's attitude towards cultural activity there seems to have been an inability or unwillingness to recognise that what was common practice on the diplomatic front – recognising the distinctive requirements of internal and external strategy – should have been equally applicable to culture. The political scientist Tom Lodge (1988) has shown, for example, that the nature of ANC political rhetoric in internal forums like the journal *Sechaba* or the underground station Radio Freedom was markedly different from the rhetoric that characterised the movement's diplomatic work abroad. Examining the multiple ideological and organisational strands that constituted the liberation movement, Raymond Suttner has similarly argued that particularly in the context of exile, '[w]hat was made public tended to conceal what diversity there may have been, behind official statements presenting a face of unity to the public' (2003: 306). It seems obvious and inevitable that internally- and externally-focused strategies had distinct functions: while there was ongoing discussion within the movement about a range of tactical and organisational issues, the intricacies of these internal debates were entirely separate from the public face of the movement's campaign for international support. For international audiences, the struggle needed to be kept on simple and translatable terms.[35]

On the subject of culture, however, such distinctions were less clearly articulated. In the case of Mayibuye, agitprop was the unashamed and open agenda: culture was primarily a vehicle for conscientising the international community and raising funds. Amandla was more complicated, because although it was designed primarily for international audiences, it was conceived and promoted with the same rhetoric used to describe culture's internal role in the struggle.[36]

Both the content and character of Amandla's shows reflected the increasing shift during the 1980s towards 'people's art' and connection with the 'broad masses'. The group travelled widely in Africa and frequently performed for South African exiles in Angola, Zambia and elsewhere;[37] its records were also available (albeit illegally) within South Africa, and were frequently broadcast on Radio Freedom.[38] The language of protest, the militaristic culture of the MK camps, and the depiction of life under apartheid were important components of the show, as we have seen, and parts of the performance deliberately resonated with the musical and theatrical ideas that defined 'people's culture' back home.

At the same time, considering Amandla in comparison with cultural trends within South Africa helps to situate it more clearly in terms of the internal-external paradigm. Black musical theatre flourished in 1970s South Africa, as previously mentioned, but it was far from a monolithic phenomenon – by contrast, it was a terrain of not only commercial but also political and ideological rivalry. Government-sanctioned 'tribal musicals' like *uMabatha* (1973), *Meropa* (1973), *Ipi Tombi* (1975), and *King Africa* (1987) effectively celebrated the apartheid status quo (Peterson, 1990: 234). There were several more genuinely collaborative interracial ventures, such as Ian Bernhardt and Barney Simon's Phoenix Players, Athol Fugard and the Serpent Players in Port Elizabeth, and Workshop '71, as well as a thriving black commercial theatre dominated by Gibson Kente and Sam Mhangwani. Black Consciousness cultural organisations rejected both collaboration with whites and the theatre of Kente and Mhangwani; they advocated 'serious' political theatre, and became influential amongst the increasingly politicised and militant youth.[39]

Although these developments emerged in the repressive context of apartheid, the paradoxical distinction is that while such diversity was possible in the broader social setting of South Africa, Amandla – as an official political vehicle – was more constrained as far as cultural expression was concerned. Ultimately, Amandla's most important objective was to create a polished, entertaining piece of musical theatre that would educate and win over foreign audiences – a priority that came with its own obstacles and implications. Writing about local South African 'adversarial' theatre that was marketed abroad during the 1980s, Ian Steadman points to the problems of theatre that 'is made out of the struggles of the people but not consumed by the people'. In particular, the image of the country presented to foreign audiences is necessarily a selective one, which as a result sometimes 'reinforces the very stereotypes that it seeks to undermine' (1990: 227-8).[40] With regard to film, Rob Nixon similarly argues that popular representations intended to deepen outrage over apartheid and mobilise foreign audiences needed to make certain modifications in order to render the struggle not only accessible, but also acceptable, to those audiences (1994: 78-9).

An evocative example of Amandla's focus on affirmative representations of South Africa for international audiences, and the sublimation of more violent or radical expressions, can be found in the discrepancy between its music and lyrics. The song texts – primarily in Xhosa and Zulu – often express defiance, vengeance, and commitment to the armed struggle, as in the example of 'Kulonyaka' ('In this year'):[41]

Kulonyaka sizimisele
Ukugwaza lamabhunu
ngoMkhonto we Sizwe

Asikhathali noma sibulawa
Sizolilwela ilizwe lomzantsi

Hlanganani nina ma-Afrika
Sowanqoba simunye wona lamabhunu

[This year we are prepared / To stab Boers / With MK ... We do not care even if we are killed / We are going to fight for the land of the South ... Unite you Africans / We will be victorious over the Boers when we are one]

The accompanying music, however, projects a rather different character: upbeat and melodious, with no signs of the aggression or combativeness suggested in the lyrics. Many of Amandla's songs reflect a similar dynamic. 'Mogosi wala' ('The call has been made'), for example, combines revolutionary lyrics in the verses – the 'Wathint'abafazi wathint'imbokodo' ('You strike a woman, you strike a rock') slogan famously chanted by women demonstrators at the Union Buildings on 9 August 1956 – with the somewhat sentimental English-language refrain 'Side by side, women of the world, side by side, fight for freedom', on a similarly light-hearted, melodious musical background.[42] For listeners unable to understand the lyrics – the bulk of international audiences, in other words – Amandla might conceivably be described as an entertaining musical with a clear but not overly heavy-handed political message, beautiful costumes, compelling dances, and memorable tunes. For all its legitimate emphasis on people's culture, the image that it presented of black South Africa was in parts a somewhat superficial one: for example, the idyllic precolonial life; the women fighting 'side by side' for freedom; even the traditional dances, which despite intentions might have served to perpetuate Western conceptions of unsophisticated 'tribal' Africa. Although its motivations were entirely antithetical to apartheid propaganda creations like *Ipi Tombi* and others, this distinction might not always have been clear to uninformed international audiences.[43] The show was an upbeat, energetic, toe-tapping, full-of-life musical that was partly about the struggle against apartheid, but perhaps more importantly about exposing and celebrating the vitality of South African culture and having audiences rocking in their seats.

Such tendencies are unsurprising and unavoidable in a popular musical of this kind. As Nixon concedes, in order for a popular representation to be politically useful, 'authenticity' cannot be the only criterion (1994: 94-5). International awareness-raising and internal nation-building are largely distinct tasks. While it took pains to present some of the most vibrant current elements of black South African culture, and genuinely affirmed many of the movement's most important cultural ideals, Amandla's primary function was ultimately mobilising international support. It was this objective, necessarily and inevitably, that surely governed the bulk of its artistic and narrative choices.

The difference between culture's internal and external functions – more precisely, the frequent lack of distinction between them within the movement – perhaps offers some insight into why, despite ample interest, the initiative to revive Amandla in early 1990s and post-apartheid South Africa was unsuccessful. A host of potential factors inform this issue, including probable financial limitations, and a more general difficulty in promoting the history and culture of the liberation struggle through the media (which was still, in the early post-apartheid years, largely controlled by the old establishment) (Ntombela, 1993; Feinberg, pers. comm., 4 July 2005). It also seems possible, however, that it was in part because Amandla did not resonate with the emerging identity and culture of the new South Africa, or that once liberation had been achieved it could speak very little to the complexity that followed in the wake of transition. It seems understandable, given the purpose for which it was created, that Amandla would have a limited contribution to make to the process of nation-building. Nonetheless, the frustration of those who hoped to resume its work seems to have stemmed from the unrealistic expectation that it could do both: dazzle international audiences and win their support; and simultaneously project a vision that expressed the deepest hopes and aspirations of the movement and the masses, in the momentous transition from the struggle against apartheid to the birth of a new nation.

REFLECTIONS ON CULTURE AT THE THRESHOLD OF A NEW ERA

By 1989, at the height of a decade in which culture was promoted, debated, and celebrated with increasing intensity, Albie Sachs declared that a shift was necessary. His comments sparked a lengthy debate that was, as Ingrid de Kok has suggested, probably on the threshold of expression anyway (1990: 11). In several interviews and writings in 1990 clarifying his position, Sachs referred to the political transition that was in progress, arguing that culture needed to move in tandem with the shift from struggle to nation-building. His intention was to open up debate within the movement and encourage members to move beyond the 'tight, defensive posture' that had been necessary to survive repression and exile, towards considering how culture might perform the more complex, affirmative role of envisioning the emergent new South Africa (Langa, 1990: 30-1; Sachs, 1990: 146-7).

Although Sachs's paper focused on culture's role in the context of transition, the debate that exploded around it repeatedly returned to the division between culture's internal and external roles. Several of his critics drew attention to Sachs' status as an exile, arguing that he was out of touch with what was happening in South Africa, and defending the vitality and diversity of cultural developments inside the country. Some made a clear distinction between the latter and work geared towards the international community, which was more likely to tend towards the shallow and formulaic.[44] Their concerns were later echoed by Barbara Masekela, who in a 1993 interview claimed that while the ANC had used culture successfully 'as a kind of showpiece or slogan', it ultimately did not recognise the value of culture as an internally-focused medium for strengthening community and building national self-esteem (Masekela, 1993.). Was Sachs basing his remarks about slogans and formulae primarily on the cultural activity with which he had come into contact in exile? Was he thinking about art geared towards the international community rather than that being produced by the oppressed masses at home, as some of his critics implied? These issues remain open to debate, but nevertheless illuminate how the internal-external dynamic affects the way in which the role of culture in the struggle might be conceived and understood. The cases of Mayibuye and Amandla reaffirm that while diversity and inconsistency were possible (and even desirable) within South Africa, political and cultural work in exile necessarily had distinct priorities and aims.

As ambassadors for the ANC, Mayibuye and Amandla made valuable contributions to the movement's work and successfully brought the anti-apartheid struggle to international audiences. Though the differences between them on the levels of form, content, approach, and presentation were dramatic, their shared, overriding objective was diplomatic – projecting an image of South Africa that would encourage the international community to lend its political and financial support. Sachs's comments offer a valuable point of reflection regarding the larger context of culture's relationship to the struggle and point towards a new phase in that relationship: the process, beginning in the late 1980s, of 'preparing ourselves for freedom'. To what degree did cultural activity adapt itself to the changing needs of this nascent era? Was culture primarily conceived as a vehicle for externally-focused propaganda, or was there substantive recognition of its value to the internal struggle for liberation? Further, did culture ever achieve equal status with 'real' political work? The extent to which cultural activity contributed to the political transition of the 1980s and 90s, as well as the ongoing process of nation-building in South Africa, is an area ripe for further discussion.

ENDNOTES

1. This essay first appeared in the *Journal of Southern African Studies*, 33(2), 2007, pp. 421-41, and is reprinted by permission of Taylor & Francis Ltd.
2. The word 'culture' occupies an important place in ANC vocabulary. While in a wider intellectual context the term bears multiple and contested meanings, within the movement its usage indicates a fairly clear conceptualisation of culture, in the words of Raymond Williams, as 'the works and practices of intellectual and especially artistic activity'. The word was used to refer to music, literature and poetry, graphic arts, theatre, dance, as well as beadwork, crafts and other popular 'people's' arts. The widespread use of terms like 'cultural journal', 'cultural ensemble' and particularly 'cultural workers', as well as the ANC's conceptualisation of art more generally as a 'weapon of struggle', derives from Soviet ideas about art and the rhetoric of socialist realism. While I have attempted to minimise my use of more outdated terminology in the article (preferring in particular the more neutral 'cultural activity'), my use of the word 'culture' parallels its connotations within the movement itself, and is used interchangeably with the word 'art'.
3. *Umkhonto we Sizwe* (Spear of the Nation), popularly known as MK, was the ANC's military wing.
4. In addition to several oral interviews and a collection of private papers, my documentation is based primarily on archival materials held at the University of the Western Cape–Robben Island Mayibuye Archives. These materials are surprisingly extensive, and include sound and video recordings of performances; recordings broadcast by the ANC's underground radio station, Radio Freedom; performance scripts, programmes and reviews; photographs; ANC newspapers and journals; interviews with group members and ANC representatives, many conducted in exile; and other miscellaneous documentation.
5. The existing literature on South African freedom songs is sparse and variable. See, for example, Kivnick (1990); and Pollard (1999); and for elsewhere in southern Africa, Vail and White (1983).
6. For a range of early responses to Sachs's paper, see De Kok and Press (1990).
7. Barry Feinberg's private materials: Mermaid Theatre Programme for *Poets to the People*.

8 Script for Mermaid Theatre *Poets to the People* production, University of the Western Cape–Robben Island Mayibuye Archives [hereafter MA], Historical Papers, MCH89. Further references to this performance and to Mayibuye's activities more generally are drawn from the same archival source, which consists of hundreds of uncatalogued documents: correspondence, press clippings, programmes and flyers, scripts, and other miscellaneous materials relating to Mayibuye.
9 At that time, Kasrils was writing and performing under the pseudonym ANC Kumalo.
10 Barry Feinberg's private materials: *Poets to the People* promotional pamphlet.
11 MA, Historical Papers, MCH89: B Feinberg, 'Mayibuye Report'. The struggle between these positions persisted for much of Mayibuye's existence, though professionalisation came increasingly to be recognised as the only viable option as the group experienced increasing demand in the late 1970s.
12 Those who came to play principal roles in the group included Godfrey Motsepe, Zarina Chiba, Melody Mancube, James Madhlope Phillips, Pallo Jordan, Bongi Dhlomo and Poppy Nokwe.
13 As Mayibuye was a voluntary organisation, the size of the group depended on where the performance was to take place, the funds available and which members were available to travel.
14 In the US context see, for example, Seeger (1965: 11); and Hsiung (2005: 23-6).
15 MA, Historical Papers, MCH89: various performance scripts; MA, Oral History & Sound, RF 491. Thanks to Brenda Mhlambi (University of the Witwatersrand, Johannesburg) for these and subsequent translations.
16 MA, Film & Video, M5 and M6; MA, Photographs, A24-3-4 and uncatalogued print.
17 MA, Oral History & Sound, RF 491.
18 MA, Historical Papers, MCH89.
19 The record, titled *Spear of the Nation*, was produced in Hilversum, Holland as Varagram ET44.
20 MA, Historical Papers, MCH89: Feinberg, various drafts of report, c.1978-9.
21 The funding for Amandla's travels generally came from solidarity groups in the countries where they performed. ANC representatives in those countries would co-ordinate expenditure and part of the funds raised would be left there to support further solidarity work. Some funds were also devoted to supporting the Solomon Mahlangu Freedom College (Somafco) in Tanzania (Gwangwa, 2004).
22 These and further references to Amandla's activities are drawn from a range of archival sources: MA, Film & Video, VA11, VA30 and VA31; MA, Oral History & Sound, MCA5-1333, MCA5-1351, MCA5-041, MCA5-042, MCA5-043, MCA5-045, MCA5-156, MCA5-158, MCA5-159, MCA5-160, MCA5-161, MCA5-162, MCA5-163.

23 Mayibuye did, however, produce new musical arrangements for many of the freedom songs it performed.
24 MA, Film & Video, VA30, VA31; MA, Oral History & Sound, MCA5-1333.
25 MA, Oral History & Sound, RF267, RF163, RF 356, MCA5-1333.
26 MA, Film & Video, VA30. The Freedom Charter was the historic manifesto adopted at the Congress of the People at Kliptown on 26 June 1955. In this scene, around 20 performers stood in formation on the stage, one by one declaiming key phrases from the Charter: 'The people shall govern!', 'All national groups shall have equal rights!', 'The people shall share in the country's wealth!', 'All shall be equal before the law', and so on. The United Democratic Front (UDF) was formed in 1983 as an umbrella organisation to co-ordinate resistance activities inside South Africa (see Seekings, 2000).
27 The refusal of apartheid notions of 'tribalism' was widespread in ANC discourse, particularly on the subject of culture; see for example Mompati (1986: 20). Tambo also explicitly articulated this idea in an interview for the launch issue of *Rixaka*, arguing that while the apartheid government tried to separate non-whites into 'ancient "tribal" entities', the ANC conceived of a single people with a rich, diverse cultural heritage, and saw these diverse cultural forms as the possession of the people, rather than divisive forms of tribal identification (1985: 22).
28 The *toyi-toyi* is a militant dance that ANC exiles probably learned from Zimbabwean guerrillas when they joined forces with ZAPU in the late 1960s. The Oxford *Dictionary of South African English on Historical Principles* defines the *toyi-toyi* as 'A quasi-military dance-step characterised by high-stepping movements, performed either on the spot or while moving slowly forwards, usually by participants in (predominantly black) protest gatherings or marches, and accompanied by chanting, singing [of freedom songs], and the shouting of slogans' (1996: 730).
29 *Kwela* is a popular improvisational style that developed on township streets during the 1950s and 60s, its primary instrument the cheap and portable penny whistle. As Louise Meintjes has suggested in a different context, the *kwela* sound brings with it particular associations as one of the most important expressive forms in the black townships during one of the most repressive decades of apartheid (1990: 43-4). *Mbaqanga* is a distinctively South African hybrid, composed of a blend of American swing, *marabi* (popular music that developed in shebeens during the 1930s) and a syncretic melodic style more closely related to 'neo-traditional South African music' than American jazz. Lara Allen explains that the term *mbaqanga* (Zulu for stiff maize porridge) was used disparagingly by musicians to refer to African jazz, particularly

in its recorded form, because they played it in order to earn quick 'bread money' (2003: 240; Ballantine, 1991: 150).
30 At least one of the group's most prominent members, Ndonda Khuze, had been actively involved with Black Consciousness cultural activities inside South Africa (Khuze, 1985).
31 MA, Oral History & Sound, MCA5-1351 and MCA5-1333.
32 *Song of the Spear* was produced by the London-based International Defence and Aid Fund for Southern Africa (IDAF) in 1986, was jointly sponsored by the ANC and IDAF, and was directed by Barry Feinberg.
33 These ideas appeared increasingly frequently, often almost verbatim, in a wide range of contexts. See, for example, Mooki (1986); Williams (1980); Tambo (1985); Masekela (1986).
34 MA, Film & Video, S9: *Song of the Spear*.
35 Further analysis of this issue lies beyond the scope of this article, particularly given the range of contexts in which the ANC was operating outside South Africa for over three decades. For more on exile and internal-external relations, see Suttner (2003); Lodge (1988); Lodge (1983: chap. 12); and Seekings (2000).
36 In an interesting parallel, a similar conceptual blurriness seems to have characterised the cultural boycott, probably the most visible dimension of culture in the international arena. Rob Nixon has argued that while the internal movement advocated using culture to reshape social life and institutions inside South Africa (in anticipation of transition), international representatives were focused on maintaining support for anti-apartheid activities abroad – a persistent conflict of approach that rendered the boycott 'symbolically powerful but strategically vexing' (1994: 157).
37 The questions of how Amandla might have modified its performance for different audiences, particularly South African versus foreign audiences, and to what extent its historical narrative changed over the ten years of its existence, are difficult to answer precisely. Recorded evidence (both video and audio) of the performances is sparse, and only fragmentary details emerge from interviews with former members. A fuller reception history of the group's international performances would enrich this research in important ways, but lies beyond the scope of this article.
38 *Rixaka* reported, for example, that one Derek Tsietsi Makomoreng received five years' imprisonment earlier that year for possessing a cassette of Amandla's music (1986: 29).
39 On theatrical trends inside South Africa during the 1970s and 1980s, see Kavanagh (1985); Kerr (1995); Orkin (1991); Peterson (1990); Steadman (1990). On Kente and township musical theatre, see also Coplan (1985: 207-15).

40 Steadman argues that plays that toured overseas, like *Woza Albert!*, *Bopha*, and *Sarafina*, presented a simplified, 'marketed' image of political struggle, using familiar images like the *toyi-toyi*, the 'necklace' and freedom songs. For more on how South African musicians and shows were 'Africanised' for foreign audiences, see also Ansell (2004: 225-6).

41 MA, Oral History & Sound, RF541.

42 MA, Oral History & Sound, RF349 and RF433. 9 August 1956 marked the apex of the women's anti-pass campaign, when some 20 000 women converged to demonstrate at the Union Buildings in Pretoria. Among the freedom songs sung at the event was the chant 'Wathint'abafazi, wathint'imbokodo, uzakufa' (You strike a woman, you strike a rock, you will be crushed), which was quickly appropriated in popular discourse, and became a powerful symbol of women's involvement in the struggle.

43 For discussion of *Ipi Tombi* and similar productions see Peterson (1990: 234); also Ansell (2004: 181).

44 See in particular R Siers, 'Vampire Bats of Ambiguous Metaphors'; G Younge, 'Running in the Sackrace'; and F Meintjies, 'Albie Sachs and the Art of Protest'; all in De Kok and Press (1990).

Bibliography

Allen, Lara. 2003. 'Commerce, Politics, and Musical Hybridity: Vocalizing Urban Black South African Identity During the 1950s'. *Ethnomusicology*, 47(2), pp. 228-49.

Ansell, Gwen. 2004. *Soweto Blues: Jazz, Popular Music, and Politics in South Africa*. New York & London: Continuum.

Ballantine, Christopher. 1991. 'Music and Emancipation: The Social Role of Black Jazz and Vaudeville in South Africa Between the 1920s and the Early 1940s'. *Journal of Southern African Studies*, 17(1), pp. 129-52.

Coplan, David B. 1985. *In Township Tonight! South Africa's Black City Music and Theatre*. Johannesburg: Ravan Press.

De Kok, I, & K Press (eds). 1990. *Spring is Rebellious: Arguments about Cultural Freedom*. Cape Town: Buchu Books.

Feinberg, Barry (ed.). 1974. *Poets to the People: South African Freedom Poems*. London: Allen & Unwin.

_. 1977. 'Mayibuye – Cultural Weapon of the ANC'. *Sechaba*, pp. 41-45.

_. 2004. Author's interview. Cape Town, 28 April.

Gastrow, S. 1995. *Who's Who in South African Politics*. Johannesburg: Ravan Press.

Gwangwa, Jonas. 1985. Interview with Barry Feinberg. MA, Oral History & Sound, MCA5-153.

_. c.1989-1991. Interview with Hilda Bernstein. MA, Oral History & Sound, MCA7-1511.

_. 2004. Author's interview. Johannesburg, 13 August.

Hsiung, DC. 2005. 'Freedom Songs and the Modern Civil Rights Movement'. *Magazine of History*, 19, pp. 23-26.

James, Deborah. 2000. *Songs of the Women Migrants: Performance and Identity in South Africa*. Johannesburg: Wits University Press.

Kavanagh, RM. 1985. *Theatre and Cultural Struggle in South Africa*. London: Zed Press.

Kerr, D. 1995. *African Popular Theatre*. London: James Currey.

Khuze, Ndoda. 1985. Interview, MA, Oral History & Sound, MCA5-161.

Kivnick, HQ. 1990. *Where is the Way: Song and Struggle in South Africa*. New York: Penguin.

Kumalo, ANC. [Ronnie Kasrils]. 1974. 'Red our Colour'. In Barry Feinberg (ed.). *Poets to the People: South African Freedom Poems*. London: Allen & Unwin, pp. 41-2.

Langa, M. 1990. 'Interview with Albie Sachs'. *Rixaka*, 1, pp. 30-1.

_. March 1988. 'The Quiet Thunder: Report on the Amsterdam Cultural Conference'. *Sechaba*, pp. 26-7.

Lodge, Tom. 1983. *Black Politics in South Africa since 1945*. London & New York: Longman.

_. 1988. 'State of Exile: The African National Congress of South Africa, 1976–86'. In P Frankel, N Pines & M Swilling (eds). *State, Resistance and Change in South Africa*. London: Croom Helm, pp. 229-58.

Masekela, Barbara. 1993. Interview with Wolfie Kodesh. MA, Oral History & Sound, MCA6-312.

_. 1985. Interview with Barry Feinberg. MA, Oral History & Sound, MCA5-168.

_. 1986. 'Isolate Apartheid Culture'. *Rixaka*, 3, pp. 7-9.

Mbeki, Thabo. 1985. Interview with Barry Feinberg. MA, Oral History & Sound, MCA5-166.

Meintjes, Louise. 1990. 'Paul Simon's *Graceland*, South Africa, and the Mediation of Musical Meaning'. *Ethnomusicology*, 34(1), pp. 37-73.

Moema, T. 1980. 'Editorial'. *Medu Newsletter*, 2(1), pp. 1-3.

Mompati, Ruth. 1986. 'Interview with Ruth Mompati'. *Rixaka*, 2, pp. 19-22.

Mooki, B. 1986. 'Popular Theatre and Struggle'. *Rixaka*, 2, pp. 4-7.

Nixon, Rob. 1994. *Homelands, Harlem and Hollywood: South African Culture and the World Beyond*. New York & London: Routledge.

Ntombela, Man (Santana). 1993. Interview with Wolfie Kodesh. MA, Oral History & Sound, MCA6-343.

'Obituary' [Nomkhosi Mini]. 1986. *Rixaka*, 3, p. 25.

Orkin, M. 1991. *Drama and the South African State*. Johannesburg: Witwatersrand University Press.

Peterson, B. 1990. 'Apartheid and the Political Imagination in Black South African Theatre'. *Journal of Southern African Studies*, 16(2), pp. 229-45.

Pollard, AB. 1999. 'Rhythms of Resistance: The Role of Freedom Song in South Africa'. In AMS Nelson (ed.). *'This is How we Flow': Rhythm in Black Cultures*. Columbia: University of South Carolina Press, pp. 98-124.

'Render South Africa Ungovernable! Message of the National Executive Committee of the African National Congress on the 73rd Anniversary of ANC'. 8 January 1985. http://www.anc.org.za/ancdocs/history/or/or85-1.html, accessed 27 May 2004.

Sachs, Albie. 1998. 'Preparing Ourselves for Freedom'. In D Attridge & R Jolly (eds). *Writing South Africa: Literature, Apartheid, and Democracy, 1970-1995*. Cambridge: Cambridge University Press, pp. 239-48.

_. 1990. 'Afterword: The Taste of an Avocado Pear'. In I de Kok & K Press (eds). *Spring is Rebellious: Arguments about Cultural Freedom*. Cape Town: Buchu Books, pp. 145-48.

Seeger, P. 1965. 'You Can't Write Down Freedom Songs'. *Sing Out!*, 15(3), p. 11.

Seekings, J. 2000. *The UDF: A History of the United Democratic Front in South Africa, 1983-1991*. Oxford: James Currey.

Seidman, Judy. 2004. Author's interview. Johannesburg, 21 July.

Steadman, Ian. 1990. 'Towards Popular Theatre in South Africa'. *Journal of Southern African Studies*, 16(2), pp. 208-28.

Suttner, Raymond. 2003. 'Culture(s) of the African National Congress of South Africa: Imprint of Exile Experiences'. *Journal of Contemporary African Studies*, 21(2), pp. 303-20.

Szymczak, C. 2003. 'Music as a Cultural Weapon in the Life of Jonas Gwangwa'. M. Mus. diss., University of the Witwatersrand.

Tambo, OR. 1985. 'Interview with OR Tambo'. *Rixaka*, 1, pp. 21-22.

Vail, L, & L White. 1983. 'Forms of Resistance: Songs and Perceptions of Power in Colonial Mozambique'. *The American Historical Review*, 88(4), pp. 883-919.

Williams, T. 1980. 'An Interview with Thamsanqa Mnyele'. *Medu Newsletter*, 2(1), pp. 23-40.

'World Federation of Democratic Youth'. http://www.wfdy.org, accessed 4 June 2004.

9

'NKOSI SIKELEL' IAFRIKA'

STORIES OF AN AFRICAN ANTHEM

DAVID B COPLAN AND BENNETTA JULES-ROSETTE

Footprints of cultural artefacts travel across borderlands and boundaries of multiple inscription, from villages to towns and back again, between territories of the imagination and fetishised, armed and dangerous national states, imprinted in landscapes of experience and practice.[1] Anthropologists and oral historians have recently become fascinated with how rumours, fantastic tales, songs, and images become enshrined in a mobile African popular culture taken for granted by many of those who partake of it.[2] Children's songs, for example, have in their resilience played an important role in the indexical transmission of African history. So the demarcation of Basutoland's colonial borders by the British Resident Major Warden is memorialised in the satirical Basotho children's verse, 'Majoro Wardene, Majoro Wardene, Nka thipa ea hao u sehe naha' ('Major Warden, Major Warden / Take your knife and cut the country'). The objects circulating in this mobile popular culture blur the boundaries between sacred and secular, as well as public and private social life. In music, as with other popular arts, the framing of images through lyrics, harmonies, and melodies inscribes historic moments in what Johannes Fabian calls a remembrance of the present (1996: 226-77).[3] Each rendition of a song is connected to the community or context in which it is performed, imbuing the piece with a distinctive, historically emergent social and political meaning.

The hymn 'Nkosi Sikelel' iAfrika' ('God Bless Africa'), known as the African as well as South African national anthem, occupies a field of such experience and practice at the intersection of public religion and popular culture. Two decades ago, one of us wrote that '"Nkosi Sikelel' iAfrika" has come to symbolise more than any other piece of expressive culture the struggle for African unity and liberation in South Africa' (Coplan, 1985: 46). Yet the song's popularity extends beyond the borders of South Africa and the confines of the liberation struggle, especially during apartheid, that it so actively animated. Composed in the form of a blessing, the hymn offers a message of unity and uplift and an exhortation to act morally and spiritually on behalf of the entire African continent. A closer examination of the variations in both the hymn and its contexts of performance, however, reveals the complexities of its messages as they are presented in different performative spaces. The image of Africa and the conception of the blessing may be called into question depending on the groups performing the song and their intended audiences. So the field of song becomes a mutable *gestalt* that changes not only across linguistic and cultural categories and performance frames, but also within a single performance as 'Nkosi' moves from prefatory blessings to its closing exhortations (Gurwitsch, 1964: 144-146). In this regard, it is possible to question whether the first printed version of the song constitutes the 'original', and to examine the relationship of this text to the various settings in which 'Nkosi' is performed.

Songs are contextualised through their histories, fields and occasions of performance, and the presence of other songs and rituals performed in their immediate environment. Analysing a song as a single tune and text in terms of its fixed verse structure misplaces its concreteness in, in this case, a Western format and establishes the song as a cultural object about which claims of authorship and authenticity may be made. And so to deal, inescapably, with such claims: In 1897, Enoch M Sontonga, a teacher at a Methodist mission school in Nancefield, Johannesburg, composed 'Nkosi' as part of a repertoire of songs prepared for the students in his school (Jabavu, 1949: 56-58; Coplan, 1985: 44-45). Sontonga was a Tembu Xhosa of the Mpinga clan, born near Uitenhage in the eastern Cape colony in 1873 and trained at the Lovedale Mission Institution. He wrote the opening stanza of the song in isiXhosa, and the song was first performed publicly in 1899 at the ordination ceremony of Reverend M Boweni, the first Tsonga to become a clergyman in the Methodist or indeed any mission church. Sontonga was a man of parts; not merely a teacher but an accomplished poet, composer, choirmaster and lay preacher for the Church of Reverend PJ Mzimba, and an amateur photographer. He wrote the first verse and chorus of 'Nkosi Sikeleli' iAfrika' when he was 24, and later the same year composed the music.

Sontonga's choir sang the song around Johannesburg and KwaZulu-Natal, and other choirs followed them. Seven years after Sontonga's death in 1905, on 8 January 1912, after the closing prayer at the first meeting of the South African Native National Congress (SANNC, later the African National Congress (ANC)), it was sung by the Ohlange Institute Choir under Reuben T Caluza. The song was used in political street protests in Johannesburg as early as 1919. Solomon Plaatje, a founding member of the ANC and a writer, recorded the song in London on 16 October 1923, accompanied by Sylvia Colenso on the piano. In 1925, when the organisation changed its name to the ANC, it also adopted the song as its official anthem, to be sung at the close of all its meetings. 'Nkosi's' more universal and timeless vision thus replaced Reuben Caluza's 'iLand Act', a song protesting the dispossession embodied in the 1913 Natives Trust and Land Act, which was thought outdated and too topical. In 1927 the Lovedale Press in the eastern Cape published all the verses of 'Nkosi' in pamphlet form. It was included in the Presbyterian Xhosa hymnbook, *Incwadi Yama-culo Ase-rabe*, in 1929, where it was given the unique benefit of transcription in staff notation, and also published in a newspaper, *Umteteli wa Bantu*, on 11 June 1927, as well as in a Xhosa poetry book for schools. According to Alan Buff, Sontonga's wife Diana sold rights to the song for a sixpence before her death in 1929 (cited in Davie, 2002). It is rather a shame that no other Sontonga compositions are extant. One story goes that Sontonga used to lend his notebook of hand-transcribed songs to fellow teachers, one of whom failed to return it, leading to its disappearance. Ivy Rabotapi, Sontonga's granddaughter, also explained that she had an exercise book with three of the composer's songs when she lived in Sophiatown, but lost it in the removals to Soweto in 1955 (Rabotapi, 2000).

The additional seven stanzas of 'Nkosi', composed by poet Samuel EK Mqhayi, appeared in the author's first collection of poetry, *Imihobe Nemibongo* (Anthems of Praise), published in 1927. Mqhayi was a major literary figure in his own right, often referred to in his time as the 'Xhosa National Poet', and an avatar and embodiment of the 'New African'. The New Africanist movement was a response to whites' rejection of black middle-class aspirations, exposing the need for African unity across class as well as ethnic boundaries. Educated cultural leaders addressed these divisions in part by attempting to create a model African national culture for all classes of African townsmen (the 'New Africans'), and the performing arts played an important role in effecting the necessary synthesis.

Mqhayi was eulogised in 1945 by HIE Dhlomo, himself a leading New African figure:

> He was the last link, perhaps, between the tribal bard who could extemporise and declaim long lines of poetry at the spur of the moment, and the modern African who only writes his verse. Mqhayi could do both; and even some of his written work is reminiscent of izimbongi [praise singers]. Never will the writer of these notes forget the deeply moving experience he had each time he listened to Mqhayi composing and reciting poetry all at once (*Ilanga lase Natal*, 1 September 1945).

Tellingly, New Africanist author Jordan Ngubane emphasised Mqhayi's cross-ethnic black nationalist appeal: Mqhayi has been discovered not only to have been an outstanding poet among the Xhosas, but to have been a son of whom the Zulu, Sutho were rightly proud ... In other words, he lit the torch for the younger generation of African writers (*Inkundla ya Bantu*, 31 August 1945).

Mqhayi combined in his upbringing and education both a deep immersion in Xhosa law and custom (he was a descendant of Mqhayi, the great councillor to Chief Ngqika) and commitment to Presbyterian Christianity. It is perhaps no coincidence that one of his prose works, the African utopian narrative of *U-Don Jadu* (1929), foresees an integrated system based on a blend of indigenous political and legal principles and Christian prescriptive values in the realm of his pan-Africanist philosopher king (Gerard, 1971: 53-62). It is precisely this style of political and religious integration that we argue characterises the fundamental spirit of Sontonga's original verse, and that Mqhayi continues faithfully in his additional stanzas of 'Nkosi Sikelel' iAfrika'.

The original song reflects patterns of both Methodist hymnody and African praise singing, and we cannot know whether, in the common practice of African composers, Sontonga might have been inspired by an existing folk melody. Nevertheless, he took the step of combining generic Victorian hymn-tune harmony with an African blessing. As John Blacking put it, 'the appropriation of the triads and cadences of European hymn tunes expressed the new relationships and values of urban groups, who expected fuller participation in the social and political life into which they had been drawn economically' (cited in Erlmann, 1991: 198). Further, the hymn's invocation of the Holy Spirit (*Moya*) combines a fundamental Protestantism with African traditions of ritual cleansing.

Such spiritual as well as musical symbiosis enhanced the song's profound appeal across a variety of religious and secular settings and communities. After the ANC adopted it officially, the hymn accompanied and galvanised the organisation's victories and struggles as it travelled across borders into exile. The cast of the all-black musical play *King Kong* sang the anthem at

Johannesburg's airport upon their departure for London in 1960. Both non-African language speakers in the internal anti-apartheid movement and their comrades abroad recall the role that learning the anthem played in building solidarity and providing a stirring call to action. Yet as late as 1969, the apartheid government, having already banned the song, was still trying to deny its political status. Yvonne Huskisson, then director of music programming for the state's South African Broadcasting Corporation's Bantu Radio services, added a note to her entry for Sontonga in her biographical survey of black southern African composers: 'An abortive attempt was made by the African National Congress, using 'Nkosi Sikelel' iAfrika' to close their meetings, to insinuate that the ordinary Bantu singing this anthem were doing so in support of their organisation, its aims and policies' (Huskisson, 1969: 273). Yet not long before, the apartheid regime had cynically attempted to appropriate the symbolic status of 'Nkosi' by declaring it the national anthem of the 'independent' Xhosa homeland of the Transkei (Act of Parliament, No. 48 of 1963, Section 5; Comaroff and Comaroff, 1991: 3).

As the first verse of the national anthem of South Africa since 1997, 'Nkosi Sikelel' iAfrika' has been published officially in isiXhosa, isiZulu, Sesotho, English, and Afrikaans (Coplan, 1985: 46). Here is the full Sontonga-Mqhayi text:[4]

Nkosi, sikelel' iAfrika	Lord, bless Africa
Malupakam' upondo lwayo;	May her horn rise high up
Yiva imitandazo yetu	Hear Thou our prayers and bless us.
Chorus	Chorus:
Yihla Moya, yihla Moya	Descend O Spirit,
Yihla Moya Oyingcwele	Descend, O Holy Spirit
Sikelela iNkosi zetu;	Bless our chiefs
Zimkumbule umDali wazo;	May they remember their Creator.
Zimoyike zezimhlouele,	Fear Him and revere Him,
Azisikelele.	That He may bless them.
Sikelel' amadol' esizwe,	Bless the public men,
Sikelela kwa nomlisela	Bless also the youth
Ulitwal' ilizwe ngomonde,	That they may carry the land with patience
Uwusikilele.	And that Thou mayst bless them.

Sikelel' amakosikazi;	Bless the wives
Nawo onk'amanenekazi;	And also all young women;
Pakamisa wonk'umtinjana	Lift up all the young girls
Uwusikilele	And bless them.
Sikelela abafundisi	Bless the ministers
Bemvaba zonke zelilizwe;	of all the churches of this land;
Ubatwese ngoMoya Wako	Endue them with Thy Spirit
Ubasikelele.	And bless them.
Sikelel' ulimo nemfuyo;	Bless agriculture and stock raising
Gzota zonk'indlala nezifo;	Banish all famine and diseases;
Zalisa ilizwe nempilo	Fill the land with good health and bless it.
Ulisikelele	
Sikelel' amalinga etu	Bless our efforts of union and self-uplift,
Awomanyana nokuzaka,	Of education and mutual understanding
Awemfundo nemvisiswano	And bless them.
Uwasikele.	
Nkosi Sikelel, Afrika;	Lord, bless Africa
Cima bonk' ubugwenza bayo	Blot out all its wickedness
Neziggito, Nezono zayo	And its transgressions and sins,
Uwazikelele.	And bless us.

Sontonga's original song was an appeal beyond the injustice of powerful men (specifically the white rulers of the then Transvaal) to the all-powerful blessing and judgement of God. As part of South Africa's rising black elite at the turn of the century, Sontonga wished to impart a sense of hope and dignity to his students. The 'melancholy' and musical yearning of the song emerges, we explore below, from both Sontonga's likely social discontent and from his efforts to bring together two musical and cultural traditions with an air of solemnity and reverence (Coplan, 1985: 46).

From 1890 to 1898, Orpheus M McAdoo, a talented African-American who had attended Hampton Institute in Virginia, toured South Africa with a musical ensemble revived from Frederick Loudin's Fisk Jubilee Singers (Erlmann, 1991: 24-27; Martin, 1999: 85-89).[5] McAdoo, who had been a member of a quintet consisting of the original Fisk Jubilee Singers, formed his own group called the Virginia Jubilee Singers in 1889. The group's South African tours coincided with the emergence of a worldwide interest in black spirituals and minstrelsy as popular forms of entertainment.[6] The Virginia Jubilee Singers' repertoire consisted largely of spirituals and songs of uplift sung in four parts (Martin, 1999: 87). Although the style of singing that the Jubilee singers introduced was new to South Africa, it contained elements of call-and-response and rhythmic patterns that could easily be homologated onto traditional African tunes.

McAdoo's controversial tours overlapped with the beginning of the South African Anglo-Boer War, the arrival of an influx of black and white American Protestant missionaries, and the stirring of a heightened sense of political consciousness among South Africa's emerging black elite of clerks, teachers and professionals. The messages of the Virginia Jubilee Singers echoed the social aspirations of this class (Erlmann, 1991: 42).

The Virginia Jubilee Singers' tours also coincided with the expansion of the African Methodist Episcopal Church (AMEC) in South Africa, which welcomed McAdoo's presence as a valuable source of contact with the United States and a vehicle for reviving its liturgy. Gifted black South African students such as Simon Hoffa Sinamela managed to obtain scholarships to study in the United States through these networks. Sinamela also formed a group of African Jubilee

Ex. 1. 'Nkosi Sikelel' iAfrika' by Enoch Sontonga (Mutloatse, 1987: 165).

Singers who performed in South Africa and abroad. Veit Erlmann (1991: 49) reports that Sinamela produced a series of hymns that combined the Jubilee spirituals and songs of uplift with local forms of oratory and praise poetry. The result was a novel form of syncretic music.

Both the musical form and the content of Jubilee-style songs conveyed messages of spiritual and social protest masked under religious decorum and solemnity. The solemn sonorities and spiritual yearning characteristic of Sontonga's 'Nkosi Sikelel' iAfrika' were thus products, we may conclude, of an urban Afro-Christian syncretism (in isiXhosa: *isidolophu*) at a time of changing social consciousness and increasing cosmopolitanism among South Africa's black elite.

But the hymn goes beyond expression of simple frustration towards the expression of protest and resistance, albeit in a circumscribed manner. The ANC perhaps perceived this sense of protest and worked to enhance it in adopting and promoting its performance. Over the years, not only the ANC but countless other organisations and public gatherings made various uses of the song for political mobilisation and fundraising. Throughout the anti-apartheid struggle, ANC cultural groups such as Amandla toured and made recordings of 'Nkosi' in Europe and the United States to promulgate its political cause.[7] As migrant labourers moved into South Africa from other colonies and territories, they too were exposed to 'Nkosi' as a song of veiled protest that they took home with them, connecting the music and lyrics to new communities. The multidirectional stylistic voices of 'Nkosi' derives from its primary spiritual ethos of 'blessing' that allowed it to be appropriated and translated by institutions of mission education while serving as an anthem of protest for resistance movements and oppositional independent churches.

Changing frames: Is it the 'same old song'?

While missionaries moved north into what was at the time the Rhodesias, African migrant labourers travelled south in search of work in the mines, railroads, and industries of colonial South Africa. Within South Africa, rural-urban migration created a new mobile labour force whose religious and social outlets were fulfilled by neither traditional religion nor the missions. From the Zionists of Natal to the charismatic Apostolic groups ranging from Durban to Harare, a new type of Protestant hymnody arose, its compelling appeal in its capacity to link traditional 'sacred' songs, familiar rhythms, and Christian modalities. Two focal cases, discussed below, highlight contrasting versions and uses of 'Nkosi Sikelel' iAfrika' as a religious song, each of which have different ideological implications for the communities concerned. Although undoubtedly aware of Sontonga's anthem as the generative source of the song, the independent religious reformulations of the hymn infused its field with unique visions of Africa and its redemption.

The first case is that of the Nazarite Church of the prophet Isaiah Shembe. Born in 1870 in Natal, Shembe evolved into one of the most flamboyant and influential independent religious leaders of his day (Sundkler, 1961: 110). From 1906 to 1911, Shembe was part of William Mathebule Leshega's Baptist congregation on the Rand (Ibid.: 164-165). After the South African War, Leshega was ordained as a Baptist minister and set up a refugee camp at Boksburg, where he sought a number of acolytes to help him. Shembe joined the group and remained in the fold until 1911 when he experienced a dramatic prophetic revelation through a near-death experience in which he was called to found his own church. Thus did Shembe establish the Church of the Nazarites at Ohlange, eighteen miles north of Durban, building a religious centre known as *Ekuphakameni*, 'the Elevated Place' and the gate to heaven. In addition to developing a complex liturgy with healing rituals, rites of passage, and elaborate oratory, Shembe composed his own praise, poetry, and hymns under divine inspiration (Muller, 1999: 92-94).

Shembe claimed to hear voices that would dictate songs and rhythms to him whether he was awake or asleep (Sundkler, 1976: 187). Church members would then transcribe and type up the inspired hymns (Muller, 1999: 92). These songs had a dream-like quality and they translated spiritual messages for application to the daily lives of Shembe's followers. Shembe thus claimed spiritual authenticity for the hundreds of songs and hymns that he composed to frame and invigorate Nazarite rituals. After Shembe's death, Galilee Shembe is said to have inherited his father's charismatic powers and his musical ability. Galilee Shembe was a graduate of Fort Hare College, and he took the intellectual responsibility for inscribing, into a hymnal, aspects of Nazarite liturgy and song (Sundkler, 1976: 187-188).[8]

Carol Muller (1999: 150) explains that Galilee Shembe composed most of what she terms the 'Westernised' Nazarite hymns influenced by the four-part harmonic structure of mission church songs. Among Galilee's pieces is Hymn 242, 'Nkosi Yethu'. This hymn of invocation appears to be a variation of 'Nkosi Sikelel' iAfrika'. It asserts the readiness of the Nazarites to stand before God and calls on the Holy Spirit (*Moya*) for help and divine intervention. Muller presents the following text for Hymn 242 with elements added by Nazarite evangelist Mvangeli Mpanza (Ibid.):

Nkosi yethu simakade	Lord, our Eternal One
Simi phambi kwakho;	We stand before you;
Siyacela ubekhona	We request Your presence,
Nawe kanye nathi.	You, together with us.
Nawe kanye nathi.	You, together with us.
Yehla Moya oyiNgcwele,	Descend, Holy Spirit,
Ngena wena kithi	Enter into us.
Usebenze kubo bonke	And work within everybody
Loko okuthandwa nguwe.	In the manner you desire.
Loko okuthandwa nguwe.	In the manner you desire.
Zonke izono maziphele	May our sins be wiped away,
Nazo zonke izifo.	And all diseases.
Ubumhlophe nobumnandi	Let purity and sweetness
Mabuhlale nathi.	Dwell with us.
Mabuhlale nathi.	Dwell with us.

'Nkosi Yethu' differs in key and rhythmic patterns from 'Nkosi Sikelel' iAfrika', but the essential characteristics of the composition are similar, as are the lyrics, making it possible to view Galilee Shembe's hymn as an interpolation of the earlier song. Galilee Shembe's interpolation may be viewed as similar to musical improvisation in which the emotional quality and mood of the piece dictate further performative variations (Berliner, 1994: 232-234). The spiritual inspiration of Galilee Shembe's hymn was influenced by his musical environment and the overall configuration of the song as an invocation. Nevertheless, the legitimacy of the religious claims of divine authorship must be recognised with reference to the intended uses and audiences for 'Nkosi Yethu', which assumes its own autonomy and integrity within Nazarite liturgy.

John Maranke, born Muchabaya Momberume in 1912 near Bondwe Mountain in the Maranke Tribal Trustland of Southern Rhodesia, began to preach in his area after a near-death experience resembling Shembe's (Jules-Rosette, 2001: 38-40). Considering himself a divine messenger (*mutumira*) and African prophet, Maranke had a vision about his spiritual calling on 17 July 1932. During his youth, Maranke had attended the local Methodist mission (Daneel, 1971: 316; Jules-Rosette, 1987: 24).[9] Maranke's preparation for his calling included dreams and visions recorded in his spiritual journal, the *Humbowo Hutswa we Vapostori* (New Revelation of the Apostles), which serves as a foundational ecclesiastical text of the group, much in the manner of Galilee Shembe's hymnal. In providing a record of his visions and spiritual instructions, Maranke states:

> The Voice told me that all I had seen was going to happen and that a lot of people were going to be converted and fear God. The Voice said that It was Jesus Christ. The following morning I went out and a lot of people followed me. The Voice told me that I had seen the heirs of the Heavenly Kingdom. The rod which I had seen and had flashed with light was held upright in the building. The rod shone with light whenever I was told or given a thing. Whenever I wanted to do the work of the Lord or wanted to pray, I was told to sing the following song:
> 'Everywhere we see people who do not know the Lord. They sin. Oh, Lord! Our God of strength, Hear us when we pray. Send us Thy Holy Spirit and send it also to those who do not have it'.
> The other song I was commanded to sing was as follows: 'Lord bless Africa. Listen to its Prayers. Bless us its family. Come the Holy Spirit come. Come and bless us we servants of the Lord'.
> (*Humbowo Hutswa*: 16).

The first hymn, known as 'Kwese Kwese', opens the Apostolic sabbath ceremony, or *kerek*, while the second, 'Mwari Komborera Africa', is an inspired version of 'Nkosi Sikelel' iAfrika', which designates the Apostles as spiritual saviours of Africa. By 1932, when Maranke experienced his vision, 'Nkosi' was widely distributed in printed form and had become part of southern African vernacular and religious cultures. As with Shembe's hymns, the Vapostori performed 'Mwari' as a sacred song issuing from Maranke's divine revelations. It is paired with 'Kwese Kwese' which exhorts Apostles to evangelise, and it ends with the affirmation: 'We are here to meet You', which goes beyond 'Nkosi's' original blessing by designating the Vapostori as chosen messengers, just as 'Nkosi Yethu' elects the Nazarites. In an interview by Jules-Rosette with Apostolic song leaders, members stated that Maranke first sang 'Mwari' as 'God Bless Israel' and then changed the words to 'God Bless Africa', with the connotation that the Vapostori were the chosen elect, designated to intervene on behalf of the continent, hence the notion of standing in readiness as religious soldiers with a mission (Jules-Rosette, 1975: 131). The parallel between Africa and ancient Israel implicit in Maranke's version of the song also echoes the invocation portion of Sontonga's original text. Maranke's notion of the 'Heavenly Kingdom', like Shembe's ideal of *Ekuphakameni*, is a space out of time and a utopian theodicy promising the fruits of spiritual redemption. This space is the spiritual transfiguration of 'Africa'.

John Mushawatu, a leader and composer of songs among the Maranke Apostles in Zimbabwe, explained the variations in the performance of 'Mwari Komborera Africa' in contemporary Apostolic ceremonies (pers. comm., 6 November 2002):

> There is no standard version or translation of the song, and the words vary from place to place and occasion to occasion. Apostles in Zimbabwe sing it differently from the rest of the country, and even within the church, Manyikas and Ndebeles do not sing it the same way. You go to Congo, and it's another version, although with all attempts to sing it in the Zimbabwean language. The Manyika [a Shona dialect] version is getting prominence here.

The Manyika version of 'Mwari Komborera Africa' is transcribed and translated into English by John Mushawatu:

Mwari komborera Africa,	Lord bless Africa
Inzwai minamato yedu	Hearken to our prayers
Mwari Baba na Jesu	Lord God and Jesus
Mutikomborere	Bless us
Kudai matikomborera isu	We wish you to bless us – those that are here
tavepano	Being your Apostles.
Vapositori venyu	
Tumirai Mweya	Send the Spirit
Uya Mweya komborera,	Come Holy Spirit and Bless
Tumirai Mweya	Send Holy Spirit
Uya Mweya komborera	Come Holy Spirit and Bless
Uya Mweya,	Come Holy Spirit
Mwari Baba na Jesu	Lord God and Jesus
Mutikomborere	Bless us
Kudai matikomborera isu	We wish you to bless us – those that are here
tavepano	Being your Apostles.
Vapositori venyu	

Ngaisimudzirwe zita rayo	May its name be uplifted
Inzwai minamato yedu	Hearken to our prayers
Mwari Baba na Jesu	Lord God and Jesus
Muti Komborere	Bless us
Kudai matikomborera isu tavepano	We wish you to bless us – those that are here Being your Apostles.
Vapositori venyu	
Mwari Batsirai Africa	God help Africa
Ngaisimudzirwe zita rayo	Hearken to our prayers
Inzwai minamato yedu	Lord God and Jesus
Mwari Baba na Jesu etc.	Bless us etc.
Tumirai Mweya, etc.	Send the Holy Spirit, etc.
Tiripano nerusando rwenyu.	We are here on your mission being your Apostles

Within the Apostolic *kerek*, 'Mwari Komborera' is considered to be an invocation of the Holy Spirit to bless Africa and its chosen people and an exhortation to Apostles to act on behalf of their own and the continent's salvation. The specific addition of 'Vapositori venyu' ('We, your Apostles') makes this version of 'Mwari' stand apart from other religious and political renditions. Variations across Apostolic congregations remain similar in intent. All Maranke Apostles attempt to sing 'Mwari' in a Shona dialect. Local vernaculars, however, intervene, creating a creolised version of the hymn with slightly different tempos, harmonic patterns, and spiritual resonance. In 1971, Jules-Rosette field-recorded a version of 'Mwari' performed by non-Shona Zambian and Congolese church members, which differs in significant ways from both Maranke's original hymn and Mushawatu's Manyika version (see 1975: 268-269).

This performative variation of 'Mwari' includes an 'Alleluia' in the first line and the addition of 'Hosanna' in each refrain, embellishments which point to a more charismatic performance of the song, and mask the fact that non-Shona singers do not always know the exact words, and that the text itself is a polyglot simulation of the original Shona when performed in the outlying Zambian and Congolese Apostolic congregations. None of these changes affect the identity of the song or the inspiration of its heartfelt performance. Instead, they point to its widespread appeal and the connection of its core message to each community in which it is performed. As a result, 'Mwari' has become one of the crucial ceremonial building blocks for grass-roots ecumenism across Apostolic congregations in southern Africa.

As independent churches began to spread and consolidate their bases, various efforts at grass-roots ecumenism emerged. In Lusaka, Zambia, two major Apostolic groups, the Maranke Apostles and the Masowe Apostles, joined forces for local and external political reasons. Their co-operative efforts involved joint worship ceremonies and domestic healing rituals in which 'Mwari' played a key symbolic role. Emerging as a prophet in the Hartley District of Southern Rhodesia in 1932, John Masowe, who preached an apocalyptic and millenarian message, moved en masse with his followers to the Korsten suburb of Port Elizabeth, South Africa in 1948. His followers, who engaged in various self-supporting activities, such as furniture building and basket-making, were known as the 'Korsten Basketmakers'. Masowe reportedly became involved with the South African labour movement through contact with one of its influential members, Charles Mzengeli (Dillon-Malone, 1978: 23-24).[10] It is possible that the version of 'Mwari Komberera Africa' adopted by the Masowe Apostles was influenced by variations of 'Nkosi Sikelel' iAfrika' performed at labour union rallies.

In any case, the version of the song performed by the Masowe Apostles was more strident and upbeat than the Maranke rendition. Describing their reactions to Maranke hymnody in ecumenical ceremonies, Masowe Apostles stated: 'The Marankes sing too slowly. They don't teach their members how to sing either. You have to open your mouth very wide, like this' (Jules-Rosette, 1981: 51). Although Maranke and Masowe ecumenical ceremonies were infrequent and marked by mutual criticism, the message of 'God Bless Africa' created a bond uniting the two groups in common ideals of spiritual protest and change. In the interpretations of both churches, the Africa to be blessed was the province of misguided political leaders, including those of the apartheid state, and remained to be recaptured as part of a religious utopia.

POPULAR MUSIC, RELIGION, AND POLITICAL CULTURE

'Nkosi Sikelel' iAfrika', a song originally composed for school children, was adopted by political and religious leaders across the African continent as an emblem of hope and unity. The song itself occupies a unique cultural space in the landscape of memory. It stands at the crossroads between utopian visions of African unity and political action. The formulation of the term 'bless' (*mutikomborere*) in the subjunctive voice in the Manyika religious version of the song points to the wish for utopian freedom in a virtual Africa that does not yet exist. The substitution of the terms 'save' and 'remember' for 'bless' in a number of versions of the song suggests that Africa has been lost or forgotten and is in need of redemption. The independent religious leaders position themselves as intercessors waiting to bring about this utopian change, while political performers of the song wait for blessings to fall upon their chiefs and leaders. In all cases, the hymn is a preamble (in contrast to South African political events, where it is sung as a closing anthem or hymn) that sets the stage for more dramatic events: religious ceremonies, political rallies, funerals, and celebrations. As John Mushawatu described it for the Vapostori, the song 'solemnises' events in its transformation from an oration to an anthem.

Ceremonial framing plays a critical role in political action. It serves as the basis for shaping a civil religion and civic culture across which dialogues can take place. Yet this civic culture may be as fragile and mutable as the changing lyrics and melodies of a song. The terms of dialogue and coalition shift with personal, communal, and institutional memories. Robert Bellah (1970: 186) remarks: 'Behind the civil religion at every point lie biblical archetypes: Exodus, Chosen People, Promised Land, New Jerusalem, and Sacrificial Death and Rebirth'. These images emphasise not only the 'transcendent goals of politics' (Ibid.: 173), but also the political goals of religion. In Sontonga and Mqhayi's early version of 'Nkosi', Africa (as opposed to any particular subgroup or nation) is blessed, and its colonial and potentially revolutionary leaders are held accountable to transcendent goals that go beyond those of the state. Spiritual intervention is invoked as the method to achieve the desired end. The last stanza of 'Nkosi', however, is the most variable because it contains the ambiguous narrative outcome of the exhortation to act. Who assumes the ultimate agency and responsibility for change, and who benefits from it? This question is posed and answered differently in each variation of the hymn as it moves from one context and population to another across the African continent. The change in agency points to shifts in the loci of power and in the spaces and arenas for political debate.

Thomas Turino (2000: 58) argues that popular songs contain 'highly mediational signs' that reinforce a sense of community and group identity. At issue is not merely 'imagined communities' (Anderson, 1991: 144-145), or what Terence Ranger (1975: 32) has termed a desire for political 'wish-fulfilment' but, instead, the conscious construction of a solemn and sacred intermediary space where groups meet, weld, and mobilise in a shifting political environment.[11] The blessing in 'Nkosi' sacralises unity by drawing upon a powerful religious archetype that calls for justice beyond the bounds of the state in the name of empowered, sacred communitarian groups. This call for justice and redemption is present in both the 'political' and more strictly 'religious' versions of the song. 'Nkosi's' blessing links religion to politics as a source of transcendent morality. This is why radical political emotions could be galvanised by a song that exhorted, in Sesotho, *'Morena boloka sechaba sa Jesu'* ('God bless the nation of Jesus') (Comaroff and Comaroff, 1991: 3). The mediative space constructed by the song is wide enough to allow various versions to develop and survive across cultural contexts. These contemporary variations are further enhanced by the song's established status as an official anthem and a popular cultural artefact that reinserts itself back into vernacular culture. Further, Nicholas Cook observes that:

> 'Nkosi Sikelel' iAfrika' has a meaning that emerges from the act of performing it. Like all choral performance, from singing a hymn to chanting at a football match, it involves communal participation and interaction. Everybody has to listen to everyone else and move forward together. It doesn't just symbolise unity, it *enacts* it ... Through its block-like harmonic construction and regular phrasing, 'Nkosi Sikelel' iAfrika' creates a sense of stability and mutual dependence, with no one vocal part predominating over the others ... It lies audibly at the interface between European traditions of 'common-practice' harmony and African traditions of communal singing, which gives it an inclusive quality entirely appropriate to the aspirations of the new South Africa ... Enlisting music's ability to shape personal identity, 'Nkosi Sikelel' iAfrika' actively contributes to the construction of the community that is the new South Africa. In this sense, singing it is a political act (1998: 75-76).

Indeed, whether the religious or political meanings come most to the fore may depend on the context of performance. When sung by a choir or other formal ensemble, the performance of the full four-part arrangement might tend to provide a more hymn-like, Afro-Christian religious sensibility. Conversely, in the heat of political demonstration and mobilisation the song tended to become a booming musical volley fired in apparent melodic unison, giving a more political emphasis not only to the occasion but to the sound of the anthem itself.[12]

During the anti-apartheid struggle of the 1980s, American bassist Charlie Haden and his Liberation Music Orchestra issued a jazz version on their album, *Dream Keeper*, and the white End Conscription Campaign used the version sampled by Bright Blue in their song 'Weeping', even though the song was still banned in South Africa. As early as 1962 jazz composer, pianist, and band leader Gideon Nxumalo worked a version of 'Nkosi', much disguised, into the track 'Second Movement: "Home at Night"' for his live performance of *Jazz*

Fantasia at the University of the Witwatersrand in Johannesburg.

Later, post-apartheid white pop groups also cited 'Nkosi'. For parodic or satirical purposes, Sons of Trout included it in 'Kom Psalm' (1998) and Danny de Wet in 'New National Anthem' (1998/1999) (see Ballantine, 2004: 120). And in 1998, the sexy township group Boom Shaka rocked the seemingly unrockable and produced a catchy, booty-shaking *kwaito* version that made the old hymn instantly relevant to hedonistic urban black youth.

In 1997 a combined isiXhosa–Sesotho version, coupled awkwardly to the old anthem of white South Africa 'Die Stem van Suid Afrika' ('The Voice of South Africa') in Afrikaans and English, became South Africa's new national anthem. Here is the 'Nkosi' section of the anthem in its present guise:

Verse 1: isiXhosa

Nkosi, sikelel' iAfrika	Lord, bless Africa
Maluphakanyisw' uphondo lwayo	May her spirit rise high up
Yizwa imithandazo yethu	Hear Thou our prayers
Nkosi sikelela, thina lusapho lwayo	God bless us, we her children

Verse 2: Sesotho

Morena boloka setjhaba sa heso	God protect the nation of Jesus
O fedise dintwa le matshwenyeho	End wars and tribulations
O se boloke, o se boloke setjhaba sa heso	Oh protect, oh protect our nation
Setjhaba sa South Afrika – South Afrika	The nation of South Africa

We might note that this conglomerate version omits the original African feature of a response answering the verses ('Yihla Moya, yihla Moya'), sometimes nevertheless included by black ensembles and audience members in actual performance. Further, the word 'horn', referring to the medicine horn of indigenous, non-Christian Xhosa diviners, has been replaced by the more universalised, Western notion of 'spirit'. The second verse, entirely new and not derived in any way from Sontonga's or Mqhayi's Xhosa verses, provides different lyrics and a somewhat different melody due to differences in semantic tone in Sesotho. This Sesotho verse was apparently composed and first published in 1942 by Moses Mphahlele, in the midst of the intellectual fervour of the New Africanist movement of the time.

In 1994, at the time of South Africa's first multiracial elections, the independent churches, including the Zion Christian Church (ZCC), the

Nazarites, and others, were considered by political analysts to compose South Africa's 'silent majority' (Keller, 1994: 34-41). The fact that the churches did not remain silent but voted in some numbers for the ANC as well as for other parties (in Kwa-Zulu-Natal for the provincially victorious Inkatha Freedom Party) surprised many of the same analysts. Symbolically, the Zionists 'voted' for their utopian vision of Africa, portrayed as an imaginary landscape in suspension and waiting for redemption. For Zulu Zionists evidently, this was not the same 'Africa' as the political space championed by the ANC, since the Shembe Church has close relations to the Zulu royal house, and the majority of its members voted for the Zulu nationalist Inkatha, but the two forces were at least brought closer by, among other things, a song that created a mutable field of political discourse.

Conclusions: What's in a song?

'Nkosi Sikelel' iAfrika' is not alone in its status as a religiously linked song of protest that has become a political anthem. 'Lift Every Voice and Sing', the so-called Negro national anthem, composed by James Weldon Johnson and J Rosamond Johnson in 1896, occupies a similar position as a song of protest and uplift in the United States (Johnson, 1933: 154).[13] The message of suffering, hope, and veiled protest in the song resembles Sontonga's version of 'Nkosi', and the doctrinal roots of the song in liturgical music and in the African-American struggle for freedom are similar.

Although the Johnsons' anthem was adopted by the National Association for the Advancement of Coloured People and performed in black schools and churches on solemn occasions, it did not acquire the political prominence or cross-national appeal of *Nkosi*. Nonetheless, the origins and messages of both anthems position them as mediational signifiers uniting and mobilising regional groups for a common cause. While it has a very different history, the civil rights anthem 'We Shall Overcome' could also be analysed as a mediational signifier that unifies various groups as it shifts and assumes multiple meanings across contrasting contexts of performance. Gerald Platt and Rhys Williams (2002: 343-344) suggest that the wording and uses of these anthems in the United States were intended to counteract the notion that segregation was a divinely ordained and morally sound plan of political action. In this sense, 'Nkosi' and the other anthems are redemptive pleas for social justice and reconstruction.

In his brief essay 'Save the African Continent', VY Mudimbe (1992: 61-62) suggests moving beyond 'anti-colonialist' and 'decomposing' critiques of African politics to develop concrete projects and new programmes to somehow extract black Africa from its continuing cycles of conflict, dependency and underdevelopment. It is interesting to speculate about the extent to which such projects might find roots in the creative power and energy displayed in popular culture, projects with an organic momentum of their own pushing beyond the purposes of a strategically constructed self-and-other critique. The movement of songs, stories, and works of art across borders and boundaries reflects this organic momentum and embodies the ongoing cultural mediations that assume their shapes beyond the confines of variously defined communities.

The utopian vision implicit in 'Nkosi' does not refer to a specifically bounded, or even an imagined community, but rather to the protean reworking of landscapes of collective emotional experience painted in cultural memory and solidary spaces. As we have travelled America and South Africa presenting this paper at conferences and seminars, we have been struck by how many auditors of widely divergent background and experience have approached us with their own personal stories of the place of 'Nkosi' in their past: at demonstrations, ANC cell meetings, student rallies, religious revivals, training camps, union meetings, in exile on four continents; wherever the freedom of South Africa, and through an extended ideological geography, that of all southern Africa was the focus. The strains of Sontonga's solemn but stirring melody are the accompaniment to countless personal and public images that compose the collective memory of the struggle against apartheid and the ceremonial emergence of the new nation. Across South Africa's borders, the same melody creates a network of significance and association with a common aspiration: the freeing of Africa from the clutches of a seemingly immortal, protean imperialism and the centrality of South Africa's liberation and success to that historical process.

Sontonga's vision of freedom, the ANC's call to liberation struggle, the nation-state's exhortations, and the dreams of independent church prophets represent different versions of a virtual Africa yet to be born. Emerging out of a profound sense of discontent with a social world in which the creative process of self-definition and re-definition was forcibly denied, all the transmutations of 'Nkosi Sikelel' iAfrika', even in these post-triumphant days, conclude with the hope for change. But what has changed perhaps as much as anything, always a stalking horse for newly emerging political realities, is the song itself as its strains drift through the century of collective memory between Sontonga's untimely death and South Africa's too-long delayed rebirth.

Endnotes

1 We wish to express our appreciation for the collaboration on this paper of John Mushawatu, Archivist, Apostolic Church of John Maranke, Zimbabwe. Earlier, somewhat different, versions of this article are published in *Cahiers d'Etudes Africaines*, 44(1-2), 2004, pp. 343-368; and in *African Studies*, 64(2), 2005, pp. 285-308.

2 Jan Vansina (1985: 70) emphasises the importance of analysing formal texts such as anthems and praise poetry as reflections of the communities in which they develop. Luise White (1990: 418-438) applies a similar approach to rumour. In the study of music and memory, these concerns may be traced to Maurice Halbwachs (1939: 136), who describes music as a critical aspect of the social construction of collective memory. Music is woven into the symbolic universe and stock of shared knowledge that informs individual experiences (see Schutz, 1964: 162-164; Berger and Luckmann, 1966: 102-103).

3 Johannes Fabian's study of popular Congolese painting via the work of Tshibumba Kanda-Matulu provides another example of the social construction of memory through cultural objects. Although Fabian (1996: 276) rejects the notion of collective memory as a theoretical approach to the interpretation of painting, he clearly demonstrates how memory is socially constructed through images.

4 The format and punctuation of the original text, including English translation, of 'Nkosi Sikelel' iAfrika', as published in 1904 by the Lovedale Press, has been preserved. This version includes the two verses that were part of Enoch Sontonga's original song. It is likely that the sheet music was available to various African religious and social organisations at the turn of the century. John Mushawatu points out that 'Nkosi' in the Xhosa version translates as 'Lord', while 'Mwari' translates into English as 'God'. This difference may also be based on missionary transliteration of the Bible.

5 Denis-Constant Martin (1999: 85-88) describes Orpheus McAdoo's South African tours with the Virginia Jubilee singers during the 1890s. He points out that the term 'jubilee' has often been confused with Queen Victoria's jubilee celebrated in 1887 in commemoration of the emancipation of the South African slaves. In the American context, jubilee was used to describe the spiritual songs of uplift such as those performed by the Fisk Jubilee Singers and McAdoo's troupe. The jubilee tradition influenced the harmonic and melodic structure of South African religious music; see also Erlmann (1991: 24-27).

6 The jubilee songs continued to influence South African religious and secular music well after Orpheus McAdoo's departure. The African Jubilee Singers

founded by Simon Hoffa Sinamela added new variations to the music and increased its popularity (Erlmann, 1991:48-49).

7   See Shirli Gilbert's essay in this volume for more on the ANC-in-exile's uses of culture during apartheid.

8   Galilee Shembe recalls that his father would often compose sacred songs after hearing a woman's or a girl's voice in a dream. He could not see her, but as he woke from a dream or walked along the path in Zululand, meditating, he heard that voice which gave him a new hymn (Sundkler, 1976: 186). Isaiah Shembe would either write down the words or instruct someone else to do so. After Shembe's death, Galilee Shembe too composed hymns through visionary inspiration and undertook the project of compiling all of the Nazarite hymns (Sundkler, 1976: 187; Muller, 1999: 92-94).

9   Over the years, Apostolic informants have maintained that John Maranke was baptised as Roston in a Methodist mission in eastern Zimbabwe. Some group leaders, however, feel uncomfortable about any suggestion that the Vapostori were connected to the Methodists. The church itself had no formal affiliation with Methodist missions (Jules-Rosette, 2001: 38-39).

10 Clive Dillon-Malone (1978: 23-24) asserts that while he was in Port Elizabeth, John Masowe came into contact with Charles Mzengeli, a member of the Independent Industrial and Commercial Workers' Union of South Africa (ICU). The ICU was active in its criticism of the educational and labour policies of South Africa and Southern Rhodesia. South African authorities viewed Masowe's group as threatening because of its leader's association with ICU members.

11 Benedict Anderson (1991: 143-145) points to the importance of music and song in emphasising a sense of nationalism in 'imagined communities'. Song creates a national landscape that transcends internal borders and connects, in different ways, with each community performing a musical piece.

12 Still, there are contrary cases. Among my favourite renditions is that by the London Symphony Orchestra under André Previn, with an introductory solo by the professional Zulu cabaret artist Thuli Dumakude, featured in Richard Attenborough's film *Cry Freedom* (1987). With full orchestral backing and a classically-trained choir at its disposal, this 'Nkosi' is among the most politically stirring, least obviously religious versions of the anthem.

13 Acknowledgments and thanks are extended to Paula Marie Seniors (2002) for her remarks on James Weldon Johnson and J Rosamond Johnson's 'Lift Every Voice and Sing'. Her research on this anthem will contribute valuable information to the study of cultural objects and collective memory.

Bibliography

Anderson, Benedict. 1991. *Imagined Communities: Reflections on the Origin and Spread of Nationalism*. London: Verso.

Ansell, Gwen. 2004. *Soweto Blues*. New York & London: Continuum.

Attali, Jacques. 1985 [1977]. *Noise: The Political Economy of Music* (trans. Brian Massumi). Minneapolis & London: University of Minnesota Press.

Ballantine, Christopher. 2004. 'Re-thinking "Whiteness"? Identity, Change and "White" Popular Music in Post-apartheid South Africa'. *Popular Music*, 23(2), pp. 105-131.

Bellah, Robert. 1970. 'Civil Religion in America'. In *Beyond Belief: Essays on Religion in a Post-Traditional World*. New York: Harper & Row, pp. 168-186.

Berger, Peter & Thomas Luckmann. 1966. *The Social Construction of Reality*. Garden City, New York: Anchor Books.

Berliner, Paul. 1994. *Thinking in Jazz: The Infinite Art of Improvisation*. Chicago: University of Chicago Press.

Comaroff, Jean, & John L Comaroff. 1991. *Of Revelation and Revolution*, vol. 1: *Christianity, Colonialism and Consciousness in South Africa*. Chicago: University of Chicago Press.

Cook, Nicholas. 1998. *Music: A Very Short Introduction*. London: Oxford University Press.

Coplan, David B. 1985. *In Township Tonight! South Africa's Black City Music and Theatre*. London: Longman.

Daneel, ML. 1971. *Old and New in Southern Shona Independent Churches*. The Hague: Mouton.

Davie, Lucille. 2002. 'The Search for the Man Who Wrote Our Anthem'. http://www.joburg.org.za/jan_2002/anthem.stm, accessed 1 April 2007.

Dillon-Malone, Clive M. 1978. *The Korsten Basketmakers: A Study of the Masowe Apostles, an Indigenous African Religious Movement*. Lusaka, Zambia: Institute for African Studies.

Erlmann, Veit. 1991. *African Stars: Studies in Black South African Performance*. Chicago: University of Chicago Press.

_. 1996. *Nightsong: Performance, Power, and Practice in South Africa*. Chicago: University of Chicago Press.

Fabian, Johannes. 1996. *Remembering the Present: Painting and Popular History in Zaire*. Berkeley: University of California Press.

Gérard, Alfred S. 1971. *Four African Literatures*. Berkeley: University of California Press.

Gurwitsch, Aron. 1964. *The Field of Consciousness*. Pittsburgh: Duquesne University Press.

Halbwachs, Maurice. 1939. 'La memoire collective chez les musicians'. *Revue Philosophique*, 2, pp. 36-165.

Huskisson, Yvonne. 1969. *The Bantu Composers of Southern Africa*. Johannesburg: South African Broadcasting Corporation.

Jabavu, DDT. 1949. 'The Origin of "Nkosi Sikelel' iAfrika"'. *Nada*, 26, pp. 56-58.

Jewsiewicki, Bogumil. 1996. 'Corps interdits: La representation christique de Lumumba comme redempteur du peuple zairois'. *Cahiers d'Etudes Africaines*, 36(1-2), pp. 113-142.

Johnson, James Weldon. 1933. *Along This Way: The Autobiography of James Weldon Johnson*. New York: Viking Press.

Jules-Rosette, Bennetta. 1975. *African Apostles: Ritual and Conversion in the Church of John Maranke*. Ithaca: Cornell University Press.

_. 1981. *Symbols of Change: Urban Transition in a Zambian Community*. Norwood, New Jersey: Ablex Publishing.

_. 1987. 'New Religious Consciousness and the State in Africa: Selected Case Studies'. *Archives de Sciences Sociales des Religions*, 64(1), pp. 15-35.

_. 2001. 'The Apostolic Church of John Maranke (Vapostori or Bapostolo)'. In Stephen D Glazier (ed.). *Encyclopedia of African and African-American Religions*. New York: Routledge, pp. 38-39.

Keil, Charles & Steven Feld. 1994. *Music Grooves: Essays and Dialogues*. Chicago: University of Chicago Press.

Keller, Bill. 1994. 'A Surprising Silent Majority in South Africa'. *The New York Times Magazine*, April 17, pp. 34-41.

Lipsitz, George. 1994. *Dangerous Crossroads: Popular Music, Postmodernism, and the Politics of Place*. London: Verso.

Maranke, John. 1953. 'Humbowo Hutswa we Vapostori' ('The New Witness of the Apostles') (trans. JS Kusotera). Unpublished booklet.

Martin, Denis-Constant. *Coon Carnival: New Year in Cape Town, Past and Present*. Cape Town: David Philip.

Mqhayi, SEK. 1927. *Imihobe Nemibongo*. Alice, South Africa: Lovedale Mission Press.

_. 1929. *U-Don Jadu: UkuHamba yimFundo*. Alice, South Africa: Lovedale Mission Press.

Mudimbe, VY. 1992. 'Save the African Continent'. *Public Culture*, 5(1), pp. 61-62.

Muller, Carol Ann. 1999. *Rituals of Fertility and the Sacrifice of Desire: Nazarite Women's Performance in South Africa*. Chicago: University of Chicago Press.

Mushawatu, John. 2002. Personal communication. Harare, Zimbabwe, 6 November.

Mutloatse, Mothobi. 1987. *Umhlaba Wethu*. Johannesburg: Skotaville.

Page, Carol A. 1982. 'Colonial Reaction to AME Missionaries in South Africa, 1898-1910'. In Sylvia M Jacobs (ed.). *Black Americans and the Missionary Movement in Africa*. Westport, Connecticut: Greenwood Press, pp. 177-196.

Platt, Gerald M, & Rhys H Williams. 2002. 'Ideological Language and Social Movement Mobilization: A Sociolinguistic Analysis of Segregationists' Ideologies'. *Sociological Theory*, 20(3), pp. 328-359.

Rabotapi, Ivy. 2000. Interview. 'Please Rise', *Xpressions*, SABC 3, 17 September.

Ranger, Terence. 1975. *Dance and Society in Eastern Africa, 1890-1970: The Beni Ngoma*. London: Heinemann.

Schutz, Alfred. 1964. 'Making Music Together'. In *Collected Papers: Vol. II: Studies in Social Theory*. The Hague: Martinus Nijhoff, pp. 159-178.

Seniors, Paula Marie. 2002. Notes on 'Lift Every Voice and Sing'. Unpublished paper.

Sontonga, Enoch. 1904. 'Nkosi Sikelel' iAfrika'. Lovedale Sol-fa Leaflets, No. 17. Johannesburg: Lovedale Press.

Sundkler, BGM. 1961. *Bantu Prophets in South Africa*. London: International African Institute.

_. 1976. *Zulu Zion and Some Swazi Zionists*. London: Oxford University Press.

Thompson, Leonard M. 1985. *The Political Mythology of Apartheid*. New Haven: Yale University Press.

Turino, Thomas. 2000. *Nationalists, Cosmopolitans, and Popular Music in Zimbabwe*. Chicago: University of Chicago Press.

Turner, Victor W. 1968. *The Drums of Affliction: A Study of Religious Processes among the Ndembu of Zambia*. Oxford: Clarendon Press.

Vansina, Jan. 1985. *Oral Tradition as History*. Madison: University of Wisconsin Press.

White, Luise. 1990. 'Bodily Fluids and Usufruct: Controlling Property in Nairobi, 1917-1939'. *Canadian Journal of African Studies*, 24, pp. 418-438.

Discography

Boom Shaka. 1998. *Words of Wisdom*. Polygram, RBC262.

Bright Blue. 1987. *Yesterday Night*. Blue Records, BLU 1.

Charlie Haden and the Liberation Music Orchestra. 1990. *Dream Keeper*. Blue Note Records, CDP 7 95474 2.

Gideon Nxumalo. 1991. *Jazz Fantasia*. Teal Records, TELCD 2301.

10

WHOSE 'WHITE MAN SLEEPS'?

AESTHETICS AND POLITICS IN THE EARLY WORK OF KEVIN VOLANS

Martin Scherzinger

Introduction[1]

In the late 1970s and 1980s, when apartheid still held sway in South Africa, the composer Kevin Volans wrote a set of compositions entitled *African Paraphrases*. Though they were cast in a Western idiom, these works drew on distinctly African modes of music-making, such as music of the *mbira dza vadzimu* and *matepe* from Zimbabwe, *lesiba* music from Lesotho and *nyanga* panpipe music from Mozambique, to name a few representative instances. Volans' paraphrase compositions, which gained considerable success in Europe and America, posed a conspicuous challenge to the 'official' aesthetic ideology of apartheid in South Africa. In his various statements and writings Volans has addressed his musical compositions to predicaments across two intersecting political arenas: On the one hand, he argues that his early music was meant to effect 'reconciliation' between 'African and European aesthetics' (through *connecting* what was deemed culturally separate). On a local level, then, the composer regards the music as his 'small contribution to the struggle against apartheid' (Volans, n.d.). On the other hand, Volans' early music was meant to call into question the industrialised standardisation of Western culture in general; its obsession with (what the composer calls) an 'objectified and reified' sound that ultimately would end 'in a nightmare of alienation' (Volans,

1986). On a general level, that is, the composer argues that the processes of capitalist modernisation have had a largely negative impact on African music, seeking either to domesticate it ('to Westernise African music'); or to exoticise it (give it 'local colour'). Instead, Volans sought to 'gently set up an African colonisation of Western music and instruments' as if to 'introduce a computer virus into the heart of Western contemporary music' (Volans, n.d.). The principal mechanism used to achieve this reversal in his early works was quotation and, of course, paraphrase.

This article examines the hoped-for politics implied by the ways Volans' paraphrase technique allows one cultural practice to intersect and blend with another in a time of rigid cultural divisions. By borrowing some (and warding off other) African musical forms and intensities, and thereby effectively moving a carefully chosen selection of African fragments of musical text (transcriptions and performance techniques) from one place to another, Volans' early music offers a unique critical glimpse into the complex social processes through which musical rituals in various quarters were, and are, routinely understood. Cultural artefacts are obviously not static, existing instead in an evolving and contradictory history bound up with personal and institutional conflict, negotiations, and appropriations. While the argument that follows recognises the constraints upon individual intervention in social struggle, it will assess the political imagination at work in Volans' attempt to refashion and move traditional African music from one zone of display to another. Because of a deep concern about what gets marginalised by the social critique of Volans' project, the assessment tends to tease out the progressive dimensions of his political imagination. In the final analysis, however, this essay keeps the matter unresolved.

On the critics, and the extra-musical

It is easy to dismiss Volans' claims to be effecting a genuine reconciliation between separate aesthetic domains; it is still easier to dismiss his idea of a 'reverse colonisation' of the West in any robust, practical sense of the words. Indeed, while it was a commercial triumph in classical and world music markets, much of the *academic* commentary on Volans (both in South Africa and abroad) has not only dismissed Volans' aspirations, but also raised to a higher degree the critique of Volans' entire project, concluding it a political and aesthetic failure on both local and global terrains. Locally speaking, that is, far from effecting reconciliation, Volans is accused of appropriation, and, globally speaking, far from reversing the colonial moment, Volans is accused of marching in step with the demands of late capital. Jürgen Bräuninger, for example, makes both arguments: on a local level, he questions whether it is legitimate to 'sell' such music 'as original composition', and then suggests that the music is at bottom a form of 'exploitation in a modern guise' (1998: 6). The legitimacy of these questions rhetorically supports the crux of Bräuninger's argumentative leap to follow; namely, that there is no *'artistic* value in re-orchestrating the [*mbira,* panpipe, and bow] pieces' on grounds that the originals are diminished thereby (6; italics mine). Volans' earliest harpsichord works, for example, reduce away the buzzing inharmonicities of the *mbira;* while movements from the early string quartets cancel the crucial dance steps and the *ubuntu*-like philosophy (a local concept linked to an ethics of reciprocity) of the original panpipe music upon which it is based (6). Bräuninger's conclusion is tied to his critique on a global terrain: Volans' sequential quotation and paraphrase method creates 'less meaning' than vertical relationships could, sounding like 'strolls ... from one super-market shelf to the next ... the art music equivalent of MTV' (9). For Bräuninger, Volans' early work is a case of stolen goods, blandly combined in a pastiche of postmodern blurring, and ultimately becoming the very airport art it sought to critique.

This kind of disapproval is echoed in later commentary as well. In a review of a recent recording of Volans' string quartets, Chris Walton maintains that Volans' 'plagiarism' erases the 'moral claims' associated with copyright protection for the original creators (2002/2003: 23). Here Walton is not, as one might expect, referring to the actual African source materials that allegedly ground Volans' compositional endeavour. Instead, Walton recalls a moment of infighting in the 1980s to support his point, when members of the 'South African music establishment' accused Volans of 'cultural banditry' (22). On this matter, Walton's verdict is strident and clear: '"Cultural banditry"? If this means appropriating without authorial permission the music of others and re-using it under one's own name to one's own aesthetic ends, then the attack is not without substance' (23). Likewise, on Volans' claim that a 'folk tune played by a symphony orchestra is no longer a folk tune', the writer retorts: '—*Oh yes it is!* This smacks of using the act of transcription as an excuse for erasing any moral claims of copyright on the part of the original author. In other words: if I take something, then it becomes my property, because I have stripped it of its original significance in making it mine' (23; original emphasis). Walton finds this to be a 'circular argument', out of which he chooses to read 'starkly neo-colonialist implications' (23). As it is with Bräuninger, Walton goes on to affine the music's commercial success with the very market-driven 'local colour' Volans had set out to resist: 'The (South) Africa that [the quartets] evoke ... is the Africa of today's Jo'burg Airport lounge with its ethnic tourist shops:

beautifully crafted, masterfully packaged, thoroughly enjoyable, but sanitised and somewhat bland' (23). Once again, an apparently 'political' argument leapingly buttresses the case for a debased aesthetic. Unlike Bräuninger, Walton finally modifies his critique in a puzzling non sequitur: Volans' music, it seems, reminds him less of Africa than it does of Anglo-Saxon *minimalism* after all. This is a noteworthy turnaround for an argument scrupulously invested in the notion that a folk tune, no matter its instrumentation or context, remains a folk tune. And it is this later argumentative edifice that supports Walton's genuine aesthetic judgements: While not his personal preference 'Volans' music is finely wrought, ... his craftsmanship is first-rate, ... the fact that its minimalistic patterns are never overdone is proof to me of Volans' innate sense of formal rhythm', and so on (24). With minimalism sliding into the argument's central reference point (Walton mentions Michael Nyman as a representative instance), Volans' music is paradoxically redeemed.

Argumentative pastiche aside, however, the moralising conclusions of these writers are quite censorious. As an easy rejoinder, one might ask whether the paraphrase-composition of Justinian Tamasuza, Dumisani Maraire, and Bongani Ndodana, and other African art music composers, is also a case of stealing. By what inscription, one might continue? What about Haydn, Berlioz, Brahms, Mahler, Stravinsky, Bartok, Berio, Foss, Schnittke, Ligeti? Or one might question why the legalist-political failure implies an aesthetic failure. In what respect, *precisely* that is, are the Africanised paraphrases diminished, sanitised, bland? More seriously, one might ask how the music is both complicit with *and* resistant to the ideological demands of neo-colonial capitalism – and of apartheid. Far from illuminating the dialectical tensions within this body of work, what we find in the critical reception of Kevin Volans' *oeuvre* today is an ideological culture of critique, as unrestrained as it is morally assured.

It is worth noting that the American academic reception of Volans, with some notable exceptions, bears almost identical ideological traits to those described above. In a 1995 *Perspectives of New Music* article, for example, Timothy Taylor concerns himself with the question of how we can talk about music and politics using the work of Volans as a test case. He notes that music critics at large seem to have effectively weeded politics out of music, and claims that when this happens, 'audiences' of music are effaced in the binary; implicit 'meanings of all kinds' are left out (1995: 505). Taylor aims, first, to 'deconstruct' this separation (which he identifies with the late eighteenth-century emergence of aesthetic autonomy) and, second, to provide 'a theoretical model for looking at music' with Volans' music as an example (505). Broadly speaking, for Taylor, music is irreducibly social, and believing it to be otherwise – autonomous, say – a site of desire. He quotes Adorno: 'form [collated here with autonomy] can only be the form of a content' (507), while 'listening involves listen*ers*' and not only such 'objective form' (508; original emphasis). The better to reveal the content of these plural perceptions, then, Taylor recommends 'the ethnographic [a]s the next area to be explored' in our discipline; a terrain in which readers and listeners can ultimately 'read into the music whatever they want' (508).

On the topic of Volans himself, Taylor positions his method in a newly outmoded way. Resisting an argument that he sees as 'the fashion these days', Taylor says that he is going to take seriously Volans' *intentions*, because, far from being irrelevant, 'they inevitably shape the way [his] works are received' (504) via disseminating views in talk shows, interviews, and in magazines. The argument goes something like this: in the interviews of the late 1980s, Volans, drawn to the 'formal asymmetry' of African music, 'reconcile[s] African music and Western music' (511) in his compositions, and thus Volans uses African music in his work 'to show his engagement with this music and to make his political point'; that is, against apartheid's politics of separation (512). However, the argument continues, there has been a change in intention in the interviews of the early 1990s because Volans now seems to partake in the 'particular, particul*ate*, notion of self that does not appear to have arisen in societies that are not capitalist' (516; original emphasis). As a result 'his composerly individuality overrides everything "African"' (517) and, in logical step with his changed intentions, 'Volans now disavows the social and political considerations' of his work (518). 'So now Volans talks about his music in far more formal terms.' For example, Volans' characterisation of the first dance of his string quartet 'White Man Sleeps' has shifted from a telling about a concertina player in Lesotho, whose performance inspired this movement, to a telling about an exercise in writing a movement with only two chords. Taylor describes the social trends that accompany Volans 'emptying [his own works] of everything except formal values' (524). Under Thatcher/Reagan, he argues, 'looking at art as empty of politics became more acceptable' (525). Taylor seems to imply that the interpretative reception of Volans' music (once?) replete 'with overt political meanings' (526) is depoliticised under Thatcher-Reaganism. And Volans is (overtly?) party to this 'retrogressive formalism' because the 'resurgence and universalization of bourgeois European values in the 1930s has made it comfortable for [Volans] to have this "universal" belief [Adorno's alleged aesthetic autonomy], and a "universal" identity instead of a more local one' (525). It is in this later interpretation of Volans' intentions that Taylor accuses Volans of stealing music from other people.

For all their differences, these critical accounts share a common confidence that *extra-musical* matters are adequate to the task of musical judgement. Bräuninger draws actual musical sound closer to the substratum of his critique than do Walton or Taylor, but, even here, this sound is barely audible. Thus we hear about failures of re-orchestration and the loss of musico-philosophical content, but only in the most general sense. There is one revealing moment, however: at bottom, it seems, Bräuninger prizes 'vertical relationships' over sequential quotation and paraphrase (on grounds that the latter create 'less meaning' than do the former). While creating the conditions for undermining a certain brand of postmodernism, this kind of critique is not substantial. What are 'vertical' relationships? Are they harmonic? Under what conditions can (any) music have no vertical relationships? Why are these relationships more 'meaning'-producing than other ones? What kind of meaning is envisaged here? The questions go on and on. One surprising symptom of lending pride of place to vertical relationships is that it recapitulates the hierarchic European (and American) value of harmony (over rhythm) that is in strong tension with Bräuninger's apparent respect for African culture. Noteworthy too is the way the movement of the argument recapitulates the very strolling pastichism ('from one idea to the next') that is the object of Bräuninger's musical criticism. The strictly *musical* moment remains uninterrogated, assumed; it appears merely as an unwarranted postmodern fragment. Unlike the carefully substantiated ethico-political argument in Bräuninger's text, music's vertical relationships are better simply because they are. And thus the author's aesthetic stance resonates, ultimately, in the tones of political disapproval alone.

As for the substance of Walton's order of values, this is clearly grounded in aesthetics of an abashedly universalist sort (even if this fact is not demonstrably known by the author). For while we find a genuflection towards a context-driven theory of art ('Is there a single composer of quality who is not marked by some degree by where he comes from?') and a protest against a context-free one ('There is surely no place on earth where one might be able to pretend a complete absence of knowledge of one's place in it'), the argumentative weight Walton ascribes to this heterogeneity is not at all clear. It may be that geography is constitutive of musical creativity in Walton's understanding, but the author seems to prefer art that keeps such a 'sense of place' in the closet. Walton dislikes Volans' 'exotic African' titles (like 'White Man Sleeps') because, he claims, they are designed as a 'selling-point': a position that opens space for a latent critique of a 'marketing machine' (2002/2003: 23). Why the striking three-word title 'White Man Sleeps' – a translation of an African dance step – is merely exotic is not up for discussion in Walton's text. Nor is the fascinating aesthetic, historical and conceptual imaginary at work in these three words given any thought. Nor does Walton explain why 'Highlights of Potgietersrus' (a title he rhetorically conjures as a substitute for the exotic African one) is either less exotic or more interesting on *non*-exotic terms (be they aesthetic, historical, conceptual, or whatever). Of course, Walton's argument against Volans' apparently foregrounding 'local colour' comes to contradict his deliberately uninteresting rhetorical substitutes, advanced to clinch the point about the pressures of the market: they are equally (actually, more) local: Potgietersrus! The point is that only a diminished view of African aesthetics would limit the conceptual dimensions of the words 'white man sleeps' to the logic of exoticism. Instead of noticing what the composer deeply admires, the thoughtful play in these words, the critic simply offers an injunction: one need not wear one's 'passport on one's sleeves' (a 'tag of origin') to reflect geographical locale, claims Walton; it is ultimately the '*quality of the ends*' that counts (24; italics mine).

This last point reveals the latent aesthetic universalism as the ultimate principle of value in Walton's thinking. For an author seemingly concerned about the politics of neo-colonialism, this (not self-evidently progressive position) is an ironic turn. But the greater contradiction of course lies elsewhere. For an account that elevates musical *quality* to an aprioristic position, there is a remarkable absence of *musical* discussion. Apart from occasional remarks (the music is 'finely-wrought' and has a captivating 'urgency'; it resembles 'minimalist Anglo-Saxon speak', and so on) most statements of value are *extra-* or *non*-musical. (As an aside, it is noteworthy that the author *opposes* Volans' resemblance to minimalism, at this point of his review at least, with Volans' resemblance to African music, apparently unaware of minimalism's great debt to African music.) The point is, one might expect detailed discussions of musical content following from an overarching interest in musical quality. *Analysis*, concrete musical engagement, surely a minimal task attending any coherent claim to musical *quality* (in its universalist moment), is withheld or deferred in this writing: it is present as a key argumentative plank, but functions only as a rhetorical figure. The musical content of Volans' music is unable to impose itself upon the critical imaginary. The music is silenced by *extra-music*.

This deafness to the actual music is as true for Walton as it is for Taylor. Taylor's article is particularly guilty of this absence because he does not even identify the actual music he accuses Volans of stealing. The article is further complicated by an allegiance to a crude psychological model of 'intentions' that becomes the primary site of the music's 'politics'. Taylor is disturbed by what he considers to be Volans' formalistic representation of African music. His suspicion of Volans' aesthetic claims about his own music carries interesting overtones of desire. Believing African music to be, at bottom, functionalist and 'nonformal', Taylor wants its appearance in the context of a Western medium to articulate a (kind of postmodern) critique of formalism in America (1995: 511). Failing that, it becomes 'conservative'. Of course the case of Volans' use of African music is ironic in the light of this form/function dichotomy because the composer's explicit interest in 'formal asymmetry' (or what Taylor mistakenly thinks of as the 'nonformal' as such) owed more to the influence of Morton Feldman and painters like Philip Guston than it does to African principles of composition. In his description of his 'The Songlines' quartet, for example, Volans explains that 'in an effort to get away from form and into the material, [Philip Guston] stood close up to the canvas, working quickly and not stepping back to look until the work was finished. In the main body of this piece ... I juxtaposed very different kinds of music in the order that they occurred to me, not thinking ahead, and allowing the material to unfold at its own pace' (1994: 3). The irony is that the form Volans is getting away from in this quartet is precisely African form, and on principles that are in alignment with modern Western artistic ideals.

On the problem of form and function, for example

As I have argued in various contexts, I do not think we should trivialise the perplexing prevalence of this kind of false binary ossified by cultural geography; the fantastic opposition between a *formalised* north Atlantic and a *functionalised* Africa. The form/function dichotomy has become a commonplace capable of spawning a host of subsidiary myths. For example, in his article 'Musical Structure and Human Movement', John Bailey argues that the perceptual focus on musical structure is an exclusively Western idea that cannot be readily applied to non-Western music (1985: 237-258). Using the *kalimba* music of southern Africa as an example, Bailey identifies the physical patterns of fingering (instead of the sounding forms) as central to the organisation of the music. Like Gerhard Kubik, who asserts that, whereas 'in Western music the movements of a musician playing his instrument generally have meanings only in terms of the sonic result, in African music patterns of music are in themselves a source of pleasure, regardless of whether they come to life in sound in their entirety, partly, or not at all', Bailey emphasises the kinaesthetic dimensions of African *kalimba* music above the formal-perceptual ones (1985: 241).

But does this distinction successfully divide musical-cultural continents? On the one hand, it is odd to suggest that hearing the formal organisation of a Western piece of music can be figured apart from a kinaesthetic dimension; that hearing a formal gesture on the violin, say, is not also hearing physical work done by a performer. Recent composers frequently explore the mismatch between the physical actions used to create the music, on the one hand, and the sounding forms that result. In György Ligeti's piano etudes, for example, we find a systematic music that seems to encounter its formal limits by way of a physical constraint. Ligeti's fascination for music in which the systematic aspect encounters a physical limit is well-known. Regarding the piano etudes in particular, he writes: 'Given the anatomical limitations, it was necessary to allow the music to arise, so to speak, from the position of the ten fingers on the keys' (1988: 6).

Likewise, in recent scholarly writings, theorists recognise the irreducible physicality of all music. As Suzanne Cusick and Andrew Mead have argued, a kind of 'kinaesthetic empathy', in which listeners identify with a sound as an embodiment of physical work done, is a central factor in the experience of Western music (Mead, 1999: 13). In addition to examples that bring the mode of production of sound into explicit formal play (like the backstage oboes or horns in symphonies by Berlioz or Mahler), even the music of one of the West's ostensibly most formalistically-minded composers, Anton Webern, is saturated with extreme expressive directions, *ponticelli*, harmonics, rhythmic complexities, difficult bowings, sudden dynamic changes, and angular voice-leading that cannot but invoke a kinaesthetic hearing and sometimes even obscure the formal mirrorings and symmetries that generate the pitch-structure. This is not to say that formal considerations are necessarily antithetical to kinaesthetic ones. In 'Bodily Hearing', for instance, Mead demonstrates how the physical hand-crossings in the second movement of Webern's 'Variations for Piano, Op. 27', play a structural role in articulating the principal motivic returns, which appear in addition to the canonic unfolding (1999: 13). In this way, the physical movements involved in performing the work indicate an aspect of the music's structure. As Mead notes, 'Music, in large part, is indeed something we do ... That the mind can be ravished by the patterns we perceive in sounds I would never deny. But how we perceive those sounds, and how we make those sounds, cannot help but carry part of the message ... The study of music has its own rewards, but it is good to remind oneself occasionally that music's path to the mind is inevitably through the body' (15).

On the other hand, it is also odd to suggest that the kinaesthetic dimension of an African piece of music can be figured apart from *any*

Ex. 1a. *Kushaura* of 'Ngozi Yemuroora' as performed by Tute Chigamba (transcription: Martin Scherzinger).

Ex. 1b. *Kushaura* of 'Nhimutimu' as performed by Tute Chigamba (transcription: Martin Scherzinger).

formal organisation. Consider the example of a simple *kushaura* ('leading part' in Shona *mbira dza vadzimu* music) for the song 'Ngozi Yemuroora' (transcribed in Example 1a) from Tute Chigamba's repertoire. Notice how the anomalous absence of a bass note on the eighth pulse of the third and fourth measures coincides with the doubling of D in the right hand. If kinaesthetic considerations were logically prior, we would not expect the doubling in the right hand and we would expect the left hand to play some or other note on those silent pulses. Now, the lower note D cannot be found on either of the two left-hand manuals of the *mbira*. But, in order to maintain the integrity of the harmonic motion (which calls for a dyad built on G during this span of the cycle) and the registral integrity of the bass line, it is played by the right hand instead. (I should note here that the experience of irregularity in executing this passage on the *mbira* is minimal.) In effect, then, a physical fingering pattern is broken to accommodate a formal consideration of the music. This kind of adjustment in hand movement is a staple technique in *mbira* performance practice. In another simple *kushaura* for the song 'Nhimutimu', for example, Chigamba once again omits a bass note, this time only on the first pulse of the fourth measure (see Example 1b). At this moment in the cycle the melodic-harmonic flow calls for the D# that can only be played by the right hand.

The general idea that kinaesthetic-and-not-formal considerations are to the fore in African music while formal-and-not-kinaesthetic ones prevail in Western music strikes me as false. Indeed, *mbira* performers frequently report a sense of complete disorientation when they perform pieces on instruments with a different tuning layout (see Berliner, 1973: 70-71). This would be unlikely if fingering patterns were as primary as Bailey and others suggest. Shorthand cultural oppositions of this sort cannot be sustained in the face of rigorous comparative work. Nor can they be sustained in the face of carefully crafted creative work, of which Kevin Volans' work is an exemplary instance.

The political imagination at work in Volans' use of African musical sources in the context of a Western instrumentarium is one of its highest achievements. While seemingly aestheticising the source material and thus denying its concrete history, the music also puts into urgent question and doubt various racialising commonplaces about African music. Tethered to questions recently raised by African musicologists (Kofi Agawu, Akin Euba, Zabana Kongo, and others) about common (but false) 'Africanist' topoi generally held in the West, Volans' music issues social thought in its very sounding forms. And Volans was twenty years ahead of the curve. The topoi under critical scrutiny by these African writers today include the alleged primacy of rhythm and timbre in African music (over, say, melody and harmony) no less than the apparently functionalist (instead of contemplative) and kinaesthetic (instead of formal) essence of African music. The point is that Volans' music – effectively translating the sounds and patterns of African music in a new idiom – draws attention to values in the traditional music that uniquely menace such invented topoi. And this kind of progressive imagination is open to actual *listening* experiences; it is open to a critical reception that is acutely attuned to the music's inner workings. It is in the recesses of its sound, finally, that the music's political ambitions are fully understood.

On the music

For many southern Africans, Volans' early works, especially the *African Paraphrases*, are heard *as* quotation. The source material is overt, vivid, literal, almost tangible. Even the titles are pre-given: 'She Who Sleeps with a Small Blanket', 'Cover Him With Grass', and 'White Man Sleeps', for example, are taken from African song titles – the last a translation of *Nzungu agona*, one of the silent dance patterns of the *Nyanga* panpipe dance of the Nyungwe at Nsava, Tete, Mozambique – while later Volans works like 'Dancers on a Plane' or 'Cicada' are taken from middle period works of Jasper Johns. It is precisely because of the immediacy of this recognition that the African originals themselves recede from earshot and our listening is drawn to something else. The content of the original music, one might say, metamorphoses thereby into formal play, issuing an aesthetic hearing. At the centre of Volans' 'African Paraphrases' lies a phenomenological reversal, a paradoxical moment of transition from the *interpretation* of musical content (attending to its contextual coordinates and referents) to the *experience* of musical form (listening to the flow as vibrantly patterned sound alone). The orientation of this music is thus directed less towards whatever citation the music is able to engender and more towards its regularly patterned displacement, which yields aesthetic by-products that are never quite predictable.

This way of hearing aligns Volans' work with an artist like Jasper Johns. Johns too is interested in what he describes as 'pre-formed, conventional ... factual, exterior elements' (such as flags, maps, and targets in his early work), and 'things which are seen and not looked at, not examined' (1996: 1). The tension between the thing depicted and the depiction yields the possibility of 'looking at' what was previously merely 'seen'; of examining the found schemas in terms of their independent aesthetic aspect. 'Seeing a thing,' says Johns in 1982, 'can sometimes trigger the mind to make another thing.' (1996:

Ex. 2. *Kushaura* of 'Mutamba' as performed by Ephat Mujuru (transcription: Andrew Tracey).

6) Analogously, Volans encourages *hearing* the borrowed image in itself, apart from its original source; the immediately recognisable taken as a handhold for the ear, which might guide us into the unknown, the purely aesthetic, in this modernist sense. Volans' own description of Johns' flag painting is instructive: 'These are not paintings of flags but flags in paint' (pers. comm., January 2007). While this is just what some may think of as a case of 'looking at art as empty of politics'; or a case of a 'settler colonist' inhabiting 'the nation of Art' (Taylor, 1995: 525, 522); free from politics, society, and cultural context; and worse, at the cost of 'appropriating' from others and thus of 're-enacting colonialism' (514, 516), I want to suggest that this music is an effort to think African music outside of the metaphorics of indigenous 'cultural practice' – and is, therefore, an implicit critique of apartheid thinking.

Take an example from the second string quartet 'Hunting: Gathering'. In this work, Volans juxtaposes a variety of pieces of African music – *kora* music from Mali, *lesiba* music from Lesotho, an Ethiopian folk tune, and so on – which 'come and go in a random fashion like images or events on a journey' (a feature of the music that Bräuninger associates with a kind of meandering postmodernism) (1998: 3). In the middle of the second movement, the *mbira* tune 'Mutamba' appears in its traditional form. This was the song played by Zhanje for Pasipamire, the legendary spirit medium for Chaminuka, during the time of the nineteenth-century Shona/Ndebele wars. Legend has it that the song endowed Pasipamire with super-human strength in the face of certain death (see Example 2)

Volans' rendition in 'Hunting: Gathering' combines two parts in a characteristic hocket (see Example 3). The note-for-note patterns produced by this combination of parts recapitulate precisely the traditional mode of improvised performance on the *mbira dza vadzimu*, in which one *mbira* part (often referred to as the *kushaura* part, meaning 'to lead') falls in the spaces of a second *mbira* part (referred to as the *kutsinhira* part, meaning 'to follow'). Far from mere postmodern pastiche, then, the point of this quotation is to allow the traditional *mbira* patterns to issue the music's most poignant *melodic-harmonic* statement in the piece thus far. By framing the quotation with agitated modernist music – extreme bowings, extended passages of *ponticello* and *pizzicato*, complex and unpredictable rhythms, desolate tapestries of harmonics, and so on – the *mbira* tune paradoxically comes to sound like gently undulating nineteenth-century European song. It is as if African music – appearing as unadulterated quotation – ushers in a phantom world of Schubertian *Biedermeier*. Traditional African music suddenly reappears, as if from a great distance, in illusory domesticity. At the very least,

Ex. 3. 'Mutamba' as it appears in Kevin Volans' 'Hunting: Gathering', bars 338-95.

'Mutamba' therefore comes to propel the work's most significant melodic and harmonic movement, and hence to offer a sensuous deconstruction of the customised ethnographic idea that African music is at bottom timbre-oriented and rhythmically complex.[2]

Take another example: In the second movement of 'The Songlines' quartet, the music, 'built on various running and walking rhythms' probably inspired

Ex. 4. 'Nyamaropa' as performed by Gwanzura Gwenzi (transcription: Andrew Tracey).

by San bow music, seems at the same time to be preoccupied with an *mbira* tune throughout. The tune is known as 'Nyamaropa' ('Bloody Meat'), and is associated, in traditional parlance, with a successful hunt or a successful battle. Example 4 depicts one incarnation of 'Nyamaropa', based on the playing of Gwanzura Gwenzi.

This time Volans breaks with African tradition by adding wrong notes (perhaps to conjure the unique tuning of the *mbira?*) and by including occasional metric irregularities to the original. In bars 1-12 (see Example 5), a version of 'Nyamaropa' that cannot decide on the quality of its third degree is introduced as a kind of groaning *ostinato* in the viola. The *pizzicato* cello begins by doubling one or other of the viola's polyrhythmic lines, while the highly dissonant violin harmonic on G# seems to conjure the timbre of the *mbira*. (The iron rods of the *mbira*, known as *lamellae*, tend to sound out, not the overtone a perfect fifth above the fundamental, but the overtone lying a sixth above it.) As the four-bar cycle progresses, the music seems to forget about the overtone, and the cello line falls increasingly out of sync with the 'Nyamaropa'-carrying viola. By bar 10 the cello has fallen in the spaces of the viola's lower line. While this kind of interlocking is a traditional *mbira* compositional device, the gradual pitch disalignment in 'Songlines' is not. It is as if the cello grows increasingly deaf to the tune it was miming and repeats forth absent-mindedly instead. The repeated Cs in bar 10 are late and, after a brief rest in bar 11, as if to catch wind of the sound it was forgetting, the cello plays the F to E-flat move a few beats late and then seems to quit.

When the music starts up again, the cello sustains a hocketing and vaguely un-co-ordinated imitation of a viola line, resulting in some spiky minor seconds around E-flat. Only this time, the viola, seemingly ruffled by the cello losing track of its line, forgets to mutate to the second quarter of the 'Nyamaropa' cycle in bar 22, and repeats instead a version of the first quarter, before skipping to the fourth quarter in bar 23. The length of the cycle has thus been cut from four to three measures. This issues a new response in the cello – a repeated F# – groping for contrapuntal direction in the face of musical disalignment. In bar 28 the 'Nyamaropa' cycle is cut (probably quite literally given the indentation of the staff at this 4/4 measure of the original hand-written score) thereby offsetting the metric regularity of the 6/4 measure, after which F# sinks back to its opening pitches, and finally dances away – still in slightly wrong notes – with the upper dotted note line of the viola.

Ex. 5. Volans' 'The Songlines' quartet, II, bars 1-12.

I am describing these details to emphasise the fact that the music's 'formal asymmetry' (to quote Taylor's phrase) is the result not of its use of African music, but of its absent-minded disalignment with it. In fact, the harmonic sequence guiding the patterns of the piece under investigation is, according to certain analytic perspectives, highly symmetrical. Consider the progression of 'Nyamaropa' depicted in Example 7 as two six-dyad progressions, the second of which is an inverted retrograde of the first. Put differently, if we call the first dyad G(D) 0, the cycle runs 024025035135, which is RT5I of itself.[3]

Now, by cutting, splicing, and adding wrong notes to this progression, Volans effectively undermines this symmetry in 'The Songlines'. And, as the piece progresses, it seems to undertake a reverse journey. It gradually feels its way back to the original, as if to elaborate found fragments that eventually, albeit fleetingly, encounter tradition – music not of evolution, but of de-composition. In bars 89-100, the second violin holds the 'Nyamaropa' passage, while the surrounding instruments articulate a much more traditional interlocking part than before. While there is still less consistency in the patterning of the violin line than there would be in a more traditional rendition of this part on the

19
Violin 1
Violin 2
Viola
Cello
pizz. half pont.
mf
p
pp
gliss.
24
pp

Ex. 6. Volans'' The Songlines' quartet, II, bars 19-29.

mbira, there are relatively fewer false notes, and these gradually melt away over bars 97-100. Notice how the 'Nyamaropa' pattern, as if to betray its orientation towards the fading interlocking part, seems to trip over itself in bar 100 where it is extended by two pulses. And finally, we get a traditional variation for four measures without wrong notes, without skipped beats or added parts and with a regularised interlocking part – a part once played by Gwanzura Gwenzi in Harare. It is here that the music finally wisps away under that voice.

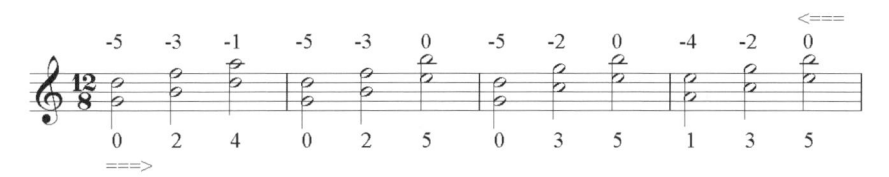

Ex. 7. The 'Nyamaropa' cycle expressed as a retrograde inversion of itself.

The point is that where we find harmonic and rhythmic asymmetries and displacements we find the voice of Volans, not that of Gwenzi. In fact, the distortions of traditional music in 'The Songlines' underscore a Western preoccupation and not strictly an African influence. I am reluctant to call even these asymmetries 'nonformal' (as in Taylor's lexicon) because the melodic and rhythmic disalignments bring lightness and co-ordination to the 'traditional' passage in bars 101-104. They make us arrive somewhere; they offer a momentary clearing; they make aesthetic form.

Volans makes similar alterations in other works as well. For example, in the third movement of the string quartet version of 'White Man Sleeps', Volans slows down and overholds various pitches of the 'Nyanga' panpipe dance from

Mozambique to such an extent that the original is lost in a haunting mat of sound that slowly invades the ears, bristling in a desolate dreamworld, while in the first movement, he recasts a traditional concertina song from Lesotho in an asymmetrical 13/4, with myriad twists and turns into 14/4 or 10/4 or 11/4 – a solid unmoving pounding between two chords that brutally affirm new proportions in unpredictable places. Again, in these examples, Volans distorts the original music to produce a more asymmetrical flow. It will not do to wishfully think *African* music as an aesthetics of 'asymmetry' alone, still less as the 'nonformal' per se. This is not to say that all African music inclines towards symmetry; it does not. West African bell patterns, for example, are, under some analytic perspectives, inherently asymmetric – although, even in these cases, the asymmetry depends on how we are hearing and thinking.[4] San bow music, to name a less debated example, in which ternary rhythms frequently run agilely beneath two-beat groupings, is highly unpredictable in its patterned displacements over time. The last movement of 'White Man Sleeps' is inspired by this bow-playing technique.

Interestingly, where Volans does quote an African piece verbatim and throughout a movement, it is often an African song that exhibits some kind of asymmetry. Take the second movement of 'White Man Sleeps', which is a rendition of the 'Nyanga' panpipe dance performed by the Nyungwe people of Mozambique. This music, played on various sets of bamboo pipes interlocking with voiced tones involves a 24-pulse chord progression (see Example 8). Notice how closely the 'Nyanga' cycle resembles the 'Nyamaropa' cycle. If we begin on Nyamaropa's sixth dyad, leave out the fourth dyad and approximately halve the harmonic rhythm, we produce 'Nyanga' (see Example 9). So 'Nyanga' can be summarised as 'Nyamaropa' (with a piece lopped off) in fast forward. 'Nyanga' also starts in the middle of a chord's unfolding and has a more elastic harmonic rhythm than 'Nyamaropa'. Again, this is not a case of 'nonformal' music as such, even if one might say it is no longer symmetrical (or not yet lopsided).

A brief word on how the 'Nyanga' dance works. There are different groups of players, some performing in groups of three pulses, and others in groups of two. Within a group, each player performs a different pattern that starts at a different point. These have different names, such as *Kwarira Mvuu*, *Pakira*, *Kabombo*, *Mbite*, and so on. In 'White Man Sleeps' for two harpsichords and viola da gamba, Volans juxtaposes *tutti* sections with different combinations of individual parts. In his 'Section B', for instance, Player 1 combines *Kwarira Mvuu* and *Mbite Ngono*, while Player 2 performs the part *Pakira*. Despite the literal quotation, Volans' piece differs from the original in a few respects. First, the *tutti* sections include an irregular distribution of silences in each part, which inhibits the performers from getting into a simple physical groove. Again we witness an imposed asymmetry but this time one that paradoxically conjures the course-grained, almost convulsive, dynamic instability of the original. This sound is consistent with Volans' understanding of African music, which in his view does not 'groove' as much as 'flow' (pers. comm., January 2007). Second, occasionally Volans omits or changes a note, such as the 20th and 21st pulses of player 1's 'Part B'. In this respect too, Volans is quite 'traditional' because the performance of 'Nyanga' is not as fixed as the notation implies – players tend to listen and react to each other, leaving out notes, overholding or splitting others, adding new ones, varying the dynamics, delaying and anticipating, always adjusting to the drifting hockets of the surrounding ensemble.[5]

ON APPROPRIATION, IN CONCLUSION

The richness of Volans' early music lies in its open embrace and subtle translation of values found in traditional African music by way of a *paraphrase* technique. Volans' paraphrases sometimes offer literal borrowing and other times show marks of alteration and tampering with the original. In the first case, African music is rendered in tone colors whose very familiarity (in the West) can convey a sudden and paradoxical sense of wonder about music of the non-West, and in the second, African music is rendered in revised form to recapitulate some of the very qualities of its original context in a new one. Is this kind of work politically *appropriate*? And how does it articulate, in particular, with the politics of apartheid? On the word *appropriate*, the *Oxford English Dictionary* writes: 'that which is suitable or proper to or for'; or 'to take to oneself without authority'. Can knowing that 'cultural practice' (rather than formal value) is the suitable and proper methodological gaze for understanding African music also be a case of taking such music to oneself without authority? Can such knowledge be a methodic prior idealisation of a music we claim to get to know through that method? Perhaps not – but only maybe if that 'cultural practice' is presented in great detail and shown, in the robust sense, to contradict other approaches and methods. In contrast, can taking some African dances to oneself without authority also be a case of hearing something that is suitable and proper to it? Perhaps not – but only maybe if that music is explored in great detail and shown, in the robust sense, to be exhausted by its socio-political significance instead. Close examination of the socio-political contexts of the African music in question suggests a less robust approach.

Consider the role played by music in the spirit possession ceremonies of the Shona, for example, whose *mbira* music is perhaps the most important source for Volans' paraphrase compositions. These ceremonies, known as

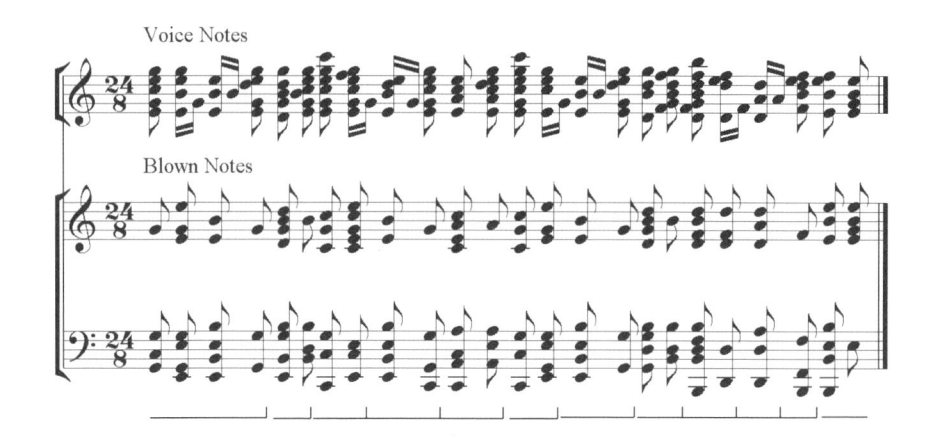

Ex. 8. The 'Nyanga' progression (transcription: Andrew Tracey).

bira, have the function of addressing social ills, such as conflict and dispute between members of a community, or affliction caused by disease, drought, technology, or social upheaval. The aim of the ceremony is to invoke the ancestral spirits so that they may assist in the negotiating process among villagers; ameliorating differences of opinion in the case of dispute, and so on. Before a Shona ancestor enters the body of a *homwe* (medium), s/he needs to be coaxed forth by specific musical tunes on the *mbira*. This frequently involves an all-night ritual of *mbira* playing, dancing and singing. When the requisite spirit comes, the music stops and the negotiations begin. It is counter-intuitive not to construe the *bira* ceremony as a case of aesthetics bringing possibilities into imaginative play; of negotiating the antagonistic demands of reality and ethics in a manner not entirely at odds with a Western construal of the problem. Even Immanuel Kant's formulation of the (logically) autonomous faculty of the imagination in the freeplay of aesthetic contemplation was still heteronomous insofar as it had the power to bring moral man in contact with the scientific world. Only an account of aesthetic autonomy that is prepared to forget the crucial bridging role played by the *Critique of Judgement* (between the *Critiques of Pure* and *Practical Reason* respectively) can fail to notice the imagination's ability to connect objective with subjective experience. For the purposes of this argument it suffices to note that cultural *differences* across the terrain of aesthetics cannot be aprioristically assumed.

It is precisely this default position *assuming* difference – an idea that flourished under apartheid – that Volans' paraphrase compositions put into question and doubt. While it must be acknowledged that Volans' musical *appropriations* are double-edged – both taking without authority *and* offering something suitable and proper to African music – I want to emphasise and exaggerate the importance of the latter in relation to the politics of apartheid. Volans' music draws attention to aesthetic qualities of African music that can be systematically veiled not only by an ideology of separateness and difference, but also by a well-intentioned anthropological gaze. It dares to imagine, one might say, a then-impossible sound of post-apartheid South Africa. It revitalises a sense of wonder and sensuous attention to historically buried details about African music. By enclosing African music in new formal boundaries it thereby reaches beyond such boundaries to a larger political world, evoking in the listener a new perspective on the cultural forces from which it emerged and for which it may be taken to stand. This resonance illuminates the complex, dynamic conditions of the music's making. That is, Volans' unfettered paraphrase of African music discloses aspects of the history of its appropriation; it paradoxically reinstates the fragile openness, the negotiable permeability of the music's social and historical meanings in the first place. This reinstatement occurs not (only) on the banal grounds of the music's removal from a traditional context, but because its particular resonance in the context of the new work menaces the very concept of tradition. The music can awaken in the listener a sense of the contingency of the exclusions by which certain cultural practices come to be conceptually separated from other practices, which they partially resemble.

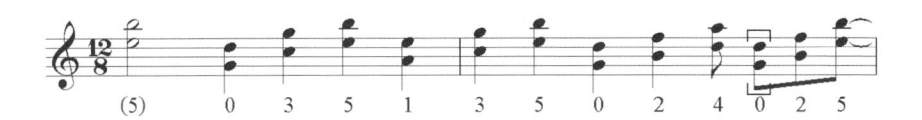

Ex. 9. Harmonic reduction of 'Nyanga' and its relation to 'Nyamaropa'.

For instance, the ability of 'Hunting: Gathering' to reinstate the harmonic genius of African song is one corrective to such hardened historical oppositions. By casting a new aesthetic perspective on African harmony 'Hunting: Gathering' challenges the time-worn commonplace about the primacy of harmony in the West. Three centuries of harmonic development are frequently enlisted in traditional Western music histories and theories to distinguish Western forms of music from other forms. Take an example from the days of apartheid: 'Bantu music ... lacks a particular dimension: its harmony has remained rudimentary:

it has remained a tail-stump instead of developing' (Arthur Wegelin cited in Levy, 1992). For all the ironies of the metaphor of a tail-stump in the context of evolutionary *regression*, the characteristic foregrounding of 'rhythm', 'timbre', 'inharmonicities', and so on, in analyses of the music of Africa may resonate more closely than it seems at first sight with this awkward evolutionary position. Volans' 'African Paraphrases' refuses such racialised topos formation.

On the other hand, as the critics remind us, Volans' music also gained traction on the logic of apartheid, did little to allay the drastic inequality of apartheid, and even effaced the African authors of the original music. Did it thereby *compose* apartheid, to borrow a phrase from the title of this book? Did it merely form part of its repertory? Or worse, did it in fact constitute and compile apartheid ideology through arrangements of sound? Still worse, did it in fact calm the convulsive madness of apartheid? Did it allow ideology to collect itself in the face of political excess? Did it render the blight of apartheid palatable, stabilise an order of things? Perhaps it did. Perhaps Volans' music functioned as an efficient ideological mechanism for apartheid thinking, offering fantasy transgressions in place of real ones, to a mostly white audience mostly in the northern hemisphere. As such, Volans' work could be said to recapitulate the outmoded vision of high culture as harmonising a domain of reconciliation grounded in aesthetic labour that ultimately transcends its precise economic and political determinants. The criticism described (and criticised in turn) at the outset of this paper tends towards this interpretation.

And yet, it is important to exercise caution in this rush to judgement. The critics' gestures of apparent dissent may also be an element in a larger process of legitimation, while Volans' apparent stabilisation of the ruling order may turn out, in the long run, to subvert it. Political overtones and valences are in constant flux, sometimes abruptly so. There are no formal guarantees that what seems progressive in one social conjuncture will not become conservative in another. The *criticism* of Volans' project, largely disconcerted as it is by the (Western) problem of ownership alone, may be useful in addressing various historical inequities in various quarters – the uneven handling of Western and non-Western music by copyright law, to name one obvious example – but this use should not hide from view the many battles in Africa's ongoing struggle for justice, equality, and freedom.[6] Volans' compositional actions, which in the critique of them appear as singularly appropriative, are in fact multiple. They cannot, to use Bahktin's term, be reduced to the monological self-uttering expression of a single artist's intention, even if some of the most progressive qualities of the work are not fully grasped by the artist.

It is deceptive to withdraw the relations of power, politics and economy that are sublimated in the composer's works, but it is a further deception to interpret these works as unmediated reflections of these relations. For Volans' art gives unmistakable voice to an aesthetic hearing of African music – a form of wonder and admiration – that to an extent escapes the structures of politics and the market. In 'Of White Africans and White Elephants', Volans writes: 'From our privileged position in this country we can and must learn something of the spirit of traditional African culture – the exuberance, extravagance and unexpectedness; the sense of order and pattern – the need to make every part essential to the whole; the assurance, humility and lack of guilt that comes of a knowledge of one's place and value in society' (1986). This passionate openness to the aesthetics of African music, however invented these aesthetics may be, is directly linked in the composer's mind to social values and even ethics. African music, for Volans, can teach the elite class about the social values of interaction, assurance, humility, guiltlessness. His music sets out gently to reveal this lesson. By no means fully autonomous and yet not reducible to the complex social forces by which it is shaped, Volans' music is fundamentally centered on a certain *way of listening* to the other, a listening grounded in art's ability to generate surprise, admiration, delight. In so doing, the music encourages a different listening experience from that encouraged by mainstream ethnography, which has sacrificed sensuous pleasure (centred on aesthetics) on the altar of socio-cultural description (centred on anthropology). By permeating its textures with African music, and yet resisting the cultured 'cultural' experience that encourages listening right through the music – *being unsure enough not to delimit the space for the expression of the other* – Volans' 'African Paraphrases' paradoxically open unanticipated perspectives on the African music it appropriates. In the words of Jeanette Winterson, 'We have to recognise that art, all art, is not our mother-tongue' (1995: 4). Volans' respect and admiration for the unguessed-at aesthetic genius of others, an admiration deeply embedded in his paraphrase compositions, is a response worth cherishing, enhancing, and celebrating still today.

Whose 'White Man Sleeps'? Who is the one whose white man remains oblivious, unaware? Does that one recognise oneself in the object of anthropological benevolence? A speech act is not complete without a concomitant *listening*. How much less so for a musical one! Said a cobra spirit in the region near Tete, where the 'Nyanga' is danced: 'The one who will not listen will be poisoned!' Now maybe the one who will can help the white man awake.

Endnotes

1. Portions of this essay have appeared in the author's essays 'Of Sleeping White Men: Analytic Silence in the Critical Reception of Kevin Volans' (2005); 'The Form is/in the Function: Situating the African Keyboard Music of Kevin Volans' (2005); 'Art Music in a Cross-Cultural Context: The Case of Africa' (2004); and 'Notes on a Postcolonial Musicology: Kofi Agawu and the Critique of Cultural Difference' (2003). They are reproduced here with permission.
2. On the invention of African rhythmic complexity, see Agawu (2003).
3. RT5I refers to a retrograde inversion at a transposition of 5. On the time-transcending symmetries and near-symmetries of 'Nyamaropa', see my 'Negotiating the Music Theory/African Music Nexus' (2001).
4. On the asymmetry of west African timelines, see Arom (1991).
5. On the *Nyanga* panpipe dance, see Tracey (1971).
6. On the ambiguities of copyright protection of non-Western music, see my 'Music, Spirit Possession and the Copyright Law' (1999).

Bibliography

Agawu, Kofi. 2003. *Representing African Music: Postcolonial Notes, Queries, Positions.* New York & London: Routledge.

Arom, Simha. 1991. *African Polyrhythm and Polyphony* (trans. Martin Thom, Barbara Tuckett & Raymond Boyd). Cambridge: Cambridge University Press.

Bailey, John. 1985. 'Musical Structure and Human Movement'. In P Howell, I Cross & R West (eds). *Musical Structure and Cognition.* London: Orlando, pp. 237-258.

Berliner, Paul. 1973. *Soul of Mbira: Music and Traditions of the Shona People of Zimbabwe.* Berkeley: University of California Press.

Bräuninger, Jürgen. 1998. 'Gumboots to the Rescue'. *South African Journal of Musicology*, 18, pp. 1-16.

Johns, Jasper. 1996. *Jasper Johns: A Retrospective.* New York: Museum of Modern Art.

Levy, Michael. 1992. 'Three South African Cross-Cultural Orchestral Pieces'. Presentation for the International Society for Contemporary Music, World Music Days, Warsaw.

Ligeti, György. 1988. 'On my *Etudes* for Piano', and 'On my *Piano Concerto*' (trans. Sid McLauchlan). *Sonus*, 9, pp. 3-13.

Mead, Andrew. 1999. 'Bodily Hearing: Physiological Metaphors and Musical Understanding'. *Journal of Music Theory*, 43, pp. 1–18.

Scherzinger, Martin. 1999. 'Music, Spirit Possession and the Copyright Law: A Cross-Cultural Comparison'. *Yearbook for Traditional Music*, 31, pp. 102-125.

_. 2001. 'Negotiating the Music Theory/African Music Nexus: A Political Critique of

Ethnomusicological Anti-Formalism and a Strategic Analysis of the Harmonic Patterning of the Shona Mbira Song *Nyamaropa*'. *Perspectives of New Music*, 39(1), pp. 5-117.

_. 2003. 'Notes on a Postcolonial Musicology: Kofi Agawu and the Critique of Cultural Difference'. *Current Musicology*, 75, pp. 223-250.

_. 2004. 'Art Music in a Cross-Cultural Context: The Case of Africa'. In A Pople & N Cook (eds). *Cambridge History of Twentieth-Century Music*. Cambridge: Cambridge University Press, pp. 548-613.

_. 2005. 'The Form is/in the Function: Situating the African Keyboard Music of Kevin Volans'. In C Tse Kimberlin & A Euba (eds). *Towards an African Pianism (Volume 1)*. Richmond, CA: MRI Press, pp. 157-165.

_. 2005. 'Of Sleeping White Men: Analytic Silence in the Critical Reception of Kevin Volans'. *NewMusicSA: Bulletin of the International Society for Contemporary Music, South African Section*, 3, pp. 22-26.

Taylor, Timothy. 1995. 'When We Think about Music and Politics: The Case of Kevin Volans'. *Perspectives of New Music*, 33, pp. 504-536.

Tracey, Andrew. 1971. 'The Nyanga Panpipe Dance'. *African Music: Journal of the African Music Society*, 5(1), pp. 73-82.

Volans, Kevin. n.d. 'White Man Sleeps: Composer's Statement'. http://www.kevinvolans.com/kv_arti_whit.shtml; accessed 8 April 2007.

_. 1986. 'Of White Africans and White Elephants'. http://www.kevinvolans.com/kv_arti_ofwh.shtml; accessed 8 April 2007.

_. 1994. 'Notes to CD: *String Quartet No. 3*: The Songlines'. Performed by the Balanescu Quartet. Decca /Argo 44029-2.

Walton, Christopher. 2002/2003. 'CD Review: Kevin Volans' String Quartets Nos. 1, 2 & 6'. *NewMusicSA: Bulletin of the International Society for Contemporary Music, South African Section*, 2, pp. 22-24.

Winterson, Jeanette. 1995. *Art Objects: Essays on Ecstasy and Effrontery*. London: Cape.

11
STATE OF CONTENTION

RECOMPOSING APARTHEID AT PRETORIA'S STATE THEATRE, 1990-1994. A PERSONAL RECOLLECTION

Brett Pyper

Introduction[1]

In the maelstrom of cultural debate that attended South Africa's transition towards non-racial democracy in the early 1990s, few institutions were more vocally held to symbolise the apartheid cultural apparatus, at least as far as the performing arts were concerned, than Pretoria's State Theatre. Even if one never entered the complex, adjacent to a domed plaza housing a larger-than-life bust of former apartheid prime minister JG Strijdom, the massive modernist structure situated solidly in the centre of the apartheid capital architecturally and symbolically bespoke a familiarity with Pretoria's bureaucratic and political establishment, and reciprocally invested a city often caricatured for its civil servant mentality with the conspicuous trappings of Western high culture.

As a schoolchild growing up in the city, I was among the many Pretorians marshalled to line Church Street for the grand opening of the facility in the week of Republic Day in 1981.[2] I had dutifully donned my Boy Scout uniform, and what I recall as an early lesson in the banality of public pageantry reached a personal anticlimax when the black limousine of then-State President Marais Viljoen raced past me. The president hardly deigned to be seen, let alone to wave triumphantly as I had expected, as fanfares echoed out from the balconies of the self-proclaimed 'new world centre' and dignitaries arrived by the Mercedes-full.[3]

Associations between the State Theatre and the apartheid order extended, of course, well beyond physical proximity and the semiotics of public space. The State Theatre was the headquarters of the Performing Arts Council of the Transvaal (PACT), the largest of the four provincial performing arts councils, and offerings presented on its stages were among the few to receive a government subsidy in the old South Africa. Viewed from the outside, at the most commonsensical level, the State Theatre and the apartheid state were clearly on intimate terms.

Yet, with one notable exception, much has been assumed and relatively little documented about the place of South Africa's publicly funded theatres in promulgating 'apartheid culture' on the shifting terrain of national cultural politics during the apartheid era.[4] For one thing, PACT and its counterparts in other provinces (PACOFS in the Free State, NAPAC in then-Natal and CAPAB in the Cape) were established in the mid-1960s on cultural terrain that had already irrevocably been shaped by colonialism and apartheid's coercive physical and cultural removals of the 1950s. White racial hegemony having been long entrenched by the 1960s, the performing arts after this time were afforded a degree of liberal licence under high apartheid,[5] though the threat of state censorship always hovered in the background.[6] Furthermore, responsibility for the apartheid state's flagship cultural institutions (including the Nico Malan Theatre in Cape Town, the Playhouse in Durban, and the Sand du Plessis complex in Bloemfontein – monuments to culture, rather than cultural centres, as I once heard South African composer Kevin Volans pertinently put it) devolved to the provinces rather than the central government, making them relatively minor instruments for shaping public opinion when compared to, for example, the national broadcaster. While I don't mean to suggest that provincial and local politics were any less invested in Afrikaans or, later, a more generalised white cultural and political hegemony than they were at the national level, my impression of the State Theatre when I entered it as a junior music administrator in the watershed year of 1990 was of an organisation in which a particularly situated network of artists and arts administrators had, within the structural constraints that pervaded apartheid society in general, significantly been left to their own devices by the state. That this relatively autonomous if officially sanctioned art world had come, I increasingly came to realise, by varying degrees to perpetuate apartheid, was less because it responded to official dictates and more because it espoused a particular *cultural* politics that brought it into broad alignment with apartheid writ large.[7]

This chapter is informed by my partial perspective as a relatively junior PACT employee in its music department during the volatile transitional years of the early 1990s and supplemented by archival material, including public pronouncements of the former PACT's management.[8] I move towards an understanding of the ways in which certain primarily aesthetic investments adopted by a sector of South Africa's performing arts community occasioned this ideological alignment with a profoundly racist and exploitative order. I will focus on the period between the unbanning of liberation movements in 1990 and the official end of the apartheid era some four years later, not only because it spans the duration of my association with PACT and affords me a certain perspective on how my colleagues within the organisation responded to the unfolding political transition, but because it was a period in which debates around the status of the performing arts councils, the public theatres in which they resided, and the socio-political relevance of the art forms which they promoted were intense and far-reaching, becoming an important flashpoint for broader social contestation over the meaning of cultural democratisation in South Africa.

A PACT with apartheid?

The vaunted image of the performing arts council based at the State Theatre with which I grew up was in fact a latter-day instantiation of an organisation that was originally rather different in its scope and pretensions.[9] Though one must of course hedge any assessments with several caveats about the egregious racial policies of the time, one might go so far as saying that the early PACT was oriented towards fostering a kind of community-based cultural infrastructure, at least within the racially exclusive population that it saw as its primary constituency. PACT was founded in 1963 and originally comprised a drama and a music department; and its focus in the 1960s and into the 1970s lay, in addition to establishing English and Afrikaans resident drama companies, in bolstering or facilitating the creation of amateur music societies throughout the former Transvaal, which it then organised into a circuit through which a selection of South African and foreign artists regularly toured.

The reach of this organisation, whose offerings eventually came to include ballet and opera productions, within the white population of the Transvaal is hard to imagine in the light of the narrow association of PACT with the State Theatre after 1981. A tour in 1968 by the Vienna Boys' Choir featured no fewer than 54 concerts over more than a four-month period across the length and breadth of the province, most of which were one-night engagements in small-town church and school halls.[10] One might imagine what this kind of public-sector support and infrastructural vision might, under different political circumstances, have meant to the likes of Gibson Kente and untold numbers of emerging black artists of the time similarly attempting to reach audiences beyond the mainstream urban theatres. PACT's offerings were, however, oriented almost exclusively towards white audiences, and artists and repertoire were drawn almost exclusively from the European canon. That PACT significantly collaborated in its formative years with local concert clubs located in civil society should be noted, not least because since the demise of the performing arts councils in the late 1990s, local concert clubs have been re-emerging across the country as a feature of the post-apartheid cultural sphere.

Since the internal distribution of activities within PACT over time located operas, musicals and orchestral concerts outside the purview of the music department, PACT Music was seen within the organisation to be a relatively minor player by way of attendance, income, and subsidy, as its Head Schalk Visser admitted (*Annual Report*, 1968). Nonetheless, over time the department's presentation of solo, chamber, and on occasion larger ensemble concerts across the province to no small degree supported PACT Director Eghard van der Hoven's claim that in its first decade, the organisation presented 13 069 performances of 838 programmes for an audience of almost five million people (1973). A decade later, these figures were set at 31 000 performances attended by almost twelve million people over twenty years ('Preface', 1983). PACT Music's portfolio of presentations over its first two decades featured a series of predominantly European-based classical instrumental ensembles (the German Male Voice Choir, Ensemble Vocal de Lausanne, Johann Strauss Ensemble der Wiener Symphoniker, Chilingirian String Quartet, and so on), folk touring companies (the Mercedes Molina Spanish Dance Theatre, the Kasatka Cossacks, Los Paraguayos, et cetera), South African (white) university choirs, and a long list of soloists, some internationally renowned, many of them South African or based in South Africa, and many others lesser known. In a relatively early statement on its programming policy, Visser avowed a two-fold approach comprising, on the one hand, popular programmes likely to draw 'the man in the street' (Salzburg Marionettes, and local artists like soprano Nellie du Toit and tenor Gé Korsten, and of course the Vienna Boys' Choir), and, on the other, 'the less popular or connoisseur programme' presented at the University of Pretoria's Musaion venue and a few other centres (*Annual Report*, 1968). Visser declared it the objective of his department 'eventually to win over many people from the lighter type of programme to the more serious type', apparently on the assumption that the one would organically lead to the other. In the same report, Visser noted 'a stage of crisis' with respect to the presentation of local artists; practically all PACT's best artists were allegedly being 'absorbed' by the Opera Department during the first three terms of the year, and PACT was reportedly receiving complaints that it was presenting 'the same artists over and over again'. Against this background, Visser resolved to 'make more use of popular groups from overseas'.

In a mix, then, of middlebrow and more 'serious' offerings, PACT Music adopted a moderately populist stance in conjunction with a more curatorial, avowedly developmental programming policy. The time would come when PACT would justifiably be accused of elitism in a broader national context, but its capacity to countenance and respond to such a critique would for decades be framed by its image of itself as a body that brought the high European opera, ballet, orchestral and drama repertoire to white middle-class audiences, including rural ones, for prices significantly lower than those associated with these and other more commercial genres in other national settings. As the 1970s waned, however, the international oil crisis made the cost of extended tours prohibitive, and the belated introduction of television to South Africa offered audiences on the *platteland* an alternative source of entertainment.[11] The reach of PACT's productions shrunk considerably as its aspirations became focused on the sumptuous facility that was being built for it in the centre of Pretoria. By the time that the organisation took occupation of the State Theatre in 1981 its priorities had clearly shifted, with the emphasis falling on producing lavish productions that could showcase the technical facilities of the venue, which were reported to be among the most advanced in the world, and bringing audiences to the arts, rather than the other way around, as had formerly been the case.

The apogee of the State Theatre in the 1980s coincided, of course, with the intensification of the anti-apartheid struggle and renewed political repression throughout South Africa, even as the latter was accompanied by a relative ideological liberalisation under PW Botha's presidency. When the State Theatre opened, it was announced, contrary to what remains common wisdom in some quarters, that the facility would be open to all races, a response, apparently, to the controversies and boycotts occasioned by the earlier designation of Cape Town's Nico Malan Theatre as a whites-only venue.[12] Nevertheless, there is little denying that PACT ever catered to more than a small, racially homogeneous fraction of the Transvaal's population, and there is a significant difference between nominally granting people of colour admission to theatres and developing an ethos and policy that could advance the cultural interests of the population at large, which could hardly, given the broader South African context of the time, overlook artists voicing political dissent. Faced with these challenges PACT, for the most part, looked in the other direction as it planned an extensive roster of productions that were often critically praised as technically and artistically accomplished, but increasingly disconnected from the social and cultural priorities of the broader society beyond its walls in whose name it claimed to operate, and from whose taxes it indirectly received its funding. PACT's programmers unilaterally ignored and actively undermined cultural embargoes by bringing foreign artists to South Africa, while the efflorescence of politically engaged performance genres that audiences were encountering elsewhere at venues like Johannesburg's Market Theatre hardly registered on the State Theatre's main stages; though some variance could be discerned in this respect between PACT's resident companies, with the drama and later the contemporary dance companies taking significant steps in this direction. The council's management remained entirely white, and the culture of the organisation was not devoid, in my experience, of the taint of racial hierarchy or *baasskap*.

Nevertheless, by the early 1990s, when I arrived at PACT, alongside the canonical Western repertoire of opera, ballet, classical drama, symphony concerts and instrumental recitals, PACT offered appearances by several leading exponents of the counter-cultural Afrikaans rock and cabaret florescence of the late 1980s, innovative presentations by its multiracial contemporary dance company, a jazz series that belatedly featured established and emerging African jazz musicians, and a sponsored mobile stage that took an admittedly selective set of educational and repertoire programmes to black townships and schools. Though still predominantly targeted towards its white audience base in Pretoria, and virtually entirely divorced from debate within black cultural and political organisations concerning the role of the arts in the transition towards democracy, it didn't feel like too much of a stretch of the imagination to some of us working within the organisation to imagine that PACT might build on these emerging trends within its programming to engage the social and political transition taking place beyond its walls, now that the government had unbanned the political organisations with which several progressive arts bodies were affiliated, and in view of the fact that face-to-face interaction with formerly exiled anti-apartheid activist-artists had been legalised.

Indeed, a cursory look at what documentary evidence remains of contemporary debates within the cultural flank of the anti-apartheid struggle suggests that organisations like PACT might have identified not only challenges to its mandate but also several points of convergence, if not opportunities for collaboration, with at least some progressive organisations, as questions were increasingly raised about its capacity to survive the transition to democracy. At the Culture in Another South Africa (CASA) conference convened by the

African National Congress (ANC) in Amsterdam at the end of 1987, while recognising the existence of an alternative, democratic, people's culture that had developed in opposition to the apartheid regime, delegates articulated a decidedly catholic vision of South African culture in which existing Eurocentric artistic disciplines and performance spaces might be afforded a role (see Campschreur and Divendaal, 1989: 214, 223). Patrick Fitzgerald's 'reflection on ruling-class culture in South Africa' included the observation that '[m]uch or most cultural production in the present conjuncture in South Africa cannot be simply packaged into democratic and non-democratic containers and shipped into contemporary political theory in neat analytical bundles' (Ibid.:162). And while Barbara Masekela's keynote address on behalf of the Department of Arts and Culture of the ANC was more willing to speak of 'a dichotomy' between progressive and reactionary cultural forces, she too warned 'against relegating to irrelevance the contribution of our white democratic compatriots. We must encourage the trend of Afrikaner cultural workers of the past and present, take cognisance of and support their efforts to identify with the national democratic struggle' (Ibid.: 254). Speaking on behalf of the National Executive Committee of the ANC, Pallo Jordan argued that 'While we require propaganda art, we do not demand that every graphic artist and sculptor become a prop artist. We would urge our artists to pursue excellence in their respective disciplines – to be excellent artists and to serve the struggle for liberation with excellent art' (Ibid.: 265). And at the Zabalaza Festival organised by exiles in London in mid-1990, Junaid Ahmed, General Secretary of the Congress of South African Writers, mentioned PACT by name in trenchantly critiquing mainstream adherence to narrow definitions of South African theatre, while recognising the skills of theatre practitioners working in organisations like the State Theatre and calling on them to make their skills broadly available through public education and workshop programmes (cited in Oliphant, 1993: 117).

Recomposing apartheid

Since several of the calls from outside the organisation for broadening access to learning and culture expressed values that PACT's management claimed to espouse,[13] I and several of my colleagues felt that there was merit in the organisation revisiting its programming policies and engaging in dialogue, parallel to the concurrent national political negotiation process, with the broader performing arts community, including the cultural desks of the formerly exiled liberation movements. Yet PACT's management displayed considerable reluctance on both counts. As far as artistic policy was concerned, PACT recommitted itself to its historical investment in developing what its general director called a 'universal arts culture *('n universele kunskultuur)'* in South Africa, foregrounding the European-derived so-called 'classical theatre disciplines' and *de facto* overlooking most contemporary black South African theatre, music and dance (*TRUK/PACT Info*, November 1991-January 1992: 2). Indeed, in voicing weak repudiations of the charge of Eurocentrism in PACT'S programming, spokespersons sometimes seemed to be wholly ignorant of, let alone prepared to invest in, what the CASA conference had called the 'other South African culture' that by then had acquired its own kind of canonical status from Broadway to Berlin. PACT's official pronouncements of the early 1990s continued to imply that the African performing arts were yet to come of age, implying their dependence on European-derived patronage or collaboration in claims to the effect that '[b]y promoting the Eurocentric and so-called Afrocentric art forms in tandem, an art form of the future will be brought into being' (*TRUK/PACT Info*, August-October 1992: 2), going so far, on occasion, as quoting and thereby endorsing the characterisation of Afrocentric performing arts as 'some nebulous and unproven culture of limited international appeal'.[14] Instead, PACT's leadership exhorted audiences across apartheid divides to invest in a universalist, transcendent, apolitical view of art: 'The performing arts transcend all boundaries and differences, whatever they may be. When we all attend a presentation of one or another theatre discipline, regardless of our political persuasion, religious belief or race, such an audience is brought together in an experience that is often referred to as "food for the soul"' (Ibid.; my translation).

The tension between these aesthetic investments and the national cultural environment was exemplified in 1991 when PACT Music elected to celebrate its tenth year in the State Theatre by inviting a major German orchestra to tour South Africa under its auspices. Having hosted the Bamberger Symfoniker on the occasion of the facility's opening in 1981, the department now invited the Sinfonieorchester des Südwestfunks Baden-Baden to perform seldom-heard landmarks of the late Romantic orchestral repertoire in Pretoria, Johannesburg, Durban, Cape Town, and Bloemfontein. Within classical music circles at least, this tour became a flashpoint for debates as to whether, when, and how the Unesco-endorsed cultural boycott of South Africa might be ended, with the Baden-Baden orchestra assuming what *The Star* newspaper described as 'the dubious title of cultural isolation-breaker No 1' (18 April 1991). The Cultural Desk of the ANC expressed opposition to the proposed tour, a sentiment that was articulated by various progressively positioned bodies elsewhere in the country. In Cape Town, the Federation of South African Cultural Organisations (Fosaco) and the Cultural Workers' Congress condemned the visit, named some of its European-based sponsors 'for their collusion in breaking the cultural boycott', and called for a full boycott of CAPAB, which hosted the local concert (*Weekly Mail*, 19-25 April 1991). The Performing Arts Workers Equity (PAWE) wrote to the management of the Baden-Baden orchestra pointing out not only that the tour would be a unilateral infringement of international embargoes but also, as reported in the *Weekly Mail*, that the importing of the 105-member ensemble would 'usurp the rights of South African musicians'. PAWE's objections went to the heart of the State Theatre's significance on the national cultural landscape:

> Classical music, they [PAWE] say, is virtually unknown in the townships and rural areas, and has become the exclusive prerogative of affluent whites. PAWE's objection was compounded by the fact that the orchestra was brought out to celebrate the anniversary of the State Theatre, which has become a hated symbol of the state-sponsored arts (*Weekly Mail*, 5-11 April 1991).

Despite such opposition, the tour went ahead, underwritten by a reported array of more than 30 sponsors in Germany, Switzerland, and South Africa, the latter notably including the Department of Foreign Affairs, which evidently saw the tour as a means of promoting the international legitimacy of the De Klerk political dispensation (*Pretoria News Tonight!*, 16 April 1991). The concerts in Johannesburg and Cape Town attracted demonstrators in opposition to the tour, prompting conductor Michael Gielen to comment from the podium on the orchestra's decision to accept the invitation and announcing a music development initiative to flow from the tour; to my knowledge, little ever came of this commitment. PACT Music Artistic Director Schalk Visser was quoted in the Afrikaans press as saying that the tour would take the sting out of the cultural boycott and that further orchestras were likely to follow (*Rapport*, 24 March 1991).[15]

Perusing the folder of press clippings that PACT compiled at the time, one is struck by the disconnect between these burning contextual questions and the sentiments evoked by the Baden-Baden orchestra's renditions of works by Mozart, Bruckner, and Mahler. Critics wrote in superlative terms of 'remarkable orchestral playing' (*Pretoria News Tonight!*, 16 April 1991), 'an unforgettable aesthetic experience' (*Applous*, 12 April 1991), 'almost painfully beautiful' (*Beeld*, 23 April 1991). The elder statesman of Afrikaans composers, Stefans Grové, wrote of conductor Gielen's outstanding balanced treatment of the greatest contrasts of texture and emotional colour (*Rapport*, 14 April

1991), while another critic noted his 'mastery of structure' (*Citizen*, 19 April 1991). Two critics referred to the presence of dissonant social voices in their reviews. One, with no apparent irony, referred to 'the hurdles of separation set by anti-apartheid movements', reporting that '[f]rom across the comfortable divide of President Street, concert-goers watched, snorted and generally turned their backs on the demonstration' (*The Star Tonight!*, 18 April 1991). *Vrye Weekblad*'s reviewer provided somewhat more substantive engagement with the charges of the protesters, specifically a placard reading 'We do not need racist culture. Baden-Baden go home', offering the liberal rejoinder that in a new democratic dispensation people should have the right to freely practise their cultural preferences (26 April-2 May 1991). The closer one was to the music, it seems, the harder it was to reconcile patent artistic excellence with an awareness that aesthetic achievement could not in itself dispel the divisions that cross-cut South African society. Indeed, looking out from the first floor of the City Hall at the protesters on the corner with Mahler ringing in my ears, the distance across President Street felt not comfortable, but rather like a disquieting and profoundly consequential gulf.

My sense that PACT's future survival depended on bridging such gaps increasingly felt like a minority view within the State Theatre's corridors. Consistently rejecting calls that implicated PACT in broader socio-political transformation, the organisation's senior management cast the latter as 'attacks on a regular basis on the performing arts' (*Annual Report*', 1991/92: 3). PACT's leadership nevertheless found it expedient, on occasion, to appropriate political discourse for its own ends. Celebrating the crumbling of cultural boycotts, the Council's General Director Dennis Reinecke argued that '[c]ultural embargoes were responsible for limiting artists locally and abroad from exercising their "democratic right" or "human right" to perform where and when they wished – political persuasion should never be allowed to curb the development of the arts' (*TRUK/PACT Info*, February-April 1992: 2). This kind of ostensibly apolitical double-speak reached bizarre extremes in the organisation's then deputy, later general, director's statements. In a foreword to a publicity brochure he, on the one hand, rejected efforts to 'drag PACT into the political arena' and, on the other, claimed that 'PACT was a non-racial organisation long before any of the current advocates of equal rights had even thought of it'.[16] On a later occasion, he asserted that PACT was being democratic by not negotiating with 'the ANC alliance' since democracy entails government by all the people and the ANC represents one of 'more than twenty different political groups' that then existed in the Transvaal (*TRUK/PACT Info*, November 1992-January 1993: 2-3).

This type of baldly ignorant and increasingly intransigent management stance made PACT few new friends in progressive cultural circles at the same time that the organisation was fighting legal battles relating to its occupational safety standards (following actress Gaynor Young's serious injury on its main stage) and a protracted labour dispute following the dismissal of the majority of its black staff. What was sobering, from within the organisation, was the implication that the stance of senior PACT officials as nay-saying apartheid apologists implicated many accomplished actors, musicians, dancers, technicians and other theatre professionals in opposition to broader efforts to reimagine and reshape the South African cultural landscape. In the process, the predominantly latent cultural racism espoused within certain South African arts circles was exposed, and a parastatal organisation like PACT found itself to the right of the very political dispensation that had nurtured it. In short, apartheid was recomposed at the State Theatre as its resident council and the art forms it promoted came to be seen, ensconced in their stronghold in Pretoria, to be in the rear guard of social transformation.

Epilogue 1

PACT and the State Theatre remained flashpoints for debates over the meaning of cultural democratisation well beyond the period on which I have focussed here. It became increasingly obvious that as the broad consultative process that led up to the formulation of South Africa's post-apartheid cultural policy gained momentum, PACT would become an object of, rather than an active agent in, attempts to democratise the public theatre sector in South Africa. After I left the Council at the end of 1993, the decline of the organisation could periodically be followed in public news reports and national policy statements.

This backdrop did not, however, deter PACT's management from a rather surprising, apparently last-ditch attempt to signal a willingness to transform itself. After ascending to the post of general director, the former deputy director, who had claimed that PACT had thought of non-racialism before anyone else, appointed none other than Hugh Masekela, veteran South African jazz musician, composer and anti-apartheid icon, as his deputy. Whether one reads this as naïve or as a transparent attempt at institutional co-option, the appointment struck me as ironic, given that I had some years previously presented a proposal to PACT's directorate to invite Masekela and other prominent exiled jazz musicians to appear in its main concert season, a proposal which had been rejected out of hand. But granting Masekela's musical and political stature, at a time in his career when he faced a court-ordered lien against his earnings in the United States and was still adjusting to being back in South Africa after three decades of exile, the latter compounded, as he frankly describes in his autobiography, by various addictions, the decision to appoint him to an administrative position at executive level remains hard to justify. The two pages which Masekela devotes to his year at PACT in his autobiography read like a series of dystopian South African arts management vignettes:

> Later that year [1995] I was appointed deputy director of the Performing Arts Council, with executive offices in Pretoria's State Theatre. I had to be at work every morning at eight. I was provided with the penthouse apartment atop the State Theatre, a brand-new Mercedes-Benz sedan, and a full bar for entertaining guests. The entire staff of 750 was headed by the director and me, and I had every possible perk. I would have a couple of tots of brandy before going down to my office. Part of my portfolio was to help in the transformation of the arts in South Africa. At first I was excited over my new job and very enthusiastic to make things happen. I soon discovered that my energies were futile (2004: 359).

Masekela ascribes the futility of his efforts to government bureaucracy above him and an intransigent middle management below him, which he equated with the apartheid civil service remaining intact in the immediate post-apartheid years, deliberately slowing down the transformation of the government's services to discredit the new dispensation. He also writes of discovering that the State Theatre's maintenance department, most of whom were black, worked under horrendous conditions, and moreover that a special locked toilet remained set aside for whites. Among the achievements of his stint at the State, Masekela claims a role in bringing African performers such as Rebecca Malope, Brenda Fassie, Afro-fusion group Bayete and Pretoria-raised musician Don Laka to the theatre, all of whom he avers were never allowed to showcase their talents there during the apartheid years. He also played a role in organising 'the 1996 independence celebrations', during which a 'cultural potpourri of traditional groups representing all ethnic groups marched and danced through Pretoria's streets and parks' (Ibid.: 361)

Epilogue 2

When the post-apartheid government adopted the recommendations of the Arts and Culture Task Group (ACTAG) in its cultural policy blueprint, the White Paper on Arts, Culture and Heritage of 1996, the transformation of the four performing arts councils was described as the subject of 'more controversy than any other issue facing the Ministry [of Arts, Culture, Science and Technology]' (White Paper). Citing the findings of a specially commissioned study of the four councils, the White Paper went on to stipulate that venues such as the State Theatre should be restructured in such a way that the infrastructure and skills built up over decades were not to be lost, but redirected to serving the artistic and cultural priorities established by a newly constituted National Arts Council. Whether the proposed redirection of such skills in fact took place is a topic for another study, but in the three years after the publication of the new policy, under the rubric of 'budgetary rightsizing', the existing arts councils received steeply declining subsidies to the point where only their core infrastructure and staff were guaranteed, effectively turning them into receiving houses or venues for rent with no resident performance companies.

Yet even in this circumscribed role, the State Theatre remained mired in controversy. Members of the transitional board in 1995 revealed that PACT's senior management had, in its twilight years, established a secret reserve fund, skimmed from its public subsidy, apparently to secure their pensions in the event of the organisation not surviving the transition to the new South Africa. Once discovered, the fund was reinvested, with post-apartheid ministerial approval, in what turned out to be a high-risk fund which in turn led to financial disaster. This led to a cabinet-level decision to shut down and 'mothball' the State Theatre in the middle of 2000. This could hardly have been followed, a few years later – on none other than the former Republic Day – with a more appropriate *Götterdämmerung*: the collapse of the dome on the adjacent square and the disappearance of Strijdom's infamous bronze bust into the bowels of the State Theatre's parking garage.

Epilogue 3

At the time of writing in 2007, the State Theatre has been reopened for some years and reclassified – marking a step back towards its former official status – as a state-funded body under the Cultural Institutions Act of 1998. The parking garage has been painted with Ndebele motifs, the interior decorating has been redone and the automated voice on the telephone switchboard proclaims that the State Theatre is 'a theatre for all South Africans'. Official publicity describes the facility as an 'unusual, stylish, centrally located venue' that can accommodate almost any event, including performances, conferences, festivals, product launches, fashion shows, film festivals, weddings, parties, matric dances and farewells, lunches and dinners. While the theatre's status as a receiving house has entailed an orientation towards what its publicists cite as 'blockbuster shows' like *Cats, Sarafina!, The Phantom of the Opera* and *The Sound of Music*, its National Lottery Board-funded

'52 Seasons' and 'Residency' programmes have provided emerging companies with a developmental platform and the mentoring of new work. Though the narrative recounted on the theatre's website elides much of the bumpy history sketched above – 'The opening of the theatre complex in May 1981 was a milestone in South African theatre and marked the beginning of great things to come' – one awaits with interest the outcome of the claim that 'The South African State Theatre has an important and necessary part to play in the daily lives of everyone and is definitely here to stay!' (www.statetheatre.co.za/about_us.htm).

Conclusion

For all their initial Eurocentrism and the elitist connotations that have accrued to them in various national settings, the art forms promoted by organisations like PACT have not necessarily been articulated to racist political ideology at all times and in all places and had in many instances been quite well established in South Africa before the apartheid era, sometimes, it is often overlooked, among sectors of black communities. If we agree with a significant body of poststructuralist cultural scholarship that the political valence of a particular expressive form is never guaranteed and immutable but rather sustained by a range of culturally, historically, and geographically contingent factors, then it becomes important to understand precisely how the Western cultural canon was made to serve the interests of the apartheid state, all the more so because, as I have argued here, the ideological work was largely done by artists and art professionals who saw themselves as working outside of its strictures. As we look to the ways in which the aesthetic was, and potentially continues to be, implicated in the political in South Africa, I believe that looking at the now defunct performing arts councils and the theatres that housed them offers a valuable illustration of the principle that apartheid perpetuated itself through certain sectors of the arts community less through overt intervention and propagandistic symbolism (though there were surely examples of this, as the opening of the State Theatre clearly demonstrated) than more subtly and implicitly, below the level of state politics, in institutional cultures and the day-to-day processes of artistic production as many artists accommodated themselves to the prevailing socio-political order.

Endnotes

1 This material is based upon work supported by the National Research Foundation. Any opinions, findings and conclusions or recommendations expressed in this material are however those of the author, and therefore the NRF does not accept any liability in regard thereto.

2   While at least one notable commentator reports the opening to have been on Republic Day, the official commemorative brochure dates the opening as 23 May 1981.
3   The claim to world stature was prominently made on posters advertising the opening in 1981. Even in the more defensive position in which it found itself on the eve of the end of formal apartheid, the theatre's general director would describe it as 'the largest theatrical management on the African continent' (*TRUK/PACT Info*, May-July 1993: 3).
4   The exception is Carol Steinberg's excellent master's thesis, 'Towards the Transformation of the Performing Arts Council of the Transvaal' (1993), parts of which are summarised in Steinberg (1996). Though the conference paper on which this chapter is based was written before I had read Steinberg's thesis, it will be evident that the personal account offered here, from my position as a music administrator within PACT, is to a significant extent congruent with hers, written from her position as a drama practitioner and negotiator with the State Theatre management on behalf of the Performing Arts Workers' Equity.
5   My analysis in this respect diverges somewhat from Steinberg's contention that the performing arts councils were a product of 'the newly constituted Republic of South Africa' (1996: 247). Not only does this overlook some of the shifts in Afrikaner nationalist cultural policy in the fifteen years marking the transitions between the Malan, Strijdom and Verwoerd eras, it also leaves unexplored the partial origins of the performing arts councils in predecessors like the National Theatre Organisation.
6   For a detailed study of music censorship in apartheid South Africa, which had particularly far-reaching consequences on broadcasting if not live performance, see Drewett (2004).
7   Steinberg points out that the management of PACT and the State Theatre were drawn from a relatively homogeneous stratum of middle-class whites whose collective disposition was to accommodate themselves voluntarily to the prevailing apartheid order.
8   I am especially grateful to Bronwen Lovegrove for her assistance in accessing what remains of PACT's archive of the period.
9   For a nuanced historical overview of PACT's operations and racial politics, see Steinberg (1993).
10 According to PACT's 1968 *Annual Report*, the Vienna Boys' Choir was heard by 39 858 people during its tour of that year. The itinerary of performances is worth listing in full: Windhoek, Nylstroom, Potgietersrus, Louis Trichardt, Pietersburg, Tzaneen, Phalaborwa, Lydenburg, Sabie, Nelspruit, White River, Waterfalboven, Middelburg, Witbank, Warmbaths, Brakpan, Brits, Germiston,

Bloemhof, Kerksdorp, Potchefstroom, Lichtenburg, Zeerust, Heidelberg, Bethal, Ermelo, Piet Retief, Standerton, Carletonville, Verwoerdburg, Vanderbijlpark, Vereeniging, Kempton Park, Rustenburg, Johannesburg, Edenvale, Benoni, Krugersdorp, Boksburg, Pretoria, Springs, Bulawayo, Salisbury.

11 My account here is informed by discussions with former colleagues during the period of my employment at PACT. Steinberg points out that throughout the 1970s, PACT's management complained about the difficulties of country tours, especially for the ballet and opera companies, to the extent that the 1977 Niemand Commission drew attention to its responsibility to continue catering for rural audiences.

12 On racial admissions policies at the State Theatre and its counterparts, see Fuchs (2002: 4-7).

13 For example, in his foreword to the publicity brochure *TRUK/PACT Info* (February-April 1993: 3), General Director Dennis Reinecke claimed that, while bound by the laws of the country and the circumstances of the day, 'it has always been PACT's earnest endeavour to develop the various disciplines of the performing arts to the benefit of all'. For evidence to the contrary, see Steinberg (1993; 1996).

14 The quote is from Julius Eichbaum's editorial '"Democratising" the Arts: The Poisoned Chalice', which appeared in the arts magazine *Scenaria*, reprinted in *TRUK/PACT Info* (November 1992-January 1993: 38-9).

15 Translations from the Afrikaans in this and subsequent quotations are mine.

16 See Steinberg's discussion of the competing understandings of non-racialism at play in public discourse at the time (1993: 250-1).

BIBLIOGRAPHY

Campschreur, Willem, & Joost Divendaal (eds). 1989. *Culture in Another South Africa*. London: Zed Books.

Drewett, Michael David. 2004. 'An Analysis of the Censorship of Popular Music within the Context of the Cultural Struggle in South Africa during the 1980s'. Ph.D. diss., Rhodes University.

Fuchs, Anne. 2002. *Playing the Market: The Market Theatre, Johannesburg*. Amsterdam: Rodopi.

Masekela, Hugh, & D Michael Cheers. 2004. *Still Grazing: The Musical Journey of Hugh Masekela*. New York: Crown Publishers.

Oliphant, Andries Walter (ed.). 1993. *Culture and Empowerment: Debates, Workshops, Art and Photography from the Zabalaza Festival*. Johannesburg: COSAW & ANC.

Steinberg, Carol. 1993. 'Towards the Transformation of the Performing Arts Council of the Transvaal'. M.A. diss., University of the Witwatersrand.

_. 1996. 'PACT: Can the Leopard Change its Spots?' In Geoffrey V Davis & Anne Fuchs (eds). *Theatre and Change in South Africa*. Amsterdam: Harwood Academic, pp. 246-259.

White Paper on Arts, Culture and Heritage. 1996. Chapter 4, Section 11. www.dac.gov.za/white_paper.htm; accessed 16 April 2007.

PACT PUBLICATIONS

Performing Arts Council Transvaal. 1968. *Annual Report*.

Performing Arts Council Transvaal. 1973. Director's preface in *Decade: A Pictorial Review. Performing Arts Council Transvaal 1963-1972*. Special anniversary publication. Pretoria: PACT, n.p.

Performing Arts Council Transvaal. 1983. Director's preface in *Decade 2. A Pictorial Review. Performing Arts Council Transvaal 1973-1982*. Special anniversary publication. Pretoria: PACT, n.p.

Performing Arts Council Transvaal. 1991/2. *Annual Report*.

TRUK/PACT Info, February-April 1992.

TRUK/PACT Info, August-October 1992.

TRUK/PACT Info, November 1992-January 1993.

TRUK/PACT Info, February-April 1993.

TRUK/PACT Info, May-July 1993.

NEWSPAPERS

Applous. 1991. ''n Onvergeetlike estetiese ervaring.' Daan du Toit, 12 April.

Beeld. 1991. 'Pencz se vertolking byna pynlik mooi.' Henning Pieterse, 23 April.

Citizen. 1991. 'Gielen's mastery of structure.' Michael Traub, 19 April.

Pretoria News Tonight! 1991. 'Baden-Baden concert is indeed one to remember.' Willem Scott, 16 April.

Rapport. 1991. 'Duitse orkes wys angel is uit boikot.' Paul Boekkooi, 24 March.

Rapport. 1991. 'Ryk tekstuur, skakeringe in Baden-Baden.' Stefans Grové, 14 April.

The Star Tonight! 1991. 'Baden-Baden gives a Mahler to dream about.' Pieter Smit, 18 April.

Vrye Weekblad. 1991. 'Dié Duitsers wys jou wat jy mis.' Henning Viljoen, 26 April-2 May.

Weekly Mail. 1991. 'Pawe angry over 105 imported musicians.' Raeford Daniel, 5-11 April.

Weekly Mail. 1991. 'Full boycott of Capab demanded.' Gaye Davis, 19-25 April.

12

DECOMPOSING APARTHEID

THINGS COME TOGETHER.
THE ANATOMY OF A MUSIC REVOLUTION

Ingrid Bianca Byerly

Musical markers in life histories[1]

Nobody plays Chopin quite like my father does. When I was eight, I believed he was the reincarnation of Chopin. At night I would fall asleep to the sounds of nocturnes, polonaises and etudes being played down the hall. My favourite was the 'Revolutionary Etude', Op. 10 No. 12 in C Minor, with the thrilling suspense of its unmistakable opening chord, followed by the spectacular descending cascade of notes as it transitioned into the desperate *appassionato* melody. A frail Chopin, I was told, had composed this dramatic piece as his contribution to the people's uprising when Russia occupied Poland in 1831. Both the piece and the motivation behind its composition captivated me, not only for the aesthetics of the sound, but also for the intensity of the sentiment that lay within that sound. To this day, it serves as both a nostalgic 'umbilical chord' connecting me to the music of my childhood, and as a symbol of my earliest recognition of the power of music in a political context. It was the first of many masterpieces that have presented themselves as musical markers across my lifetime.

Musical markers punctuate people's lives, whether consciously or not. These markers entertain, inform, influence, and instil personal memories that serve as symbols of meaningful demarcations in any life history. For some, associations with music are deepest when related to relationships. For others, they define seminal rites of passage in their lives. For others still, musical markers define cognitive awakenings that alert them to social realities they were previously unaware of. The latter case has the ability to influence thinking subtly or blatantly, drastically change minds, or even dramatically alter worldviews.

So, too, do musical markers punctuate the lives of societies, whether they are individually or collectively conscious of them or not. These markers similarly entertain, inform, influence, and instil cultural memories that preserve cultural attributes, and mobilise change. They reveal relationships within the group, indicate rites of passage within the community, or define affective or intellectual awakenings through pieces that culturally or politically influence or affect the group as a whole. The latter case has the ability to either maintain, or transform, the vision and the workings of their world. Such is the influence of musical markers, and it is this power that I discuss here, for its consequences not only delineate and change individual lives, they also define and transform social histories.

A CALL TO ARMS

The history of any country is revealed in its art,
and the history of any art is revealed in its influences (Clarke, 2004).

In this statement, South African artist John Clarke challenges the misleading tendency, in attempts to record history, of highlighting the more definable markers of armed conflict in favour of the more abstract markers of artistic initiative. He suggests that while historical scrutiny is typically documented through markers of war, if one were to shift the angle and focus of observation, it would uncover a wealth of clues to history hidden within the sights and sounds of art and music. Such a shift would reveal telling incidences of dramatic turns of events that affect the course of history. It would, moreover, reveal patterns and parallels between histories from a perspective not previously considered.

A striking example could be found in juxtaposing two historical 'Crossings of the Rubicon': the first being Caesar's military passage in 49BC from Roman into Gaul territory, the second being FW de Klerk's metaphorical passage in his 1990 speech transitioning South Africa from apartheid to democracy. Both events symbolised points of no return, and resulted in redirecting the course of history, yet they differed in pertinent ways. First, while Caesar expressed uncertainty in his decision, realising the enormity of the consequences, De Klerk's intentions were clear, following his now-renowned 'moment of truth' and 'change of heart' that led to his 'spiritual leap away from apartheid' (De Klerk, 1990). Second, while Caesar's move symbolised a shift *away* from democracy in the creation of the Roman Empire, De Klerk's move resulted in a transition *towards* democracy through the abolishment of apartheid. Third, while Caesar positioned himself to gain his control as emperor, De Klerk prepared himself to lose his command as president; and finally, while Caesar was aware of his option to retreat, De Klerk knew there was no turning back. The single most striking similarity that marked both occasions however was the influence of music surrounding the event. The mysterious piper who sounded the final call to arms on the banks of Caesar's Rubicon had counterparts, two millennia later, in the form of reprobate musicians who adamantly and persistently challenged the status quo in the years leading up to De Klerk's Rubicon. It was these musicians, amongst others, who had long negotiated change and demanded reform through the sounds and sentiments of their song, pre-empting the unofficial negotiations between South Africans themselves, relying on their own tactics to reassess past and future, and negotiating optional routes to non-violent confrontation, strategic conciliation, and a peaceful transition to democracy.

Music, communication and transformation

Everyone comes to a subject from varying angles of observation and interest. Ethnomusicologists perceive the world through the tools of cultural enquiry, while they hear the messages of societies through their music. They believe people can be more effectively understood when observed through the lens of their culture, and heard through the earpiece of their music. Ethnomusicology, or the anthropology of music, scrutinises the cultural and the auditory, the cerebral and the aesthetic, the academic and the artistic. The music *indaba* of the South African transition is a particularly rich arena within which to explore these phenomena, as it contains all the elements of a multifaceted music revolution within a complex political sphere, leading to a negotiated social resolution. It also offers an unmatched site of enquiry through which to redress the more consequential oversimplifications of previous historical enquiry regarding the anti-apartheid movement.

An *indaba*, in African terms, is a meeting place where topical matters are updated, or where members of a society contribute towards the solution of a problem. It suggests shared efforts of collaboration, and endeavours towards consensus through a discussion of matters concerning the group as a whole. The *indaba* of song and sound, at the height of political dissent, involved not only every sector of the South African population, but also, importantly, musicians abroad (whether South African exiles, or foreign musicians) who joined the struggle. The final years of the music *indaba*, leading up to De Klerk's Rubicon speech, were efforts of unprecedented contestation and collaboration that added many voices to the protest, such that the initial mono-cultural discord had been transformed into polycultural polyphony.

The confrontational and conciliatory role of music in helping to abolish apartheid and ensuring that 'things come together' serves as the opposite bookend to Chinua Achebe's description of the insipient and fragmenting influence of religion in *Things Fall Apart* (1958). The ingenious strategies of musicians, and the unique language of musical dissent (whether through altercation or collaboration), could communicate and achieve what previous attempts at revolution and change could not. Prior to musicians' powerful use of song as catalyst and communicator in the liberation struggle, things had already fallen apart to a large extent in South Africa. In his poem 'The Second Coming' (1921), Yeats coined the original phrase 'things fall apart' in his depiction of the disintegration of social cohesion, where increased chaos and decreased communication causes the organisation of society to fall apart, and 'the falcon cannot hear the falconer' anymore:

> Turning and turning in the widening gyre
> The falcon cannot hear the falconer;
> Things fall apart; the centre cannot hold;
> Mere anarchy is loosed upon the world,
> The blood-dimmed tide is loosed, and everywhere
> The ceremony of innocence is drowned;
> The best lack all conviction, while the worst
> Are full of passionate intensity.

In the face of certain anarchy, and with both conviction and intensity, music gradually became the unofficial forum that served the role of the archetypal African *indaba*. Communication through music, therefore, had resulted in a unique *music indaba* in which all South Africans could participate, whether as contributors or audience. It remains a deep irony that, amidst all the strategic and meticulously co-ordinated efforts of politicians to keep apartheid in place while things fell apart, it was the intuitive and largely un-co-ordinated endeavours of musicians that made things come together. By prompting 'moments of truth', and encouraging consequent 'changes of heart' through both brutal honesty and compassionate convictions, musicians and their music challenged a society experiencing both doubt and fear in changing times. This was primarily achieved through the gradual collaborations between musicians of diverse genres: a concerted strategy resulting in what has come to be the 'collaborative' music of the era, and a harbinger of the social and political collaborations to come. While social segregation, originally the result of blinkered ideologies and ethnocentric world views, had been supplanted by official strategies to 'compose apartheid' through the careful appropriation, eradication, imposition, monitoring, and censoring of art forms, it was these very art forms that managed to reverse the process, and 'decompose apartheid'.

Musical osmosis and social diffusion

Music has always been a seminal form of communication in South Africa. This has been the case for both black and white South Africans – whether in solitary environments (a mother's Zulu or Afrikaans lullaby to a child), in social scenarios (a Xhosa work song or an English folksong) or as religious offerings (a Sotho prayer or an Afrikaans hymn). An important element at play in the early stages of protest is what could be termed musical osmosis. In scientific terms, osmosis refers to the movement of a liquid from an area of high concentration to low concentration through a permeable membrane. However strictly the laws of apartheid were enforced, the imaginary boundaries that separated groups, as suggested by Benedict (1983), were inherently permeable, especially to influences like music. Music could easily be fashioned by astute musicians to slip through the porous barriers put up by the regime, and flow between two areas efficiently and effectively. South Africans, whether they realised it or not, had been immersed in the influences of the music around them since birth.[2] The seemingly 'soundproof' walls that censorship and separate development built between races weren't sufficient to make provision for the fact that apartheid's imposed infrastructure not only *allowed* for, but made *provision* for, constant musical osmosis between those walls. Once protest had become part of the fabric of society, the unpredictability of dissent (in both prompt and outcome) challenged the notion that social movements are usually carefully organised, strategically planned, and meticulously rational. Strang and Soule (1998) and Myers (2000) point out that *diffusion* processes such as fads, epidemics, and contentious innovations are so socially embedded that established network lines are needed to spread anything from a source to an adopter. Social diffusion, then, played an enormous part in the gradual escalation of protest through the music *indaba*, and the established networks persistently branched into secondary networks in uncharted areas, continually compounding the influence across society.

While a great deal of music passed between cultures through natural osmosis, what developed as the liberation struggle became more fervent was the move towards a more concerted effort at diffusion, not only to share songs across established networks, but to create new music cross-culturally. After seemingly irredeemable political destabilisations, social schisms and ethnic erosions, music served as a means of both conversation and conversion. In analysis, music presents an elegant yet complex model of non-violent conflict resolution that stresses the essential bi-directional nature of protest and resolution. It also reveals the importance of exposure to alternative environments, styles, and social groups, so that striking or meaningful musical works have the opportunity to be heard. These then have the prospect of becoming musical markers in individuals' lives, potentially leading to 'moments of truth' and consequential 'changes of heart'. Many South Africans would be able to trace their own path and find parallels in the maze of music that challenged their thinking, changed their minds, and expanded their tastes in song during the height of the apartheid era. Furthermore, as John Clarke suggested in calling to arts (instead of calling to arms) in investigations of history, their views would be as varied as the angles from which they are observed. As Achebe says:

> I believe in the complexity of the human story, and that there's no way you can tell that story in one way and say, 'this is it.' Always there will be someone who can tell it differently depending on where they are standing ... this is the way I think the world's stories should be told: from many different perspectives (cited in Brooks, 1994:5).

MOMENTS OF TRUTH AND CHANGES OF HEART

Whether tracking individual stories, or social histories, the perspectives from which accounts can be forged are innumerable. My own musical journey, like many in my social sphere in South Africa at the time, started in a home filled with the sounds of European art music. My own ventures into pop and rock were tinged with a combined sense of fear that my standards may well be dropping, and of hope that there had to be some redeeming features to these popular forms of artistic expression. It was only as a university student that my fears were mitigated, and my hopes realised. Four seminal events transformed my thinking about the motives of music in general, and the meaning of music in particular. The first, representing stylistic contestation, was on hearing Ali Rahbari's controversial ethnoclassical composition *Half Moon* (1982), fusing the symphonic traditions of the South African Youth Orchestra with black choral traditions from Soweto.[3] It was an aesthetic revelation of the possibilities and significances of cultural fusions that challenged all my pre-conceived notions regarding the boundaries of art. The second, representing lyrical revelation, was on encountering the banned song by the British musician Peter Gabriel, simply called 'Biko' (1980). The song triggered a political awakening and turning point that forever caused me (and others around me) to listen to music with different ears: hearing both the sound and sentiment of song. The third event, representing anthemic contestation, occurred at Jameson's, a live music venue in Johannesburg, where the band Bright Blue was performing the song 'Weeping' (1987).[4] It revealed how a 'harmless' pop song could integrate and camouflage banned themes (in this case, the anthem 'Nkosi Sikelel' iAfrika') and outwit censorship effectively and cunningly. It was the same anthem that brought me to my fourth epiphany many years later, after the official transition to democracy. Before the commencement of the final round of the International Piano Competition in Pretoria, in January 1996, the orchestra launched into a magnificent symphonic arrangement of the new national anthem, 'Nkosi Sikelel' iAfrika', (previously banned, and now official), followed by a seamless transition into the old anthem of apartheid South Africa, 'Die Stem'. The two, I realised, were now one. Both anthems had taken on profoundly new meanings (and seemed to take on a new sound as a result), and for me music had come full circle. Through these four events, representing memorable musical markers, the insular world of sound as I had known it had burst open at the seams, and there was nowhere it couldn't go.

A single personal journey into the protest music of the resistance movement is but one of the innumerable instances where individuals could encounter their moments of truth, and subsequent changes of heart, through the ingenious creations of musicians, and the infinite capacities of music. It was, eventually, the combined journeys of individuals that gradually created an unofficial forum, the music *indaba*, where things came together through moments of transformation, and consequential changes in the behaviour and actions of increasingly larger groups, and eventually the nation as a whole.

In the same way that one can trace defining musical markers in a personal history, so too can one trace defining moments in a social history. Some say the *Graceland* album (1986) and concert (1987) were shared turning points, each bringing attention to a political crisis and social inequities, while ushering in new awareness of the potential of musical and social fusions. Others might say the tipping point was Peter Gabriel's 'Biko', or that the *doodskoot* (death-shot) was in one of the self-critical Afrikaner introspections such as the revue 'Piekniek by Dingaan' (1987), the controversial Kerkorrel album *Eet Kreef* (1989) or the groundbreaking *Voëlvry* tour of 1989 across campuses. Each of these was responsible for not only breaking the seal between the powerful and the disenfranchised, but especially for eroding the cohesion between members of the ruling party, and in so doing, splitting and weakening the stronghold of the elite. Whatever one interprets as the defining moment in a cultural revolution, it is a moment that bursts open a sluice gate and pours a tide of discontent over both the privileged and the disenfranchised. This turned tide, once it gains momentum, eventually forms a powerful wave, demanding discourse and collaboration (whether confrontational or conciliatory) between both dominant and subordinate groups.

Focusing the lens and amplifying the earpiece

The resolve of musicians, and the capacity of music to forge change, has long presented an arena of interest to those trying to understand the 'mystery of the miracle' that was the South African transition to democracy. Besides the earlier, more academic research, recent investigations have taken on more popular formats. Most of these depictions, however, are problematic in their over-simplification of both the players and the process, and none more so than the internationally acclaimed documentary *Amandla!* by American filmmaker Lee Hirsch, and its presentation of a 'revolution in four-part harmony'. The film convincingly demonstrates the effectiveness and strength of the black struggle through music. But, I argue, a revolution in which only the disenfranchised features is not the full story, and *Amandla!* is a prominent case of failing to recognise the complexity of the revolutionary process. By neglecting an acknowledgement of the other stages of the process, or other players in the arena, the representation simplifies the process, distorts the picture, and denies seminal musical dissidents their rightful place in the history of the *indaba*.

Hirsch's approach presents flawed deductions regarding the South African protest movement in particular, and consequently suggests potentially dangerous conclusions for protest movements in general. First, it suggests that effective protest simply consists of uni-directional thrusts of contention, by the dissidents, against a regime. Second, it suggests that such a strategy results in a long-term resolution (rather than a temporary 'changing of the guard', as is generally the case with uni-directional 'overthrows'). Third, it posits that the struggle could exist as an autonomous movement insulated from those outside of the movement in the achievement of its goals, and fourth, it fails to recognise the complex yet inevitable 'swings' between both antagonistic and conciliatory strategies, on the parts of the powerful and the powerless, in the achievement of the goal. The film, critically, fails to acknowledge that the call to arms of the black struggle was only the beginning of the music revolution, not the entire revolution itself. This call of the disenfranchised was, undeniably, critically important in expressing grievances, defining allegiances and drawing attention to the struggle and the atrocities of apartheid, but it did not, as the film suggests, end apartheid. What mobilised final actions, catalysed consensual changes, and ensured historical transitions was not a uni-directional 'revolution in four-part harmony' by a single group, but a multi-directional '*indaba* in polycultural polyphony' involving both the powerful and the powerless.

Another case in which only a selective (and in this case, more marginal) segment of the protest movement is held up as the core of the revolution is Frank Tenaille's book *Music is the Weapon of the Future* (2002). In his representation of the musicians in the struggle against apartheid, Tenaille follows the trend of many non-South African scholars in holding up exiled musicians as the key revolutionaries in the struggle. 'Like many writers, Tenaille highlights internationally acclaimed artists like Makeba and Masekela, who left South Africa during apartheid to find commercial success abroad. He follows a trend that largely neglects the influences within the country throughout apartheid, in favor of the few recognisable and more luminary names' (Byerly, 2003: 423). Tenaille opens himself to critique within the current debate amongst many (black) musicians who remained in South Africa throughout the struggle, and who resent the spotlight given to exiles who were away during the height of the struggle, leaving, as the singer Dolly Rathebe pronounced, 'us "inziles" to keep the home fires burning'.[5]

Where selective pockets of resistance are held up as the superior or definitive moments of protest, the approach fails to tell the full story, not only regarding the rest of the players who joined the struggle, but also regarding the process of protest. In late-apartheid South Africa, dissent developed from a call to arms of the disenfranchised, into complex and full-blown protest: a music *indaba* involving both the powerless and the powerful, the poor and the privileged. The deceptive tendency of culturally-insular inquiries inadvertently (or sometimes intentionally) suggests one group's undisputed supremacy of achievement over another's in the eventual success of the liberation struggle. Instead of suggesting 'who did more' or 'who did less', we should ask 'who did anything?' 'what did they do?' and 'how did they do it?' It is insufficient to suggest that Africans *toyi-toyi-ed* around the Wall of Jericho until it tumbled, or that only those musicians recorded on the Shifty record label said or achieved anything of consequence at the height of artistic censorship.[6] The tendency of presenting black protest as the sole force in the anti-apartheid movement has gradually been redressed through the recognition of novel forms of musical protest from within other cultural groups, most notably the

Afrikaans *alternatiewe* music movement (see Smit, 1992; Byerly, 1996, 1998; Grundlingh, 2004; Laubscher, 2005), the English protest of the 'Hidden Years' (as dealt with by Dave Marks of 3rd Ear Music and the Hidden Years Project), and more recently 'white protest' within a complex political context (see Drewett, 2002, 2003, 2004, Hopkins, 2006).

While such investigations are essential to our understanding of the process, and gradually reveal the wider spectrum of players in the field of anti-apartheid movements, there are two critical dangers of approach in the presentation of the music revolution. The first is in suggesting that the process was simply and persistently redemptive and conciliatory, when, in fact, the path of progress was a hard-fought one, rife with musical confrontations and lyrical altercations of harsh truths and bitter allegations. As William Blake wrote: 'Without Contraries is no progression. Attraction and Repulsion, Reason and Energy, Love and Hate, are necessary to Human existence' (*The Marriage of Heaven and Hell*). The musicians of the *indaba* followed the credo of Blake's assertion, determined to mobilise progress in their struggle through the constant friction between logic and optimism, respect and disdain, appeal and disgust. Theirs was not a communal sing-along driven by the economic machinations of recording studios. As Afrikaans alternative musician Johannes Kerkorrel put it: 'People mustn't think we all came together in a studio, held hands, sang "We are the World" and apartheid ended. It was called a struggle because it was a struggle. *Vir almal. Veral ons musikante wat siek en sat was vir die speletjies*' (For everybody. Especially us musicians who were sick and tired of the games) (Kerkorrel, 1996). Musicians, then, did not trivialise their music into a light, social pastime through which to optimistically bond with 'the other', but rather viewed it as a space of both contention and concession through which to expose realities of identity and ideology, renegotiate relationships, and mobilise change. For some, 'change' meant sabotaging the direction of the anti-apartheid movement, and causing the momentum to falter, while old ideologies were reinforced or strengthened. For others, change meant excluding others from their vision of the future, and making no secret of this in their music. The revolution, therefore, occasionally lost ground, and backlashes or marginalisations pushed the waves of dissent back, from where dissidents had to regroup their energies, and reformulate their strategies.

The second danger in the presentation of the music revolution is in suggesting resistance was constituted of insular pockets of dissent. Continuing to represent forms of musical dissent as existing largely as separate entities, rather than acknowledging and exploring the links between them throughout the liberation struggle, camouflages the fact that collaborative endeavours in music could be responsible for collaborations within society at large, that musical confrontations between individuals and groups were essential to the exposure of certain tough truths, and that musical appropriations and transpositions themselves were mimetic of greater social appropriations and transformations. Therefore, while solid, focused studies may well be invaluable in contributing individual tiles to the larger mosaic, they may also fail to reveal the critical importance of certain antagonistic musical approaches that were taken, crossovers between genres that were adopted, or the collaborative nature of the final stage of the revolution that revealed itself.

STRATEGIES AND STYLES IN SOUNDING THE REVOLUTION

It is difficult for most non-musicians to imagine the many creative ways through which musicians can fashion music to express dissent and negotiate change. The sheer volume and variability of its components, however, makes it an unparalleled site within which creative individuals can explore outlets of outrage and passages of protest. The increased use of 'code-switching', both linguistic and musical, could echo social tensions and suggest conflict resolutions in song, while the critical presentations of irony and humour could further expand the boundaries of meaning, while outwitting censors. The ingenious use of folk themes, traditional instrumentations and anthems could signify desires for group autonomy or social re-formations, while the frequent merging of intercultural musical components increasingly suggested the desire for non-racial nationalism. Black musicians continually crafted ingenious methods of resistance through sound, while simultaneously taking their shows 'on the road' through even more subtle tactics of behavioral manipulation, cloaked in the games they played with authorities to bend the laws that intended to keep them artistically and politically subservient and contained. On the other hand, the 'entitled trailblazers' who had broken rank and moved away from the ideologies of the powerful elite used their songs to be 'openly critical of the apartheid regime, shockingly scornful of sacred identity, iconography, tauntingly transgressive of *suiwer* (pure) language usage, and flauntingly dismissive of seemingly entrenched moral and religious prescriptions' (Laubscher, 2005: 313). Some interesting comparisons grow out of the juxtaposition of these two opposing 'casts' – the superior and the subordinate – and while the Comaroffs (2004) explore the play-acting of police in everyday scenarios to achieve their ends in suppressing resistance, many performers used play-acting in everyday scenarios to mobilise change. Often, while superiors used theatre of horror, subordinates used theatre of humour; while the one used forceful drama, the other used light diversion; and while the one demanded behavioural deference, the other offered false compliance. Many dissenting musicians, both powerful and disenfranchised, played the proverbial 'fool' to outwit the authorities, and their strategised conniving was rewarded through both access to performance in otherwise outlawed spaces, the avoidance of arrest, or insightful commentary in the guise of idiocy.[7]

Two challenges dogged the musicians of the *indaba*. The first lay in the matter of 'agency', where the constant adaptation of styles was necessary to suit the particular situations, varied audiences and diverse genres of fellow musicians involved in the struggle. This dilemma was dealt with, primarily, through the careful monitoring, recognition and identification of widely shifting tastes and ever-changing opinions. Once these variables were acknowledged, musicians could strategically fashion their work to suit the 'moment' of reality between oscillating poles. Convictions had to be addressed, especially where frozen perceptions needed to be unthawed, and musicians could address them through complex configurations within musical composition. These took the form of either the intricate weaving of cross-cultural melodies (as in Coenie de Villiers' fusion of the Afrikaans 'Sien Jou Weer' and the Shangaan worksong 'Shosholoza'), a superimposition of traditionally separate harmonies (as in the blending of Beethoven's Ninth Symphony with African descant in *Half Moon*), the overlay of culturally diverse rhythms (as in the reworked version of Laurika Rauch's song 'Kinders van die Wind' with the superimposition of African rhythms), and the increased use of code-switching, both linguistic and musical, where words or phrases from different languages are strung together within sentences (as in the songs of both the Afrikaner Kerkorrel and the Zulu Khanyile). The ingenious interlacing of folk themes (Casper de Vries's grotesque reworks of nursery rhymes, and van der Spuy's orchestral arrangement of 'Bobbejaan Klim die Berg'), traditional instrumentations (Clegg and Mchunu's experimental fusions in the early Juluka albums), and anthems ('Die Stem' and 'Nkosi Sikelel' iAfrika') could signify desires for group autonomy or social re-formations, while the frequent merging of intercultural musical components increasingly suggested the desire for non-racial nationalism. Humour, cynicism, criticism, and irony were all expressed through the careful revival, reconstruction, manipulation, and superimposition of varied themes (such as in Koos Kombuis's disturbing re-arrangement of the traditional 'Ver van die ou Kalahari' and Kerkorrel's disconcerting lyrics to the national anthem 'Die Stem' in 'Swart September'), and interplays between seemingly unrelated rhythms, timbres, and harmonies (such as in the collaborations of the Kalahari Surfers and Lesego Rampolokeng). Some adaptations were more difficult than others, as the aesthetics of some musical forms are more closely related than others.

Synthesising certain African rhythms within the Western symphonic tradition, for example, required skill, and shortcomings would cause an intentionally syncretic piece to sound fraudulent. Afrikaans music, in particular, underwent a dramatic transformation in the decade leading to democracy. Here, a great deal of the problem lay in the Afrikaans language itself, and in particular with forcing the language into a musical mould that did not suit its intonation, invariably producing a result that could sound both synthetic and disjointed. Afrikaans music critic André Brink explains: *'Omdat daar iets lomp aan Afrikaans is, is dit 'n baie moeilike taal om in te komponeer, maar dit wil voorkom asof meer en meer musikante dit wel begin regkry'* (Because there is something clumsy to Afrikaans, it is a very difficult language to compose in, but it seems as though more and more musicians are getting it right) (pers. comm., 5 May 2006). As was the case with any genre, adaptations attempting to merge, synergise, or make provision for alternative circumstances within which to make an impact, needed time to develop, through continual moulding, into strategies of effective communication. *'Dis amper asof dit 'n tegniek is wat sy weg moet vind'* (It's almost as if it's a technique that must find its way) (Ibid.). By a certain stage, musicians had become adept at 'finding their way' and adapting their style (both across time, and across genres) to become more accessible to a wider audience outside of their own group. Traditional African music leaned more towards a compatibility with Western pop and rock, and previously stoic Western styles opened avenues to greater Africanisation.

The second dilemma musicians faced was in 'reception', and the innumerable 'ways of listening' across such a diverse population. Just as every person has their own unique set of musical markers that punctuate their lives, so too every person experiences a unique response, attaching individual meanings to a particular piece of music. During the music *indaba* it was crucial to acknowledge that, even if their reception of it differed, people could appreciate others' music, and relate to it in a distinctive way, no matter how seemingly removed from a group or style they may be. The question was, to what extent could the divide be bridged through either exposure, or adaptation, and to what extent could musicians effectively appropriate styles that were convincing to the audiences they were trying to reach?

Waves of dissent and currents of contention

It can be argued that the single most important factor in the success of the music *indaba* was that, at some point, musicians realised their mission was not to preach to the converted, but to convert. Their strategy was not merely to reiterate concerns with like-minded people on the one hand, or to level their protest against those they disagreed with on the other, but to reveal realities and ideologies they opposed in the most convincing ways they knew how, through music, and thereby to steadily and tirelessly assimilate others in their protest against social inequalities through ever-expanding networks of contention. The capacity of musicians to be creative and candid, and music to be malleable and communicative, facilitated the process, as musicians could optimise and adjust existing forms in any way that would speak to the widest audience possible, and so build a united front. This resulted in increasing incidences of collective behaviour, as the groundswell expanded and affected society as a whole. Collective behaviour has been defined as 'extra-institutional, group problem-solving behaviour that encompasses an array of collective actions, ranging from protest demonstrations, to behaviour in disasters, to mass or diffuse phenomena, such as fads and crazes, to social movements and even revolution' (Snow and Oliver, 1995: 371). For the duration of the music *indaba*, one of the most difficult challenges that dissidents faced in securing collective action was the constant shifts in the political arena, and the consequent expectation to engage in mutable social protest through relentlessly modifying their focus and strategies to match the instability within which they were working. An upsurge of political dissent is never an autonomous period of contention. It is dependent on matters of time and space and is therefore simultaneously the result of an ever-shifting political arena, of the complex history of dissent that preceded it, and the convoluted reality of dissent surrounding it. Ruud Koopmans, a leading expert in wave theory in the field of protest, stresses the importance of recognising that a revolution is not an autonomous event:

> We must move beyond single movements, and consider dynamic interactions among a multitude of contenders, including not only challenging protestors, but also their allies and adversaries – elite and non-elite – as well as the whole range of forms of claims-making from the most conventional and institutionalised, to the most provocative and disruptive (2004: 21).

This brings us to an important theoretical point regarding the anatomy of a successful revolution. Contrary to depictions of insular protest movements, two of the fundamental requirements of successful protest are the *connectedness* of protest initiatives, and the inevitable existence of *waves* of protest within the grand scheme of contention:

> Instances of collective action are not independent. They are neither

understandable in their own, unique terms, nor are they merely interchangeable instances of general classes of events. The most fundamental fact about collective action is its connectedness, both historically and spacially, and both with other instances of collective action of a similar kind, and with the actions of different claim-makers such as authorities and counter-movements (Ibid.: 19).

As a form of collective action, where a common goal is pursued through shared effort, a social movement cannot then simply be seen as a powerful, contained, individual 'event' which marks the beginning and end of a transition, or which singularly represents a revolution. Instead, it must be seen as dependent on the events that precede and surround it, and as encompassing numerous waves of dissent within an expansive area of revolutionary activity. It is always connected to numerous other events of history, is usually preceded or followed by variations of itself, and involves a web of linkages between complex playing fields and multiple players.

The consequences of involvement in musical protest in South Africa, whether through joining street *toyi-toyi*, or creating original works of resistance, were usually unpredictable. They varied from music being ignored (as inconsequential to society) to musicians being arrested (as dangerous to the state). As such, every approach, or series of events, was essentially unique. Innovative borrowings, and collaborations on approaches, strategies, and styles of protest across various contingencies of contention, were crucial to the quest towards a common goal. In an authoritarian society, the flow of information is constantly checked and, as such, dissidents within protest movements have to account for vigilance and scrutiny, and outwit the censors at every turn in how they strategise collective action. At a certain point, in order to optimise and expand their political opportunity, dissidents have to become aware that 'beyond a certain threshold of deviation from habitual patterns of interaction, centripetal forces rapidly erode and make place for a much more disorderly, unpredictable and innovative course of events' (Koopmans, 2004: 33). Consequently, protestors have unexpectedly to contend with a more disorderly, unpredictable and innovative course of protest. Because of the constant shifting of the field of contention, the goal becomes a continuously moving target. The complexity of strategies involving numerous protest groups operating at any given time complicates the equation still further, and most dissidents feel as though they are constantly moving in the dark, unaware of strategically-placed obstacles, and unsure of the exact distance and whereabouts of their goal.

Within each revolution, then, waves take on variations on a theme of dissent, rather than existing as separate, contained entities. Only if circumstances were identical, which they never are, could a wave be repeated, and even then it would be foolhardy not to improve on the strategies of a previous effort towards an incomplete revolution. The most effective protest occurs when individuals show dissent within the context of their groups, and the strength of their networks determine their actions to achieve their goals. And yet, the most powerful and successful waves of dissent are those in which people do not merely get swept up in the emotional energy of a single incident of collective action, or lose their individuality under the spell of the crowd, but where their strategy is conceptualised with caution and confidence.

The mechanism by which music moved within the confines of South African society was a constant combination of sheer chance and strategic mobilisation, depending on obstacles and opportunities within the ever-shifting cultural landscape. Music served as a relentless vehicle of communication for dissidents trying to communicate, in spite of hindrances. The nature and form of song and sound could slip though both real and imaginary divides of society, and it was through these porous filters that difficult questions could be posed, and 'alternative thinking' could be presented, allowing for both individual and group 'moments of truth', which in turn would lead to 'changes of heart'. Unlike the dynamics of spoken conversations, where interruptions, counter-arguments and superfluous disturbances are frequent, in a musical piece or song, the artist is offered an uninterrupted space to express a sentiment, and the audience is presented with an opportunity, if not an obligation, to listen to the sentiment in its entirety. In this way, 'optional sensibilities' could filter in to the listener – either through passively receiving revolutionary ideas, or actively searching for them.

Every wave of dissent holds its own unique perils, and when dissidents commit to a revolutionary event, it is seldom without grounded fears, for strategy is never guaranteed success in relation to the particular moment in time within which it is employed. Most groups, whether part of the elite or part of the subordinated, approach protest with contradictory anticipations of success. It is never known whether an event will result, successfully, in the fall of the Berlin Wall, or, catastrophically, in the Tiananmen massacre. Another reason protest functions on a slippery slope is that the unpredictable is always prevalent – whether to the advantage or disadvantage of the movement. Some routes are suddenly closed off, while others are opened to dissidents, and some efforts are instantly foiled, while others don't even have to be made in the event of a fortunately unforeseen political opportunity.

While earlier references to 'protest cycles' suggest recurrent 'patterns' within repeated movement, Tarrow (1994) points out that the ending of each cycle is essentially different from any other, and consequently the next attempt at protest is varied to compensate for the successes and errors within the previous one. By this time, of course, the field of contention has also been altered and shifted somewhat, and that has to be factored in the new strategy of approach towards the next attempt. For this reason, the term 'wave' (suggesting a unique parabola of rise and fall in dissent) is more apt than 'cycle'. Waves never end where they began, and waves are never unproductive, for they carry their cause a little further each time. Even those waves of dissent that failed to reach a desired goal contribute to an increased knowledge of which strategies were effectual and productive (through expanding the base of dissent and nearing a goal or eroding counter-movements), and which were ineffectual and counterproductive (through narrowing the base of dissent as a result of antagonism, and causing increased suppression or a counter-movement). Waves are either suppressed or redirected, but only the last wave, punctuated by victory, can claim closure. It is, in fact, seldom known which wave of dissent will be the one defining the revolution, until after such a revolution has reached its conclusion.

THE ANATOMY OF THE MUSIC *INDABA*

In an earlier paper (Byerly, 1998), a depiction of the two main waves of resistance and protest in the music *indaba* (see the peaks in Figure 1) suggested both the placement of the waves of dissent in relation to each other across four decades, as well as their parabolic rises and falls in relation to the regime's attempts at suppressing them.

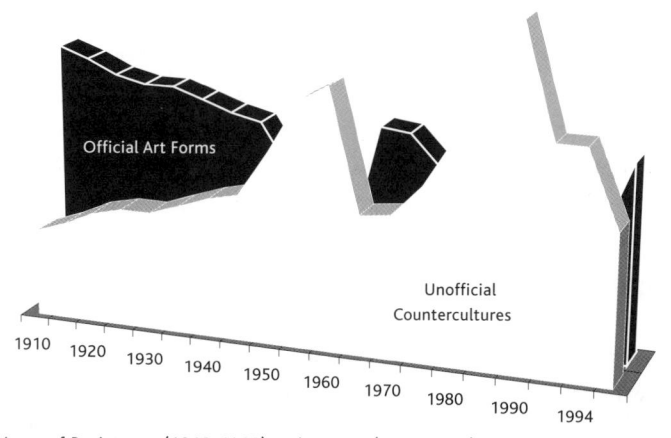

Figure 1: Waves of Resistance (1912-1960) and protest (1960-1990)

A closer analysis of the complex nature of the waves of dissent would present a more detailed model in which each wave contains two or more *currents of contention*. The first wave (which was suppressed) is followed by an essential demarcation, or 'tipping point', which was crucial to the successful strategies of the second wave (which was successful). The demise of the first wave occurred because of the counter-move (stronger clampdown and censorship of music) on the part of the apartheid regime, whereas the second wave ended voluntarily because the goal (the announcements in the Rubicon speech, and the impending transition to democracy) had been reached. Equally importantly, the suppression of the first wave by the regime was also the cause of heightened protest in the second wave, as, in most revolutions, 'high levels of repression increase the likelihood of future collective action' (Olivier, 1991: 113). Looking at the model as a whole, resistance moved into protest, causing revolution, which eventually resulted in resolution.

THE FIRST WAVE: FROM RESISTANCE TO PROTEST

The call to arms, the earliest current within the first wave, involved primarily the music of the disenfranchised. Styles like the early *marabi* and *tsaba-tsaba* became increasingly popular with the later *mbaqanga*, and while a great deal of it focused on sentiments expressed between members of the same groups in articulating resistance to the status quo, it also included the increasing use of *toyi-toyi* in street protest. This move, to take the songs from private spaces into public ones, signaled the initial call to arms, through, amongst other things, the call to arts. In every revolution, however, innovations of protest and resistance need to be carefully assessed with regards to their length and effectiveness, and if an innovation is used for too long, or not followed through by others, it can have destructive or counter-productive effects on the revolution itself. It can have varying effects on parties uninvolved with that strategy of resistance, through alienating some (within the group), and antagonising others (outside of the group). It may also not be the strategy all feel comfortable being part of, and therefore it could be an obstacle to those who are interested in joining the revolution. 'Innovations may be helpful for one group, but be seen as useless or inapplicable to another' (Koopmans, 2004: 26).

The success of the first current is undeniable in that it drew strong attention to the dire situation that the majority of South Africans found themselves in. Whereas most other forms of communication, especially the media, were not as effective in relaying outrage and protest (because of strong censorship), the music of the disenfranchised, and especially public street protests, were constant reminders to those who shared power that others were suffering, and that political instability may, as a result of increasing dissent, unimaginably replace the steel hold of apartheid. When the second current of contention rose up, it carried with it a new set of dissidents, namely protestors from within the empowered elite, albeit mostly those who were converts already. While they may not have been members of the regime, they represented difference, or a shift in allegiance from within the ranks of those who had the vote. The strongest voices at the time were those of the renegade English 'folk' movement, also known as the troubadours (the Tracey brothers, Jeremy Taylor, and Des and Dawn Lindberg), and later, the bitter protest in more contemporary popular genres, like rock (the prime example here is the music of Roger Lucey, who was personally persecuted while his music was banned). The music contained in this current, while often using double meanings in its lyrics, was still autonomous, played mostly in isolation from other groups, and consisting of clearly defined genres affiliated with the different groups playing them. They were largely muted implications, often in the form of camouflaged allegories, that all was not as it should be, rather than angry demands. The cry of the disenfranchised, sung in united voice, was becoming accompanied by the hum of the elite, sung in varying independent voices.

THE TIPPING POINT: 'OPENING THE DOOR FROM THE INSIDE'

So here we stand – wailing on our saxes and beating on our drums outside the music-hall. You guys have to open the door from the inside if you don't want us to break it down (Nkosi, 1998).

These words, spoken by the saxophone player Sipho 'Smile' Nkosi of the Afro-fusion band *Tswelopelo* (meaning 'progress'), offer a critical clue to the success of the South African transition. It presents the tipping point in the wave model, in which the ideological seal is broken, the powerful break rank, and 'the door is opened from the inside'. As in most revolutions, there is a critical moment of realisation that continued force exerted from either side causes decreased progress, and increased counter-movements. 'Countermobilisations', as discussed by Meyer and Staggenborg (1996), occur when signs of successful mobilisation threaten to affect, or directly impinge on, the interests of those within the group, or those of another group. The result of such continued oppositional pressure is either inconclusive stalemate, or violent overthrow. It is never peaceful transition. A relatively peaceful transition occurred in South Africa because, between the first and second waves of dissent, negotiation was mobilised from within, and across opposing factors of society, as increasing numbers broke rank from the stronghold of the reigning ideology, and joined the dissidents in their fight to end apartheid. 'When elites are divided among themselves, factions among them may choose to mobilise popular support in order to strengthen their position *vis-à-vis* rival elites, either by directly sponsoring or even initiating protest campaigns, or by encouraging dissent in more subtle ways' (Koopmans, 2004: 24). The Rubicon was unofficially crossed within the populace when the tipping point was reached, and signs of schism between the elites began to show – long before De Klerk officially crossed it in his parliamentary speech of 1990. The first signs of such a schism became apparent when the Afrikaans *lekkerliedjie* morphed into the *luisterliedjie* (literally, 'listen song'), and lyrics changed from detached commentary on flora and fauna to impassioned introspections of a more personalised and political nature.[8] The turning point had occurred, as the balance was tipped in favour of the currents of contention, rather than the dogma of apartheid.

The second wave: From revolution to reconciliation

The second wave of dissent in the music *indaba* took up the challenge of strategising stylistic means by which to mobilise the revolution to its full strength. In order to succeed, the *indaba* needed to ensure that, as Hunter Thompson described American protest in the 1960s, 'the energy of a whole generation comes to a head in a long fine flash… We had all the momentum; we were riding the crest of a high and beautiful wave' (1971: 67). It involved the vigour and contributions from musicians of every spectrum of the population and mobilised the movement to its zenith. While the first current recognised and acknowledged the voices and genres of other groups, and incorporated them, in innovative ways, into their own genres, the second, representing the

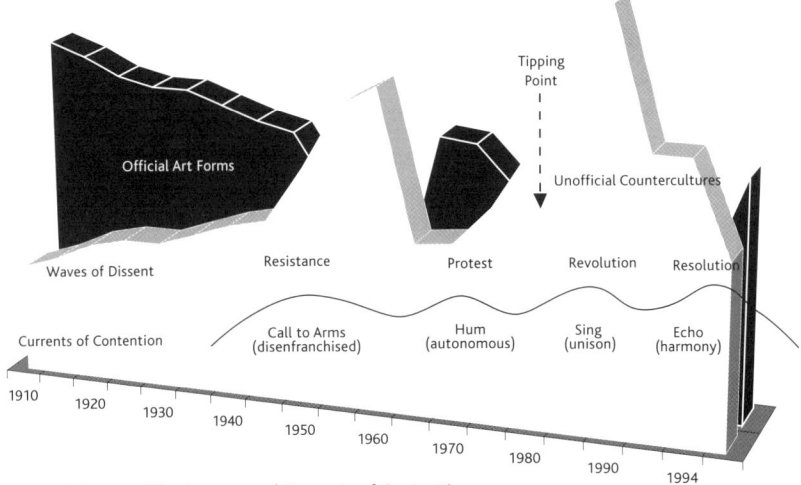

Figure 2: Waves of Resistance and Currents of Contention

summit of the music *indaba*, and the height of the revolution itself, contained collaborations of such syncretic allegiance that they morphed, harmonised, and echoed into creations of new polycultural, polyphonic music genres: styles mimetic of the collaborations being forged socially too. These styles contained everything from contrapuntal revivals and superimpositions of traditional styles,[9] to ethnoclassical fusions,[10] from progressively alternative Afrikaans forms,[11] to unexplored frontiers of fusion.[12]

The call and hum of the first wave, then, were joined by the song and echo of the second. When the music *indaba* had reached its goal of including the majority of the population as dissidents, or converts to the struggle, the revolution was complete.

Contrary to the earlier discussed depictions of a uni-directional 'revolution in four-part-harmony', the music *indaba* was a multi-directional 'revolution in polycultural polyphony', involving dissidents from every sector of the population, and moving through certain essential waves of dissent to arrive at its goal. The players involved, whether powerless or privileged, shared the conviction that change was both necessary and inevitable and employed their talents in the pursuit of this cause. One of the notable characteristics of the music *indaba* was that the players revealed an important attribute of a successful revolution – that waves of dissent can be initiated not only by the visible De Klerks and Mandelas of the world, but also by the less visible freedom fighters.

It is undeniable that the players involved in the struggle were a motley crew, and their roles within the critical waves of protest varied as much as their backgrounds. Kriesi (2004) sees three components in the 'configuration of actors' of a social movement: the protagonists (or allies), the antagonists (the adversaries), and the bystanders (those not involved, but affected). In fact, 'contention is always a multi-actor process that cannot be adequately understood by focusing attention on one actor and reducing the others to the role of context variables. Instead, interactions between actors become the fundamental units of analysis' (Koopmans, 2004: 40). Just as a revolution is defined by the *connections* between the waves of dissent and currents of contention within the movement as a whole, so too the players should be lauded as much for their individual efforts as for their dealings with each other. The music *indaba* reinforced the importance of individual courage in mobilising collective action towards change in an unequal society. Whether the *toyi-toying* crowds of the earliest resistance, or the lone trailblazers and troubadours of the sixties, whether the peacekeepers and patriots of the 'hidden years', or the camouflaged commentators of the cabaret circuit, whether the elite dissidents breaking rank from the ruling party, or the exiles and inziles from the townships; each played an essential role in the process of 'things coming together'.

CONCLUSION

By exploring both the flagrant machinations of the apartheid government (by 'composing apartheid'), and the camouflaged manoeuvres by which individuals utilised music to break rank, and join a cause (by 'playing apartheid'), and finally, the ingenious means by which a protesting populace can employ music to contest and conquer (by 'decomposing apartheid'), a new model of conflict resolution can be found. Such an investigation exposes how the intricate components of mindful, challenging, and collaborative musical composition and performance can suggest corresponding non-musical tactics of conflict resolution. It offers a model through which to appreciate the prospects of political change, while understanding the requirements of social harmony in societies in transition. It simultaneously stresses the imperative collaboration between individual initiative and collective action, reminding us that revolution is not a single event by a single player, but a complex process involving dissidents on either side of the battlefield.

In this essay I have attempted to rectify certain misconceptions regarding the history and nature of the anti-apartheid movement in South Africa, especially through the earpiece of the music *indaba*. I have endeavoured to stress the importance of unbiased inclusiveness in the acknowledgment of the players involved, and of ensuring that the predicaments and the processes of the struggle are revealed from the conception of dissent to the attainment of conciliation. I have also attempted to avoid the tendency of some accounts to represent the revolution as a single movement involving an autonomous group of dissidents, and rather to reveal the complexity of the process. Primarily, I have tried to redress previous historical records that highlight only violent calls to arms in revolutions, rather than acknowledging the potential success of a non-violent call to arts in struggles towards democracy.

It would be both remiss, and irresponsible, not to conclude on a more reflective note. The transition to democracy in South Africa was, although an undeniable triumph of the human spirit, not the end of the story either. For all the fanfare and accolades that accompanied the demise of apartheid in South Africa, and for the irrefutable fact that South Africans have arrived at a social reconciliation unprecedented in its history, the aftermath of the transition carries with it a cautionary tale. A real danger lies in the dream of South African peace and prosperity gradually being transformed into an unanticipated nightmare of violence and economic instability. The realities of the present cannot, and should not, be ignored in an exploration of the past, as such an oversight would merely repeat the flaws of previous investigations that present autonomous moments in history as definitive and conclusive. Can South Africa still be held up as the 'miracle' of social transformation if 'things fall apart' again, and would a new *apart*-heid replace the previous divide between black and white with one between rich and poor, healthy and dying, perpetrator and victim? How effective is a social movement in which the focus has shifted from art as a crime, to crime as an art?

And so, the transition continues. Like our investigations into the history of the anti-apartheid movement(s), investigations into post-apartheid South Africa need to be made from the conception of new ideologies to constantly changing social dilemmas, through all the gestational states of renewed protest against looming inequities, to the successful birth of a new status quo and a peaceful resolution. Only when stability in its broadest sense is achieved will the waves of discontent have reached their destination, and the dishonour of the past have been overturned by the integrity of the present.

> The longed-for tidal wave of justice can rise up,
> And hope and history rhyme (Seamus Heaney).

ENDNOTES

1. This chapter has been adapted from an earlier version presented as the keynote address at the Composing Apartheid conference in Grahamstown, South Africa, on 1 July 2004. I would like to acknowledge the many salient suggestions from fellow ethnomusicologists at the conference regarding the early draft of this work. Particular gratitude is extended to Louise Meintjes of Duke University for critical feedback regarding the final piece, and André Brink, for helpful insights during the writing process.
2. An old photograph captures some of my fondest childhood memories: sitting with my black nanny Mickie on the lawn with her old gramophone player, and listening to 'Wimoweh' and *kwela* penny whistle music. In an otherwise segregated world, music provided a space that could be shared, and a bond that could be explored.
3. It is important to stress that several (white) South African art music composers had already been integrating 'African' elements into their music; see Scherzinger's chapter in this volume on the composer Kevin Volans. The visibility of this particular event, in 1982, therefore caused contention among local musicians who felt overlooked by the touting of the work as the 'first' of its kind. The

sponsor of the work, Adcock-Ingram, was also criticised for commissioning a foreign (Persian) composer instead of a local composer, and the work itself received mixed reviews.

4 Jameson's was one of the locations where music increasingly either honestly eradicated, or brutally explored, issues of race and politics in the country.

5 This subject was prominent during numerous interviews between myself and 'inzile' Dolly Rathebe (held in Pretoria, Indiana, and North Carolina) between 1999 and her death in 2004. It was also the subject of a heated exchange between Senegalese host Bouna Ndiaye and exile Hugh Masekela on the radio show *Bonjour Africa* (on WNCU 90.7 in the United States) on the 16 April 2006.

6 *Toyi-toyi* is a style of street protest consisting of united, rhythmic marching, accompanied by chanted slogans, high-pitched ululating, and spontaneous song. The Shifty label represented a maverick music studio that recorded and distributed cutting-edge protest music, much of which was banned.

7 This tactic was particularly the case with the prominent black female vocalists of the fifties and sixties, like Dolly Rathebe and Thandi Klaasen (who avoided many a scrape with the law through comical play-acting and light-hearted deference), as well as the later antics of Afrikaner cabaret artists like Casper de Vries and Nataniël (who feigned naïvety and ironic conformity to reveal absurd realities).

8 The *luisterliedjie* 'movement', launched by Merwede van der Merwe, spotlighted singers like Laurika Rauch, Anneli van Rooyen, and Anton Goosen.

9 Albums of pop groups Juluka and Malombo, and the *Graceland* album, revealed the potential of fusing (neo)traditional black South African genres and styles (like *isicathamiya* and *maskanda*) with the Western pop idiom.

10 Art music composers Stefans Grové, James Khumalo, Hans Roosenschoon, Peter Klatzow, Christopher James, Barry Jordan and others incorporated African music into the Western art music aesthetic of their compositions.

11 The *'alternatiewe* Afrikaner' movement, launched by Dirk Uys, was popularised by Johannes Kerkorrel (Ralph Rabie) and Koos Kombuis (André le Toit), among others.

12 These were represented by new fusions between musicians like Nico Carstens (of Afrikaans *boeremusiek* fame) and Ray Phiri (of the group *Stimela*), as well as by diverse fusion groups like Tananas, Orchestro Mondo, and Intsholo.

Bibliography

Brooks, Jerome. 1994. 'Chinua Achebe: The Art of Fiction'. *The Paris Review*, 133, pp. 142-166.

Byerly, Ingrid. 1996. 'The Music Indaba: Music as Mirror, Mediator and Prophet in the South African Transition from Apartheid to Democracy'. Ph.D. diss., Duke University.

_. 1998. 'Mirror, Mediator and Prophet: The Music *Indaba* of Late-Apartheid South Africa'. *Ethnomusicology*, 42(1), pp. 1-44.

_. 2003. 'Music is the Weapon of the Future: Fifty Years of African Popular Music' (Review of book by Frank Tenaille). *Notes*, 60(2), pp. 422-425.

Clarke, John. 2004. Author's interview, Pretoria. 18 February.

Comaroff, J, & J Comaroff. 2004 'Criminal Obsessions, After Foucault: Postcoloniality, Policing and the Metaphysics of Disorder'. *Critical Inquiry*, 30, pp. 800-824.

De Klerk, FW. 1990. Address by the State President at the opening of the Second Session of the Ninth Parliament of the Republic of South Africa. Cape Town, 2 February. http://www.info.gov.za/speeches/1996/101348690.htm, accessed 16 May 2007.

_. 1990. Interview Frederick van Zyl Slabbert, February.

_. 1999. *The Last Trek*. London: Macmillan.

Drewett, Michael. 2002. 'Satirical Opposition in Popular Music within Apartheid and Post-apartheid South Africa'. *Society in Transition*, 33(1), pp. 80-90.

_. 2002. 'It's my Duty, Not my Choice: Narratives of Resistance to the South African Border War in Popular Music'. In C van der Merwe & R Wolfswinkel (eds). *Telling Wounds: Narratives, Trauma and Memory: Working through the South African Armed Conflicts of the 20th Century*. Proceedings of the conference held at the University of Cape Town, 3-5 July, pp. 127-133.

_. 2003. 'Battling over Borders: Narratives of Resistance to the South African Border War Voiced through Popular Music'. *Social Dynamics*, 29(1), pp. 26-47.

_. 2004. 'Aesopian Strategies of Textual Resistance in the Struggle to Overcome the Censorship of Popular Music in Apartheid South Africa'. In B Müller (ed.). *Censorship and Cultural Regulation in the Modern Age*. Amsterdam: Rodopi Press, pp. 1-18.

Grundlingh, Albert. 2004. 'Rocking the Boat? The "Voëlvry" Music Movement in South Africa: Anatomy of Afrikaans Anti-Apartheid Social Protest in the Eighties'. *International Journal of African Historical Studies*, 37(3), pp. 483-508.

Hirsch, Lee (dir.). 2002. *Amandla! A Revolution in Four-Part Harmony*. Lions Gate.

Hopkins, Pat. 2006. *Voëlvry: The Movement that Rocked South Africa*. Cape Town: Zebra Press.

Kerkorrel, Johannes. 1996. Author's interview, Cape Town. 4 January.

Koopmans, Ruud. 2004. 'Protest in Time and Space: The Evolution of Waves of Contention'. In David Snow, Sarah A Soule & Hanspeter Kriesi (eds). *The Blackwell Companion to Social Movements*. Oxford: Blackwell, pp. 19-46.

Kriesi, Hanspeter. 2004. 'Political Context and Opportunity'. In David Snow, Sarah A Soule & Hanspeter Kriesi (eds). *The Blackwell Companion to Social Movements*. Oxford: Blackwell, pp. 67-90.

Laubscher, Leswin. 2005. 'Afrikaner Identity and the Music of Johannes Kerkorrel'. *South African Journal of Psychology*, 35(2), pp. 308-330.

Meyer, David S, & Suzanne Staggenborg. 1996. 'Movements, Countermovements and the Structure of Political Opportunity'. *American Journal of Sociology*, 101, pp. 1628-60.

Myers, Daniel J. 2000. 'The Diffusion of Collective Violence: Infectiousness, Susceptibility and Mess Media Networks'. *American Journal of Sociology*, 106 (1), pp. 173-208.

Nkosi, Sipho 'Smile'.1998. Author's interview, Johannesburg, 23 March.

Smit, Brendon. 1992. 'Afrikaans Alternative Popular Music 1986-1990: An Analysis of the Music of Bernoldus Niemand and Johannes Kerkorrel'. B.Mus. thesis, University of Natal.

Snow, David, & P Oliver. 1995. 'Social Movements and Collective Behaviour: Social Psychological Dimensions and Considerations'. In K Cook, G Fine & J House (eds). *Sociological Perspectives on Social Psychology*. Boston: Allyn & Bacon, pp. 571-599.

Soule, Sarah A. 2004. 'Diffusion Processes within and across Movements'. In David Snow, Sarah A Soule & Hanspeter Kriesi (eds). *The Blackwell Companion to Social Movements*. Oxford: Blackwell, pp. 294-310.

Strang, David, & Sarah Soule. 1998. 'Diffusion in Organization and Social Movements: From Hybrid Corn to Poison Spills'. *Annual Review of Sociology*, 24, pp. 265-290.

Tarrow, Sidney. 1994. *Power in Movement: Social Movements, Collective Action and Politics*. New York: Cambridge University Press.

Tenaille, Frank. 2002. *Music is the Weapon of the Future: Fifty Years of African Popular Music*. Chicago: Lawrence Hill.

Thompson, Hunter S. 1971. *Fear and Loathing in Las Vegas: A Savage Journey to the Heart of the American Dream*. New York: Random House.

13

ARNOLD VAN WYK'S HANDS

STEPHANUS MULLER

It does not seem to me, Austerlitz added, that we understand the laws governing the return of the past, but I feel more and more as if time did not exist at all, only various spaces interlocking according to the rules of a higher form of stereometry, between which the living and the dead can move back and forth as they like, and the longer I think about it the more it seems to me that we who are still alive are unreal in the eyes of the dead, that only occasionally, in certain lights and atmospheric conditions, do we appear in their field of vision (WG Sebald, *Austerlitz*, 2002: 185).[1]

When I was asked to participate in the conference from which this book was born, my initial reaction, after giving it some careful thought, was to decline the invitation. I told myself: I am too busy to do this. But in reality, I was discomforted by the conference theme and the sentiment that seemed to drive it. A press release of 30 April 2004 by NewMusicSA, under whose auspices the conference was organised, left little doubt of what that sentiment was. In this press release, the South African composer Michael Blake (then president of NewMusicSA) was quoted as saying:

> While everyone in music and the arts has been looking at the achievements of the past 10 years, NewMusicSA felt it was a good time to reflect on composition in the years of apartheid when white composers – the current whingers! – were having a pretty good time, thanks to their great patrons the old National Party, the Broederbond, the SABC and Anton Hartman, and the apartheid system itself. Never before (or since) had so much mediocrity reached such heights ...

It was difficult to see how open and explorative the conference could be in the face of such provocative and simplistic views. Nor was it clear how research on white composers who lived during apartheid (in my case Arnold van Wyk) could be presented unless it accepted (even, or especially, in opposing) this already established master-narrative of apartheid complicity and aggrandisement.

But my reservations went deeper still. I was reluctant to prepare yet another academic paper in English at this time. I had recently decided that I wanted to create more of a balance in my professional writing between English and Afrikaans, my mother tongue and the language in which I am also writing my biography of Van Wyk. The decision to revisit the possibilities of writing in Afrikaans was not only prompted by the promise of a broadening of register, a change of style, a discovery of spaces hidden in the nuances of a different vocabulary and semantics, although these considerations with their echoes of belief in an admittedly Herderian *Urwüchsigkeit* of language were important to me. But I also found that when I wrote in Afrikaans I instinctively wrote for a different audience. This would happen without any intent or planning. Writing the language I grew up in, I found that I (also) spoke to people like my parents and siblings, my school friends, aunts and uncles, or rather: 'ooms en tannies'. Writing in the language, English, I have grown more proficient in professionally, I invariably found that I addressed colleagues. I wanted to see how my writing would change (the 'what' as well as the 'how') after an enforced change of tongue. 'My use of "constituency", "audience", "opponents", and "community",' writes Edward Said, 'serves as a reminder that no one writes simply for oneself. There is always an Other; and this Other willy-nilly turns interpretation into a social activity, albeit with unforeseen consequences, audiences, constituencies, and so on' (2001: 120).

In South Africa, Afrikaans academics have to negotiate the linguistic tightrope between Afrikaans and English with, in the best of views, a broadening of perspectives on the work language can do. But let it also be said that it is a painful process, bifurcating between an honest desire for communication with a broader scholarly community in which the *lingua franca* is English (and the flipside fear of parochialism), and the desire to think and write and conduct verbal retrospection in the language of one's home and therefore inevitably coupled with the politicised responsibility of Afrikaans academics to maintain Afrikaans as an academic language, and ultimately as a spoken language, for future generations of South Africans. The responsibility I speak of is not a responsibility to a political idea, at least it is no longer so to me, but to all who might be driven out of themselves in future by finding the doors of the past locked in strange accents and unknown combinations of sounds. More controversially, I would claim, it is to keep the options open of positioning oneself in a discursive space with the potential to stake out in an authentic voice a postcolonial South African position in a global discourse shaped by English. And more respectably, finally, it is tethered to the problem of nomenclature set out classically in Marc Bloch's incomplete work *The Historian's Craft*, a rather intractable problem I can only mention here but that has to be left unexplored.

After I had declined the invitation to go to Grahamstown, where the conference was held, I was unable to banish the conference working title from my thoughts: Composing ApARTheid. During this time I also received the proofs of a correspondence I conducted in an American musicological journal, in which I had replied at some length to an article written in a previous edition by a South African-born composer, David Hönigsberg, then resident in Switzerland, now deceased. Reading through it, this correspondence seems to me now to be extremely defensive and even apologist to a degree, although I do not want to distance myself from the substance of what I wrote, forwarding for my defence the notion of advancing a more balanced 'understanding' than the undifferentiated 'explanation' that was offered in Hönigsberg's article. Because of its relevance to the conference title, I should like to recount some fragments of this correspondence with Hönigsberg. About South African music history under apartheid, Hönigsberg wrote as follows:

> To this end [legitimation of white racial superiority], the cultural apparatchiks set about finding and promoting white talent. As of 1948 the search for the South African Bartók/Kodály had begun ... Much time and debate was spent attempting to define the exact parameters that such a composer would have to fulfill. To try to define the more-or-less officially required style in South Africa is troublesome. I would readily call it Christian National Realism, taking advantage of the corresponding meaning envisaged by Soviet Social Realism. Christian National Realism refers to music that meets all the requirements demanded of it by the 'culture controllers' of the National Party (1999: 140).

I felt a need to respond to these and other statements, and did so at some length, a reply that I cannot repeat here in its entirety. Here, however, is part of my response:

> Who were these 'cultural apparatchiks'? The writer won't say. Neither does he venture an opinion on how they 'set about finding and promoting white talent'. Nor does he inform the reader whether this Boer-Bartók was ever found, and who he was (it would have to be a 'he'), or what these traveling talent scouts or their controllers did when two gay, non-Calvinist, non-Nationalist Afrikaner composers (Arnold van Wyk and Hubert du Plessis) emerged as among the most important standard bearers of the so-called 'Christian National Realism.' Hönigsberg provides no documentary or even anecdotal evidence to support the notion of musical style 'debates' and, not surprisingly, the 'officially required style' that he finds so troublesome to define, is not illuminated by examples or a source-based indication of official guidelines or preferences – a tag (this time linking Afrikaners with the totalitarianism of the Soviet Union) suffices. It seems that for Hönigsberg Afrikaners can only ever be understood in analogy to other ideological evils (2002: 252).

Implied in my reasoning, and more explicit in the actual correspondence, is my belief that in white-dominated South Africa, music was not a primary parameter of cultural style (to use the terminology employed by Leonard Meyer [1989: 21]).[2] I think that many of the erroneous generalisations regarding art music in South Africa stem from the tendency to disregard, probably with the best of methodological intentions, this discontinuity between 'black' and 'white' culture. Whereas, in the case of the former, I think that it can be argued persuasively (as has been done in the work of David Coplan, Veit Erlmann, Lara Allen, Grant Olwage and others) that music was and is indeed a primary shaping force in culture, a manner of expression definitive of black cultural struggles and aspirations, in the case of the latter I believe this to be untrue. One consequence of this hypothesis would be a differentiated positioning (and consequently a differentiated analysis) of different musics *vis-à-vis* the other cultural parameters like politics and ideology in a synchronic sense. Being a primary shaping force in a specific cultural field (as was and is music in black South African culture), music must be considered more productively politically and ideologically relational within such a field (even as an institutionally/

structurally marginalised discourse) than music that constitutes a secondary parameter in a specific cultural field (as was and is art music in white South African culture) but is nevertheless institutionally ensconced or at least protected. In the case of apartheid, one would therefore expect black music-making to be amenable to historiographical and stylistic analysis with regard to effects of this ideology by virtue of it being such an important vehicle of expression for its constituents. Conversely, even though art music was, as a marker of European high culture, a desired form of musical expression for the white political elite, its relative unimportance to the constituency supporting that political structure and for the political structure itself (and here lies the burden of proof for the historian) makes it somehow more removed from the social, political, and economic processes of that culture, so that an analysis conducted from that perspective might yield unsatisfactory or confusing results. This way of thinking might be seen to perpetuate a kind of binary thinking – them and us, black and white – but I believe the opposite is in fact true. As soon as we realise that the contingencies for an existentialist voice *vis-à-vis* ideology and politics can inhere in one kind of musical expression and not in another occupying the same synchronic space, it is lack of differentiation that perpetuates ethnic divides.[3]

The correspondence quoted above marks only the latest salvo in my English-speaking involvement with apartheid and a specific body of South African music. It is clear that in generalising, I nevertheless try to import a sense of the uniqueness of the South African situation, a process that needs to be taken further by music historians in order to deal with these kinds of naïve allegations that amount to little more than political posturing. The perspectives offered in my doctoral work are clearly also very personal instances of coming to terms with a specific cultural inheritance and the burden of guilt and historical responsibility Afrikaners have to shoulder for apartheid (see Muller, 2000). When I was busy writing these case studies, it seemed to me as if I was writing my way out of an existential dilemma. I took the deconstructionist possibilities of stretching the text to the utmost in unashamedly strategic readings intended to reclaim part of my cultural inheritance for a discourse that was intent on excluding it. From this point of view, it was a thoroughly conservative enterprise, as well as a rather ambitious one. It moved beyond scholarship as a 'science' aimed at clarifying the 'truth' and became a narrative refiguring truths to create livable new identities. In one such a reading I placed Arnold van Wyk's *Missa in illo tempore* into orbit within a constellation of texts in order to read, strategically, Adornian-formulated immanent critique in its *a cappella* textures. This reading has subsequently been critiqued and stabilised in other readings prompted by the iconoclastic potential of my methodology. Personally, my scholarship has therefore been tied inextricably to apartheid and its effects on the music that interests me most, and I have spoken about this at length in English to a mostly English scholarly audience. This scholarship contains elements of confession, of retrieval, and of defence.

Reciting this history as the context of the above scholarly altercation has the purpose, firstly, of putting on the table the documented arguments necessitating defence of a kind with regard to the music I study, lest my concerns are seen as purely personal and psychological. Of course, they are *also* that, but in that sense I at least control the agenda to the extent that I could theoretically 'move on' once my personal business had been transacted to my own satisfaction. Even though apartheid, and in a broader sense colonialism in general, is destined to remain a paradigmatic conceptual framework for South African (musical) culture of the twentieth century and well beyond, I find myself at a personal junction where defining a position with respect to apartheid – whether it be one of atonement or justification or revelation – can no longer be the sole reason for my visitations to my, and our collective, pasts. I find the apartheid-framed skirmishes and debates directed at audiences gathered together by a global English-speaking consensus mentality – an apartheid spelt but rarely pronounced in the Afrikaans fashion, as though English wishes to distance itself from the word even when using it to English-language effects – ApARTheid – to be indifferent, if not antagonistic, to my own research interests. And while I do not imply that our scholarship can take place in a space where politics do not intrude or are not important, I should like to think that it can be practised without us all becoming politicians. If you detect in this a degree of exasperation with the conference topic, you are correct. It is, however, exasperation accompanied by the full knowledge that we have not even begun to articulate adequately the impact of apartheid-thinking on our musical landscape.

But my short exposition of my own scholarship's fascination and involvement with apartheid is intended also, secondly, to register clearly and briefly that the agency implied in the conference title 'Composing ApARTheid' rests perhaps more convincingly in the concerns and preoccupations of scholars today than in the hands of the creators of musics during the apartheid era. Perhaps we are the true composers of apartheid in the construction of a retrospective historical discourse that veers from polemics to apologetics without going to the trouble to explore the fascinating spaces within these polarities.

II

When I returned from my doctoral studies in England, I started researching the project which has been occupying me for the past three years, and which is likely to occupy me for at least as long in the future: the life of Arnold van Wyk. Why exactly I turned to biography I cannot justify or explain. Some sort of inner compulsion drove me away from the fraught scholarly involvement with my past, intimately connected with apartheid and the reckoning made with apartheid by South African society. I now read the material I wrote during that period with a feeling of near revulsion, a circumstance which has led me to experience what seems like an insurmountable estrangement from my past academic work. I think that biography held out the promise of a more solid and neutral historical activity. An intellectual cliché, I know. Perhaps, taking my Calvinist bent into account, I could venture the description more 'honest'. But more importantly, I think that I always realised – and this is a feeling to which my years of residency abroad lent depth and persistence – that once my individual demons had been confronted, I would still need to find my 'home ground', to invent a narrative of myself as a 'member' of some kind of 'society'. I think that writing in Afrikaans about an Afrikaans composer, whose music, at first, I have to admit, did not move me intellectually or emotionally, held out the promise of constructing a narrative about the ordinary things that make up a culturally compatible past life in the present: the places, the memories of people, the books, the letters, the diaries, and from the musical perspective the recordings, the reviews, the manuscripts, the sketches. Of course the choice of this particular life, the life of Arnold van Wyk, was not an arbitrary choice, but one which was similar to my own in crucial historical and personal respects, making him sympathetic to the tenor of my historical enquiry. Eventually my active involvement with my subject's estate led to my not only embarking upon the project of researching and writing his biography, but also ordering his literary estate and compiling extensive catalogues thereof. I found myself in the dual role of archivist and biographer, of neutral observer and interpreter, of list maker and listless and somewhat desperate grappler with a history always bursting out of the narrative constraints I devise. And I am still having to negotiate this dual role as I write here, as well as the anxieties and accumulative fatigue of a project that seems to grow larger and less manageable the more time and effort I devote to it.

It was during one of the morning sessions that I usually spend working on the piles of documents taking up ever more space in the Special Collections section of the JS Gericke Library in Stellenbosch that I discovered a grey envelope with no letter included, containing five photographs. The envelope was in a plastic bag, among other photographs, and had recently been sent to Stellenbosch on permanent loan by the Nasionale Afrikaanse Letterkundige Museum en Navorsingsentrum (NALN) in Bloemfontein, where a large part of my subject's literary estate had languished in boxes for many years.[4] The envelope bore the date stamp of 1954 and was posted in Johannesburg to 38 Charles Street, Pretoria, the address of Harry and Freda Baron, where Van Wyk was on holiday at the time.[5] He often visited the Barons, whom he had met during his frequent holidays in De Rust in the Klein Karoo as a teenager in the early 1930s and who had played an important role in his development as a composer. The photographs are black and white images of different positions of a pianist's hands – Arnold van Wyk's hands, as it unsurprisingly turned out to be – on a Steinway grand piano. They were all taken from the right hand side, from a position slightly behind the pianist. One is taken from a point higher than the pianist's own head, two from a vantage point one could assume almost level with the pianist's head, and two from a lower vantage point, more level to the figure seated at the piano than behind him. The photographer, whose stamp appears on the envelope and at the back of each photograph, is Derik Worman from Johannesburg, and the respective photographs sent to my subject are clearly marked on the images as 'Proofs/Proewe'.[6]

I was oddly touched when I held these images in my hands, and sat at my overcrowded library desk for a very long time staring at them. It was clear that the hand positions, close together, had been chosen to show the hands to their best effect. It was also clear, the longer I looked at them, that the hands were depressing keys that had no logical, that is syntactical or linear, sense. The hands on the pictures were merely contracted or expanded to provide better angles, or indicate the size and reach of each hand. Thinking of the textures of much of Van Wyk's piano music, it is clear that the physiology of these hands is a clear explanation for the nearly unplayable textures of this music.[7] It also dawned on me that in order for the photographs to be taken in these musically illogical positions, the hands would have had to be extremely still, that is placed into position and kept there until the photograph had been taken.

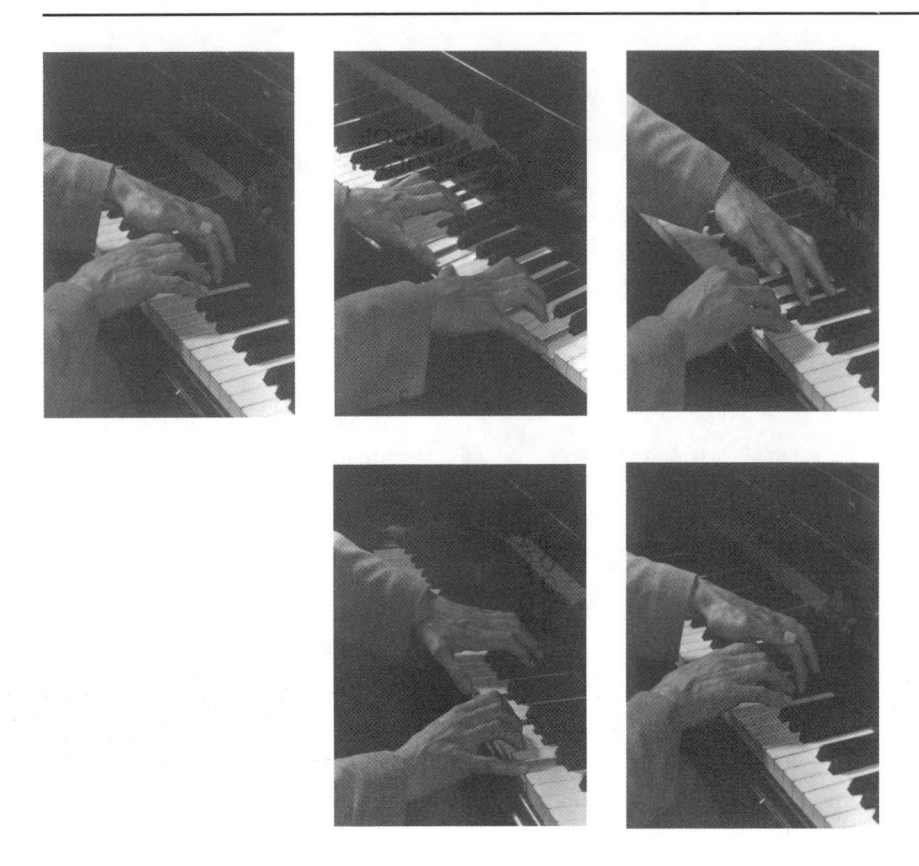

What moved me in these images, I think, was not the undoubted elegance of the hands as they appear suspended in a seemingly natural state in the habitat of the keyboard, or their composed positions, their oddly disembodied air and iconographic, de-socialised quality, but the fact that my subject, whom I had got to know quite well over the course of the last three years, was prepared for these photographs to be taken. Almost involuntarily I recalled an apocryphal story of how, when Arnold van Wyk had died, a musicological colleague and Beethoven scholar had tried to get access to the body to have a death mask made in the style of the Beethoven mask by the painter Joseph Danhauser.

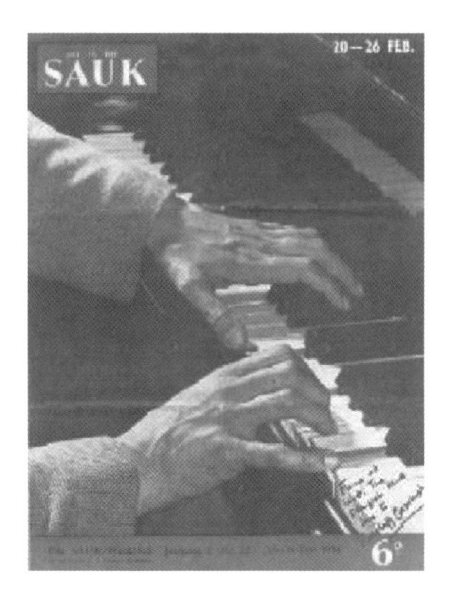

The suggestion was indignantly rejected by the close friend of the composer, I believe because the feeling was – rightly so, if I take into account what I have learned from my subject over the years – that he would have found the idea revolting. Due to liver failure, Van Wyk's face had also become uncharacteristically bloated in his final days. Of course, I cannot vouch for the accuracy of this story. The reason for agreeing to the photographs, whatever their purpose, could not be vainglory or pretensions of fame. By the way, the actual purpose of their existence later proved to be a cover page for *Die SAUK Weekblad* (20-26 February 1954), where a single, blown-up photograph appears with the following description on the inside of the cover: 'This striking photograph of the composer Arnold van Wyk's hands was taken when he recently performed with the SABC-orchestra in Johannesburg' (my translation).[8] On a copy of this cover page included in a letter to Howard Ferguson dated 26 April 1954, Van Wyk had written 'Fame at last! The Starfish send love to Falstaff Gorsebush'. 'Starfish' was the affectionate nickname the British pianist Myra Hess had given Van Wyk's hands when they became good friends during his war-time stay in London (1938-1946), and 'Falstaff' and 'Gorsebush' were two (seldom combined) nicknames Van Wyk used to refer to Howard Ferguson. 'Long awaited fame' aside then, it is undeniable that the photographs signify the kind of Romantic – with a capital 'R' – adulation of an individual as something special, perhaps even genius, that the Beethoven death mask also communicates to us 180 years after it was made. I think that the subject of Arnold van Wyk's Romanticism is convincingly ushered in by these photographs. I have said before that there was a congruence between the ideologies underlying apartheid and the idea of Western art music as a medium of expression for white South African composers, but I think that a case could also be made for a more specific consonance between the kind of Romantic that Arnold van Wyk was and the basic tenets of white superiority. The area of greatest consonance is, I believe, the typically Romantic preoccupation with the unique, the peculiar, the idiosyncratic, and the fostering of diversity. Certainly

Van Wyk's music can be said to embody a strange mixture of the ideals of beauty characterising the early nineteenth-century musical aesthetic and the philosophical-prophetic *Weltanschauungsmusik* of the latter part of the century: a tension between the delicate and beautiful on the one hand and the meaningfully new and original on the other.

Even though Van Wyk was not a political animal, as all who knew him testify, he did have the occasional brush with politics. One such occasion was reported in the *Somerset Budget* under the title 'A bomb thrown at S.A. culture':

> Cape Town – The Afrikaans composer Arnold van Wyk has thrown a bombshell into the annual conference of the Suid-Afrikaanse Akademie at Stellenbosch. He said in the Stellenbosch newspaper Eikestad Nuus that a Nationalist M.P. had asked him 'to end his perversity and compose boeremusiek.' Mr. Van Wyk said that as a composer of serious music he lived in a cultural desert among his own people.
>
> Referring to Afrikaans audiences at the 'Wonder of Afrikaans' festivities in the Cape Town City Hall, he said Afrikaners reacted only to speeches and popular ditties. Serious music meant nothing to them. Mr. Van Wyk said Silas Marner, the first full-length opera by a South African composer (John Joubert) will be staged in Britain – not South Africa. (The Festival of Union Committee concerned with the selection of music rejected the opera as unsuitable.) 'Now that our Akademie is 50 years old and the Union will soon reach its half-century, it is a suitable time to say that the South African composer lives in a desert,' says Van Wyk. The little oases are 'even scarcer than those for the painter and author' (1959).[9]

That Van Wyk was not entirely indifferent to matters pertaining to politics and music is clear from two broadcasts he did for the Afrikaans Service of the BBC from London on Friday 25 May 1945 and 1 June 1945 respectively, entitled 'The Music of the Future'. Van Wyk spoke about the responsibility of the creative artist in the battle for self preservation in the light of the imperative for reconstruction and healing ('to prevent humanity from destroying itself') in the wake of the Second World War:

> Now, I know that artists today – or those of them who matter in my opinion – are not in touch with normal people; and there are moments when Mozart against machine guns is about as effective as a *kleilat* against tanks – nevertheless it remains a fact that the creative artist

has a mighty weapon with which to join battle – regardless of what the disbelievers might say. It was Einstein (if I remember correctly) who said: 'How can we despair of humanity when we remember that Mozart was human?' And here I can also recount Sir Thomas Beecham's strong faith – the faith that the world's many problems could be solved by simply forcing every soul to listen – for half an hour every day – to the works of Mozart (my translation).

Clapping the natives in irons to enforce a strict diet of *divertimenti* is hardly a programme with which to ignite the African *uhuru*, I concede, but it is also too generally humanistic and universal a vision to be easily incorporated into a narrow Afrikaner nationalist, at times fascist, ideology. According to Nicol Viljoen, erstwhile student and life-long friend of Van Wyk, Arnold was the kind of person who got on extremely well with all people on a personal level, but who was extremely naïve politically and largely oblivious to the injustices of apartheid that surrounded him. Viljoen never heard him speak negatively of the National Party's leaders, and is convinced that he would have voted for the National Party as the political structure that could maintain the kind of order he felt was necessary to guarantee the space for great music to act as a 'civilising force' for the advancement of the whole of society – the vision he formulated in his two BBC broadcasts. I have become convinced that Viljoen is wrong about this. Van Wyk had little patience or sympathy for Afrikaner Nationalism, his attitude to Nationalism being shaped in war-ravaged London. Scathing remarks about the National Party government abound in his correspondence to his life-long friend Freda Baron, who, as a Jew forced to flee with her family from the rural anti-semitism of De Rust, was a safe ear for Van Wyk's criticisms. In one such letter from London, Van Wyk writes:

> I wish it could be possible for you to stay on at De Rust, but nothing would please me more than to hear that you have managed to escape to another place where there is more tolerance & less pig-headed Nationalism. We are having a thoroughly unpleasant time in London, but I don't think I'd very readily exchange the dangers of present-day London for the 'serenity' of De Rust for instance. As a matter of fact, I do not feel that I want to come back to South Africa at all now. At least people in England have enough sense to recognise a serious threat to freedom & to do all in their power to neutralise that threat. But when a responsible body of churchmen like the Synod

of the O.F.S. D.R.C. [Orange Free State Dutch Reformed Church] declares that Hitler is fighting for Christianity & a Minister profanes his cloth & pitilessly exposes the quality of his mind by saying that Mein Kampf ought to be regarded as the Bible of South Africans and read as such, I feel stifled and outraged. It is no exaggeration to say that after reading some of the Nationalist S. African papers, my first impulse is to go and have a Lysol bath!![10]

More evidence of a strong antipathy with regard to the Afrikaner political establishment is found in a letter of 29 May 1961, when Van Wyk writes to Freda Baron about the impending declaration of a Republic:

I haven't much to complain of, either, always excepting the terrible times we live in and that we are only two days from our glorious republic ... Anyway, there is nothing I can do but carry on: nothing that is except saying a word here and there to shake complacent Nats. But it is like talking to a wall. Anton [Hartman] expects a period of *'ongekende bloei'* [unprecedented growth] – an unfortunate word, since as you know, it can also mean bleeding.

However, the more public criticisms expressed by Van Wyk in documents and letters against the government or government structures are related to the meagre opportunities and inadequate support for South African composers and do not involve direct political comment. In a letter to a certain Mrs Field, President of the South African Federation of Business and Professional Women, Van Wyk writes on 25 February 1957:

The State has thusfar (sic) not spent one single farthing to help a SA composer to get a work printed. If it has, it must be in some indirect way: for instance, an organisation which receives State support may have, on occasion, used some of the money to help with printing. But I know of no instances. It is safe to say, I think, that as far as the State is concerned, the South African composer just does not exist.

One might have thought that things would have changed under the stewardship and patronage of Van Wyk's friend and Broederbond member Anton Hartman at the SABC from 1961 on.[11] But little more than a year before he died on 27 May 1983, Van Wyk wrote a letter to Mrs Jacobs of the SABC:

I (and, I can assure you, *all* South African composers) feel convinced that the SABC and especially SATV are not really interested in us and that it is meaningless to try to change the situation. And should there be sense in trying again, I am bitterly upset that I have to devote precious time and energy at this late stage of my life to the unpleasant necessity of writing this (very difficult) letter. The strongest feeling that I have at the moment is that I wish to inform you that I should in future choose to have nothing to do with the SABC – especially because the disparagement and humiliation that one has to endure from the Corporation is not worth the few stale crumbs it throws one. Or let me put it like this: if I look back to the near half-century that I have had dealings with the SABC, I see more unpleasantness and disparagement than anything else. In the last ten years things have worsened, and in the last four years especially the SABC has made abundantly clear what it thinks of me. I now feel very strongly that I never really managed to be successful at the SABC, that I will never be able to be successful there and that I don't want to try, because if I look at some of the people that enjoy your favour I feel rather proud that I am not one of them (20 November 1981; my translation).

Naturally one need not take Van Wyk's word for the treatment supposedly meted out to him, which many today would feel was quite royal. Also, the last sentence of his letter to Jacobs could suggest patronage of a political kind and a certain resentfulness that he was excluded from this. Certainly the idea that an artist could work within apartheid structures, and even perpetuate apartheid thinking while believing himself to stand outside such structures, is not inconceivable. However, the facile notion of some latter-day propagandists of the existence of a comfortable and mutually profitable relationship between the 'apartheid regime' and 'white composers' in general is hereby at least qualified to an extent. More research into this murky area is palpably needed.

If it is historically more or less true that Arnold van Wyk was not a willing participant in the projects or ideologies of Afrikaner Nationalism, particularly apartheid, and that his Romantic eschewing of hierarchy and class distinction, his egalitarianism, and his formalist abhorrence of art in service of language and by implication politics *could* be construed as markers of an anti-establishment position, we should nevertheless be careful to note that the exact opposite is in fact more probable. When Van Wyk made statements about the philistinism of his own people, as he did when that Nationalist MP berated him for his musical perversity with the advice to start composing *boeremusiek*, this criticism was of course absorbed by the establishment as the paradoxical affirmation of a centuries-old Western conception of the artist as a lonely and idiosyncratic genius. As Leonard Meyer has written about the nineteenth-century artist: 'Artists wanted to be different and special, and their claims to singularity were supported both by the mysteries of musical creation and by the mythic opposition of the Philistines. Yet even as they scorned and mocked the middle class, the artists of the nineteenth century created for it, representing subjects, symbolizing beliefs, and advocating values consonant with those of the elite egalitarians' (1989: 183). And there is little doubt that Arnold van Wyk was in many respects a nineteenth-century composer in the twentieth century in a colonial society embracing many nineteenth-century values, not the least of which was of course a virulent nationalism. So perhaps my musicological colleague did not, after all, have the wrong end of the stick when he tried (and failed) to preserve in plaster Arnoldus Christiaan Vlok van Wyk's sad features for posterity.

III

Looking at the photographed hands on the day I found them, the thing that disturbed my archival complacency, that grabbed my thoughts and would not let go for days and weeks until I started writing about them, was the thought that these photographs in their coagulated state were about communicating something to the future, my present, that was of some deep and not entirely intelligible significance. In *Time and Narrative*, Paul Ricoeur writes with regard to his third category of mimesis, which he calls mimesis$_3$, that aesthetic reception of something cannot take up the problem of communication without also taking up that of reference. 'What is communicated,' Ricoeur continues to say, 'in the final analysis, is, beyond the sense of a work, the world it projects and that constitutes its horizon. In this sense, the listeners or readers receive it according to their own receptive capacity, which itself is defined by a situation that is both limited and open to the world's horizon' (1990: 77).

A situation both limited and open to the world's horizon.

I think that this explains to an extent not the 'what' or the 'why', but the 'how' of the emotional appeal these photographs made on me in their prenarrative quality of experience that hints at the existence of music. For all their extreme alienation to the reality of an historical world in which they 'composed' and 'played' – a world of social engineering, desperate poverty, broken lives, and ruined futures – extreme alienation is still a case of intersection (Ibid.: 79). I think that the acontextualism of these hands, firstly with respect to their distance from real performed music and secondly with respect to the space of their Steinway keyboard and its obvious 'remove' from society, convey only the particular *modality* of the intersection with the society where the hands and piano 'lived'. That which could be construed as indifference towards society is in fact a Romantic – again with a capital 'R' – engagement with it. An engagement that set itself apart from the same society validating its existence by espousing all the symptoms of Romanticism: the unimportance of context, the mistrust of language, the aspiration to emulate the truth and elegance of nature, the prizing of the unique person and the diversity implied by this, the ideological scaffolding of a formalist point of view proclaiming the possibility, nay, the imperative of complete meaning in the work of art stripped of its context. Ricoeur speaks of the intersections contained in a work being both limited and open to the world's horizon, and I think he intends this to be read as intersections that exist synchronically. However, I sense that today, when we speak to a title like 'Composing ApARTheid', we are still inhabiting the old world to such an extent that we cannot address the subject as if it were some historical event, or series of events. We – I – have to treat it in the sense that I am now, at this present and in this discourse, composing apartheid or a version thereof that I can live with. We have to stretch Ricoeur's meaning to encompass the limited historical context *and* the ever expanding horizon of time intersecting with it. It is a more complicated view of apartheid than is allowed for in granting it a beginning and an end, and the narratives we devise to tell our story might not most profitably be confined to ones with happy endings/beginnings at Victor Verster or diachronic listings mostly confined to tracing the Marxist faultlines of social structures and cultural production, however sophisticated we make these perspectives. My wish would be for narratives about apartheid that recognise both our need to tell, and our humble and honest recognition that we can never tell it all. Fundamentally, it is a wish that depends on Ricoeur's insight that 'time becomes human time to the extent that it is organised after the manner of a narrative; narrative, in turn, is meaningful to the extent that it portrays the features of temporal existence' (Ibid.: 3). Following from his reading of Augustine's *Confessions* (Book 11), Ricoeur realises that the conversion of time ('the past', for my purpose) into narrative does not solve aporias, but only resolves them poetically (and not theoretically) (Ibid.: chap. 2). 'The question of the relationship between time and narrative culminates in this dialectic between an aporetics and a poetics' (Ibid.: 71). The past is accessible as a modality of the present in which the writer and the reader, anchored in the world of action (the present), interacts with the world poetically mediated by narrative (the past). Central to this transaction is the refiguration that takes place through Ricoeur's constructed categories of $mimesis_1$, $mimesis_2$ and $mimesis_3$. It exposes a notion of historical complexity that is indispensable to South African stories. 'This South African word,' writes Graham Pechey on apartheid in the context of the migrancy of South African words, 'has a lot more travelling to do' (2004: 15).

In this spirit I think that these photographed hands indicate an action – the motionlessness should not be confused with a lack of action, of motivation to pose – that points to a place and time other than its own present. A place and time where, of course, it is not and will not be, as it was not *then* as a prior side to narrative, ethically neutral. But an infinitely extended moment of intersection where the hands signal the sensual – for the fingers, and the pads of the fingers are for pianists sensual endings or extensions of the keys – points of contact between what is inside and what is allowed to flow to the outside. What is referenced as 'flowing' in these photographs is of course music. These photographs of Arnold van Wyk's hands constitute an iconic visual preservation of an articulated gesture of aesthetic transmission in something refusing words and pointing to a meeting of private and public space. It asserts the primacy of its agent and his music intersecting with our world – my world – in a manner that, I maintain, I cannot approximate under a subject potentially assuming so much historically as 'Composing ApARTheid'; a set of circumstances that assumes conclusions so confidently that it induces paralysis in those whose stories do not coincide with the endings imposed by the historical cut-off dates, or who wish to arrive at different conclusions. There exist things from the past, sometimes incomprehensible and inexplicably significant, that cannot become part of the story this book wishes to tell, and in this, constitute a crucial, discordant part of its plot.

Endnotes

1 I am much indebted to Sebald's writing in constructing a narrative voice for this article, including his evocative use of photographs.
2 The rest of this paragraph also makes use of Meyer's conceptual framework.
3 Discussing the prose of Naguib Mahfouz, Edward Said contrasts it to prose by Palestinian novelists Ghassan Kanafani and Emile Habibi (within the collective of 'Arab writing') by drawing parallels between the differences in geographical and political instability in Egypt on the one hand and Palestine and Lebanon on the other. The point that the subjects in the latter two countries are 'urgently political and its concerns radically existential' compared to that of Mahfouz has something to do with the different relationality of prose production in the three situations (2001: 317-26). I think that a similar understanding needs to be cultivated in heuristic constructions of South African culture, where the 'one nation' idea is an anachronistic and political imposition on the divided realities

of South African cultural production and differentiated relationality to politics and ideology. I suspect, for instance, that Afrikaner cultural production is now, for the first time since the early decades of the twentieth century, again becoming more and more existentially explorative.

4   Van Wyk's literary estate was only officially donated to the University of Stellenbosch by his executors (Jan du Toit and James May) on 16 September 2002. Substantial documentary material from Van Wyk's estate (including letters, diaries, photographs, and lectures) was held by NALN in Bloemfontein. As part of a permanent loan agreement between the two institutions it was transferred to the University of Stellenbosch in March 2004 to be integrated with the rest of the Van Wyk collection.

5   Van Wyk left for Pretoria on 28 December 1953. He travelled, as he frequently did, on the famous Blue Train. Van Wyk stayed with the Barons for six weeks, only travelling back to Cape Town on 11 February, after having received the news on 18 January that his song cycle *Van Liefde en Verlatenheid* had been selected for performance at that year's International Society for Contemporary Music Festival in Haifa, Israel.

6   Unless stated otherwise, all letters, photographs, and other documentary material used in this article are held in the Arnold van Wyk collection (no. 320) in the Special Collections section of the JS Gericke Library at the University of Stellenbosch. These documents have not yet been catalogued and therefore do not possess reference numbers. All material is published with permission.

7   The actual size of Van Wyk's left hand is illustrated in a letter to his sister, Minnie Hahn (nicknamed 'Mintel'), dated 29 August 1939. On the first page of this letter Van Wyk traces the outline of his left hand, revealing not only a large hand but also a wider than average stretch between the fingers.

8   The performance was a recording of Mozart's K. 449 piano concerto with the SABC Symphony Orchestra, conducted by Anton Hartman. The recording was made on 18 January 1954.

9   There is an irony here. As early as 1939, Van Wyk had written to 'Oom' Charlie Weich about a planned concert of South African music in South Africa House in London, ending his plans with the sentence: '*Ons moet die Rooinekke wys dat ons die "Vat-jou-goed-en-trek-Fereira"-stadium al verby is*'. ('We have to show the Rednecks that we have progressed beyond the "Vat-jou-goed-en-trek-Fereira" [a popular Afrikaans folk tune] stage.'); see letter to Charles Weich, 27 February 1939, Documentation Centre for Music (DOMUS), Music Library, University of Stellenbosch.

10 Letter to Freda Baron, 18 October 1940. The Barons left De Rust for their new address in Baileys Muckleneuk, Pretoria, in 1941. This is the address (38

Charles Street) to which the photographs of Van Wyk's hands were sent. The reason for the relocation was local Afrikaner anti-semitism; this was confirmed to me in a conversation with Charlotte Perold, Freda Baron's daughter. In a letter of 6 June 1941, Freda Baron wrote to Van Wyk in London: 'Yes, dear, at last the incredible has happened, and we are going to live in Pretoria. We are actually going to leave De Rust – a place I am vaguely attached to for I have spent many happy years here but the memory of these was often wiped out by the last few years of hell. I wonder whether I'll be able to forget it or even whether my soul will ever straighten out again completely.' Van Wyk replied in a letter of 20 July 1940: '... did not the greatest thing in my life – meeting you and Mr. Baron – happen there?'.

11 For more on Hartman, see Walton (2004).

Bibliography

'A bomb thrown at S.A. culture'. 1959. *Somerset Budget*, 29 July.

Hönigsberg, David. 1999. 'Chamber Symphony 1998'. *Current Musicology*, 67-68, pp. 139-56.

Muller, Stephanus. 2000. 'Sounding Margins: Musical Representations of White South Africa'. D.Phil. diss., University of Oxford.

_. 2002. 'Letter to the Editor'. *Current Musicology*, 74, pp. 250-54.

Meyer, Leonard B. 1989. 'Toward a Theory of Style'. In *Style and Music: Theory, History and Ideology*. University of Chicago Press: Chicago, pp. 3-37.

Pechey, Graham. 2004. 'On Trek'. *The Times Literary Supplement*, 30 April, p. 15.

Ricoeur, Paul. 1990 [1983]. *Time and Narrative* (trans. Kathleen McLaughlin & David Pellauer). Chicago & London: University of Chicago Press.

Said, Edward. 2001. *Reflections on Exile and Other Literary and Cultural Essays*. London: Granta.

Sebald, WG. 2002. *Austerlitz* (trans. Anthea Bell). New York: Modern Library.

Walton, Chris. 2004. 'Bond of Brothers: Anton Hartman and Music in an Apartheid State'. *Musical Times*, 145(1887), pp. 63-74.

CONTRIBUTORS

A former Junior Research Fellow at Girton College, Cambridge, **Lara Allen** is presently a researcher at WISER (the Wits Institute for Social and Economic Research) at the University of the Witwatersrand. Recent publications include 'The Gallo Music Archive: Popular Music and the Refiguring of Post-apartheid South African Archives', *Fontes Artis Musicae* (2006); 'From Rights to Responsibilities: Identity Politics and Ethnographic Methodology, Dialogues with South African Musicians', *Social Dynamics* (2006); and 'Circuits of Recognition and Desire in the Evolution of Black South African Popular Music: The Career of the Penny Whistle', *South African Journal of Musicology* (2005). Allen is working on a book on *kwela*, and a book on women in black South African popular music and jazz.

Gary Baines is an Associate Professor in the History Department at Rhodes University. His areas of research include South African urban history and culture, especially film and music. His monograph, *A History of New Brighton, Port Elizabeth, South Africa, 1903-1953: The Detroit of the Union*, was published by Edwin Mellen (2002). He recently co-edited (with Peter Vale) *Beyond the Border War: New Perspectives on Late-Cold War Conflicts* (Unisa Press, 2007).

Presently Visiting Assistant Professor in the Department of Cultural Anthropology at Duke University, **Ingrid Byerly** has lectured in Oxford, England, and in the United States and Russia. Academic awards in America include, amongst others, an American Council of Learned Societies Fellowship and a Fulbright Award, and she received the Charles Seeger Prize from the Society for Ethnomusicology for her paper 'Mirror, Mediator and Prophet: The Music Indaba of Late-Apartheid South Africa', *Ethnomusicology* (1998). She is currently working on two books, including one in ethnomusicology titled *Things Come Together: The Music Indaba of Apartheid South Africa*.

Christopher Cockburn lectures in music theory at the University of KwaZulu-Natal, and is well known in South Africa and the United Kingdom as a concert organist and choral conductor. His doctoral research focuses on the performance and reception history of Handel's *Messiah* in South Africa, and his article 'A Distinctive Politics: Handel Becomes Historically Informed in South Africa' appeared in the *South African Journal of Musicology* (2003).

David Coplan is Professor in Anthropology at the University of the Witwatersrand and a veteran of scholarship on South African music. While he is best known for his 1985 study, *In Township Tonight! South Africa's Black City Music and Theatre* (Ravan Press), he has lectured and published widely for three decades on southern African performing arts in Africa, North America and Europe. Other major publications on music include *In The Time of Cannibals* (University of Chicago Press, 1994). An updated and revised edition of *In Township Tonight!* is due out from Jacana in late 2007. **Bennetta Jules-Rosette** is a Professor in the Department of Sociology, University of California, San Diego. Her research interests include semiotic studies of religious discourse, tourist art, and new technologies in Africa. Her most recent monograph is *Two Loves: Josephine Baker in Art and Life* (University of Illinois Press, 2006).

Michael Drewett is a Senior Lecturer in the Department of Sociology and Industrial Sociology at Rhodes University, where he teaches courses in gender and popular culture. His central research interest is in the censorship of popular music (especially in South Africa). He has co-edited (with Martin Cloonan) a book on *Popular Music Censorship in Africa* (Ashgate, 2006), and has an essay, 'Music in the Struggle to End Apartheid', in *Policing Pop*. Drewett has also produced a film documentary dealing with an instance of South African music censorship for the Danish Film Institute, and is a member of the Freemuse Advisory Board.

Shirli Gilbert is lecturer in history at the University of Southampton, where she teaches courses in modern Jewish history, the Holocaust, and music and resistance. She gained a DPhil in Modern History and a Masters in Music from the University of Oxford. Her book *Music in the Holocaust: Confronting Life in the Nazi Ghettos and Camps* was published by Oxford University Press in 2005.

Christine Lucia is London-born and has taught music in South African universities for 32 years. She published the anthology *The World of South African Music: A Reader* (Cambridge Scholars Press) in 2005 and is editor of the journal *SAMUS: South African Music Studies*. Until the end of 2007 she was Professor and Chair of Music at the University of the Witwatersrand, Johannesburg.

Carol A. Muller has taught at the University of KwaZulu-Natal, University of North Carolina at Chapel Hill and New York University, and is currently Associate Professor of Music at the University of Pennsylvania. Her book publications include *Rituals of Fertility and the Sacrifice of Desire: Nazarite Women's Performance in South Africa* (University of Chicago Press, 1999), and most recently *South African Music: A Century of Traditions in Transformation* (revised edition, Routledge, 2008), a book co-authored with Sathima Bea Benjamin, *Musical Echoes* (Duke, 2008); a world music text, *Musically Connected* (Oxford University Press, 2008), and she edited *Shembe Hymns* (University of KwaZulu-Natal Press, 2008). Muller is engaged with issues of music and community in Philadelphia (see http://ccat.sas.upenn.edu/music/westphillymusic) and is a gumboot dancer.

A graduate of Balliol College, Oxford, where he completed a DPhil on 'musical representations of white South Africa', **Stephanus Muller** is a lecturer in musicology at the University of Stellenbosch. His research has focused on music in South Africa and identity politics and he is currently writing a critical biography of the South African composer, Arnold van Wyk. He is co-editor of *Gender and Sexuality in South African Music* (SUN Press, 2005) and *A Composer in Africa: Essays on the Life and Work of Stefans Grové* (SUN Press, 2006).

Grant Olwage is a Senior Lecturer in the Wits School of Arts at the University of the Witwatersrand, and was Edison Visiting Fellow at the British Library, London, for 2004-2005. His research interests span Victoriana, the voice, South

African music, and contemporary popular music. Recent essays appear in the *Journal of the Royal Musical Association* (2006) and *Ethnomusicology Forum* (2004), and he has a chapter on black choralism as musical colonisation in *Music, Politics, and Power* (Routledge, 2005). As Dr G, he has (in the past) fiddled on the turntables, and more recently developed a hobbyist interest in electronic music production.

Brett Pyper is a Fulbright scholar and doctoral candidate at New York University, researching the role of music in South Africa's transition since the early 1990s. For much of the 1990s he worked as a public arts administrator, and later as a freelance facilitator of musical projects geared towards exploring the emerging post-apartheid environment. Among the latter was the collaboration between British vocal ensemble I Fagiolini and the Soweto-based SDASA Chorale. Pyper was Head of the Division of Heritage and Cultural Management in the Wits School of Arts from 2005-2007 and is currently CEO of the Klein Karoo National Arts Festival.

Martin Scherzinger, Associate Professor of musicology and music theory at the Eastman School of Music, is a South African-born music theorist and composer. His current research includes large-scale projects on the political hermeneutics of absolute music as well as the globalisation of musicology and music theory. Awards include fellowships from the Princeton Society of Fellows (2004-2007), AMS 50 (2000), ACLS (2003-4), Paul Sacher Foundation (2006), Tuck Foundation (2006), and the SMT Emerging Scholar Award (2003-4). He has written chapters for the following books: *Cambridge History of Twentieth-Century Music* (Cambridge University Press, 2004), *Beyond Structural Listening* (University of California Press, 2004), and *Postmodern Music/Postmodern Thought* (Routledge, 2000).

INDEX

aesthetics 5, 43, 90-91, 93, 209-221, 227-228, 230-233, 239, 244-246, 250, 255, 257, 260, 266, 291, 295, 297
African Jubilee Singers 191-192
African National Congress (ANC) 6, 56, 68-70, 81, 155-160, 162-164, 166-167, 169-174, 177, 187-188, 192, 202-203, 243-244, 246
    Amandla Cultural Ensemble 156-158, 161, 164-174, 176-177, 192
    Mayibuye Cultural Ensemble 156-161, 163-166, 168-171, 173, 177
    Medu Art Ensemble 165
    Radio Freedom 173
    Umkhonto we Sizwe (MK) 156, 162, 164-170, 175, 203
African unity 186-187, 198
Africanisation/Africanist 63, 68-70, 187, 219, 267
    Black Consciousness Movement 68-69, 170, 174
    New Africanist movement 187-188
    Pan Africanist Congress (PAC) 56, 68-69
Afrikaans counter culture/*alternatiewe* music movement 242, 264, 266, 274
    Vöelvry 108, 130-131, 261
Afrocentric art forms 244
Afro-Christianity/independent churches 192, 197-198, 200-202
    African Methodist Episcopal Church 191
    African prophet 193-194, 198, 203
    Apostolic Church 192, 194-198
    grass-roots ecumenism 197-198
    Holy Spirit 188-189, 193, 195-197
    Nazarite Church 193-194, 202
    Presbyterian Church 188
    Zion Christian Church 192, 201-202

Agawu, Kofi 3, 219
Alexandra township 92
American music, influence of 42-44, 84, 190-191
    blues 43
    jazz 140, 142-146, 149-150
    rock 'n' roll 83-88, 94
Amu, Ephraim 28
anthems 57, 193, 199, 202
    national (See also Sontonga, Enoch: *Nkosi Sikelel' iAfrika*) 7, 186-189, 200-201, 261, 266
    political/of protest 192, 199, 200, 202-203
    praise singing/poetry 187-188, 192-197, 199
anti-apartheid movement/resistance/ liberation struggle 6, 24, 68, 74, 80, 83, 87, 107, 121, 130-131, 155-178, 186-188, 192, 200, 203, 209, 213, 221, 230, 241, 243-244, 257-258, 260-265, 268-276
    cultural boycott 244-246
    Defiance Campaign 83
apartheid
    censorship 7-8, 104, 107, 115-119, 121-125, 127-129, 131, 146, 189, 238, 259, 263, 269, 272-273
    as construct/discourse/ideology 4, 47, 55-56, 62-66, 73, 80, 86, 93-94, 107-108, 111, 115-119, 125, 127, 129-131, 174, 230-232, 259, 282-283, 290, 294
    education 5, 12, 22, 24, 158
    as historical era 1-3, 5-7, 12-13, 20, 24, 26, 35, 39, 41, 47, 56, 59, 64, 66, 72, 80, 117, 142, 169, 282-287, 296-297

institutions/infrastructure 4-7, 39, 104, 238, 250, 259
liberalism 6-7, 41, 63-64, 68, 70-72, 74, 81-82
'long apartheid' 4, 6
militarisation 119-122, 130
tribalism 40-42, 63, 106-107, 127-128, 174
as word 1-2, 209
appropriation 7, 101, 107, 111, 188-189, 192, 210-211, 221, 229, 231-233, 246, 259, 265, 267
arrangement 11, 14, 20-21, 43-44, 47, 107, 168, 200, 232, 261, 266
art music 13, 24, 27, 43, 284-285

Bantu Men's Social Centre 41
Baron, Freda 288, 292
Bayete 248
Benjamin, Sathima Bea 3, 7, 137-140, 146
Bhabha, Homi K 8, 20
Bikitsha, Basil 86
biography 189, 282, 287-288
black South African music 4-5, 20, 22, 36, 79, 82
'third space' 20
Blacking, John 3, 188
Bokwe, John Knox 11, 13, 44
Bouws, Jan 38
Bräuninger, Jürgen 210-212, 214, 221
Breytenbach, Breyten 163
Bright Blue 110, 261
Brooks, Ike 80
Brutus, Dennis 158

Caluza, Reuben 12-13, 187
canon 3, 21, 43, 145, 149-150, 216, 240, 242, 244, 250
Carstens, Nico 89
Cele, Willard 83
Chakrabarty, Dipesh 144-145
Chigamba, Tute 218-219
choralism
black 4-5, 11-14, 17-22, 24, 27-30, 35-40, 43-47, 55-63, 66-67, 69, 71-74, 161, 187, 200, 260

17th century Italian/French 29
Clarke, John 256, 260
Clegg, Johnny 3, 6, 106-108, 110, 129-130, 266
indlamu dance 106
Juluka 107, 128-129, 266
collaboration 8, 67, 79, 107, 174, 240, 242, 244, 257-259, 262, 264-266, 269, 275-276
colonialism 3, 5, 68, 169, 172, 238, 287, 295
neo-colonialism 211-212, 215
Comaroff, Jean and John 189, 200, 265
composition 5, 8, 11, 14, 17-19, 21-22, 28-30, 44, 47, 194, 209-210, 212-233, 266, 276, 282
hocket/hocketing 221, 223, 229
paraphrase technique 209-212, 214, 220, 229-233, 238, 291
cosmopolitanism 145, 192
counterpoint 18, 20-21, 26, 28-29
Cultural Workers' Congress 244
Culture in another South Africa conference (CASA) 165, 244

Dahlhaus, Carl 27
deconstruction/deconstructionist 2-3, 13, 212, 222, 285
de Klerk, FW 245, 256-258, 274-275
Rubicon 256-258, 272, 274
Derrida, Jacques 1-2, 4, 8
de Vries, Casper 266
Dhlomo, HIE 187
Dishy, Leslie 57-59, 70-71
du Toit, Andre (Koos Kombuis) 108, 110
du Plessis, Herbert 284
Dywili, Nofinishi 18

Erlmann, Veit 12, 19, 40, 47, 146, 192
ethnocentrism 115, 259
ethnomusicology 5-6, 17, 45, 257
Euba, Akin 219
exiles/'inziles' 3, 6-7, 140, 146, 150, 156-157, 159, 168, 173, 177, 188, 203, 247-248, 258, 263

Fassie, Brenda 248
Federation of South African Cultural Organisations (Fosaco) 244

Feinberg, Barry 158-159, 161, 164-166
Feldman, Anne 59
Ferdinand, Osborne 58
Fisk Jubilee Singers 190
folk/traditional music
  African traditional/folk music 13-14, 16-18, 37-38, 43-47, 66, 88, 106, 128, 188, 200, 210-211, 213, 215-217, 219, 221, 223-224, 226-227, 229, 231, 233, 267
  Afrikaans/*boeremusiek* 38, 89-91, 93-94, 105, 267, 295
forced removals 7, 72, 82, 238
formalism/formal 13, 29, 43, 212-213, 216-217
Fort Hare, University of 18, 193
Freedom Charter/charterists 70, 170
  Congress of the People 70
Friedland, Joseph 57-59, 61, 70
Fugard, Athol 174

gender 115
  heterosexism 115, 120-1, 124
  sexism/chauvinism 115, 121-122, 125, 131
globalisation 7, 109-110, 140, 144-145, 150
  global imagination 146, 149
Griffin, Brian 116
Gwangwa, Jonas 156, 166-169
Gwenzi, Gwanzura 223, 227
Gxashe, Stanford 57-58

Hamm, Charles 39, 85, 87-88
Handel's *Messiah* 7, 55-75
Harlem Renaissance 41, 145
harmony 13, 17-21, 23-24, 26, 28-29, 193, 200, 214, 218-219, 224, 231
Hartman, Anton 282, 293
Hartmann, Friedrich 26
Herbert, Alf 80
homeland states 7, 30, 39-40, 189
Hönigsberg, David 283
Huskisson, Yvonne 47, 189
hybridity 56

Ibrahim, Abdullah 137-138, 149
identity/ethnicity 68, 74, 94-95, 103-106, 110, 199, 264
  Afrikaans 38-39, 93, 102, 105-106, 108-110, 131, 282-283, 292-293
  Jewish 70-71
  national non-racial/nation-building 23, 100, 102, 157, 170, 172, 176-178, 265-266
  racial 86, 88, 93, 107, 111, 147, 284-285
  traditional/tribal African 63-64, 104, 106, 125, 127, 170, 188, 233
  urban African/black 64, 81, 88, 90, 104, 170, 192, 201
  white 80-81, 99-102, 105-111, 121-122, 125, 127
  Zulu 106-108
imagined communities 109-111, 199, 203
  nation-states 109
imperialism
  British 38, 68
  cultural/Eurocentrism 43, 56, 125, 145, 203, 243-244, 250
  imperialist capitalism 35-36, 40
immanent critique 285
Inkatha Freedom Party 202
International Defence and Aid Fund 164

Jabavu Choristers 57
jazz, South African 3, 88, 137-140, 142-147, 149, 170, 200-201, 242, 247-248
Johannesburg 41, 55-60, 80, 83-85, 90, 93, 131, 187, 189, 201, 242
  Bantu Music Festival 57
  Market Theatre 242
Johannesburg African Music Society (JAMS) 59, 61, 63-64, 66, 69-70, 72-75
Johns, Jasper 220-221
Jordan, Pallo 243
Junod, family of missionaries 45-47

Kalahari Surfers 129-130, 266
kalimba 216
Kant, Immanuel 230
Kasrils, Ronnie 159, 165

Kente, Gibson 170, 174, 239
Kerkorrel, Johannes 110, 261, 264, 266
Khumalo, Mzilikazi 14, 22
Khuze, Ndonda 168
kinaesthetics 216-219
King Kong 59-60, 67, 81-82, 84, 166, 188
Kirby, Percival R 5, 13-14, 17, 20-21, 24, 26
Kongo, Zabana 219
Kramer, David 105-106, 110, 128
Kunene, Mazisi 158
kwela 4, 79-94, 170
    politics of pleasure 79-80, 83, 86, 88, 93-95
Kwela, Allen 90

Laka, Don 248
Leroli, Jake 88
Leshega, William Mathebule 193
Letanka, Iris 58
Leyden, John 93
Liberal Party 70, 81
Liberation Front of Mozambique (FRELIMO) 164
Ligeti, Gyorgi 212, 217
Lindberg, Des and Dawn 273
literacy 5, 46
living history 147-148
Locke, Alain 43
Lodge, Tom 173
Lovedale Press 187
Lucey, Roger 273
Luthuli, Albert 81

Madzunya, Josias 69
Magogo, Princess Constance 18
Magwaza, Duze 91
Makana, Peter 84
Makeba, Miriam 166, 263
Makibinyani, Josias 14
Malahela, Saul 90
Malan, Robin 104
Mali *kora* music 221
Malope, Rebecca 248
Mankwane, Marks 90
marabi tradition 79, 88, 90, 272
Maraire, Dumisani 212

Maranke, John 194-198
    Kwese Kwese 195
    Mwari Komborera Africa 195-198
    Manyika version 196-198
Marivate, Daniel 36, 40, 44-47
Masekela, Barbara 172, 177, 243
Masekela, Hugh 166, 247-248, 263
masculinity 106-107, 120-121
Mashiyane, Spokes 83-84, 87, 90, 92
maskandi 107
Masote, Michael 60
Masote, Sheila 60, 69
Masowe, John 198
Matshikiza, John 159
Matshikiza, Todd 89
Matyila 13, 24
Mazibuko, Jabulani 57
mbaqanga 88, 170, 272
Mbeki, Thabo 166, 171-172
McAdoo, Orpheus 190-191
McClary, Susan 27-29
McClintock, Anne
McGregor, Chris 149
Mchunu, Sipho 107, 129-130, 266
mekorotlo (See folk music: African/traditional)
Memorable Order of Tin Hats (MOTHS) 57, 67, 71
memory, collective
Mhangwani, Sam 174
mimesis 295-296
Mini, Nomkhosi 167
Mini, Vuyisile 167
mission church schools 12, 41, 43, 45-46, 192-193
Mngoma, Khabi 69
Mnomiya, Phelelani 28-29
Mnyele, Thami 168, 173
modernity/modernism 5, 11, 14, 19, 21, 26, 35, 38, 43, 46-47, 109, 145, 221
    African/Afro-modernism 19, 21, 30, 43-45, 47
    capitalist modernisation 210
    postmodernism 214, 221
Modiga, Mabel 58
Modisane, Bloke 4

INDEX

Moerane, Michael 5, 14, 22, 24, 26, 28-29
Mohapeloa, Joshua 5, 14, 16-21, 23, 28-29
Molekane, Tumi 8-9
Mollson, Alice 58
Mompati, Ruth 171
Monkoe Itala 58
Mothopeng, Urbaniah 69
Mothopeng, Zeph 69
Motsieloa, Griffiths 36
Mozambique
    nyanga panpipe dance 3, 209, 220, 227-228, 233
Mphahlele, Ezekiel 41
Mqhayi, Samuel EK 187-188, 199, 201
Mthethwa, Barney 28
Mtshali, Oswald 158
Mushawatu, John 196, 199
music education 5, 12, 21-22
music revolution 255-258, 262-265, 268-272, 275-276
    currents of contention 272, 274-275
    countermobilisations 273-275
    moments of truth/changes of heart 270
    music *indaba* 257-258, 260-262, 264, 266-268, 271, 274-276
    musical markers 255-256, 261, 267
    tipping points 261, 272-274
    waves of dissent 264-275
musical echoes 140-143, 145, 148-149
musical osmosis 259-260
musical surrogacy 139, 146, 148

National Party government 13, 24, 62-64, 67-68, 71-72, 103-104, 282, 292, 294
    Broederbond 282, 293
nationalism 2-3, 104, 119, 122, 265-266, 295
    Afrikaner 62-64, 68, 102, 292-294
    black/African 41-42, 63, 68, 88, 187-188
Negro spirituals 43-44, 192
NewMusicSA 181-182
    Blake, Michael 281-282
New Negro 42-44
Ngubane, Jordan 188
Nkosi, Ben 79, 84

Nkosi, Saul 90
Ndodana, Bongani 212
Nokwe, Duma 70
Nortje, Arthur 158
notation 5, 12, 229
Ntombela, Man 167
Nxumalo, Gideon 200

Ouseley, Sir Frederick Gore 21

Paff, WP 20-21
patriotism 119-123, 130-131, 275
Pebbles, RnB songster 9
Pieterse, Cosmo 158
Plaatje, Solomon 187
polycultural polyphony 258, 263, 275
Popular Movement for the Liberation of Angola (MPLA) 162, 164
Posel, Deborah 64
post-apartheid 5, 7-8, 13, 23, 29-30, 56, 99-100, 111, 158, 176, 200-201, 240, 247-248
    transition/social transformation 4, 6, 8, 99, 108, 155, 158, 177-178, 203, 237, 239, 242, 247-249, 256-257, 261-262, 265, 269, 273, 276-277
postcolonial/postcolonialism 2, 56, 66, 283
Progressive Party 56
Protestant hymnody/hymns 7, 23, 28, 161, 188, 192-195, 198-199, 201
Pukwana, Dudu 166

quela dance 89

race
    commodity racism 36, 45
    discourse of representivity 2
    historicity of 101
    musical constructedness of 3-6
    racism/racial stereotypes/prejudice/exclusion 2-4, 13, 71-75, 101, 115, 121, 125, 127-128, 169, 174-175, 239-242, 247, 250, 283

records/classification 106, 158
race-ethnicity 2-5, 27, 35-41, 44-47,
    64, 66-67, 104, 115, 119, 122,
    125, 127, 128, 170, 238
  segregation 4, 8, 35-36, 38-41,
    44-47, 59-60, 63, 65, 68, 72-74,
    80, 86, 94, 118, 128, 130, 149,
    158, 170, 202, 213, 248, 259
  whiteness 3, 99-102, 105-111
Rachabane, Barney 88
Radano, Ronald 2
Rahbari, Ali 260
Ralulimi, Albert 84, 90-92
Rampolokeng, Lesego 266
Ramsey, Guthrie 43
rap music 8
Rathebe, Dolly 263
recording/publishing industry 8, 12,
    24, 35-41, 45, 47, 79, 83, 90, 93,
    115-117, 119, 122-125, 128-130,
    146, 150
  Gallo Records 83, 90-91, 146
  Shifty Records 129-130, 263
redemption
Reineke, Dennis 246
religion
  and censorship 128-129, 189
  nationalist Christianity 128, 283
rhythm 17, 21, 62, 83, 89-91, 169, 191-194,
    212, 214, 217, 219, 221-223, 227-228,
    232, 266-267
Romanticism 4, 290, 294, 296
Rosenschoon, Hans 23, 26
rural-urban migration 18, 36, 106, 130,
    169, 192

Sachs, Albie 155-158, 176-177
Sampson, Anthony 82
San bow music 223, 228
Sankomota 128
Saxophone jive 80, 88
Schulman, Jeremy 59, 70
Schwartz, Harry 70
Scott, Lucas 58
Scott, Tony 79
Semenya, Caiphus 166

serial techniques/serialism 11, 19
Serote, Mongane Wally 158
Shembe, Galilee 193-195
  Nkosi Yethu 193-194
Shembe, Isaiah 193-194
  Ekuphakameni 193, 195
Shangaan 36, 40, 45, 47
Sharpeville 56, 68, 72
Shona 3, 229, 196-196, 218, 221,
    229-230
  mbira 3, 209, 211, 218-219, 221,
    223-224, 227, 229
Simon, Barney 174
Sinamela, Simon Hoffa 191-192
Smith, Faye 60
Sobukwe, Robert 69
social diffusion 8, 259-260, 268
Solven Whistlers 79
songs 13-14, 17-18, 20, 23, 26, 28, 36,
    45-47, 186-187, 197, 199, 218-219,
    228
  freedom 157, 159-161, 163, 168-170,
    174-175
  Sotho 20
  Xhosa bow 18
  Zulu 18, 40
Sontonga, Enoch 13, 186-190, 192-193,
    195, 199, 201-203
  African blessing 186, 188, 190,
    192, 195, 199
  'God Bless Africa' 186, 195, 198
  Nkosi Sikelel' iAfrika 7, 185-195,
    198-203, 261, 266
  Xhosa version 186-189, 192, 201
Sophiatown 58, 72, 166, 187
Sotho music 3, 14, 18, 21, 26, 185
  lesiba 3, 209, 221
  verse 20-21
South African Academy 22
South African composers
  black 5, 7, 11-13, 17-18, 22, 24, 26-28,
    36, 44-47, 84, 186-189, 196, 200
  white 2-3, 5-7, 290-291, 293-294
South African Indian Congress 159
South African Information Service 82
South African Institute of Race Relations 5

INDEX

South African Broadcasting Corporation (SABC) 39, 104, 107, 128, 146, 189, 282, 294
    Radio Bantu 39, 47, 104, 128, 129, 189
    Springbok Radio 103, 122
South African Music Rights Organisation (SAMRO) 12, 22
Sowden, Dora 73-74
Soweto uprising 161-162, 170
State Theatre (Pretoria) 6, 237-239, 241-242, 245-250
    Performing Arts Council of the Transvaal (PACT) 238-250
Stradling, Leslie 74
Sundkler, BGM 193
Suttner, Raymond 173
symbols/symbolism 67, 72, 75, 100-102, 121-122, 130, 186, 189, 198, 200, 202, 237, 245, 250, 255-257, 295
syncretism 20, 93-94, 161, 192, 267, 275

Tamasuza, Justinian 212
Taylor, Jeremy 104-105, 273
Taylor, Timothy 212-216, 225
Tenaille, Frank 263
theory of music 5, 11, 17-18, 21, 27-29, 212, 217, 231
Tomlinson, Gary 27, 29
tonality 11, 17, 21, 27-29, 82
Tracey, Hugh 17
Transvaal African Eisteddfod 44-45
Tutu, JP 58

United Democratic Front (UDF) 170
United Party 81
Union of South African Artists 80
universalism 56, 70, 213-215
utopian vision 188, 195, 198-199, 203

van der Hoven, Eghard 240
Van Rooyen, Jacobus 117-118, 122, 125

Van Wyk, Arnold 3-4, 6, 281-282, 284-285, 287-295, 297
Vapostori 195, 199
    Vapositori venyu 197
vastrap dance 89-91
Verwoerd, HF 13
Viljoen, Nicol 292
Virginia Jubilee singers 190-191
Visser, Schalk 240-241, 245
voice/voicing 17-18, 21, 23-24, 26, 29, 66, 141-142, 148, 192, 217, 227-228
Volans, Kevin 2-3, 6-7, 209-216, 219-221, 223, 225, 227-233
    'Hunting: Gathering' 221-222, 231
    'Mutamba' 220-222
    'Ngozi Yemuroora' 218
    'Nhimutimu' 218-219
    'Nyamaropa' 223-225, 227-228
    Pasipamire, spirit medium for Chaminuka 221
    'The Songlines' 216, 222-227
    'White Man Sleeps' 3, 209, 213-215, 220, 227-228, 233

Walton, Chris 211-212, 214-215
Webern, Anton 19, 217
Wolkers, Jan 163
World Black Festival of Arts and Culture (FESTAC) 166

Xatasi, Ben 57-58
Zabalaza Festival 243

Zambi, Billy 90
Zimbabwe African People's Union 163
Zimbabwean music
    matepe 209
    mbira dza vadzimu 209, 218, 221
    tsaba tsaba 90, 272